LANGUAGE AND GENDER

Routledge Applied Linguistics is a series of comprehensive resource books providing students and researchers with the support they need for advanced study in the core areas of English Language and Applied Linguistics.

Each book in the series guides readers through three main sections, enabling them to explore and develop major themes within the discipline:

- Section A, Introduction, establishes the key terms and concepts and extends readers' techniques of analysis through practical application.
- Section B, Extension, brings together influential articles, sets them in context, and discusses their contribution to the field.
- Section C, Exploration, builds on knowledge gained in the first two sections, setting thoughtful tasks around further illustrative material. This enables readers to engage more actively with the subject matter and encourages them to develop their own research responses.

Throughout the book, topics are revisited, extended, interwoven and deconstructed, with the reader's understanding strengthened by tasks and follow-up questions.

Language and Gender:

- presents an up-to-date introduction to language and gender;
- includes diverse work from a range of cultural, including non-Western contexts and represents a range of methodological approaches;
- gathers together influential readings from key names in the discipline, including Mary Haas, Deborah Cameron and Mary Bucholtz.

Written by an experienced teacher and researcher in the field, *Language and Gender* is an essential resource for students and researchers of Applied Linguistics.

Jane Sunderland teaches in the Department of Linguistics and English Language at Lancaster University. She is a key member of IGALA (International Gender and Language Association) and publishes widely in the area of language and gender.

ROUTLEDGE APPLIED LINGUISTICS

SERIES EDITORS

Christopher N. Candlin is Senior Research Professor in the Department of Linguistics at Macquarie University, Australia and Professor of Applied Linguistics at the Open University, UK. At Macquarie, he has been Chair of the Department of Linguistics; established and was Executive Director of the National Centre for English Language Teaching and Research (NCELTR); and was foundation Director of the Centre for Language in Social Life (CLSL). He has written or edited over 150 publications and since 2004 co-edits the *Journal of Applied Linguistics*. From 1996 to 2002 he was President of the International Association of Applied Linguistics (AILA). He has acted as a consultant in more than thirty-five countries and as external faculty assessor in thirty-six universities worldwide.

Ronald Carter is Professor of Modern English Language in the School of English Studies at the University of Nottingham. He has published extensively in the fields of Applied Linguistics, Literary Studies and Language in Education, and written or edited over 40 books and 100 articles in these fields. He has given consultancies in the field of English Language Education, mainly in conjunction with the British Council, in over thirty countries worldwide, and is editor of the Routledge Interface series and advisory editor to the Routledge English Language Introduction series. He was recently elected a fellow of the British Academy of Social Sciences and is currently UK Government Advisor for ESOL and Chair of the British Association of Applied Linguistics (BAAL).

TITLES IN THE SERIES

Intercultural Communication: An advanced resource book
Adrian Holliday, Martin Hyde and John Kullman

Translation: An advanced resource book
Basil Hatim and Jeremy Munday

Grammar and Context: An advanced resource book
Ann Hewings, Martin Hewings

Second Language Acquisition: An advanced resource book
Kees de Bot, Wander Lowie and Marjolijn Verspoor

Corpus-Based Language Studies: An advanced resource book
Anthony McEnery, Richard Xiao and Yukio Tono

Language and Gender: An advanced resource book
Jane Sunderland

Language and Gender

An advanced resource book

Jane Sunderland

Routledge
Taylor & Francis Group

LONDON AND NEW YORK

To Graham and Emily

First published 2006
by Routledge
2 Park Square, Milton Park, Abingdon, Oxon OX14 4RN

Simultaneously published in the USA and Canada
by Routledge
270 Madison Ave, New York, NY 10016

Routledge is an imprint of the Taylor & Francis Group, an informa business

© 2006 Jane Sunderland

Typeset in Akzidenz Grotesk, Minion and Novarese by
Keystroke, Jacaranda Lodge, Wolverhampton
Printed and bound in Great Britain by
TJ International Ltd, Padstow, Cornwall

British Library Cataloguing in Publication Data
A catalogue record for this book is available from the British Library

Library of Congress Cataloging in Publication Data
Sunderland, Jane, 1952–
  Language and gender : an advanced resource book / Jane Sunderland.
    p. cm. – (Routledge applied linguistics)
  Includes bibliographical references and index.
  1. Language and sex. I. Title. II. Series.
  P120.S48S863 2006
  306.44–dc22
                                        2006002240

ISBN10: 0–415–31103–9 (hbk)
ISBN10: 0–415–31104–7 (pbk)
ISBN10: 0–203–45649–1 (ebk)

ISBN13: 978–0–415–31103–8 (hbk)
ISBN13: 978–0–415–31104–5 (pbk)
ISBN13: 978–0–203–45649–1 (ebk)

Contents

Contents cross-referenced

Series editors' preface

The Routledge Applied Linguistics Series provides a comprehensive guide to a number of key areas in the field of Applied Linguistics. Applied Linguistics is a rich, vibrant, diverse and essentially interdisciplinary field. It is now more important than ever that books in the field provide up-to-date maps of what is an ever-changing territory.

The books in this series are designed to give key insights into core areas of Applied Linguistics. The design of the books ensures, through key readings, that the history and development of a subject is recognised while, through key questions and tasks, integrating understandings of the topics, concepts and practices that make up its essentially interdisciplinary fabric. The pedagogic structure of each book ensures that readers are given opportunities to think, discuss, engage in tasks, draw on their own experience, reflect, research and to read and critically reread key documents.

Each book has three main sections, each made up of approximately ten units:

A: An **Introduction** section: in which the key terms and concepts that map the field of the subject are introduced, including introductory activities and reflective tasks, designed to establish key understandings, terminology, techniques of analysis and the skills appropriate to the theme and the discipline.

B: An **Extension** section: in which selected core readings are introduced (usually edited from the original) from existing key books and articles, together with annotations and commentary, where appropriate. Each reading is introduced, annotated and commented on in the context of the whole book, and research/follow-up questions and tasks are added to enable fuller understanding of both theory and practice. In some cases, readings are short and synoptic and incorporated within a more general exposition.

C: An **Exploration** section: in which further samples and illustrative materials are provided with an emphasis, where appropriate, on more open-ended, student-centred activities and tasks, designed to support readers and users in undertaking their own locally relevant research projects. Tasks are designed for work in groups or for individuals working on their own. They can be readily included in award courses in Applied Linguistics, or as topics for personal study and research.

The books also contain a detailed Further Reading section, which lays the ground for further work in the discipline. There are also extensive bibliographies.

The target audience for the series is upper undergraduates and postgraduates on Language, Applied Linguistics and Communication Studies programmes as well as teachers and researchers in professional-development and distance-learning programmes. High-quality applied research resources are also much needed for teachers of EFL/ESL and foreign-language students at higher-education colleges and universities worldwide. The books in the Routledge Applied Linguistics series are aimed at the individual reader, the student in a group and at teachers building courses and seminar programmes.

We hope that the books in this series meet these needs and continue to provide support over many years.

The editors

Professor Christopher N. Candlin and Professor Ronald Carter are the series editors. Both have extensive experience of publishing titles in the fields relevant to this series. Between them they have written and edited over 100 books and 200 academic papers in the broad field of Applied Linguistics. Chris Candlin was President of AILA (International Association for Applied Linguistics) from 1996 to 2002 and Ron Carter has been Chair of BAAL (British Association for Applied Linguistics) since 2003.

Professor Christopher N. Candlin
Senior Research Professor
Department of Linguistics
Division of Linguistics and Psychology
Macquarie University
Sydney NSW 2109
Australia

and

Professor of Applied Linguistics
Faculty of Education and Language Studies
The Open University
Walton Hall
Milton Keynes MK7 6AA
UK

Professor Ronald Carter
School of English Studies
University of Nottingham
Nottingham NG7 2RD
UK.

Acknowledgements

UNIT B1.1

Haas, M. (1944) 'Men's and Women's Speech in Koasati', *Language* 20. Reprinted by permission of Robert Haas.

UNIT B1.2

Milroy, L. (1980) from *Language and Social Networks*, reprinted by permission of Blackwell Publishing.

UNIT B2.1

Lakoff, R. (1975) from *Language and Woman's Place*, Colophon Books. Reprinted by permission of the author.

UNIT B2.3

Fishman, P. (1983) 'Interaction: the work women do', in B. Thorne et al. (eds) *Language, Gender and Society*, Newbury House. Reprinted by permission of Barrie Thorne, Cheris Kramarae and Nancy Henley.

UNIT B3.1

Maltz, D. and R. Borker (1982) 'A cultural approach to male–female miscommunication', in J. Gumperz (ed.) *Language and Identity*, Cambridge University Press. Reproduced with permission.

UNIT B4.1

Cameron, D. (1992) from *Feminism and Linguistic Theory*, 2nd edn, Macmillan. Reproduced with permission of Palgrave Macmillan.

UNIT B4.2

Bucholz, M. (1999) from 'Bad examples' in Mary Bucholtz, A. C. Liang and Laurel A. Sutton (eds) *Reinventing Identities*, Oxford University Press. Copyright © 1999 by Oxford University Press, Inc. Used by permission of Oxford University Press, Inc.

UNIT B4.3

Nelson, C. (2002) from 'Why queer theory is useful in teaching: a perspective from English as a Second Language teaching', *Journal of Gay and Lesbian Social Services*, 14 (2): 46–53. Copyright © 2002 by The Haworth Press, Inc. All rights reserved.

UNIT B5.3

Schwarz, J. (2003) from 'Quantifying non-sexist language: the case of Ms', in S. Sarangi and T. van Leeuwen (eds) *Applied Linguistics and Communities of Practice*, Continuum. Copyright © Srikant Sarangi, Theo van Leeuwen and contributors 2003. Reprinted with the permission of The Continuum International Publishing Group.

UNIT B6.1

Sunderland, J. et al. (2002) 'From representation towards discursive practices: gender in the foreign language textbook revisited', from L. Litosseliti and J. Sunderland (eds) *Gender, Identity and Discourse Analysis*, John Benjamins, pp. 226–37, 244–9. With kind permission of John Benjamins Publishing Company, Amsterdam/Philadelphia. www.benjamins.com.

UNIT B6.2

Eckert, P. and McConnell-Ginet, S. (1992) from 'Communities of practice: where language, gender, and power all live', in K. Hall et al. (eds) *Locating Power: proceedings of the Second Berkeley Women and Language Conference*, Women and Language Group. Reprinted by kind permission of the authors.

UNIT B6.3

This is an extended abstract of an article originally published as: Puleng Hanong Thetela (2002) 'Sex discourses and gender construction in Southern Sotho', *Southern African Linguistics and Applied Language Studies* 20: 177–89.

UNIT B7.1

Sunderland, J. (2004) from *Gendered Discourses*, Palgrave Macmillan. Reproduced with permission of Palgrave Macmillan.

UNIT B7.2

Baxter, J. (2003) from *Positioning Gender in Discourse: a feminist methodology*, Palgrave Macmillan. Reproduced with permission of Palgrave Macmillan.

UNIT B8.1

Rayson, P., Leech, G. and Hodges, M. (1997) from 'Social differentiation in the use of English vocabulary: some analyses of the conversational component of the British National Corpus', *International Journal of Corpus Linguistics* 2 (1): 133–41. With kind permission of John Benjamins Publishing Company, Amsterdam/Philadelphia. www.benjamins.com.

UNIT B8.2

Stokoe, E. and Smithson, J. (2001) from 'Making gender relevant: conversation analysis and gender categories in interaction', *Discourse and Society* 12 (2). Reprinted by permission of Sage Publications Ltd and the authors.

UNIT B8.3

Kitzinger, C. (2001) from 'Doing feminist conversation analysis', *Feminism and Society* 10 (12). Reprinted by permission of Sage Publications Ltd and the author.

UNIT B9

Edley, N. (2001) from 'Analysing masculinity: interpretive repertoires, ideological dilemmas and subject positions', in M. Wetherell, S. Taylor and S. Yates (eds) *Discourse as Data: a guide for analysis*, Open University/Sage Publications. Reprinted by permission of Sage Publications Ltd and Margaret Wetherell.

UNIT B10.1

Thornborrow, J. (1994) from 'The woman, the man and the Filofax: gender positions in advertising', in S. Mills (ed.) *Gendering the Reader*, Harvester Wheatsheaf. Reprinted by permission of Joanna Thornborrow.

UNIT B10.2

Davies, B. (2003) from *Frogs and Snails and Feminist Tales*, 2nd edn, Hampton Press. Reprinted by permission of the publisher and author.

UNIT B10.3

Bucholz, M. (2002) from 'Geek feminism', in S. Benor, M. Rose, D. Sharma, J. Sweetland and Q. Zhang (eds) *Gendered Practices in Language*, CSLI Publications. Copyright (c) 2002 CSLI Publications. Reprinted by permission of the publishers.

Thanks are also due to Lilian Atanga, Paul Baker and Sibonile Ellece for their help with different aspects of the text.

How to use this book

Language and Gender: An advanced resource book provides a rich diversity of material for students in this field, particularly those who wish to contribute through their own research as well as learn about and appreciate the significance of others' work.

Like other resource books in this Routledge Applied Linguistics series, *Language and Gender* is divided into three sequential sections: 'Introduction' (Section A), 'Extension' (Section B) and 'Exploration' (Section C). (See also the series web site: <http://www. routledge.com/rcenters/linguistics/series/ral.htm>.) This particular resource book is additionally divided into four parts – Background, Gender, Language and Research – and into ten units, one or more of which constitutes each of the four parts. Each unit is developed over the A, B and C sections.

The Introduction 'A' units establish key terms and concepts, provide a discursive summary and overview, and preview what is to come in the corresponding extension ('B') and exploration ('C') units. The extension 'B' units provide extracts from a range of original texts, the majority 'classic' and influential, others less known but nevertheless showcasing excellent illustrative work. The exploration 'C' units allow students to engage very actively with the subject matter of the 'A' and 'B' units and to take their study further in a range of independent ways, through desk and field research.

It is not necessary to have read the corresponding B unit before undertaking a research project from a C unit, neither is it necessary to have read the corresponding A unit before reading the extracts in a B unit. However, these preparatory uses are recommended. It is also not necessary to work through the ten units sequentially; they can be chosen according to interest and purpose, and according to the reader's experience in the field to date. There is extensive cross-referencing throughout the book.

Language and Gender: An advanced resource book does the following:

- It shows the development of the field, in particular the changing foci: from 'sexist language' and 'gender differences in talk' to *discourse* (informed both by post-structuralism and critical discourse analysis [CDA]) and the social/textual/ linguistic construction of gender.

- It highlights the interdisciplinary nature of gender and language study, in particular by focusing on different theoretical approaches: CDA, conversation analysis (CA), feminist post-structuralist discourse analysis (FPDA), discursive psychology and corpus linguistics.
- It gathers together influential key readings as well as illustrative new work, from, *inter alia*, Robin Lakoff, Mary Bucholtz, Sara Mills and Celia Kitzinger.
- It encourages students' own critical questioning and problematising of work in the gender and language field.
- It facilitates students' own research in a range of ways and promotes their own contributions to gender and language study.
- It includes a very substantial Bibliography, as well as many references throughout the exploration 'C' units. These allow students to follow their interests and to take their studies forward on an independent basis.

The ten unit topics are as follows.

Part 1 'Background', comprising:

- early work on gender and language (Unit 1)
- the influence of feminism and feminist linguistics (a) (Unit 2)
- the influence of feminism and feminist linguistics (b) (Unit 3).

Part 2 'Gender', comprising:

- developing understandings of gender (Unit 4).

Part 3 'Language', comprising:

- developing understandings of language: language change (Unit 5)
- developing understandings of language: context (Unit 6)
- developing understandings of language: discourse and discourses (Unit 7).

Part 4 'Research', comprising:

- approaches to gender and language research (Unit 8)
- data and data sites (Unit 9)
- written texts (Unit 10).

Needless to say, the four parts are not mutually exclusive in their concerns. Research is a feature throughout, becoming an explicit focus in Part 4.

Much of the documented research on gender and language today has been done by, and even with, people from 'Western' countries, and 'language' often means 'English'. Although this book cannot rectify this situation (and, like others, is probably guilty of perpetuating it), it is emphasised throughout Section C, 'Exploration', that the language researched by readers, in most of the research projects, does not have to be English – and researching other languages is encouraged.

Students' own experience is drawn on throughout the book. It would be bizarre if this were not the case. As Deborah Cameron writes, 'Men and women are members of cultures in which a large amount of discourse about gender is constantly circulating' (1997a: 60). Although not everyone may not see it in this way, anyone who reads newspapers, watches television and indeed converses with others can hardly escape participating in that 'discourse about gender'. One aim of this book is to see that participation is itself a valuable resource for gender and language study, and to help readers articulate and theorise their experience accordingly.

SECTION A: INTRODUCTION

The 'Introduction' units, distributed across this resource book's four parts – 'Background', 'Gender', 'Language' and 'Research' - are written not only for those relatively new to the gender and language field, but also for those who would benefit from an updated summary of the unit topic. Broadly, they deal with relevant concepts and terms (in particular, meanings of 'gender', but also 'context', 'feminism', 'discourse'), and lay the foundations for the 'B' and 'C' units that follow (see 'How to use this book'). Most units include some sort of historical perspective. Gender and language study may be a young field, but since the early 1970s it has developed apace, creating an expanding paradigm which draws on a wide range of disciplines and theoretical and methodological approaches. Interestingly, new developments have not only built on their predecessors but have also been premised on challenges to those predecessors. The result is a field with practitioners whose contributions can be seen as located at different diachronic points, resulting in ongoing yet hopefully productive tensions. One ongoing debate, for example, is the role of the study of gender and language in what might be described as emancipatory feminism; another is whether CA is an appropriate approach for the feminist project that gender and language study is often seen to be.

These introduction 'A' units are in part 'springboards' for the extension 'B' units, since the latter are previewed and, importantly, contextualised here. Interspersed with the texts are 'Follow-Up Tasks' and 'Reflection Tasks'. Many of these invite and encourage the reader to critically question what they are reading, to draw on their own prior reading or experience, or to develop their own perspective on an issue. Active reading is thus a desideratum of both the introduction 'A' units and the extension 'B' units.

SECTION B: EXTENSION

Following on from the introduction 'A' units, which look at key concepts and terms, and at the historical background to various approaches and foci of research, the corresponding extension 'B' units take these further through illustrative readings. For each 'B' unit readers would benefit from studying the corresponding 'A' unit first. Particular readings from the 'B' units can (sometimes, should) also be read before starting particular 'C' exploration tasks, and readers are given directions here.

Again, then, following the four-way division of the resource book, the extension 'B' units focus on 'Background', 'Gender', 'Language' and 'Research'. The different extracts are all 'key' but for different reasons, including their theoretical approach and/or methodology, as well as empirical findings. Most units contain two or three extracts. The selection has been designed to allow students to read in the original a wide range of extracts from books, chapters and articles - in some cases, almost the whole chapter or article. Importantly, although all centre on both language and gender, the meanings of 'language' and of 'gender' vary from one extract to another, and the reader is encouraged to be alert to this diversity.

As regards selection, some extracts originally identified as highly desirable or very suitable were simply too expensive as regards copyright fees, or the authors were only willing for them to be included in their entirety (impossible in a book containing a large number of extracts). The extracts eventually chosen include both 'classic' and less well-known but nevertheless indicative work. Two pieces (those by Sara Mills and Puleng Hanong Thetela) have been commissioned especially for this resource book. All but one (Alma Graham's 'The making of a non-sexist dictionary') were written as academic pieces. Most of the extracts were written in the second half of the twentieth century, but there is also earlier work (Mary Haas's 'Men's and women's speech in Koasati'), and several pieces are from the first few years of the twenty-first century. Some extracts were originally targeted at readers working in the 'obvious' disciplines of Sociolinguistics, Applied Linguistics (in the broad sense) and Women's Studies; others in the less obvious ones of Literature, Language Education and Psychology. This is in accordance with one aim of this book: to acquaint the reader with work from different disciplinary as well as different theoretical and methodological traditions.

These extension 'B' units allow the authors to make their points for themselves. As both experienced and less experienced researchers know, reading the original article after having become very familiar with references to it in other work can be a salutary and exciting experience. The reader may find that the work in question has been misinterpreted; alternatively, it may have been cited so selectively that, without the proper context, any critique is unfair. Alternatively, the work may have been celebrated without due consideration of its problematic nature, evident only in further reading. And, almost certainly, the reader will not only come across the 'famous', classic, endlessly recycled quotations, but will have the refreshing experience of coming across *other* groups of words identifiable as potential quotations for her or his own work. And, sometimes, there is the 'buzz' of simply reading first-hand, in the writer's own words, something actually written by someone who has made a real difference to the field.

Preceding, punctuating and following the extracts are, variously, 'Before you read', 'Reflection', 'While you read' and 'After you've read' tasks. These, we hope, will help the reader to engage critically with the text: to anticipate the range of directions an extract might take; to question conceptualisations; to recognise the limitations and constitutiveness of a given methodology; to distinguish problems of presentation from problems of content; and to be able to identify what an extract has to offer the gender and language field and/or the reader's own research.

SECTION C: EXPLORATION

Following the four-part structure of the book into 'Background', 'Gender', 'Language' and 'Research', the purpose of Section C, 'Exploration', is to allow readers independently to take further a selection of the topics raised in Sections A and B, and to be able to do so at various levels, in various ways and directions, and to various extents and depths. Readers do this through research tasks, which allow them to become familiarised with a range of research practices in a very immediate way. They will develop research competencies, including those of principled data selection, careful and ethical data collection, and systematic and reflexive data analysis. They will hopefully continue to broaden and raise their awareness of the diverse field of gender and language in an informed and critical way, being able to use insights gained from their own hands-on research projects to constructively critique the work of others.

Readers will draw on their own personal and academic agendas in making their selections of which research tasks to carry out. Underlying their own work may be an intention not only to understand more about the workings of language in relation to gender, but also to develop further their understanding of the multiplicity of meanings of 'gender' itself. And, for some, the relationship of gender and language research to the broader, emancipatory 'feminist project' will always be an issue.

The research tasks can be used for a variety of specific purposes. They can suggest or constitute assignments with a clear research component; they can also be the basis for more substantial and extended Masters-level research. Developed, they can provide the germ of doctoral work. In higher-education institutional contexts, some may form the basis for seminar tasks, to be done individually, in small groups, or by the seminar group as a whole. Other tasks may provide suitable extensions of seminar work.

The tasks take the form of desk research and field research, and combinations of these. Desk research often involves the tracking down of others' work beyond what constitutes usual 'library research'. Field research may also include this, but additionally requires the collection (or selection/generation) and/or analysis of empirical data. The research tasks are carefully contextualised in association with particular theoretical and methodological approaches. They also draw on the different understandings of 'gender' addressed particularly in the Unit 4 units.

These research tasks do not automatically assume that the 'corresponding' intro-duction 'A' units have been covered, although study of the corresponding 'A' unit often provides a useful starting point for those unfamiliar with the task topic. Several tasks do require the reading of at least one of the extracts in the corresponding extension 'B' unit.

The tasks make use of the World Wide Web in various ways, and it is assumed that students are familiar with search tools and are able to search creatively and to follow up links. It is probably gratuitous to remind readers of the value and relevance of the World Wide Web for academic work: there are downloadable articles, assignments and lecture notes all there for the reading. Evaluating all these and using them selectively is part of library research today. For this reason, lengthy bibli-ographies are not included with each task, although key references are included with many.

A good, general starting point is the *Gender and Genre Bibliography* (<http://www.ling.lancs.ac.uk/groups/clsl/current.htm>). Published as a *Centre for Language in Social Life Working Paper 126* at Lancaster University, UK, this covers references to gender and language in relation to a large number of written and spoken genres ('genre' is used here in a very broad sense). The current (2006) edition of the *Bibliography* is the third. This bibliography is downloadable, and free. A second useful web site is that of the 'Language and Gender' page link to the homepage of the International Gender and Language Association (IGALA) (<http://www.stanford.edu/group/igala>). This provides details of a range of publications, including several downloadable ones.

Several other web sites have been listed, although it is recognised that these are not as stable as one would like. These include the web sites of various corpora, including the British National Corpus (BNC) and the Michigan Corpus of Academic Spoken English (MICASE). Several tasks require the use of corpora, and it is hoped that readers will become familiar with this mode of investigation, if only as a supple-mentary source of data for many research projects.

The last use of the World Wide Web is as a publication outlet for the outcomes of readers' own research tasks. Members of existing 'Gender and Language' courses are encouraged to set up a web site, with links to as many other sites as possible that constitute resources for the study of gender and language (for example, the two mentioned above), and with a member or members of the course taking respon-sibility for the site. Students can then post their work on the site – and can ask for comments from readers worldwide. Alternatively, readers working with the book on their own might like to post their work on their homepage, or to set up a homepage for this purpose.

SECTION A
Introduction

Unit A1
Early work on gender and language

A1.1 PROVERBS, QUOTATIONS AND FOLK-LINGUISTIC BELIEFS

Gender and language had been linked in scholarly writings well before the second wave of the Women's Movement began in the late 1960s and early 1970s (for example, Jespersen 1922, Labov 1966). Further back, popular understandings of gender and language had existed probably for centuries before 'gender and language' was considered worthy of study. I am referring here both to prescriptive ideas of how women and men should speak, and to 'folk-linguistic' ideas about how they actually do (apparently differently). Proverbs captured these folk-linguistic ideas, often referring disparagingly to women's verbosity. Jennifer Coates (1993: 16) cites the following (some of which have fallen out of use):

- 'A woman's tongue wags like a lamb's tail' (England).
- 'The North Sea will be found wanting in water than a woman at a loss for a word' (Jutland).
- 'Many women, many words, many geese, many turds' (England).

To these we can add:

- 'Three women make a market' (Sudan).
- 'Three women together make a theatrical performance' (China).
- 'Women are nine times more talkative than men' (Hebrew).

There is, of course, no evidence to support past assumptions of women's verbosity, and claims must be seen in the wider social context of expectations of the desirability (or otherwise) of women's talk. Sweepingly, but probably with a grain of truth, Dale Spender writes 'The talkativeness of women has been gauged in comparison not with men but with silence [so that] any talk in which a woman engages can be too much' (1980: 42).

Negative representations and evaluations of women's talk may disguise a concern not so much with their use of time, or this manner of conducting themselves, as with what they were saying (and about whom). The *content* of women's talk has certainly met with conventionalised rebuttals. Examples from traditional China, Russia and Japan include:

- 'Women's and children's opinion' (China).
- 'A woman's tongue spreads gossip fast' (China).
- 'Men talk like books, women lose themselves in details' (China).
- 'Never listen to a woman's words' (China).
- 'The tongue is babbling, but the head knows nothing about it' (Russia).
- 'Three inches of a woman's tongue can slay a man six feet tall' (Japan).[1]

Also worthy of mention are those writing systems in which several characters are gendered: the Mandarin Chinese character for 'harmony' (with its implied verbal component), for example, shows one woman under one roof:[2]

Figure A1.1

Explicit reference to women's use of language can be found too in fiction, for example in the words of characters created by Sophocles, Chaucer and Shakespeare:

- 'Silence gives the proper grace to women' (Sophocles, *Ajax*).
- 'As men/Do walk a mile, women should talk an hour/After supper. 'Tis their exercise' (Francis Beaumont and John Fletcher, *Philaster*, II.iv).
- 'How hard it is for women to keep counsel!' (Shakespeare, *Julius Caesar*, II.iv.9).
- 'Her voice was ever soft,/Gentle and low, an excellent thing in woman' (Shakespeare, *King Lear*, V.iii.274).
- 'She has brown hair, and speaks small like a woman' (Shakespeare, *Merry Wives of Windsor*, I.i.48).

Fictional utterances cannot be read 'straight', or as straightforwardly reflecting the view of the author: Shakespeare may not have concurred with these representations expressed in *Julius Caesar*, or by King Lear. Further, the 'value' of these views must depend on whether they are articulated by characters who are themselves represented positively or negatively, and, of course, by how these characters are played in a given stage production. However, their articulation in these fictional texts is a reminder of the long-running, traditional discursive practice of disparaging women's talk, and constitutes a recycling of this discourse (see Unit 7 on 'Discourse and Discourses').

On a different level – since it concerns linguistic proficiency rather than language use – is John Milton's 'One tongue is sufficient for a woman', apparently his response when asked whether he would instruct his daughters in foreign languages. Samuel Johnson similarly claimed that 'A man in general is better pleased when he has a good dinner than when his wife talks Greek'. Johnson's more famous pronouncement is, however, 'Sir, a woman's preaching is like a dog walking on his hind legs. It is not done well, but you are surprised to find it done at all' (apparently a response to Boswell). This claim is often recycled to make a point about something which is not done well, but which provokes surprise in the mere fact of its being done. Both Johnson's quotations can of course be read as much as comments on men (or at least on Johnson!) as on anything else.

 Task A1.1.1: Follow-up task

➤ Try and find examples of use of the second Samuel Johnson quote on the web. For a discussion of the quote, and others, and indeed of Johnson, see <http://www.samueljohnson.com/dogwalk.html#53>.

Ideas about how women do speak tend to shade into 'prescriptive' ideas of how they should (as several of the proverbs illustrate). Saint Paul, for example, is reported to have said (presumably to an audience of patriarchally minded men): 'Let your women keep silence in the churches' (1 Corinthians 14:34). Prescriptive ideas about women's language use have also been institutionalised in etiquette books. In the nineteenth and early twentieth centuries, these routinely advised women against public speaking, to tailor their talk to the interests of their (male) guests, to ask facilitative questions, and to listen rather than speak (Cameron 1995a, Eble 1976, Kramarae 1981). Rather differently, prescription is evident in the content of well-intentioned assertiveness training courses for women (Cameron 1992b).

Task A1.1.2: Reflection task

➤ Think of and note down your own examples (in any language) of the following which focus explicitly on the way women and men do and should talk:

■ proverbs
■ works of fiction, films, plays or songs
■ religious texts
■ assertiveness training sessions or texts.

A1.2 ACADEMIC WORK ON LANGUAGE USE AND GENDER

Coates (1993: 17–19) draws our attention to several educated eighteenth-century contributors to the English newspaper *The World*:

- Richard Cambridge (1754) refers to 'a vocabulary of words which perish and are forgot within the compass of a year. That we are obliged to the ladies for most of these ornaments to our language, I readily acknowledge.'
- 'Anonymous' (1756) complains of women's excessive use of certain adverbial forms (vastly, horridly, abominably, immensely, excessively).
- Lord Chesterfield (1754) complains that women change words' meanings (vastly glad, vastly little).

Task A1.2.1: Reflection task

➤ Assuming that there is some substance to these observations, consider and note down how you might read the linguistic behaviour described here in a positive light.

➤ Can you think of any way of empirically investigating these claims about apparent gender differences in language use in the eighteenth century?

➤ Can you think of any apparently contradictory phrases like 'vastly little' that are evident in English or any other language today? Are these evaluated in any particular way? Are they associated with particular groups of speakers?

Letters to newspapers about women's language use will inevitably reflect (and recycle) folk-linguistic ideas. However, scholarly work is also prone to this. The Danish linguist Otto Jespersen has been taken to task here (for example, in Coates 1993). Jespersen included in his 1922 monograph *Language: its nature, development and origin* a chapter called 'The woman' (needless to say, this was not matched by one called 'The man'). He made various claims about gender differences or tendencies in talk: that women have smaller vocabularies, show extensive use of certain adjectives and adverbs, 'more often than men break off without finishing their sentences, because they start talking without having thought out what they are going to say', and produce less complex sentences (Jespersen 1922: 251). Jespersen's own observations were based largely on impressionistic 'data' (and literary texts), reflecting ideas and epistemologies that existed at the time for the study of language. Analyst and native-speaker intuitions were then more than acceptable substitutes for empirical data (as they continued to be for several decades, and still are in certain branches of linguistics – see Robin Lakoff's perspective on this in Unit A2).

In a very different tradition, serious empirical fieldwork on language was being carried out in the early twentieth century by contemporaries of Jespersen: ethnographers, anthropologists and linguists interested in Native American languages in particular, who also documented gender differences. Mary Haas, for example, studied Koasati (a Native American language spoken in Louisiana) by working with its speakers. Her article 'Men's and women's speech in Koasati' was published in *Language* in 1944. An extract appears as Text B1.1.

Several studies of this kind identified what later came to be called 'sex-exclusive' linguistic features, that is, features used only by women, or only by men, within a given speech community. Jespersen famously quotes the case of the Carib Indians of the Lesser Antilles (West Indies), whose language was documented by Rochefort in 1665:

> he says that 'the men have a great many expressions peculiar to them, which the women understand but never pronounce themselves. On the other hand, the women have words and phrases which the men never use, or they would be laughed to scorn. Thus it happens that in their conversations it often seems as if the women had another language than the men'.
>
> (1922: 237)

It is interesting, if Rochefort is to be believed, that the reason men avoided certain 'feminine' words and phrases was to avoid ridicule, since this was not cited as a motivating factor for women. Such 'rigid boundaries' surrounding masculinity can still be seen, including in 'Western' cultures (see Unit C9.4).

An often-quoted example of modern sex-exclusive language features is the use of certain particles and pronominal forms in standard Japanese (see, for example, Ide 2003). However, there is change and resistance here, some women intentionally producing 'men's' forms (see Ozaki 1998, Okamoto 1995). Furthermore, this phenomenon does not occur in all dialects of Japanese (McMahill 2002).

 Task A1.2.2: Reflection task

➤ Are you familiar with a language with sex-exclusive features? If so, what are these? Is this phenomenon undergoing change, in your experience?

➤ What happens if men do produce 'women's features', and vice versa? Are children, and adult learners, taught to use these features 'appropriately'? If so, how?

➤ If you are not familiar with a language with sex-exclusive features, can you think of examples of ways in which women and men *tend* to use a language with which you are familiar differently? In what way?

'Sex-exclusive' uses of language occur rarely and contrast with the much more common (and frequently studied) 'sex-preferential' uses. These refer to differential tendencies, that is, ways in which women and men tend to talk differently from each other in a given context. 'Sex-preferential' phonetic, intonation, lexical, syntactic and wider interactional tendencies have been identified (see Units A2, B2).

Importantly, any such tendencies will always be small in comparison with women's and men's tendencies to speak similarly (otherwise communication between women and men would break down). 'Tendencies' also entails variation within women and within men, that is, intra-group diversity. This diversity was underplayed in the past, and even now Gender and Language researchers (see Unit A2) have to work to stress its importance.

The topic of women's and men's speech has been of particular interest to sociolinguists. Issues include gender-differential tendencies in style-shifting (for example, between formal and casual speech), use of prestige and stigmatised variants, linguistic conservatism, who leads language change (see below) and the positive and negative evaluation of such change.

William Labov's (1966, 1972a) and Peter Trudgill's (1972a) empirical studies of variation in language use were particularly important and influential here. In his paper 'Sex, covert prestige and linguistic change in the urban British English of Norwich', Trudgill correlates 'phonetic and phonological variables with social class, age, and stylistic context' (1972a: 180). However, following Labov, he was also interested in biological sex as a sociolinguistic variable.

Trudgill's methodology was quantitative, based on a large-scale interview study (a random sample of sixty people). Looking at the variable (ng), for which there are two pronunciations in Norwich English ('walking', the prestige form, and 'walkin''), Trudgill found that women tended to use the prestige form more than men (women over thirty years of age also tended to use the prestige forms of the other phonetic variables he studied more than men). He also found that women (more than men) tended to over-report their pronunciation, that is, when asked about their pronunciation, said they produced more 'prestigious' sounds than they actually did. However, of particular interest, and a source of past controversy, is not so much these findings as his explanation. Again following Labov, this included that, 'Women in our society are more status-conscious than men, generally speaking . . . and are therefore more aware of the social significance of linguistic variables' (1972a: 182).

This has merited considerable feminist critique. Deborah Cameron in *Feminism and Linguistic Theory* (1992b) suggests rather that, 'the women's assessments might . . . have reflected their awareness of sex-stereotypes and their consequent desire to fulfil "normal" expectations that women talk "better"' (1992: 63) – something rather different. With the benefit of hindsight, then, we can legitimately question Trudgill's explanation of women's greater 'status-consciousness'. Cameron also critiqued Trudgill's research methodology, in particular the way he identified the social class of husbands and wives.

Contrasting claims have been made about women's and men's linguistic conservatism (for example, Pop 1950). Work on leadership in language change includes that by William Labov (1966, 1972a, 1972b, 1990) in the USA. Looking at use of the short vowel (a), Labov (1966) found that women in New York tended to style-shift far more than did his male informants, and that they tended to be less conservative linguistically: they were in fact initiating change by using an 'advanced' vowel form in casual speech (the merging of /ih/ and /eh/). In contrast, and a reminder of the variability of any gender–language relationship, Labov's (1962, 1972b) study of the two diphthongs (aw) and (ay) in Martha's Vineyard showed men to be leading change. In another reminder of variability, in his (1990) paper, 'The intersection of sex and social class in the course of linguistic change', Labov notes that whereas men tend to use more non-standard stable forms than women, when it comes to linguistic change, women will innovate, in part by favouring new prestige forms 'from above'.

Other relevant empirical work on linguistic variation and gender has not been carried out from a feminist perspective but has nevertheless contributed to the broader 'feminist project'. This includes work by Susan Gal (1978), Anne Bodine (1975a, 1975b) and Lesley Milroy (1980). The Gal and Bodine studies are summarised below; an extract from Milroy can be found in Unit B1.2.

In a classic study, Gal (1978) investigated language variation in the village of Oberwart, on the Hungarian and Austrian border. Looking at social networks, she found that young Hungarian women in Oberwart spoke German in a much greater range of situations than did young Hungarian men (and older Hungarian women), and that they married out of their original speech community more than the men (for whom Hungarian still had something to offer). Highlighting the importance of the local, and indeed of social practice, Gal's study anticipated the later 'community of practice' (CofP) notion. Explored in Unit 6 (with an extract from a key reading in Unit B6.2), CofP can be seen as going beyond the notion of 'speech community' to include non-linguistic social practices. It has been defined as

> an aggregate of people who come together around mutual engagement in an endeavour. Ways of doing things, ways of talking, beliefs, values, power relations – in short, practices – emerge in the course of this mutual endeavour. . . . [A] Community of Practice . . . is defined simultaneously by its membership and by the practice in which that membership engages.
> (Eckert and McConnell-Ginet 1998: 490)

CofP has become an important notion for gender and language study: as a 'site' which is meaningful for its members, it is also an 'epistemological site' which is fruitful and theoretically coherent for researchers.

 Task A1.2.3: Reflection task

➤ Think of a CofP or speech community with which you are familiar in which more than one language is spoken. Are choices and patterns of distribution of these languages gendered in any way?

Anne Bodine (1975b) carried out a survey of ethnographic work on languages in non-European societies, looking not only at the sex of the speaker, but also of the addressee, and even of the 'spoken about'. Anticipating later developments in gender and language study, she claimed that gender differentiation (especially that not occurring in the ethnographers' own languages) was often overstated (see also Hall 2003).

Gender–language relationships have been the focus of pre- and non-feminist work in several areas other than language use. These include what might be called 'linguistic gender' (for example, considerations of gender-marking, of 'natural' and 'grammatical' gender, and of 'generics' such as 'man' in different world languages, see Corbett 2004). They also include questions of verbal ability in girls and boys (largely in first-language acquisition, for example, Maccoby and Jacklin 1974) and in female and male language learners of all ages (for example, Ekstrand 1980). There is also work on gendered language use by parents with children (for example, Greif and Gleason 1980). While such work tends (if unwittingly) to be very much in the 'gender differences' tradition (see Unit 2 for critiques), it has nevertheless provided useful data, as well as a standpoint from which to develop more dynamic conceptualisations of gender–language relationships.

NOTES

1. The source of most of the Chinese proverbs is Kaye (1989). I am also grateful to Hu Yining for supplying others. Another source is Mineke Schipper's *Never Marry a Woman with Big Feet* (2003).
2. Taken from <http://www.zein.se/patrick/chinen11p.html>.

Unit A2
The influence of feminism and feminist linguistics (a): Robin Lakoff, Dale Spender, 'deficit' and 'dominance'

A2.1 THE FEMINIST CONTRIBUTION

While empirical and other work on gender and language existed well before the modern Women's Movement (see Unit A1), in the 1970s this heralded a new, important and feminist impetus to language and gender study. The 'second wave' of the Women's Movement – in its early stages known as the Women's Liberation Movement (WLM) – began in the late 1960s, prompted in large part by the Civil Rights Movement in the USA;[1] and the late 1960s and the 1970s were a time of feminist[2] protest in many Western countries.

Feminism has acquired negative associations, entailing situated notions such as 'being anti-men'. Nevertheless, progressive reforms are ongoing and worldwide, symbolised by initiatives such as International Women's Year (1975); and 'gender equality' has been substantially taken on board by aid agencies and organisations such as the World Bank and the British Council. As early as 1975, The Pacific Women's Conference, held in Suva, Fiji, passed resolutions on women and the family, health, religion, education, work, the law and politics. More recently, the 1995 Beijing Conference on Women (The United Nations Fourth World Conference on Women), had as its slogan 'Action for Equality, Development and Peace'. Although 'equality' is open to interpretation, its inclusion was crucial. Though its impact may have been marginal in the 'West', women in many African countries acclaim 'Beijing' as an important landmark and attest to its influence on the way people now think and talk about gender issues.

Language was a particular feature and target of Western women's movements. The American feminist Robin Morgan claimed strongly in 1968 in *Going Too Far* that, 'The very semantics of the language reflect [women's] condition. We do not even have our own names, but bear that of the father until we exchange it for that of the husband' (1977: 106). By 1970 Emily Toth was railing against 'one-man tents', and Germaine Greer, in her famous *Female Eunuch* (1972), notes how 'terms of endearment' for women are also terms for food ('honey', 'sweetie'). Through lexical items such as 'Mrs/Miss', 'son-of-a-bitch' and 'manageress', the English language was said to 'define, degrade and stereotype' women, and through the so-called 'generics' 'he' and 'man', to render them invisible (see in particular Miller and Swift's *Words and Women* [1976]).

Task A2.1.1: Reflection task

➤ Think of a language other than English. Do features exist in this language which can be seen as having the capacity to 'define, degrade or stereotype' women, or to render them (relatively) invisible?

➤ If so, is there resistance to such features?

➤ Are language practices changing here?

An early assumption surrounding 'sexist language' items was that language could influence both thought and behaviour. Sexist language was seen to do so for the worse. This analysis led to the adoption or creation of alternative linguistic items – for example, 'Ms' as a title for all women, married or single; 'manager', 'spokesperson' and 'chairperson' to refer inclusively to both women and men; 'he or she' and 's/he' to avoid the 'masculine bias' of the 'generic he'. These alternatives were not only used by committed individuals in their speech and writing, and documented in feminist books such as Miller and Swift's *Handbook of Non-Sexist Writing* (1989), but also appeared as elements of institutional codes of practice (with such titles as 'Guidelines for Inclusive Language'). The then UK Lancashire Polytechnic (now University of Central Lancashire) produced a 'Code of practice on non-gender-specific terminology' in 1987. This considered telephone listings, forms of address (written and spoken), procedures in meetings and letters, and noted that 'the use of "love," "dear" and "darling," to female colleagues often implies a lack of equality and mutuality' (p. 2). These interventions were not without their opponents. Commentaries and letters about this code appeared in both the local and national press, making reference to 'cultural dictatorship', the 'frustrated spinsters' (who had put the document together), and claiming that '*Luv* lacks gender, *dear* is sexless and *darling* is neutral' (italics added).[3]

The early backlash was in its turn resisted, most notably in the academic sector by critical analyses of those arguments mounted against non-sexist language. The earliest was Maija Blaubergs' (1980) 'An analysis of classic arguments against changing sexist language' (see also Blaubergs 1978). In a later, less well-known paper, Nancy Henley (1987) identified six arguments against changing the language, refuting each in turn. Challenging the argument that 'Linguistic sexism is superficial and trivial', for example, Henley writes, 'Studying sexism in language is not a diversion from study of important problems, but it does need integration with other areas of inequality so that the larger picture may be pieced together' (1987: 8).[4]

New syntactic possibilities, new lexicalisations and re-presentations of familiar ones also appeared in grammars and dictionaries (see Sunderland 1994b). *The*

Comprehensive Grammar of the English Language (1985), for example, describes 'singular they' (for example, 'Everyone should bring their deposit on Monday') as 'now increasingly accepted even in formal usage'. Non-sexist items have on the whole, however, remained alternatives to, rather than replacements for, sexist language items (see Unit 5), though they may have reduced in frequency.

As part of the campaign for non-sexist language in English, the following alternative items thus came into use:

Table A2.1

Alternative item	Intended to replace	Reason
Ms	*Miss/Mrs*	to achieve equivalence with *Mr* and to end the practice of women being 'defined' by their marital status
chairperson *spokesperson* *barperson*	*chairman* *spokesman* *barman* (especially as referents for women)	to put an end to the 'think male' phenomenon, and the 'rendering invisible' of women
s/he, 'singular *they*'	'generic *he*'	as above

To these we can add the practice of standardising 'marked' female terms:

Table A2.2

Alternative item	Intended to replace	Reason
doctor *usher* *flight attendant*	*lady doctor* *usherette* *air hostess*	to achieve equivalence with 'masculine' terms, and to end the practice of 'trivialising' and 'marking' feminine terms

 Task A2.1.2: Reflection task

➤ In what way are these alternative items used today? Complete the chart below from the point of view of your own living and working situation.

➤ Consider how (if you are female) you react to being given a title (Miss, Mrs, Ms) you do not use or like.

➤ Consider whether, as a teacher, you would (or do) teach 's/he' and 'singular they'. If 'Yes', what would/do you say about these items?

	Ms	chairperson	s/he	'singular' they	flight attendant
Do you use this, ever?					
If so, in what context(s)?					
With whom?					
To/Of whom?					
Who do you know who typically uses it?					
What is your attitude to the term? What do you see as its value today, if any?					

Other language-related practices included rather more direct action in terms of painting out sexist words and slogans on billboards and replacing them with others. The Fiat billboard ad 'If it were a lady, it would get its bottom pinched' famously received a spray-painted addition of 'If this lady was a car she'd run you down' – immortalised by photographer Jill Posener (see Sunderland 2004).

A2.2   ROBIN LAKOFF AND *LANGUAGE AND WOMAN'S PLACE*

These early feminist concerns (of both linguists and activists) were largely with the English language as an abstract system (*langue*), and with replacements (or at least alternatives) that would represent women in a more inclusive and positive way. However, feminist linguists soon took an interest in naturally occurring language use (*parole*) – particularly that between women and men. Robin Lakoff's *Language and Woman's Place* (1975, see also Text B2.1) considers questions of non-sexist language, but is best known for its explorations of what have since been widely referred to as 'gender differences in language use'. Sections of this work had originally appeared as an article two years previously, but by 1975 the political climate and developing field had more than created readiness for a book devoted to gender and language written (at least in part) from a feminist perspective, and Lakoff's was the first monograph (indeed, first complete book) on gender and language. It is now widely critiqued on many counts – including that in some ways it represents women's language use as 'deficient', relative to that of men – and is sometimes cited as exemplifying a 'deficit approach' to studies of women's talk (along with the work of Jespersen and Trudgill, see Unit A1). This is, however, to miss the clear 'male dominance' elements of the book (see below, see also Text B2.1).

Language and Woman's Place is widely acknowledged as an important pioneer work that carried (and still carries) wide-ranging influence (as the frequency of its academic citations illustrates). Its importance has been further attested by the publication of a second edition (2004). Edited by Mary Bucholtz, this includes a series of new, short contributions by key gender and language researchers, a new 'Introduction' and annotations of the original first edition text by Lakoff herself.

A2.3 DALE SPENDER AND *MAN MADE LANGUAGE*

Five years after *Language and Woman's Place* came out of the USA, a rather more hard-hitting book, Dale Spender's *Man Made Language* (1980), appeared in the UK. Spender had been a secondary-school teacher, and the book includes an important educational dimension. Aiming less at an academic and more at a popular audience, this work represented what can be seen as a radical feminist position. Writing from an explicitly feminist, committed perspective, Dale Spender was uncompromising in her early claims. Like Lakoff, Spender wrote about sexism in the English language and gender differences in language use. She saw both as operating to the clear disadvantage of women, contributing to women being effectively silenced. Largely reporting and bringing together others' findings, Spender focuses on how, in mixed-sex talk, men dominate the conversation, interrupt their conversational partners and are more successful at having the topics they bring up, taken up. This corresponds to what is now known as the '(male) dominance' approach characteristic of studies of language use and gender in the 1970s (and drawn on well into the 1980s and even the 1990s).

Through *Man Made Language*, Dale Spender did a great deal to popularise the study of gender and language in the UK and beyond. She was a prolific writer – in the same year that *Man Made Language* was published she also published (with Elizabeth Sarah) an edited collection: *Learning to Lose: sexism and education* and sustained an impressive publishing record throughout the 1980s. Her later books include (and the titles are illustrative of her stance): *Men's Studies Modified* (1981), *Invisible Women* (1982, 1989), *Feminist Theorists* (1983), *Women of Ideas and What Men Have Done to Them* (1983, 1988), *There's Always Been a Women's Movement this Century* (1983), *Time and Tide Wait for No Man* (1984), *For the Record: the making and meaning of feminine knowledge* (1985), *Mothers of the Novel*

(1986), *The Education Papers: women's quest for equality in Britain (1850–1912)* (1987), *The Writing or the Sex?: or why you don't have to read women's writing to know it's no good* (1989) and *Nattering on the Net: women, power and cyberspace* (1995).

Chapter 5 of *Man Made Language*, 'Language and reality: who made the world?' begins with a useful, and in part philosophical, discussion of the partiality of science. Spender cites with approval Chalmers' claim that 'theory precedes observation' (1978), arguing that theories and categories are not gender-neutral, and that, 'When there are a sexist language and sexist theories culturally available, the observation of reality is also likely to be sexist. It is by this means that sexism can be perpetuated and reinforced as new objects and events, new data, have sexist interpretations projected upon them' (Spender 1980: 141).

This of course begs the question of the origin of sexist language, theories and categories. Rejecting 'mere accident', Spender continues:

> I would reiterate that it has been the dominant group – in this case, males – who have created the world, invented the categories, constructed sexism and its justification and developed a language trap which is in their interest. . . . Males . . . have produced language, thought and reality. Historically it has been the structures, the categories and the meanings which have been invented by males – though not of course by all males – and they have then been validated by reference to other males. In this process women have played little or no part.
>
> (1980: 142–3)

Task A2.3.1: Reflection task

➤ In privileging patriarchy as a dominant force in shaping both cognitive and social structures, Spender is de-privileging social class and ethnicity. To what extent do you support her argument?

Spender provides some linguistic evidence for her claim that men are in part responsible for linguistic sexism, at least in the grammar of English. She cites the work of sixteenth-, seventeenth- and eighteenth-century male grammarians, who inscribed the following notions into their grammars:

▪ The male term should 'precede' the female (for example, 'husband and wife') (Wilson 1553).
▪ One reason for this was that the male was the 'worthier' gender (Poole 1646).
▪ The male gender was 'more comprehensive' than the female (Kirkby 1746).

Spender thus successfully demonstrated that 'intervention' in the language is not only something that twentieth-century feminists tried to do. These grammars may not have produced their hoped-for results, of course, but may have had other (related) effects. Spender wrote, 'the rule was there, it had been recorded, and it was extremely useful for the nineteenth-century grammarians who vehemently took it up and insisted on rigid adherence to this rule in the name of grammatical correctness – another invention of the dominant group which legitimates their prejudice!' (1980: 149).

A grammatical rule, of course, cannot legislate for understanding, and Spender provides empirical evidence that 'generic man' and 'generic he' are not (probably, cannot be) as generic (or 'comprehensive', in Kirkby's words) as is sometimes claimed. For example:

> Alleen Pace Nilsen (1973) found that young children thought that man meant male people in sentences such as 'man needs food'. . . . Linda Harrison found that science students – at least – thought male when discussing the evolution of man, they had little appreciation of the female contribution even when explicitly taught it (1975).
>
> (1980: 152)

 Task A2.3.2: Reflection task

➤ What is your own response to the utterance 'Everyone knows he has to decide for himself'? (Let us assume this is said in the context of voting in an election.) If you are female, do you feel entirely included? Do you have to 'read against the grain' (for example, do some rhetorical and/or cognitive work) to feel included by this sentence? If you are male, do you read this as referring to both women and men? Can you imagine how a woman might feel?

Like *Language and Woman's Place, Man Made Language* was thought-provoking and influential. Like Lakoff, Spender was a pioneer in the field, and, like Lakoff, her work has been widely critiqued. This was in part because of Spender's representation of the English language as a gender-biased system (as opposed to a linguistic system within which usages have acquired a masculine orientation), and in part because of her determinist stance and insufficient acknowledgement of the fact that meaning can never be fixed. Spender was articulating a form of social constructionism redolent of a strong version of the Whorfian hypothesis: that language and categories shape how people see the world, and that a sexist world has been created by men, the inventors of those categories.

Critique was accordingly voiced of Spender's view of language as somehow constructed by a conspiratorial patriarchy. And, in their classic, early post-structuralist critique, 'Linguistic, social and sexual relations: a review of Dale Spender's *Man Made Language*' (1981), Maria Black and Rosalind Coward further attack Spender's notion of gender, arguing that Spender's highly monolithic view of patriarchy and gender relations and her emphasis on 'pre-given groups' (males) 'give[s] us no real purchase on how ideologies participate in the production of groups and secure identification with the subject positions produced there' (1981: 72). Black and Coward additionally saw Spender's model of language as looking at etymological data in isolation from relevant social and linguistic changes and uses. They argued: 'We have to understand not just histories of words, but the relationship of terms to other terms, the relationship between terms in statements, the relationship between statements' (1981: 82).

If meanings are seen as produced in ideologies, so that, for example, it is not only men who may define childbirth as an 'ultimately satisfying' experience for women (as Spender claims), both men and women can be seen as capable of claiming this, as well as of emphasising the pain. Different men's and women's articulated positions depend on the discourses to which they have access and on which they draw (see also Sunderland 2004). Black and Coward were thus forerunners of a *discourse* approach to gender and language (see Unit 7); certainly they anticipated the importance the notion of discourses was to have for gender and language study.

NOTES

1. The 'first wave' refers rather Anglocentrically to the British women's suffrage movement in the early part of the twentieth century. 'Third wave' has now been applied to what might be seen as a form of 'post-structuralist feminism', in which it is fully recognised that a given form, representation or manifestation, seen as sexist by some, may have a myriad of possible alternative meanings, including to feminists (Mills 2002a, b, also Unit B5.2, Sunderland 2004).
2. The word 'feminism' had been around since as early as the nineteenth century, but now came into its own.
3. Thanks to Marilyn Martin-Jones for this data.
4. A retrospective backlash can be seen in the more recent and frequent 'knee-jerk', dismissive accusations of 'political correctness'. This notion, which seems so unproblematic to those who draw on it with a view to discrediting proponents of both non-sexist and non-racist language (and other progressive practices), has now been thoroughly problematised (see, for example, Cameron 1995a, Suhr and Johnson 2003), at least in academia. Sadly (for many), it remains triumphant in many other discourse(s) communities.

Unit A3
The influence of feminism and feminist linguistics (b): Daniel Maltz and Ruth Borker, and 'difference'

The '(male) dominance' approach to gender and language (on which Dale Spender [see Unit A2] was drawing, and to which she contributed in her emphasis on the conversational 'silencing' of women) was very much a child of its time, deriving from the concerns of the Women's Movement (with its early language of 'patriarchy' and 'sexism') and resonating with feminist interests. As Deborah Cameron later wrote, 'dominance . . . represented [a] particular moment [. . .] in feminism: dominance was the moment of feminist outrage, of bearing witness to oppression in all aspects of women's lives' (1995b: 39). Also working within this approach, Pamela Fishman (1978, 1983, see Unit B2.3) famously characterised women's contribution to mixed-sex talk as 'shitwork': 'Women do support work while men are talking and it is the women who generally do active maintenance and continuation work in conversations' (1983: 98).

Work in this tradition largely saw women's talk in relation to that of men. However, although women may tend to talk distinctively (though this will always vary with context, one contextual factor being one's interlocutor or co-conversationalists), they may also talk differently in conversation with women than with men. As Jennifer Coates wrote: 'it is very important that we do not conflate the "women's language" said to be typical of mixed-sex interaction with the "women's language" which characterizes all-female discourse' (1989: 121). Generalisations about women's talk (even assuming these are possible) cannot come out of findings about mixed-sex talk (or indeed single-sex talk) alone. Correspondingly, the nature of single-sex talk cannot be simply inferred from the way women (or men) talk in mixed conversation.

Coates has been concerned to redress the focus on mixed-sex talk with a focus on women's talk (she has written many articles on the talk of young and older women, and a book entitled *Women Talk* [1996], followed by *Men Talk* [2003]). Her work addresses her own claim that although Maltz and Borker (1982) refer to language being acquired and developed in single-sex groups (see Unit B3.1), they do not provide empirical evidence for this, evidence which is important in order to avoid the creation of new linguistic myths (1989: 95).

Work in the 'dominance' tradition has further been accused of representing women as passive and as victims and of using women's 'subordination' as a complete and 'pan-contextual' explanation for characteristics of mixed-sex talk (see Cameron 1992b, Talbot 1998). With a hindsight informed by post-structuralism, women's silence (absolute, or relative to that of men), for example, can sometimes be read as actively subversive rather than enforced, in some cases and contexts a meaningful and active strategy of resistance.

Task A3.1: Reflection task (language use and gender)

➤ Consider three contexts in which, in your experience, men and women (or boys and girls) tend to talk differently, and how. List these contexts and associated differences.

➤ Choose one 'difference in a context' from your list. Now list possible contextual features that may be relevant here. For example, who is talking to whom, where, when, doing what (Hymes 1972)? If this feature were changed, would the difference still obtain?

➤ Do you think there is an element of 'male dominance' in the 'difference' you have identified?

➤ Now describe your 'difference' to a friend. Does he or she think that this would obtain in any other context, and, if so, which, and why?

➤ What does this task suggest about linguistic variation between women and men?

The '(cultural) difference' approach, in contrast with '(male) dominance', was relatively unconcerned with masculine verbal power. It was thus more in tune with traditional variationist sociolinguistics, which was never designed to address the notion of 'dominance' and hence was ill equipped to deal with it (see Cameron 1992b). Variations on '(cultural) difference' can be seen in the work of Jennifer Coates (1996), Janet Holmes (1995) and Deborah Tannen (1991). A key influence here (particularly on Tannen) was Maltz and Borker's 1982 paper, 'A cultural approach to male-female miscommunication' (see Unit B3). Maltz and Borker claimed that girls and boys grew up largely in different 'sociolinguistic subcultures', and that any communication problems in women's and men's talk can be related to Gumperz's notion of 'interethnic communication' (for example, 1978b) – namely, that problems between people of different ethnic groups 'are the result of differences in systems of conversational inference and the cues for signalling speech acts and speaker's intent' (Maltz and Borker 1982: 201). Seeing women and men as members of different 'speech cultures' comparable to those of speakers of different languages, however, requires examination (see Unit C3).

In contrast to 'dominance', Cameron writes that '[cultural] difference was the moment of feminist celebration, reclaiming and revaluing women's distinctive cultural traditions' (1995b: 39). 'Cultural difference' researchers and theorists aimed not only to describe (rather than critique), but also sometimes to positively evaluate women's talk, in particular all-women talk (for example, some work of Janet Holmes and Jennifer Coates). Coates is concerned not to denigrate women (however unintentionally), for example not to represent them as deficient language users (which Jespersen and Lakoff have been seen as doing), or as victims (an accusation sometimes directed at '(male) dominance' work). Coates celebrates women's talk in the interesting, bold (but controversial) claim that 'All-woman conversation . . . has as its chief goal the maintenance of good social relationships' (1989: 98). Coates uses empirical evidence to support the notion of women's linguistic cooperativeness, accomplished in different linguistic ways; her paper 'Gossip revisited' (1989) concluded: 'It seems that in conversations between women friends in an informal context, the notion of co-operativeness is not a myth' (1989: 119).

There is now a myriad of non-academic books which not only embrace but enthusiastically promote the notion of 'gender differences'. The original bestseller was probably Tannen's (1991) *You Just Don't Understand!: women and men in conversation*, but we now also have John Gray's *Men are from Mars and Women are from Venus* (1992; now expanded to a whole series), as well as Allan Pease and Barbara Pease's series which includes *Why Men Don't Listen and Women Can't Read Maps* (2001), *Why Men Lie and Women Cry* (2003), and *Why Women Can't Read Maps and Won't Stop Talking* (1999). This last is described on the publisher's and distributors' web sites as a 'little book of advice for men on how to get on with their partner'. It would of course be interesting to know the proportion of purchasers who are in fact men.

Unit A4
Developing understandings of gender

A4.1   GENDER, LANGUAGE AND THE 'FEMINIST PROJECT'

Feminism has inspired gender and language study since the late 1960s (see Units A2 and A3), but there have been different feminisms, with different natures and objectives, not only historically, over time, but also at the same point in time, and this continues to be so (see, for example, Tong 1992). Different feminisms have had different impacts on gender and language study. For example, Dale Spender's (1980) approach (see Unit A2 and Unit B2.2) can be seen as a radical feminist one, embracing the notion of patriarchy as primary in women's 'struggle' – rather than, say, class, which has been of prime importance to socialist feminists.

However, as Cameron (1997b) points out, what different feminisms have in common is not just an interest in women and men, girls and boys, and gender relations, but also a critical interest. This extends to social arrangements and power relations, although notions of power (who has it, can have it and how it is exerted) similarly vary with different forms of feminism (see below).

Different phases of feminism can be seen as the driving force behind the retrospectively named '(male) dominance' and '(cultural) difference' approaches to the study of gender and talk (see Units A2 and A3). To bring together her quotes from these two units, Cameron notes that, 'Both dominance and difference represented particular moments in feminism: dominance was the moment of feminist outrage, of bearing witness to oppression in all aspects of women's lives, while difference was the moment of feminist celebration, reclaiming and revaluing women's distinctive cultural traditions' (1995b: 39).

For 'dominance', power, in a fairly monolithic sense, was a crucial analytical concept; for 'difference' it was not (though elements of power were variously acknowledged). However, of both, Cameron adds, 'Their moments have passed' and 'the theories which underpinned them are no longer sufficient' (1995b: 39). Insufficient theories had in particular precluded adequate understandings of gender.

Feminism in general and feminist theory in particular also drove the subsequent critique of 'dominance' and 'difference' as a *single* approach, with more in common than not. *Both* were prefaced on a binary notion of gender, entailing an investigative focus on differences. Though this was well intentioned ('dominance' studies attempting to expose oppressive differences, 'difference' studies to identify positive ones), both can be seen in one sense as anti-feminist with their socially essentialist focus on the binary nature of gender: conservatives too love to hear and talk about gender differences. As Cameron points out, 'every word we say on the subject of difference just underlines the salience and the importance of a division we are ultimately striving to end' (1992b: 40; see also Unit B4.1).

 Task A4.1.1: Reflection task

➤ Is the idea of 'gender differences' a popular one in your society? (Is it perhaps a positive one? Consider '*Vive la différence!*') Is it a popular idea in other societies you are familiar with?

➤ Consider different manifestations of 'gender differences'. Can you recall a recent occasion when the idea of 'gender differences' was drawn on explicitly (for example, in the media or in a conversation: 'Men are like this, women are like that')? Were tendencies (as opposed to absolutes) acknowledged?

Empirical work on contextually varying performances of gender (and indeed sexuality), including by the same individual, has thoroughly disturbed notions of gender as even socially essentialist. And gender and language study has now largely moved on from a drive to identify gender differences in all sorts of contexts. Newer understandings of gender as identity, and identity as multiple, fluctuating and continually being constructed, have made 'difference' and 'dominance' appear crude and inadequate. Subsequent challenges to the notion of identity (for example, Butler 1990, 1999), with a focus on performance, have shifted the field yet again towards a more post-structuralist concern with how gender is performed, constructed, enacted and/or displayed in spoken and written texts. Here, the sex of the speaker/ writer may be of little or no interest. To this we can add the important contribution of the notion of *discourse* to modern gender and language study, in particular discourse's ongoing constitutive potential. To quote Mary Bucholtz, 'More recent [language and gender] scholarship . . . recognize(s) that gender identity is at once more specific than most 1970s feminism realised and more fluid than much 1980s feminism allowed' (1999b: 4, Unit B4.2). This is an acknowledgement not only of the early broad-brush studies of 'women's talk' and 'men's talk', but also of the later lack of recognition of the possibility of displayed and shifting identities.

The role of theory is of interest here. Early second-wave feminism may have prompted gender and language study, but the field can be seen as having lagged behind both post-structuralist and feminist theory in terms of different possibilities for gender. Bucholtz identifies as one reason the 'scientific urge' of much linguistic research, noting that in the USA linguistic research 'has been much slower than the other social sciences to shift its focus from the "science" to the "social" aspect of its intellectual mandate' (1999b: 3, see also Unit B4.2). This is true of the UK too (where most linguists work in Faculties of Humanities rather than of Social Sciences), less so of Continental Europe. Current conceptualisations of Gender and Language (performance, construction of identity in discourse and the relevance of non-linguistic social practice – for example, in particular CofPs) though, show that the field is now being shaped quite significantly by feminist theory. These conceptualisations actively contest the idea of gender as being something other than a binary, biologically shaped or socially determined entity, consisting of a monolithic masculinity and femininity.

A4.2 UNDERSTANDINGS OF GENDER

What, then, are some possibilities for gender?

Task A4.2.1: Reflection task

➤ How many post-gender collocates can you think of? For example, the phrase 'gender role' used to be encountered frequently. What others can you think of? Make a list. Then turn the page.

➤ Here are some possibilities – add yours to the list.

gender relations	gender representation
gender identity	gender construction
gender difference(s)	gender performance
gender tendencies	gender display

Rather than relying solely on intuition, we can supplement this list by looking at uses of *gender* as shown in a corpus of spoken or written language, for example, British National Corpus (BNC), Michigan Corpus of Academic Spoken English (MICASE), as well as the LOB, FLOB, BROWN and FROWN corpora of 1960s/1990s American and British English (1 million words each). A Lancaster University web site lists still more corpora (<http://www.comp.lancs.ac.uk/ucrel/corpora.html>). Typing in 'gender' will not only confirm whether these collocates occur in actual language use (plus how frequently, and in what linguistic context), but will show still other, unpredicted collocates.

Let us take MICASE (publicly available and free of charge), <http://www.hti.umich.edu/m/micase>. Here we find eighty-two occurrences of 'gender' (compared with 142 occurrences of 'sex'). If we look at the thirty-two of the eighty-two occurrences that are followed by a content word (and are not followed by a comma), we have the following list:

```
            gender wars
    mixed gender opera troupes
    mixed gender audiences
            gender definitions
            gender-related issues
            gender issues (3)
            gender role(s) x 2
            gender role attitudes
            gender role advertising
            gender portrayals x 2
            gender analysis
            gender bigoted
            gender traditionalism
            gender stereotypes (3)
            gender relations
            gender ideas
            gender differences (2)
            gender inequality (4)
            gender boundaries (2)
            gender-bending
            gender dichotomy
```

It is of interest that 'gender differences' occurred only twice. However, several of the other concepts assume and indeed entail the notion of gender differences: 'gender role(s)', 'mixed gender opera troupes/audiences', 'gender(-related) issues', 'gender inequality' and, we can assume, 'gender wars'. Even 'gender-bending' entails some sort of 'essentialist' starting point.

'Gender relations' carries the potential not just for differentiation and differential empowerment, but also dominance, disadvantage, and economic, educational and political inequality. This is true regardless of whether women and men live, learn and work alongside each other, or live largely parallel rather than 'integrated' lives. Potentially including relations at macro-, institutional levels, at domestic, familial ones, and in small-scale, brief interactions, 'gender relations' entails the potential for those relations to be maintained and perpetuated in part through language: precisely the point the '(male) dominance' school of gender and language study was making.

'(Male) dominance' entailed a focus on actual males and females and the 'differences' between them. The collocates 'gender portrayals', 'gender stereotypes' and 'gender ideas' refer rather to how gender, including alleged differences, is talked about (and thus textually constructed). These suggest that the idea of gender as a set of differences is being (at least) supplemented by a notion of gender as a construct, or idea, dissociated from dimorphically sexed human beings.

Portrayals, I suggest, are broadly synonymous with representation (see Unit A10). Gender representation is often achieved through stereotyping – for example, women may be represented in a particular way in a joke about their alleged verbosity, which relies on this folk-linguistic stereotype. (Needless to say, there is a gulf between representation and empirically established and documented 'reality', see Cameron 2003.) Many representations seem to put women at a disadvantage. However, there is always the need for interpretation of a given representation, so that 'what is happening' in a text may be seen differently by one person and by her or his friend. This is to entertain a view of meaning as co-constructed, that is, not only by the text (and its producer), but also by the 'consumer' (the reader or listener). Given such 'co-construction', to talk about an 'effect' of any given representation (whether in fiction, on television or in a political speech) is always problematic.

Task A4.2.2: Reflection task

You may have had the experience of seeing an advertisement (for example, on television, on a billboard or in a magazine) which you did not at first understand. You may have asked someone to explain it to you. But you may not have accepted their explanation. Alternatively, two people might have explained it differently. This is because there is often more than one way of 'reading' an advertisement (indeed, any text).

➤ Consider a recent representation of women or men in an advertisement. Do you feel this representation is largely progressive, conservative or mixed? Do you think there are different ways of 'reading' the representation?

It is worth noting the distancing from 'gender role' that is achieved by the addition of 'attitudes' and 'advertising'. These new noun phrases draw on (and thus recycle) the 'gender role' notion but also crucially suggest reflexivity towards and critique of the notion of 'gender role'. Gender roles are then not just a matter of 'common sense'.

There are, however, political implications, even dangers, with a focus on gender as constructed and performed, and an emphasis on fluctuating and multiple meanings. Such a focus can lead us away from one of the original tenets of (and reasons for) feminism: the notion of the systemic disadvantaging of women and girls (Jones 1993). And while we can comfortably say that some women are now in some contexts and ways very powerful (see Baxter 2003), and that the notion of patriarchy is far too blunt an instrument to address the diversity of power in women's social practices worldwide, to abandon a concern for disadvantage completely would invalidate the broader feminist project. Hence the ongoing need for judicious use of such terms as 'gender bigoted' and 'gender traditionalism' (and even 'gender roles').

Although 'gendering' was does not occur in the MICASE data, the words preceding 'gender' include the very post-structuralist phrase 'playing with the gender dichotomy'. This, especially when seen alongside 'gender boundaries', affords an understanding of gender as not only very diverse and fluid (boundar*ies*), but also as a socially constructed (masculine/feminine) dichotomy that can be played with – so that the originally dichotomous 'either/or' may become 'both', 'neither', 'at this point in time only', 'who knows?' or even 'does it matter?' The verb phrase 'playing with' suggests both ludic intent and agency. Gender can also be seen as being 'in play', i.e. fluctuating and unpindownable, as well as being in play with other identity categories, such as ethnicity.

MICASE data comes solely from a university context (and thus cannot validly be compared with broader corpora of talk). Further, there is a limit as to how far examination of corpus data can go, since we do not know fully (beyond a few words of co-text) how the linguistic items in question were being used. Even the inclusion of a traditional phrase such as 'gender role' does not mean that it is being used in an uncritical, non-reflexive way; it may have been being critiqued (precisely what is happening in this unit). Similarly, the phrases 'gender dichotomy' and 'gender boundaries' may have referred to people's thinking about the notion of gender (the phrase 'gender definitions' certainly points to this).

Perhaps surprisingly, 'gender identity' is missing from the MICASE list. Identity has become a very important concept in gender and language study, to a large extent replacing the fixed and socially or even biologically essentialist notion of 'gender role'. However, the concept of identity has itself been challenged, and from different quarters. The philosopher Judith Butler's *Gender Trouble* (1999) is subtitled *The Subversion of Identity*; she emphasises the importance and crucial variability of performance (see below). Second, discursive psychology (for example, Edley 2001, McIlvenny 2002, Weatherall 2002, Wetherell 1998) has rejected the notion of identity as an individual's 'inner self', being concerned rather with the socially shaped accounts an individual articulates. Such accounts may be variable and even contradictory. For discursive psychology, this is not a problem, but rather can be related to the different discourses by which an individual is 'positioned' (see Unit B9, also Baxter 2003).

'Performance', 'enactment' and 'display' do not occur either as collocates of gender, but are conceptually suggested by 'playing with the gender dichotomy'. Together, 'performance', 'enactment' and 'display' point to gender as viewable as performed/ enacted/displayed differences or tendencies, and accordingly provide a new set of ways of viewing the social and linguistic practices of women and men.

A4.3 POST-STRUCTURALISM AND THE STUDY OF GENDER AND LANGUAGE

Post-structuralism has provided a major challenge to essentialist notions of gender and has been crucial in the developing understanding of gender. With its emphasis on the constitutive nature of discourse it has thoroughly informed linguistic study – and indeed has been largely responsible for the 'linguistic turn' in many other disciplines. Post-structuralism is illustrated in Cynthia Nelson's extract on 'queer theory' (Unit B4.3) and Judith Baxter's extract on FPDA (Unit B7.3, see also Baxter 2002a, 2002b, 2003).

Baxter refers to post-structuralism as entailing a 'sense of scepticism towards all universal causes, its questioning of what "true" or "real" knowledge is, and . . . loss of certainty about all absolutes' (2003: 6). A key tenet is the rejection of the idea that meaning is, or ever can be, fixed. Meaning is always provisional. Accordingly, knowledge is always (in this sense) constructed rather than discovered, hence the need for constant self-reflexivity on the part of the researcher. As regards the crucial role of language in post-structuralism, Chris Weedon famously characterised language as 'the place where actual and possible forms of social organisation and their likely social and political consequences are defined and contested. Yet it is also the place where our sense of selves, our subjectivity is constructed' (1987: 21). Seeing language as such is to work with a crucially constitutive model of language, that is, *discourse* (in the sense used by social theorists such as Michel Foucault [1972] and Norman Fairclough [2003]).

Task A4.3.1: Reflection task

➤ Consider the post-structuralist notion that language is potentially constitutive. In what possible ways can we understand 'constitutive'? Constituted where or in who/what? How? By whom or what?

Important post-structuralist work has been done by Chris Weedon (1987, 1996), Bronwyn Davies (1989a, 1989b, 1993, 1997, see also Unit B10.2) and Judith Butler (1990, 1999, 2004). Butler's influence extends far beyond the Gender and Language field, but her major contribution has been to queer theory (see Nelson's extract in Unit B4.3). Her contributions are intellectual rather than empirical. Like Deborah Cameron's, Butler's work, while feminist, is a constructive critique of different feminisms, with the aim of advancing feminism in a broad sense.

Butler is concerned to 'open up' conceptions of gender beyond those with 'hetero-normative' (i.e. assumptions of heterosexuality) underpinnings: in particular to open up 'the field of possibility for gender without dictating which kinds of possibilities ought to be realised' (1999: vi). She explores and advocates the possibility of the divorce of gender from identity, the notion of gender identity being politically unproductive, advocating the alternative gender collocates of *performance* and *performativity*.

One of Butler's most overarching intellectual contributions to gender and language study is to problematise the concept of *woman* in relation to heteronormativity. In Butler's most famous (and frequently cited) book, *Gender Trouble* (1990, 1999), she asks: 'Is the construction of the category of women as a coherent and stable subject an unwitting regulation and reification of gender relations? . . . To what extent does the category of women achieve stability and coherence only in the context of the heterosexual matrix?' (1990: 5).

In this rejection of what might be described as 'modernist' feminist politics, Butler is arguing that what the deployment of the category 'woman' can achieve will always be severely circumscribed, given the normatively heterosexual and thus limiting 'bias' of 'woman', for all women, which always recycles male–female dualism.

A4.4 GENDER AND SEX

An important relationship is that of gender to sex. Leaving aside the 'polite' use of gender to mean biological sex (and the regrettable phrase 'the two genders'), it is possible nevertheless (as many do) to see gender as a sort of social correlate of sex. In this view, biological males and biological females possess certain 'culturally' imbued characteristics which fall neatly into the same two biologically determined categories. This echoes notions of 'sex roles' (even of 'appropriate sex roles'), and sex roles being 'learned'. Thus boys 'learn' to be brave, and girls to be good listeners.

Cameron (citing Nicole-Claude Mathieu 1989, 1996) points out that a 'correlational' relationship between sex and gender is usually seen in one of two possible ways: first, that gendered behaviour is 'built on' to pre-existing sex differences (as above), and, second, that the sex–gender relationship may be arbitrary, but that there will always be gender differences in behaviour, which then come to 'symbolise' sex (1997b). This sex–gender relationship entails differences or tendencies in what women and men do and say, stemming from the notion of gender as an idea about the importance of differentiation between women and men. Mathieu observes that 'There is here an awareness that social behaviours are imposed on people *on the basis of* their biological sex (as one of the "group of men" or "group of women")' (1996: 49, Mathieu's italics). Hence the very different (but important) patterns of gendered behaviour and relations in different cultural contexts. For example, in some contexts, painting buildings may be largely a female occupation and in others largely a male.

However, current conceptualisations are frequently much more complex than this (again see Mathieu 1989). A third possibility for gender is to conceptually dissociate the notion of gender from actual 'sexed individuals' completely, and rather to see it entirely as a set of articulated ideas about girls and boys, women and men, individually or collectively. The research focus is then on the ideas themselves, rather than on behaviour.

However, this conceptual focus returns us to the first and second understandings of gender in its implications. This set of ideas is taken up, impacting on the thinking and practices of groups and individuals, and on their representations and constructions of (male and female) others. Ideas about gender may be so important that they in fact construct biological correlates of sex (for example, muscles in men who lift weights because this is 'what men do'). A second case is that of newborns who cannot be straightforwardly identified as 'female' or 'male', in which medical professionals make the decision, perhaps extending this to associated surgery (these days usually in discussion with the parents). These cases, though rare, make it possible to argue that since people see newborns through gendered, dimorphic eyes, sex, like gender, is socially constructed. The usual sex–gender distinction is similarly challenged by the practice of surgery on inter-sexed people to make them 'female' or 'male', and, more extremely by the practice of transsexualism. The question of the 'social construction of sex', and the role of gender in this construction, has been a long-running debate in gender and language studies (for example, Bergvall and Bing 1996).

Task A4.4.1: Reflection task

➤ Before you read on, consider and make notes on what other ways gender (or 'notions of gender') might be seen to 'construct sex'.

This conceptual third gender–sex relationship is more complex than the other two. Below I suggest two ways in which the analyst can separate gender from sex in his or her thinking. First, given that diversity within any group of women is always likely to outweigh the diversity between that group of women and a comparable group of men (and vice versa), and indeed that the similarities between a given group of women and a comparable group of men will always outweigh the differences, the very empirical meaningfulness of the category of gender can be called into question. It can only be socially constructed. Second, sex (in the form of a dominant sexual dimorphism) has a clear social significance, giving us gender as a culturally constructed idea or category. Sexual dimorphism is here to stay, that is, it is unlikely to change over the next (say) 10,000 years, but we cannot make this prediction of its social significance. It is possible to imagine gender disappearing if the social significance of sex declines. Sex does not have to be socially significant: eye colour, for example, and blood group, are normally not. Relatedly, Cameron (1997b) compares race (genetically transmitted) with racial categories (socially created throughout history). That the current ubiquity of gender is maintained, through the socially constructed significance of sexual dimorphism, may be because the notion/category of gender is in the particular interests of some.

The idea of sexual dimorphism losing its social significance may seem far-fetched and utopian (or, to some, dystopian) – but note its correspondence to Julia Kristeva's third model of feminism (referred to in Unit B4.1). However, sexual dimorphism losing its social significance may need to be accompanied, or even motivated, by the disappearance of what has been called, following Adrianne Rich (1980), a discourse of 'compulsory heterosexuality', the assumption that we are all heterosexual. This assumption, which underlies much discourse on gender, arguably thrives on and in turn perpetuates the notion of difference (see Butler 1999, Hollway 1984, 1995).

A4.5 GENDER, LANGUAGE AND POWER

Power interfaces with both gender and discourse. On the micro-level, power was of concern to '(male) dominance' analysts of mixed-sex talk such as Pamela Fishman (Unit B2.3); on the macro-level, it is key to critical understandings of discourse. The developmental notion of empowerment is important at both macro-/institutional and micro-/small-scale interactional levels.

Task A4.5.1: Reflection task

➤ Considering the reading and tasks you have done so far, make notes on some different ways in which the notion of power may be relevant to gender and language study.

➤ Consider the questions of (a) Who has power? (b) Can this change? (c) Might someone be simultaneously powerful and powerless? (d) What are some different forms power might take, linguistically?

Specific conceptualisations of power vary with theoretical approach. For critical discourse analysis (CDA), with its obvious applications to feminist linguistics (see Wodak 1997, Lazar 2004), power is crucially institutional (though other forms may be acknowledged), and material structures are important as well as discoursal ones. For the more recent 'Post-structural discourse analysis' (PDA), developed by Judith Baxter (2002a, 2002b, 2003, see also Unit B7.3), and the feminist variation of this (FPDA), the 'grand narratives' associated with CDA are rejected: power is in a continual state of flux, variable and multiple, so that a given participant in a given situation is positioned by and within a 'nexus' of discourses. She or he may thus be simultaneously powerful in one way and powerless in another (see also Foucault 1980). Power is not only associated with (say) hegemonic masculinity.

A4.6 SO WHAT IS GENDER? WHERE CAN IT BE FOUND?

The list below represents a starting point:

- in differences (better, 'differential tendencies') between women and men, boys and girls;
- in similarities between women and men, boys and girls;
- in diversity within women, within men, within boys, within girls;
- in aspects of linguistic dealings with (individual, and groups of) women, men, boys and girls, for example, how they are addressed, what is said to them ('hearer sex');
- in aspects of what is said and written about gender differences/tendencies, similarities and diversity;
- in aspects of what is said and written about (individual, and groups of) women, men, boys and girls (the assumption being that gender may be relevant in such spoken and written texts).

Task A4.6.1: Follow-up task

➤ Taking the above possibilities for gender, consider possible gender and language research projects with which each could be explored.

Unit A5
Developing understandings of language: Language change

A5.1 INTRODUCTION

Although the rate may vary, language is in a continual state of change: phonetic, syntactic, lexical, discoursal. 'Change' extends to such phenomena as the recent 'feminisation' of public discourse (Cameron 2000, 2003) in Western societies, and language shift in bilingual speech communities, which may sometimes be gendered (for example, Gal 1978, see also Unit A1). Although change usually refers to the way language is used, it extends to folk-linguistic views of and prescriptions about how it should be used.

Change can be seen as 'diachronic variation', that is, variation over time. Diachronic variation is related to synchronic variation – variation at a given point in time, the notion which underpins most sociolinguistic work. Prior to the 1970s, synchronic variation included 'Language and sex' – a linkage comparable to, say, 'Language and social class' and 'Language and ethnic group'. (These are chapter headings in Peter Trudgill's *Sociolinguistics* [1974, 1983, 1995].) Lesley Milroy (1980) similarly treated gender as an independent synchronic variable in her Belfast study (see Unit B1.2). However, whereas Trudgill focused on synchronic differences in language use between women and men, relating these to class, Milroy, having demonstrated synchronic differences within women, used these to show the importance of speakers' social networks (see below) as regards their work and outside-work lives.

As regards the question of which synchronic variant(s) will 'succeed' and thus contribute to diachronic variation, there has been a long-running debate on gender and language change (Trudgill 1972a, 1972b, Labov 1990). A question often asked is whether innovation is the province mainly of women or men. Labov, who has written on this at greatest length, concludes that women are leaders of most changes but in different ways (see also Cameron 2003). Whether or not innovation is valued, however, will vary with time, place and community – as well as, perhaps, with who does the innovating.

Sociolinguistics has something further to offer the field of gender and language change with the concept of 'social networks' (see Unit A1), which, together with 'speech communities', has conceptually contributed to the newer notion of CofP. Such approaches signal a move away from social class as the dominant sociolinguistic social category. Coming from the field of education, with an emphasis on learning, CofP has been drawn on significantly in gender and language study (see Eckert 2000, Eckert and McConnell-Ginet 1999). In most CofPs, some members can be seen as core, others as 'peripheral', 'on the margins' (Eckert 2000) or 'lames' (Labov 1972b). For Labov, 'lames' were members of a gang, but peripheral ones who did not follow its practices and norms in the same strict way as the core members. The role of such community members has been characterised as 'legitimate peripheral participation' (Lave and Wenger 1991), and there are implications here for change: the 'core' members may have the most non-standard speech but the peripheral members (whose speech may be more standard than the core members but less standard than many speakers outside the CofP) may then help transmit linguistic variants from within to outside the particular community (again see Eckert 2000).

Most language change occurs in ways that are unplanned and about which there is very little public or conscious awareness – and most studies of change are not concerned with conscious intervention (for example, Labov 1991). But change may be consciously sought, encoded and/or institutionalised. Interventionist change ranges from the encodings of the early grammarians to the non-sexist language items proposed and implemented in the 1970s and 1980s (Unit A2). Both come under the heading of what Cameron describes as 'verbal hygiene' (documented in her 1995 book of the same name). This refers to prescriptivism, the phenomenon of how some people think others should speak and write, and attempts to achieve this.

In practice, it is hard to bring about widespread use of new linguistic usages and even harder to eliminate particular usages. 'Legislation' may not help. The early grammarians John Kirkby (1746) and Joshua Poole (1646) formally encoded sexist notions of 'firstness' (*man and woman*) as well as use of the 'generic *he*' (in contrast to 'singular *they*') in English grammars (Unit A2, see also Spender 1980, Bodine 1975a, 1975b). However, we do not know to what extent any changes in language use were due to these interventions. (What we can assume is that their interventions were in direct response to people using, for example, 'singular *they*'.) Feminist intentions to introduce non-sexist language items have similarly faced a range of challenges (see Unit B5). Prescriptive aims may thus not be achieved, and indeed the 'law of unintended consequences' may come into play, as in the use and understanding of 'Ms' (see Unit B5.3).

Below we look at language change in the form of two recent challenges: early feminist challenges to the sexist nature of various aspects of (the English) language (particularly in the 1970s), and more recent feminist and post-structuralist challenges to those early challenges.

A5.2 EARLY FEMINIST CHALLENGES

Prompted by the identification of sexist language as language that defined, trivialised and degraded women and rendered them 'invisible', the first feminist challenges can be seen as contestations of these. 'Invisibility' referred to the use of 'generics' ('man' and 'he') and 'man'-compounds, with their masculine bias (Spender 1980, Sunderland 1991). 'Defining' referred largely to the gendered asymmetry of adult 'titles', i.e. 'Mr' vis-à-vis 'Mrs' and 'Miss', 'trivialising' to asymmetries such as 'poet'/'poetess', and 'degrading' to 'pairs' like 'Sir/Madam' (only the latter has a double meaning, see Unit A2). Also challenged were dictionaries and grammars (see for example, Stephens 1990, Sunderland 1994b). These are of course 'prescriptive' works – at least in that they need to select – but are important for their representation of what might be considered the status quo and of more progressive forms. For many, such works carry (some) authority. This is particularly true of the huge population of speakers and learners of English as a second or foreign language, many of whom often consult English grammars and dictionaries.

Task A5.2.1: Follow-up task

➤ If English is not your first language, how much authority do English grammars and dictionaries carry for you, now? Have you ever used a grammar or dictionary with a query about gender in the English language?

➤ Whether the answer is 'Yes' or 'No', find out what is said about the use of 'singular they' in an English grammar (if you wish, a pedagogic grammar for learners of English) written in the past twenty years. In the light of your experiences as an English language learner, are there any surprises here?

Contestation of 'sexist' items was accompanied by proposed alternatives. These became important institutionally in the 1970s and 1980s (for example, for publishers and universities), and documented in 'codes of practice'. Codes also often focused on age, ethnicity and disability and were sometimes seen as promoting 'inclusive language'. Many included 'checklists' of what was traditionally said (for example, 'chairman'), and how it could be improved on (for example, 'chairperson'/'chair'). These could only be, however, recommendations rather than bans and mandatory requirements.

As an example, as recently as 1998, the UK Society of Personnel Officers in Government Services (SOCPO) (<http://www.socpo.org.uk>), in conjunction with the Equal Opportunities Commission, the Commission for Racial Equality and the Royal Association for Disability and Rehabilitation, produced a document called *Language and Equality*. The sections were: 'Race and language', 'Gender and language', 'Disability and language', 'Age and language' and 'Sexuality and language'.

The 'Gender and language' section starts:

> The central issue here is the predominance of forms and terms which exclude or denigrate women. It is now accepted as sound business practice that the talents and abilities of women are fully utilised at all levels in the workplace. To be able to do this effectively, an organisation must promote positive images of women both internally and externally. This is very difficult if women are excluded by the language an organisation uses.

It suggests the following improvements to traditional job titles:

> Chairman: Chair
> Fireman: Firefighter
> Foreman: Supervisor
> Workmen: Workers
> Spokesman: Spokesperson

These five new titles are designed to address the problem of 'relative invisibility' of women (in the sense that the 'generic' compound term 'fireman', say, has for many a masculine bias). In an upbeat vein, the document notes, 'Many job titles or roles which are traditionally identified in male terms have non-gender-specific alternatives. What is required is the will to make the change. Once the change is made, the new terms will become accepted as natural and stop seeming awkward to remember'.

To linguists and social scientists, the last two sentences read naïvely. Not everyone has the 'will' to make the change, and the removal of awkwardness may only be achieved when 'traditional' titles are out of circulation altogether (within one institution is unlikely to be sufficient). However, the 'brief' of writers of such documents is normally to convince and to bring about change. Upbeat rhetoric together with a lack of problematisation may have been seen as helpful here.

Language and Equality also warns against using different titles for men's and women's jobs when there is no difference in the work, critically citing the following negative examples:

Male job title	Female job title
Assistant manager	Manager's assistant
Technician	Operator
Office manager	Typing supervisor
Administrator	Clerk
Chef	Cook

These can be seen as modern equivalents of the 'semantic derogation' pairs traditionally used as examples in gender and language study, such as 'witch and wizard' (Schultz 1975), the 'female' item of a male–female 'pair' being derogated in one way or another.

The fact that these were, and could be, nothing more than recommendations is one reason why new forms, such as 'chairperson', or 'chair', can (still) only be seen as alternatives to, rather than replacements for, items such as 'chairman'. However, given that even 'banned' words can always be used in some shape or form, any blanket ban would be counterproductive. Sexist language, for example, may need to be cited, may be used ironically or satirically, or may be used in works of fiction. Recognising this, the Australian Broadcasting Commission Code of Practice provided the following guidelines (the italics are mine):

> **2.2 Language**. Variations of language favoured by different groups of Australians are valid and have their place in programs. On occasions, the language of one group may be distasteful to another. Use of such language is permitted provided it is not used gratuitously and provided the language can be justified in the context of, for example, *news and current affairs reporting, fiction, documentary, dramatisation, comedy and song lyrics.*
>
> [...]
>
> **2.4 Discrimination**. To avoid discrimination programs should not use language or images in a way which is likely to disparage or discriminate against any person or section of the community on account of race, ethnicity, nationality, sex, marital or parental status, age, disability or illness, social or occupational status, sexual preference or any religious, cultural or political belief or activity. The requirement is not intended to prevent the broadcast of material which is *factual, or the expression of genuinely-held opinion in a news or current affairs program, or in the legitimate context of a humorous, satirical or dramatic work.*

To make two, perhaps obvious, points: a linguistic item may be the topic of a news report or be relevant to a documentary, and including a fictional character who uses derogatory terms does not mean that these are being put forward in a positive light, often the reverse being the case (allowing the reader to negatively evaluate them). Similarly, satire that ironically employs sexist language can make valuable feminist points. There remains the question of how an utterance intended as ironic will be read, or (mis)understood. Nevertheless, since non-sexist language is limited in what it can achieve (see Unit A5.3 'Later Feminist Challenges'), the 'risk' of misunderstanding or irony has to be balanced against the fact that strategies other than non-sexist language items will always be needed here.

 Task A5.2.2: Reflection task

➤ Do you think it is reasonable to have 'codes of practice' for language use in the workplace, particularly in relation to gender, at this point in the twenty-first century?

➤ If so, what would you include in terms of specific linguistic items?

➤ If not, how would you address the issue of sexist (and racist) language in the workplace? (Consider this in relation to a particular workplace.)

Task A5.2.3: Reflection task

➤ Which new and old lexical items, including phrases, would you expect to find in a 'non-sexist language' dictionary?

➤ What do you think might be some of the dilemmas facing a lexicographer with a non-sexist 'brief'?

➤ What are some different ways these dilemmas might be addressed?

➤ What would be your policy as regards these dilemmas?

➤ How would you deal with derogatory terms such as 'slag'?

A5.3 LATER FEMINIST CHALLENGES

Linguistic (word-level) sexism is the first topic addressed in the Unit B5 readings. Unit B5.1 concerns an early initiative, the *American Heritage School Dictionary* project. Its story is documented in Alma Graham's (1975) 'The making of a non-sexist dictionary'. This project began in 1969, right at the start of the 'second wave' of the Women's (Liberation) Movement.

The questions and linguistic items of concern in Graham's dictionary now sound outdated in many ways, as words and meanings have continued to change since 1975. More recent feminism (sometimes described as 'third-wave feminism'), influenced strongly by post-structuralism, has challenged previous feminist positions. What might in 1975 (or even a decade ago) have appeared unquestionably and straightforwardly 'sexist', is less self-evidently so today.

First, a given linguistic item will have more than one possible meaning, related to those of other words (and statements, and indeed discourses) with which it is textually associated (for example, Black and Coward 1981), and depending on how it is used, pragmatically. In Cameron's words, meaning is '*radically* contextual' (1992b: 192, her italics). From a post-structuralist perspective, lexical (and other) meaning is never fixed but is rather 'endlessly deferred' (see for example, Baxter 2003). At a theoretical level, this rather pulls the rug from under lexicography altogether. However, few would argue that linguistic item 'X' can mean just anything. (From a different, commercial perspective, the dictionary industry is unlikely to disappear, and it is arguably better, given the reverence that exists in some CofPs for dictionaries, to have non-sexist language items encoded than not.)

Second, given that people interpret words in different ways, a 'sexist' meaning cannot automatically be imputed. 'Reader response' can extend to listening, and to intentionally 'reading [listening] against the grain' (for example, Cosslett 1996), that is, making your own meaning for your own purposes, regardless of how you see the intentions of the speaker or writer. Relatedly, meanings can be 'appropriated' by individuals or groups, for their own, perhaps political, ends: for example the 'reclamation' of the insult 'dyke' by lesbian feminists (as well as of 'gay' and 'queer' by homosexual women and men).

Third, even 'gender neutral' words such as 'people' and 'adult' can be sexist. As an example of 'slippage', Cameron (1994) cites: 'The lack of vitality is aggravated by the fact that there are so few able-bodied young adults about. They have all gone off to work or look for work, leaving behind the old, the disabled, the women and the children (*Sunday Times*)' (1994: 30). 'Adults' thus turns out (or comes) to mean 'male adults'. This is an example of sexist use of 'adult', but we can imagine it happening in interpretation too. Such slippage happens not on an exceptional but rather on a regular basis, and not only in English, of course. At the 2002 International Gender and Language Association Conference (IGALA2), Marlis Hellinger provided the following German example:

> Vergeßliche Hotelgäste

> Wir müssen immer mit dem klassischen Fall rechnen, daß die Ehefrau nichts vom Hotelaufenthalt ihres Mannes weiß. Deshalb schicken wir die gefundenen Gegenstände grundsätzlich nur zurück, wenn der Gast darum bittet.

which translates as:

> Forgetful hotel guests

> We will always have to reckon with the classic case that a wife may not know about her husband's stay in the hotel. Therefore we return lost property only at the guest's request.

The apparently gender-neutral 'guest' means 'male guest'. This phenomenon demonstrates clear limitations on the value of the non-sexist language item. Sexist language cannot be identified, 'pinned down', controlled, contained and replaced, but will continually emerge and re-emerge in a variety of guises and genres. (Sara Mills' paper in Unit B5.2 on 'Changes in sexist language use' explores precisely this.)

Such complexity can be handled by post-structuralism, which allows for, even encourages, a text to be read in more than one way, including by the same individual. An individual may recognise what Baxter calls 'the plurality, multivocality and non-fixity of all meaning' (2003: 6). She may also know that this is what she is recognising (without necessarily seeing it in those terms). And many of us are now sophisticated consumers of irony. But while ironic texts are both interesting and challenging for the contemporary feminist linguist, irony is also a gift for sexists (who can happily 'defend' accusations of sexism) and is widely drawn on and exploited, for example, in men's 'lifestyle' magazines such as *FHM* and *Loaded* (Benwell 2002, 2004).

The 'linguistic turn' refers to the theoretical shift in the Social Sciences and Humanities away from a focus on single linguistic items to discourse, which has been embraced by feminist linguistics (as well as Linguistics more widely). A classic example here is Black and Coward's (1981) early critique of Dale Spender's (1980) *Man Made Language*, which was important in its rejection of what might be seen as a socially 'reflective' or 'expressive' model of language, in favour of a constitutive one. They proposed a different theoretical imperative (see also Unit A2):

> language, as a system of phonological, syntactic and logical structures and rules, is not inherently sexist or 'man-made' in Dale Spender's sense. Linguistic systems, however, serve as the basis for the production and interpretation of sets of related utterances – discourses – which effect and sustain the different categorizations and positions of women and men. It is on these discourses, and not on language in general or linguistic systems, that feminist analyses have to focus.
>
> (1981: 78)

Current CDA would, however, also argue that the study of discourses is greatly enriched by the detailed and systematic study of actual language use, including the use, distribution and frequency of certain linguistic items.

A5.4 ACTUAL LANGUAGE CHANGE

It is one thing to formally implement non-sexist language change, that is, to recommend, encode and document new or alternative linguistic items, for example in dictionaries or codes of practice. Questions of actual usage of non-sexist language and new progressive forms are something else again.

Evidence is sparse but not non-existent. (Note that this is quantitative evidence of change in non-sexist language items. Quantitative analysis of change in discourses would be impossible, given that a discourse cannot be 'seen', only its 'traces' [for example, Talbot 1998]; see also Unit 7.) Use of 'gender-inclusive' language has been documented in speech and writing (for example, Bate 1978, Cooper 1984, Hellinger and Bußmann 2001–2, Pauwels 1998). Cooper and his seminar group, for example, conducted a 'manual' study of 'generic he' and 'generic man' in US newspapers between 1971 and 1980, and reported a decline.

Spoken and written corpora have afforded particularly interesting research into non-sexist language use. Janet Holmes and Robert Sigley (2002a, b) looked at 'girl' and 'girls', and found 'girl' to be used in the workplace of females of subordinate status regardless of age – but not 'boy' of equivalent males (see also Sigley and Holmes, 2002). Both 'girls' and 'boys' are, however, used of groups of adults in various professions, perhaps marking in-group solidarity (see also Unit B8.1).

'Success' of non-sexist language has been patchy, varying not only with item but also with users, contexts of use and the 'biography' of the items themselves. 'Ms' use, for example, appears to vary geographically, being more widely used and more acceptable in the USA than in the UK. MICASE, the Michigan corpus of academic spoken English (<http://www.hti.umich.edu/m/micase>; see Unit A4), illustrates this patchiness. Out of the 1,848,364 words of talk in academic settings, we find no occurrence of 'chairperson' but three of 'spokesperson', none of 'she or he' but nine of 'he or she'. 'Spokesperson' was used in different academic spoken genres, each time by a female speaker; 'he or she' most frequently in small lectures, seven of the nine occurrences being produced by female speakers (again see Holmes and Sigley 2002a, 2002b). None of the occurrences of 'spokesperson' or 'he or she' appeared to be facetious or ironic. But the story is not over yet . . .

A5.5 LANGUAGE USERS' UNDERSTANDINGS

Although the non-sexist language campaign may have been theoretically naïve, flawed and limited in its achievements, one of its achievements has been to prompt people to talk about non-sexist language. Even though many did (and still do) so dismissively, some finding the whole question a big joke, quaint, naïve or completely peripheral, huge numbers of English-language users in many countries cannot now claim that they are unaware of the issue. This has personal and political implications. As Deborah Cameron wrote in 1995: 'Choice has altered the value of the terms and removed the option of political neutrality' (1995a: 119, but see Schwarz [2006] for a modification of this claim).

However, knowing about actual use tells us little about how items are conceptualised, why they are used, and what motivates a given usage at a particular moment in space and time. Is it a question of principle, politeness (for example, 'audience design'), perceived expediency, 'performing' a particular identity, or what? This is important: why something is said can tell us a lot about what really is happening. (Cameron et al. [1992] make a related point about watching a woman 'turning over the earth in a flower bed': is she gardening, or preparing to bury the budgie? If the former, is she relaxing or 'worshipping the Goddess Earth'?)

It is therefore always worth considering why people do what they do (or at least what they say about why they think they do what they do). In Unit B5.3, Juliane Schwarz asks focus group members about their 'Ms' usage, largely with the intention of ascertaining how this term is conceptualised by women of different ages. Her work contributes to an understanding of why people (say they) say what they do, and not only to improved descriptions of language use.

Schwarz's study contain pointers for future language change, but her focus group members' accounts cannot, she acknowledges, straightforwardly provide 'information' about future language use. This understanding of 'elicited' data is fully taken on board by – indeed, is the basis of – discursive psychology (for example, Wetherall 2002, Edley 2001, Wetherell, Stiven and Potter 1987). This sees accounts as co-constructed (for example, by/with an interviewer). Speakers are also 'positioned' by a range of discourses, so the same speaker may produce different 'accounts' (see Baxter 2003, also Units B7.3 and B9). Speakers draw on 'interpretive repertoires', and the fact that accounts are often similar across speakers shows these interpretive repertoires to be socially available.

Unit A6
Developing understandings
of language: Context

A6.1 INTRODUCTION

The term 'context' is used in Applied Linguistics in wide-ranging ways, broad and specific. Thousands of currently available books have 'context' in their title, hundreds have both 'language' and 'context', several are actually called *Language and Context*. The relevance of context to linguistics was established by the anthropologist Malinowski (1923), who referred to the 'context of situation' in which 'speech events' took place. He wrote (1923: 307):

> utterance and situation are bound up inextricably with each other and the context of situation is indispensable for the understanding of the words. Exactly as in the reality of spoken or written languages, a word without linguistic context is a mere figment and stands for nothing by itself, so in the reality of a spoken living tongue, the utterance has no meaning except in the context of situation.

For Malinowski and other anthropologists, Graddol et al. write, 'utterances became comprehensible only in the context of the whole way of life of which they form part' (1995: 15).

One of the most influential figures as regards context, language use, and interpretation is Dell Hymes. Unlike Chomsky, who was interested in isolated sentences, Hymes was interested in the 'rules of speaking' within a community, and the associated 'speech situations', 'speech events', 'speech acts' and 'communicative competence' (see Jaworski and Coupland 1999). Hymes's (1972) notion of the 'ethnography of communication' famously incorporates the following SPEAKING model:

Setting and scene
Participants (speaker and audience)
Ends (purposes, goals and outcomes)
Act sequence (order of components of the speech event)
Key (tone, manner and/or spirit)
Instrumentalities (forms and styles of speech)
Norms (social rules and expectations)
Genre (the kind/purpose of the event)

This model can of course also be applied to written communication.

Task A6.1.1: Follow-up task

➤ While retaining the SPEAKING acronym, adapt the descriptors (for each letter) for written communication.

➤ Then consider a particular 'literacy event' (a familiar activity in which reading and/or writing play a crucial role), which involves writing.

➤ Exemplify what is referred to by each descriptor.

In her own explanation of what is included in the 'context' of a conversation, Janet Maybin (1996) identifies the following:

- physical surroundings
- relationship between speakers
- speakers' past experiences
- current conversational goals, the social events of which the conversation is a part
- broader cultural values and expectations.

Maybin illustrates of the importance of several of these in the question of address. Focusing on 'Participants', she looks at how a young woman of twenty-one from Singapore (her full name is Lo Wing Yu) is variously addressed. These ways include:

- 'Ah Mui' (Cantonese for 'little sister') by her older sister, and by friends who find this term of address amusing;
- 'Xiao mei mei' (Mandarin for 'little girl/sister') by 'older guys who are trying to be funny, or older women who think that I am actually very, very young';
- 'Ma'am' by counter staff at fast-food restaurants;
- 'Miss Lo' by people in a more formal context, for example a job interview.

As Maybin notes (and as we can see), context-related terms of address will relate to gender, sometimes in an asymmetrical way ('older guys'). However, in a sense, such terms create as well as reflect context. Maybin comments: 'Note the way Lo Wing Yu feels positioned by certain people calling her *little sister*' (1996: 15, italics in original). This is to extend Hymes's notion of 'participants' to the (changing) relationships between them.

It is now commonplace to say that meaning is 'contextual' – even '*radically* contextual' (Cameron 1992b: 192, her italics). Sociolinguistics requires the notion of context, in the study of speech communities, social networks (for example, Cheshire 1982, Gal 1978, Labov 1966, Trudgill 1972a, 1972b), and CofPs (Eckert and McConnell-Ginet 1992a, 1992b; see also Unit B6.2). Consider a group of people who meet weekly for salsa dancing. Here, context is both social and geographical. Speech communities, networks and CofPs, however, are not restricted to geographical boundaries. The Internet has enabled these to exist independently of spatial considerations, so that, for example, academics can communicate perfectly satisfactorily on a topic with no idea of where on the globe their correspondent is writing from, and people forge genuine friendships and alliances in chat-rooms with people they have never met.

A6.2 CONTEXT, LANGUAGE AND GENDER

In 1970s gender and language study, an acknowledgement of the importance of context came with the recognition that if and when men tended to dominate women linguistically in certain ways, this had to be related, *inter alia*, to what Hymes might see as 'participants' and 'genre'. So, for example, Candace West's (1984) work on doctor–patient talk, and that of William O'Barr and Bowman Atkins (1980) on courtroom discourse, showed how professional status intersected with gender in terms of what was said. O'Barr and Atkins showed that what had been seen as 'women's language' was in large part 'powerless language': it was evident in the talk of those on trial, but not in that of the members of the legal profession involved in the trial, female or male.

Context may also extend to participants' interpretations. Mary Talbot (1992) pointed out that whether a given case of overlapping speech could be seen as an 'interruption' – unwanted and 'hostile' – could really only be established with recourse to speakers' understandings. This was important for early gender and language study since 'interruptions' – of women, by men – played an important role in findings of the '(male) dominance' tradition of investigation (for example, Zimmerman and West 1975, West and Zimmerman 1983).

Following '(male) dominance', social context was also important in gender and language study in the '(cultural) difference' approach – not only for understanding the meaning of a given utterance, but also its origin. Maltz and Borker (1982, see also Unit B3), and later Deborah Tannen (1991), claimed that girls and boys grow up largely in single-sex groups, and that these apparently very different, formative contexts entail different linguistic practices to which different tendencies in adult male/female language use can be attributed (see also Unit A3). In Unit B6, the notion of context is exemplified from three perspectives.

First, in Unit B6.1, context extends to the wider social practices surrounding the use (or 'consumption') of a written text, with an extract from a study of actual (and in many ways unpredictable) uses of a language textbook, instantiated in teacher talk. This draws on the notion of 'talk around the text', borrowed from literacy studies (for example, Jaffe 2003). The epistemological point here is that analysis of a written text alone cannot do more than suggest how it may be interpreted or responded to – which may depend in part on what is said while it is being read. Understanding that meaning is co-constructed by a text (and that text's producer) and its reader (or listener) entails that a study of meaning in the written text alone must always be inadequate.

In Unit B6.2, the second perspective on context derives from the important notion of CofP. Originating in education (Lave and Wenger 1991), with a focus on 'situated learning', this was taken up by language and gender study first by Penelope Eckert and Sally McConnell-Ginet in 1992 (1992a and 1992b), and, several years later, was the topic of a special issue of *Language and Society* (1999). Here we look at an extract from Eckert and McConnell-Ginet's influential 1992 paper: 'Communities of practice: where language, gender and power all live'.

A CofP entails shared practices (linguistic and otherwise), and thus extends the notion of 'speech community' (Graddol et al. 1995). Practices have implications for identity, which may be achieved and/or ascribed through taking part in certain social and linguistic practices. Joining an adult education class in creative writing, for example, may change that person's sense of who she is through the practices she engages in, with others; at the same time, friends, relatives and associates may 'ascribe' a certain identity to her because of her membership of the class. CofP also entails the notion of 'legitimate peripheral participation' (the subtitle of Lave and Wenger's [1991] book), meaning that whereas some members may be 'core', and relatively powerful, others are not, but are accepted as part of the CofP, and may go through a process of learning and become increasingly less peripheral. What exactly counts as a CofP (and, for example, how 'permanent' it has to be) is a matter of debate, but relatively clear examples would be a family, a football team, and the above-mentioned creative-writing class.

The CofP notion has made an important and useful contribution to gender and language study. This does not mean that as a notion it was absent before Lave and Wenger's, and Eckert and McConnell-Ginet's work. It is possible, for example, to retrospectively see Lesley Milroy's young Clonard women (Unit B1.2) as part of several CofPs: they had families, and worked and socialised outside the home. Since they both worked and socialised together, in sharing a multiplex social network, these women also shared a set of linguistic practices, and it was the linguistic details of this network that provides Milroy's explanatory power. Gender (as a variable) was thus not abstracted from practices or from the communities in which these women lived and worked.

The third perspective, in Unit B6.3, exemplifies the broad and popularly understood notion of 'culture'. While different 'cultures' are of course marked by diversity, nuancing and a myriad of CofPs, certain practices may be specific to certain cultures. One such linguistic practice is *hlonipha* (Hanong Thetela 2002, Swann 2000, Finlayson 1995), a morphological and lexical part of the language of some groups in South Africa and neighbouring countries. On the surface, *hlonipha* is about respect for women, but it also about women showing respect for others (particularly older male relatives), entailing language women are not expected to use. This largely concerns syllables in the names of in-laws, but it extends to use of euphemistic words related to the act of sex and to sexual body parts. The implications of this are the focus of Hanong Thetela's text in Unit B6.3.

Task A6.2.1: Reflection task

➤ Have you had direct experience of 'cultures' in different parts of the world in which women's and men's linguistic practices (or expectations of practices) vary, either 'sex-exclusively' or 'sex-preferentially' (see Units A1, A2 and A3)?

➤ Were these evident in single-sex or mixed-sex groupings?

Unit A7
Developing understandings of language: Discourse and discourses

A7.1 INTRODUCTION

Task A7.1.1: Reflection task

➤ Spend a few minutes making notes about some different possible meanings of *discourse*.

➤ List some collocates and closely related terms.

➤ Which writers do you associate with the notion of *discourse*?

Discourse is omnipresent. This is especially true as modes of communications increase, exponentially more texts are published year on year, and more information of different sorts becomes available. Much of this is relevant to gender and language study: as Cameron notes, 'Men and women . . . are members of cultures in which a large amount of discourse about gender is constantly circulating' (1997a: 60). The number and diversity of what might be called 'discursively gendered' sites and topics is vast, and there is no shortage of discourse to analyse.

Discourse has a variety of meanings, varying with discipline and intellectual persuasion. 'Linguistic' meanings include the broad 'stretch of written or spoken language', and the more specific 'linguistic, and accompanying paralinguistic, interaction between people in a specific context' (Talbot 1995a: 45), for example, 'Classroom discourse'. Such names can be seen as 'descriptive': 'Classroom discourse' is the language associated with the classroom.

Discourse can also refer to a 'broad system of meaning', and to 'knowledge and practices generally associated with a particular institution or group of institutions' (Talbot 1995a: 43). Given this sense of discourse, we can also talk about discourses, which have been characterised as ways of seeing the world (Sunderland 2004), and as 'ways of representing the world: the processes, relations and structures of the material world, the "mental" world of thoughts, feelings, beliefs and so on, and the social world' (Fairclough 2003: 124).

Fairclough's use of 'representing' goes beyond 'seeing' to suggest agency and intention. Indeed, speakers and writers *use* discourses – 'drawing on', 'invoking', 'producing', 'reproducing' and even 'inserting themselves' within (Foucault 1981) discourses. The different verbs imply different forms of agency. Agency does not however mean that discourses are produced ahistorically, from nothing. Rather, we can see discourses as having been around as long as there have been human, social practices, and speakers, through their language and social actions, constantly re-produce these. A given discourse may be relatively continuous and durable, over time undergoing local (and visible) transformations in written and spoken texts (Fairclough 2001), that is, manifesting changing linguistic 'traces' (see below).

Discourses themselves are neither visible nor bounded. A discourse has no objective beginning and no clearly defined end (Wodak 1997: 6). However, a given discourse may be recognisable to analysts and other language users through its manifestation in characteristic linguistic 'traces'. These 'traces' then provide 'cues' for how a text can be understood (Talbot 1998: 154). Particular discourses can be analytically 'co-constructed' from these traces with the aid of co-textual and contextual features.

Let us take as an example a 'pro-environmental discourse'. Rather than being 'descriptive', this discourse, and its name, are better referred to as 'interpretive': what for some might be a clear a 'pro-environmental discourse', for others might be a 'left-wing discourse' or discourse of 'state interference in the rights of the individual'. But, regardless of perspective, the idea of protecting the environment, for our own good and that of our descendents, is by now a familiar, recognisable one – even to those who neither positively espouse a pro-environmental discourse nor allow it to shape their practices. Characteristic lexis are words and phrases such as 'earth', 'planet', 'low impact', 'sustainability', 'biodiversity' and 'environmental footprint'. Characteristic syntax when the discourse is used with persuasive intent (for example by pressure groups) might include 'first conditional' constructions, often negative ones: 'If we do not . . . then . . .'. Such linguistic 'traces' of an environmental discourse enable us to co-construct it: what the text producers want, of course.

 Task A7.1.2: Reflection task

➤ Think of another, familiar discourse. What might some characteristic lexical and syntactic traces of this discourse be?

➤ Can you think of a familiar gendered discourse?

The same discourse may be reproduced widely, in different linguistic guises and manifestations. First, traces of the discourse can appear in both written and spoken texts. It is not hard to envisage this: there is no mode or genre restriction on either a discourse of feminism or a discourse of sexism, for example. Both can be encountered in print media, in political speeches (spoken but often scripted) and in naturally occurring talk. The same discourse can also be produced by men and by women: Wetherell et al. (1987) demonstrated that women and men both drew on a discourse of 'equal opportunities' in interviews about employment and gender and a limiting 'practical considerations' discourse. Women can also produce sexist (anti-women) discourses, and men feminist discourses. For some people this is counter-intuitive: I have several times encountered assumptions that women textbook writers will represent women in their books better than will their male colleagues, and that female researchers of Gender and Language will ask questions and/or represent their findings in ways that cast men and boys in a poor light. I do not think either is true. Women cannot be assumed to support women or to be critical of existing gendered social arrangements. Walsh, for example, has documented how in the UK complaints by New Labour women MPs of sexual harassment by their male colleagues were simply dismissed by Tory women MPs (2001: 99). That discourses are not sex-exclusive is a reason to look at what is said (and written), as well as how and by whom (the focus of earlier 'gender differences' studies).

A7.2 THE CONSTITUTIVE NATURE OF DISCOURSE

An important distinction is between what discourse is (described above), and what it does. Recognition and production of familiar (or less familiar) discourses may help the language user maintain a sense of control and make sense of the world. As regards what discourses themselves do, for both critical social theory and post-structuralism, discourses are potentially constitutive systems of meaning: 'different ways of structuring areas of knowledge and social practice' (Fairclough 1992a: 3) (from critical social theory and CDA), or, in the famous post-structuralist Foucault definition, 'practices that systematically form the objects of which they speak' (Foucault 1972: 49). Both Foucault and Fairclough (1992a, 1992b, 2003) have been influential in shaping understandings of the potential constitutiveness of discourse (see also Chouliaraki and Fairclough 1999).

Task A7.2.1: Reflection task

➤ What is your experience of language as constitutive?

➤ Can you recall occasions in which something you read, or heard, made you see things in a different way?

➤ Other than the obvious (for example, you read on a board that the last train has been cancelled, so you get a taxi home), can you recall occasions in which an encounter with language has prompted you to act in a certain way?

Discourses are constitutively potentially powerful, both in large-scale political processes and small everyday exchanges (Jaworski and Coupland 1999), and powerful in the senses of constraining and enabling (Mills 1997). The feminist discourse which names, identifies and condemns sexual harassment of women by men can be seen as empowering to women, compared with a traditional discourse in which male harassment of women was something 'natural', and therefore something women had to put up with.

Constitution can be symbolic, semiotic and/or discoursal, but is also potentially material and social, i.e. constituting effects beyond discourse. Fairclough makes a useful and important distinction between 'constructions' and 'construals': 'we may textually construe (represent, imagine, etc.) the social world in particular ways, but whether our representations or construals have the effect of changing its construction depends upon various contextual factors – including the way social reality already is, who is construing it, and so forth' (2003: 8).

As regards 'construction', J. Camille Cammack and Donna Kalmbach Phillips refer to the possibility of discourses 'binding' people 'so that they cannot see connections or construct meaning outside the set of definitions given them' (2002: 126). Claims of construction (in this sense) are, however, often theoretical and rhetorical, rather than drawing on empirical support. Accepting that a given discourse constructs language users in themselves and their practices (as opposed to in a text about them), often requires an intellectual act of faith. While accepting in principle rhetorical claims about what a discourse does (or can do), we can then also interrogate such claims. For example, 'constitute' in what sense? as evidenced in or by what? (Sunderland 2004).

Given different theoretical approaches to discourse and its workings, approaches to discourse analysis vary accordingly. Discourse analysis encompasses, *inter alia*, conversation analysis (CA), classroom discourse analysis, critical discourse analysis (CDA), critical classroom discourse analysis (Kumaravadivelu 1999), discursive psychology, and feminist post-structuralist discourse analysis (FPDA) (Baxter 2003). In FPDA, Judith Baxter stresses the possibility of different forms of power for an individual at different times (or even at the same time). Drawing on Foucauldian (rather than CDA) understandings of social 'realities' as always discursively produced, Baxter claims that our identities and subject positions as speakers are continually being reconstructed and thus open to redefinition through discourse. Unit B7.3 is an extract from Baxter's book *Positioning Gender in Discourse* (2003). Units 8 and 9 look at CA and discursive psychology, respectively. Below we look more closely at CDA.

A7.3 CRITICAL DISCOURSE ANALYSIS

CDA 'aims to show non-obvious ways in which language is involved in social relations of power and domination' (Fairclough 2001: 229). Discourses, for example, are 'non-obvious' because they cannot be 'seen', but must be inferred from linguistic cues. Fairclough goes on:

> The starting point for CDA is social issues and problems . . . it does not
> begin with texts and interactions. . . . The dramatic problems in economy
> and society . . . lie, I would argue, at the root of the problems, insecurities
> and struggles of contemporary social life. If CDA wants to address the latter,
> it has to have a picture of how language and semiosis figure in the former.
>
> (2001: 229, 232)

The social issue and 'dramatic problem' here is gender – an issue and often a problem
for women and girls, in different ways, for men and boys, and accordingly for gender
relations. CDA would thus seem to be theoretically well placed to seek and identify
gendered discourses of a 'damaging' kind (Sunderland 2004). Yet, oddly, given its
concern with power relations (see also Cameron 1998a), CDA remains relatively
marginal in gender and language research. Michelle Lazar's (2005) edited collection
Feminist Critical Discourse Analysis is the first book to explicitly bring together
achievements of this theoretical approach (but see also Walsh 2001).

Task A7.3.1: Reflection task

> ➤ As you read the next section, consider for yourself whether you think CDA
> might be an appropriate approach for gender and language study – theoretically,
> epistemologically and/or methodologically.

Crucial to CDA are notions of power and dialectical relations, in particular between
discourse and other social practices, including institutional dominance and
economic production. In addition to being constitutive, discourse is thus itself
shaped by the material and by social structures. Accordingly, analysis must consider
the extra-discursive, including the material. CDA in fact entails the extra-discursive:
there is a 'real world' where reality does not depend on discoursal constitution. For
CDA, as Chouliaraki and Fairclough claim, 'the question of power in social class,
gender and race relations is *partly* a question of discourse' (1999: vii, my italics).
Discourse is thus significant in its constitutive potential but not omnipotent,
and the potential of discourse to improve women's lives is, for CDA, seriously and
materially circumscribed.

A7.4 INTERTEXTUALITY AND INTERDISCURSIVITY

For both post-structuralism and CDA, the analysis of discourses is never straightforward in that it cannot, in contrast to the analysis of more formal or more
purely linguistic features, deal with 'bounded' units. The issue is not however the
demarcation of a unit of analysis in talk or written text, but that of intertextuality.
A given discourse is always related to others, both synchronically and diachronically.
Diachronically, 'With each word spoken, the meanings within particular discourses
are carried through time' (Peterson 2002: 352). Synchronically, similar and different
discourses exist in contemporary relation to each other. There is, for example,

a diversity of discourses of sexism (from misogyny to 'Vive la différence!'). Intertextuality may refer to 'manifest intertextuality' – for example, the use of extracts from *Taming of the Shrew* in Cole Porter's musical *Kiss Me Kate*, and the direct (if tidied up) reported speech of media reports. Alternatively, it may refer to 'interdiscursivity', the 'mixing together of different discourses and genres' (Fairclough 1992a). Discourses thus continually take on characteristics of each other, endlessly combining and recombining.

 Task A7.4.1: Reflection task

➤ Have you had the experience of becoming aware of a new discourse (articulated by a friend or relation, or in the media, perhaps through new words or phrases or combinations), becoming aware of others taking it up, and then perhaps taking it up yourself?

As an example of interdiscursivity, the following text type will be familiar to many. With the overall title of 'Project Planet', and featuring a picture of three horses on a hill in the mist or at dawn, a card with this wording was found in a city hotel bathroom:

PLEASE REUSE THE TOWELS

We invite you to join with us to conserve water by using your towels more than once. In addition to decreasing water and energy consumption, you help us reduce the amount of detergent waste water that must be recycled within our community.

Please hang towels up if you wish to participate in this program – if not, simply leave them on the floor.

The card is 'Printed on recycled paper' and is 'Laminated to reduce waste'. A 'pro-environmental discourse' can be seen here, in terms of the advocacy of the preservation of water and energy and the limitation of (presumably) polluting detergent, and the phrase 'our community'. But the 'invitation' to 'participate in this program' has been issued by a major hotel chain, whose bottom line is to succeed financially in a competitive leisure industry. It is very hard to read this text and not see the main intention of its writers to promote savings on laundry costs, and as textually 'appropriating' a familiar environmental discourse to do so. (Note that there are no linguistic traces like the serious and contingent 'If we do not . . . then . . .', suggested in the earlier discussion of pro-environmental discourse.) Behind the traces of this ostensibly 'pro-environmental discourse', and with the help of those traces, we can 'co-construct' a hard-headed commercial discourse.

When several discourses are produced in the same text, including in the same utterance (by one individual) or conversation, as they often are, these discourses can be seen not just as 'jostling' together, but also as competing, or contradictory. Contradictions are of interest to CDA (Hegel wrote on them at length), post-structuralism (including FPDA) and discursive psychology, in the shape of 'ideological dilemmas' (Billig et al. 1988). An example of a contradiction can be seen in two documented parenthood discourses in comparable texts, 'Father as line manager of the mother' and 'Mother as manager of the father's role in child-care' (Sunderland 2002). Contradictions may signal discoursal and social instability and hence act as pointers to struggle and avenues of change (Pecheux 1982), perhaps playing a 'disturbing' role themselves. They also create room for contestation in the form of, for example, explicit challenge to the speaker who contradicts him or herself, or commentary on the contradictions in one's own talk. Alternatively, they may act as a conservative force (Wetherell et al. 1987), in that articulation of a given progressive discourse invites the co-construction of a conservative or traditional one.

A7.5 GENDER AND DISCOURSE/GENDERED DISCOURSE/GENDERING DISCOURSE

'Gender' and 'discourse' appear together in the titles of several monographs and edited collections (for example, Litosseliti and Sunderland 2002, Tannen 1994, Todd and Fisher 1998, Walsh 2001, Weatherall 2002, Wodak 1997), and are both central in Wilkinson and Kitzinger's *Feminism and Discourse: psychological perspectives* (1995) and Mills's *Discourse* (1997). Discourse analyses have shown the extent to which discourse is gendered, and indeed the proliferation of work here may be precisely because of the ability of discourse analysis to challenge traditional essentialist and reductionist understandings of gender (Edley 2001).

What about the phrase 'gendered discourse'? Gender and Language theorists of the 1970s and 1980s who were adherents of the '(male) dominance' (retrospectively labelled) approach would probably see gendered discourse as referring to the nature of the interactional dominance which they found in mixed-sex conversations: Fishman (1983), West and Zimmerman (1983) and Edelsky (1977) showed men on the whole talking more than women, interrupting more, providing fewer minimal responses, asking fewer questions, and having their topics taken up more regularly (see Unit A2). This could be said to be discourse of a very gendered kind indeed. A more contemporary understanding (for post-structuralism and CDA alike) would however refer to the discoursal representation or construction of women and men, boys and girls in particular gendered ways in written text or talk – ways that may be idiosyncratic or normative, conservative or progressive.

When women and men, boys and girls are represented and/or expected to behave in particular gendered ways, post-structuralism and CDA see gendered discourses as 'subject positioning' those individuals or groups concerned. 'Subject' is used here in the double active/passive sense of 'subject' (as opposed to 'object') and 'being subject to'. Actual behaviour may or may not correspond to those representations and expectations, but people can be seen as 'taking up' (or not) particular gendered 'subject positions' (see Wetherell 1998, Weatherall 2002).

Rather than focusing on (and 'ferreting out') any 'gender differences' (or tendencies), a discourse approach would see gendered subject positions which are taken up not as an end (or the end of the investigation) in themselves, but as legitimating the 'male/female binary', and as potentially constitutive of gender more widely. Something which is gendered can thus also be gendering.

Gendered discourse may subject position women unfavourably – as in Walsh's (2001) example of the discourse of Tory (British right-wing) women concerning Labour Party (more left-wing) women (see A7.1). It does not have to do so, however. Further, to suggest that gendered discourse always constructs (as opposed to construes) gender (or that a particular stretch of discourse does so) would be to adopt a highly determinist stance which most analysts now distance themselves from. This stance was evident in some non-sexist language campaigns of the 1970s, in which one argument for 'inclusive' language was that linguistic items such as the so-called 'generic he' (a 'trace' of sexist discourse) caused people to 'think male' (see Unit A.2). While there was some evidence that thinking could be influenced by sexist language (for example, Schneider and Hacker 1973), this was by no means automatic, universal or long term (its duration was never, to my knowledge, explored). Both individual agency and the possibility of resistance need to be considered – this last might include the recognition, and rejection, of sexist discourse. To borrow from CA, an individual's orientation to a particular discourse needs to be considered before any discussion of construction in relation to that individual can take place.

In Unit B7 we look in more detail at discourses, discourse identification and discourse naming. Two extracts (B7.1 and B7.2) come from my own book *Gendered Discourses* (2004), the third (B7.3) from Judith Baxter's *Positioning Gender in Discourse* (2003).

Unit A8
Approaches to gender and language research

A8.1 INTRODUCTION

Task A8.1.1: Reflection task

➤ With what academic disciplines, in addition to linguistics, do you associate gender and language study?

➤ Is gender and language study characterised by particular sorts of data and data collection?

➤ What do you see as the role of feminism in gender and language study?

'Gender and Language' is not an approach. Rather, it can best be described as a topic, or, more broadly, 'field' of study. Within Linguistics, gender and language study has links not only with sociolinguistics, discourse analysis and language change, as we have seen, but also with stylistics, pragmatics, literacy, the history of language and even historical and descriptive linguistics (for example, Corbett 2004).

As a field, Gender and Language is highly diverse, as recent work illustrates. The programme of the IGALA3 (International Gender and Language Association) Conference of 2004 included presentations on:

- discursive creation of gendered bodies in Internet chats;
- institutionalising norms and roles of gender and sexuality in a call-in radio programme;
- positioning a mature and normative heterosexual self in 'attraction talk' in ten-year-old boys;
- 'half-Japanese' adolescent girls' display of multi-ethnic and feminine cultural capital;
- language, gender and world view: oral narrative in a Berber village;
- are psychotherapy texts gendered?
- the portrayal of women in selected Polish print advertisements.

As these titles suggest, current gender and language study is interdisciplinary. It crosses the boundaries of Linguistics into, *inter alia*, Women's Studies, Queer

Studies, Literature, Philosophy, Psychology, Cultural and Media Studies, Politics, History, Religious Studies and Education. Probably associated most closely with the Social Sciences, Arts and Humanities, Gender and Language issues are found also in Law and Management and even in the Natural Sciences, at least in their reportage (Crowther and Leith 1995). Students of Gender and Language often find the field fascinating because of its wide-ranging sphere of relevance. Much informs Gender and Language, and Gender and Language potentially informs much else.

Because Gender and Language is not a unitary approach, but rather a 'field', it can and does utilise a whole range of related theoretical approaches (for example, CA, CDA, corpus linguistics), epistemologies (views of what counts as knowledge) and methodologies.

In the 'methodologies' camp we might include:

- introspection (see Unit B2.1)
- sociolinguistic surveys (see Units A1, B1.2)
- focus groups (see Unit B5.3)
- observation, and collection/analysis of naturally occurring spoken data (see e.g. Units A8.2, B6.1, B8).

As regards 'approaches', we first look here at corpus linguistics, and then, comparatively, at CDA, CA and FPDA.

A8.2 CORPUS LINGUISTICS

Corpus linguistics is exemplified in Unit B8.1. A corpus is a representative, substantial body of systematically collected and recorded data, spoken or written, which is normally electronically stored as text on a PC. So, for example, we could have a 'classroom data corpus' or a corpus of magazine problem pages. Corpora of spoken language are often created through demographic sampling (for example, people from certain age or socio-economic groups), audio-recording, and transcription. This body of data is then normally electronically scanned, so that individual words or phrases can then be retrieved, and seen as a set. Such a corpus can be 'tagged', not only for syntactic or lexical features, but for speaker features such as age, sex, social class, occupation, place of birth, current domicile and ethnicity. Corpora are analysed using software which manipulates and sorts the data in various ways in order to uncover a range of linguistic patterns based around frequency, including keywords and collocation. An electronic corpus can be made available via the Internet, and can thus provide a shared resource for analysts. The corpus of academic spoken English MICASE, for example, exemplified in Unit A4, is free and thus widely available (<http://www.hti.umich.edu/m/micase>).

Corpus linguistics provides a valuable way to create and analyse large bodies of data. It also provides answers to questions about, for example, whether two words or grammatical structures ever occur together, how frequently (relative to other combinations, or in particular genres), and with what range of uses and meanings. Longitudinally, it can provide information about early uses of new words, and increases and decreases of certain phrasings over time. And, because it can be tagged for speaker sex, a corpus is an excellent source of data for quantitative 'gender differences' studies (for example, of whether women or men tend to use a particular term more, or differently).

Corpora have been used in CDA studies (for example, Stubbs 2001), addressing complaints of critics that CDA findings are based on very small amounts of specially selected texts. These large quantities of data also allow statistical significance to be established, that is, to show the likelihood of any 'differences' having occurred by chance. More importantly, corpora are often large enough to allow researchers to uncover unusual features of discourse, which may not appear in smaller samples of data. The most well known Gender and Language scholars to use corpus linguistics are Janet Holmes and Robert Sigley (2002a, b, Sigley and Holmes 2002; see also Unit A5), for example in their work on use of 'girl' and 'woman' in workplace talk.

A8.3 FURTHER APPROACHES TO GENDER AND LANGUAGE STUDY

Other 'approaches' characteristically used in gender and language study include:

- variationist sociolinguistics (i.e. linguistic variation within a community which correlates with some aspect of social structure) (see Unit A1)
- ethnography (see Unit A6)
- feminist theory and queer theory (see Unit B4.3)
- (critical) discourse analysis (see Unit A7)
- FPDA (see Unit B7.3)
- CA (see Units B8.2, B8.3)
- discursive psychology (see Unit 9)
- pragmatics (tag questions, compliments, apologies)
- psychoanalytical theory.

Relationships between theoretical approach and methodology are not clear cut. Some approaches – perhaps ethnography, variationist sociolinguistics and, particularly, CA – can be said to have broadly agreed-on associated methodologies. CDA, in contrast, can be seen as a broad theoretical approach, potentially 'served' by a range of methodologies – analysis of particular written texts, but also corpus analysis and even ethnography. FPDA is, at the time of writing, very new, but Baxter has suggested a set of principles and procedures (one chapter in her book is entitled 'Getting to grips with FPDA'), as well as two concrete illustrative case studies. FPDA ideally uses a combination of observation (and audio- or video-recording) of naturally occurring data, interviews with participants, and discourse analysis of the associated transcripts (see Unit B7.3).

Investigations in gender and language study can be qualitative, quantitative, or both. (It is worth making the point that both data and analysis can be qualitative or quantitative.) Much early work (for example, Fishman 1980, 1983, Zimmerman and West 1975) included a significant quantitative component. And although this work is sometimes decried for its concentration on numbers (and correlations of frequencies with the 'variable' of speaker sex) rather than on possible interpretations of what was said, this quantitative work allowed later studies to develop in fruitful qualitative directions, empirical bases (albeit using rather limited data) having already been established.

Different approaches and methodologies characteristically use certain types of data, and perhaps genres. CDA may work best with written texts designed for public consumption, and often texts are chosen for their possible ideological intent. CA (obviously) requires spoken data. Conventionally, this data has been naturally occurring, although some 'applied CA' uses elicited data (for example, ten Have 1999). Elicited spoken data, for example from focus groups or one-to-one inter-views, is however more closely associated with discursive psychology, for which participants' 'accounts' are crucial for the 'interpretive repertoires' and 'ideological dilemmas' they suggest. (We look more closely at questions of data in Unit A9.)

A8.4 LANGUAGE, GENDER AND FEMINISM

Slicing the Gender and Language cake another way, to these 'approaches' we can add (though by no means unproblematically) the categories 'feminist' and 'non-feminist'. Gender and language study does not entail a feminist approach. Neither Haas nor Labov nor Trudgill, or even Milroy or Gal, would have claimed to have been doing feminist research (some might have actively distanced themselves from it). And early research into sex differences in child language acquisition (for example Gleason 1973) was not informed by a feminist perspective. The field was however given a major impetus by the 'second wave' of the Women's Movement in the late 1960s and early 1970s, and much gender and language research since then can be characterised as 'broadly feminist'.

Different feminisms have often been translated into different forms of feminist research. To see gender differences in language use as an effect or perpetuation of masculine power, for example, may be an epistemological manifestation of radical feminism; to see any such differences as 'linguistic subcultural differences', with women and men showing different strengths, and power playing a minimal role (if any), a manifestation of liberal feminism (Cameron 1992b).

It is some time since Deborah Cameron had the experience at a job interview of hearing writing a book called *Feminism and Linguistic Theory* compared to writing one about linguistics and organic gardening (1992b: 2). The question now for Gender Studies has moved from 'whether linguistics?' to 'which linguistics?' This range of approaches, methodologies and data types raises an important question for feminist-oriented gender and language study: is a particular approach or methodology particularly appropriate (or indeed inappropriate) for feminist gender and language study? In this respect, we find books such as *Doing Feminist Research* (Roberts 1981), *Nonsexist Research Methods* (Eichler 1991), *Breaking Out: feminist consciousness and feminist research* (Stanley and Wise 1983) and *Feminist Approaches to Theory and Methodology* (Hesse-Biber et al. 1999), and articles such as 'Can there be a feminist ethnography?' (Stacey 1988; see also Nielsen 1990; Reinharz 1992). As regards language study, Ros Gill wrote: 'It seems to me that discourse analysis has an enormous amount to offer feminists', but adds, 'I want to argue that there is no *necessary* connection between discourse analysis and a progressive or critical politics' (1995: 167, 168, Gill's italics). On the other side of the coin, Stokoe and Smithson (Unit B8.2) claim that 'no method is *prima facie* incompatible with feminism (Brannen 1992, Maynard and Purvis 1994, Stanley and Wise 1983)'. Certainly it is not difficult to imagine how different approaches might each contribute to feminist ends.

Discourse analysis has both constituted and been the main 'beneficiary' of the 'linguistic turn' in the Social Sciences, including feminist theory (see Cameron 1998b). Cameron compares 'running commentary' types of analysis with 'formal analysis'. She suggests that there can be 'good' examples of each in feminist research, and against this backdrop of methodological diversity identifies a different question: 'how do we persuade one another that a given *interpretation* is more or less valid, insightful, useful?' (1998b: 970, my italics).

Post-structuralism is hotly debated (in Gill's chapter and elsewhere), in terms of whether it really means that 'anything goes' – for example, whether the account of the rapist who pleads not guilty is as good as that of the woman he raped (in which case it cannot be seen as an appropriate feminist epistemology or theoretical approach). Judith Baxter's 'Feminist post-structuralist discourse analysis' (Unit B7.3) addresses and redresses precisely this question. CA has also witnessed a lengthy and heated debate in *Discourse and Society* about its suitability for feminist study. Initiated by Schegloff in 1997, and responded to by Wetherell in 1998, subsequent contributions include those from feminist conversation analyst Celia Kitzinger, and from Elizabeth Stokoe and Janet Smithson, who argue not only that CA can be used for feminist purposes, but also that it has something unique to contribute (see Units B8.2 and B8.3). Indeed, CA is undergoing something of a revival in (feminist) gender and language study.

The same is less evidently true, however, of CDA (see also Unit A7). With its critiques of the workings of power and dominance, CDA might appear initially to be the most 'obvious' approach to feminist gender and language study. As Wodak points out, 'Many proposals and basic assumptions of feminist linguistics relate to and overlap with principles of critical linguistics and critical discourse analysis' (1997: 3). These include notions of researcher commitment, broad shared understandings of oppressive gender relations, and a recognition of the associations between masculinity, power and dominance, and between femininity and powerlessness. There is, nevertheless, a surprising lacuna here. Several articles and chapters report studies which have used CDA (for example, Caldas-Coulthard [1995, 1996], Bergvall and Remlinger [1996]), and several contributions in Wodak's collection *Gender and Discourse* (1997) and Litosseliti and Sunderland's (2002) collection *Gender Identity and Discourse Analysis* are explicitly or can be seen as forms of CDA. There is, however, to date, no monograph as such on CDA, gender and language (as Cameron noted in her 1998 'Review essay' on 'Gender, language and discourse') (1998b), although Clare Walsh (2001) follows a CDA approach, and the first edited collection on the topic has only recently been published (Lazar 2005).

One reason for this lacuna may be mistrust. Cameron characterises CDA as:

> an area of work in linguistics . . . to which feminists have made significant contributions, although its precise relationship to feminism is difficult to pin down: it is one of those broadly progressive projects whose founders and dominant figures are nevertheless all straight white men, and Wilkinson and Kitzinger (1995) specifically remark on these men's failure to give credit to feminists by citing their work.
>
> (1998b: 970)

Another reason may be CDA's concern with the material, and a rejection of the (post-structuralist) notion that discourse is radically constitutive. And a third may be that CDA is not seen as theoretically able to deal with possibilities of power and dominance as fluctuating. Comparing CDA with FPDA, Baxter refers to FPDA's 'more complex perceptions of the ambiguities and unevenness of power. While CDA is more likely to polarise the argument casting males as villains and females as victims, FPDA is more likely to argue that females are multiply located and cannot be so dichotomously cast as powerless, disadvantaged or victims' (2003: 55). Whether this is a fair characterisation of CDA is a matter for debate – and, of course, CDA, like other approaches, is not static.

In Baxter's FPDA, power is multiple, potentially enabling and – temporarily – associated with 'traditionally oppressed' groups as well as the 'traditional' oppressors (see Baxter 2003, for a fuller discussion of the similarities and differences between CDA and FPDA).

A8.5 RELATIONSHIPS WITH RESEARCH PARTICIPANTS

 Task A8.5.1: Reflection task

➤ In any empirical research work you have done in relation to a particular group of people (excluding colleagues), how would you characterise the relationship between them and you?

➤ How do you refer to them in your research reports?

➤ What was their role in the different aspects and phases of your research?

Yet another way of 'slicing the cake' in terms of approach is to look politically at the relations between researchers and those they are researching. In a 1992 collection, *Researching Language: issues of power and method*, five applied linguists, Deborah Cameron, Elizabeth Frazer, Penelope Harvey, Ben Rampton and Kay Richardson, identify three positions: 'ethics', 'advocacy' and 'empowerment'. 'Ethics' is the weakest of the three, entailing such practices as minimising damage, offsetting inconvenience to research participants and documenting the contribution of the 'researched'. This is a 'research on' model, in which the researchers do not feel accountable to their 'subjects'.

If researchers do decide to make themselves accountable, they may locate themselves in the 'advocacy' position, when the researcher researches for as well as on his or her 'subjects'. Labov's role in the Ann Arbor 'Black English' trial of 1979 is cited here: Labov acted as an 'expert witness' in court by showing that African Vernacular Black English was an actual language variety, divergent from standard English, spoken by many African American children at the school, but not their teachers. The parents eventually won their case that the specific educational needs of their children were not being met.

In the third approach, 'empowerment', the researcher does research 'on, for and with' research participants, addressing the participants' own agendas and sharing knowledge gained, in recognition that this may also enhance the research.

Without claiming that their own studies are 'models for empowering research', the authors of *Researching Language* provide case studies, in which they include consideration of the extent to which their work can be said to be characterised by the three approaches.

In Unit B8, we look at extracts from work representing two different approaches to gender and language study. (FPDA is the topic of Unit B7.3.) Unit B8.1 includes an extract from an article by Paul Rayson, Geoffrey Leech and Mary Hodges (1997) on the use of corpus linguistics to look at words most frequently used by women, and by men. Unit B8.2 continues with an argued account of how the theoretical approach of CA is relevant to gender study, by Elizabeth Stokoe and Janet Smithson (2001), and the CA of some data in relation to gender and sexuality by Celia Kitzinger (2000) is the focus of Unit B8.3.

Unit A9
Data and data sites

A9.1 INTRODUCTION

One distinction in research is between work of a primarily theoretical nature, and work which reports on an empirical study, that is, which uses data. This distinction is not clear cut. Data has a crucial role in driving theory, and primarily theoretical work often draws on empirical examples. Maltz and Borker (Unit B3) provide a good example of this, as do the extracts by Cameron and Nelson (Units B4.1 and B4.3), and Eckert and McConnell-Ginet (Unit B6.2). In turn, empirical work almost always has some theoretical base, though regrettably this may not be stated (or even clearly recognised).

Task A9.1.1: Reflection task

➤ Drawing on the work you have read in gender and language study, make one list of work you would describe as 'theoretical', and another of work you would describe as 'empirical'.

Empirical studies are based on varying amounts of data, but, for most contemporary research in linguistics, empirical data is important. Expectations of what is appropriate data have varied, however, as has the detail with which its collection is documented and the extent to which this is reflected on. Otto Jespersen, writing in the 1920s, included in his rationale for his claims about women's and men's talk his personal impressions and examples from works of fiction. Mary Haas (Unit B1.1), working in the 1940s, in contrast, collected data on Koasati from speakers of the language, though actual details of her methodology are sparse. Robin Lakoff, working in the early 1970s, used introspection as the basis for her claims about women's and men's talk, carrying out a considerable amount of rhetorical work as justification (Unit B2.1). Researchers are now increasingly 'reflexive' about their data, and data-collection methods – and are encouraged to be. The British Association of Applied Linguistics (BAAL) 'Recommendations on good practice in Applied Linguistics', for example, indicates that 'All aspects of research should be reported in enough detail to allow other applied linguists to understand and interpret them' (<http://www.baal.org.uk/about_goodpractice_full.pdf>).

A second distinction can be made between data types. 'Naturally occurring' data refers to (linguistic) behaviour that would have happened 'anyway'. This is normally collected through observation, that is, of what is visible and/or audible – which means that the observer's presence may shape the data in some way. Data on linguistic behaviour (written or spoken) can also be 'elicited', through approaches such as interviews and questionnaires.

A9.2 NATURALLY OCCURRING DATA

Most linguistic data in gender and language study has been 'naturally occurring'. The extension extracts in this resource book include several examples. Below is a selection:

- Mary Haas (we can assume) noted down occurrences of naturally occurring use of Koasati (Unit B1.1).
- Pamela Fishman audio-recorded the naturally occurring speech of heterosexual couples (Unit B2.3).
- Jane Sunderland et al. looked at naturally occurring classroom data (Unit B6.1).
- Puleng Hanong Thetela collected naturally occurring data from police stations (Unit B6.3).
- Paul Rayson et al. used a spoken corpus of everyday talk (Unit B8.1).
- Celia Kitzinger's 'coming out' data was extracts of audio-recordings of university seminars (Unit B8.3).

Jennifer Mason (2002) writes that since observation of naturally occurring behaviour can be very time- and resource-consuming, there needs to be a good reason or set of reasons to do this. Two theoretical, indeed philosophical reasons are:

1. having an ontological perspective 'which sees interactions, actions and behaviours and the way people interpret these, act on them, and so on, as central';
2. having an epistemological position 'which suggests that knowledge or evidence of the social world can be generated by observing, or participating in, or experiencing "natural" or "real life" settings, interactive situations and so on'.
(Mason 2002: 85–7)

Other reasons include conceptualising yourself as 'active and reflexive' in the research process. A general principle of research is that everything should be done (i.e. every decision made) on the basis of a principle, and indeed that the principle should be documented if the research is to be written up or otherwise presented for public consumption.

Mason's reasons suggest that, despite the time-consuming nature of observation of naturally occurring behaviour, certain topics and research questions (RQs) require precisely this. In language study, these topics and RQs are likely to focus on talk – perhaps in association with other linguistic practices (including gesture and/or proxemics), non-linguistic social practices or written texts. Examples of topics for

Table A9.1

Topic	Illustrative Research Question (RQ)
Gender tendencies in spoken interaction	If there are tendencies on the part of individuals to dominate mixed-sex team game pre-match discussions (for example, korfball), are these tendencies gendered?
Gender tendencies in non-verbal communication	Is gaze differently distributed during the talk of single-sex and mixed-sex dyads?
Construction/ performance of gender and gendered identities (masculinities, femininities) in talk	How are different masculinities constructed and performed in discourse in ante-natal classes for couples by the participants in these classes?
Parent–child talk	Do fathers use gender as a category differently in their talk with their daughters and with their sons?
Gender construction in talk in public contexts (for example, the workplace)	How is gender represented in the talk of window dressers in prestigious clothes stores?
Silence and verbosity	In a given cultural context, with which social practices or CofPs is women's (relative) silence associated, and with which women's (relative) verbosity?
Gendered talk around different text types	Does classroom 'ethos' (as evidenced in, say, an agreed classroom 'Code of Conduct') make a difference to the way collaborative group talk in the production of a written text by a mixed-sex group is gendered?

which appropriate data might be naturally occurring behaviour, with illustrative RQs, are shown in Table A9.1.

 Task A9.2.1: Reflection task

➤ Add to the chart two topics and RQs of your own that need to be addressed by naturally occurring data.

Observation has a long methodological tradition, and is well documented as a methodological approach, especially in the Social Sciences (see, for example, Allwright 1988, Lofland and Lofland 1995). It is, however, limited in what it can achieve. It cannot, of itself, directly explore what might be called understandings (perceptions, attitudes, opinions, reasons, beliefs, intentions, motivating factors) – people's 'inner workings', the focus of traditional (as opposed to discursive) psychology. So, whereas observational methods can document and describe gendered (linguistic) behaviour, any explanation based solely on the observational data will always be -*etic*, that is, the researcher's perspective, not -*emic*, that is, the participants' perspective. CA explains given cases of human spoken interaction through speakers' orientation (see Unit A8 and Units B8.2 and B8.3), but usually that orientation is identified by the analyst. And any 'piece' of behaviour (linguistic or otherwise) has many possible meanings. As Cameron et al. (1992) note (and I quote at length since this illustrates the limitations of analysts' interpretations well):

the social researcher cannot take it for granted that she knows or recognises exactly what a social phenomenon or event is when she sees it. A woman turning over the earth in a flower bed with a spade might immediately be understood by an observer to be 'digging the garden'. In fact, though, the digger's own understandings and intentions would be an important part of the reality – she might not be gardening, but preparing to bury the budgie. Even if she were gardening, the observer who simply recorded this might miss some very important aspects of the scene: the gardener might be letting off steam after a row with her children, relaxing after a hard day at the office or worshipping the Goddess Earth by cultivating her. These meanings are properly a part of the reality being observed, the question 'what is going on here' cannot be answered without reference to the agent's own understanding of what she is doing.

(1992: 11)

Further, any piece of behaviour also has an aggregate of contributory causes (consider the death of the UK's Princess Diana, for example). Claims made about the reasons for the findings of observational studies should therefore always be carefully qualified.

Naturally occurring data raises a range of issues as regards data collection (some of which we have touched on). These include:

- access
- ethics
- the 'observer's paradox'
- methods (for example, fieldnotes, audio- and video-taping, transcription)
- the role of the researcher
- researcher commitment vis-à-vis objectivity
- relationships with research participants.

None of these is specific to gender and language research, of course, and they are dealt with in many excellent books about social research (for example, Cohen, Manion and Morrison 2000, Mason 2002, Silverman 2000, 2004; see also Roberts 1981, Stanley and Wise 1983, Nielsen 1990, Reinharz 1992 and Hesse-Biber et al. 1999 on feminist research). Each issue may have particular implications for gender and language study.

A9.3 ELICITED DATA

Elicited data is found rather less often than naturally occurring data in gender and language study, with the exception of work within certain approaches, such as discursive psychology (see below). Elicited data is crucially different from naturally occurring data: it would not have existed without the research. For this reason, Mason refers here to 'data generation' rather than 'data collection' (2002: 52).

In Sociolinguistics, eliciting data in traditional 'variationist' studies has taken the form of asking respondents to pronounce words under different conditions (for example, reading word lists aloud, casual speech) (Labov 1966), and interviews: asking speakers to rate their pronunciation in terms of prestige (Trudgill 1972a, 1972b, 1974, Labov 1966); to indicate when they used Hungarian and when German (Gal 1978); and to describe their social networks (Milroy 1980). Elicited data can also be collected through questionnaires, focus groups, accounts, diaries and stimulated recall (for example, Cohen, Manion and Morrison 2000). Examples of interviews and focus groups in this resource book include:

- Lesley Milroy (Unit B1.2), who interviewed participants in Belfast about their social networks in her study of phonetic variables;
- Juliane Schwarz (Unit B5.3), who asked members of a focus group about their use of 'Ms';
- Nigel Edley (Unit B9.1), who interviewed small groups of men about their understandings of feminism.

Other possible topics requiring elicited data and illustrative RQs are shown in Table A9.2.

Table A9.2

Topic	Illustrative Research Question (RQ)
Women's understandings of the meanings of different linguistic forms of resistance to sexual harassment and unwanted sex	In what different ways do women evaluate the notion of 'Just say No' as a way of resisting unwanted sex and sexual harassment? (see Kitzinger and Frith 1999)
Students' understandings of linguistic forms of 'differential teacher-treatment-by-gender' in the classroom, for example, reasons/intentions and possible effects	What explanations do students offer for differential teacher-treatment-by-gender in the classroom (for example, if the teacher asks boys harder questions) (see Sunderland 1994c)
Gendered discourses of parenting: articulated understandings of the (different) roles of mothers and fathers (as expressed, say, in ante-natal classes, or public meetings on the role of the home in early childhood education)	How do professionals' understandings of gender in parenting differ from those of parents themselves?

Task A9.3.1: Reflection task

➤ Add two more topics to Table A9.2, together with illustrative RQs that need to be addressed by elicited data.

As indicated, studies of attitudes, feelings, beliefs, perceptions, understandings, memories and/or reasons – all notoriously difficult to define (and often to distinguish) – might best be grouped together under an overarching term such as 'understandings' or 'consciousness'. Strictly speaking, of course, elicited data is not data on understandings or consciousness at all, but rather 'reported' or 'articulated' consciousness or understandings (as in the third topic in Table A9.2). A respondent may be deceiving herself or the researcher; she may not know what her attitude, say, towards something is; she may not have an attitude towards something, but may not like to appear ignorant or indifferent, and so may report one. And, of course, different attitudes may be reported at different times, for different reasons. All this is taken as given by discursive psychologists (and by post-structuralist discourse analysts, see Unit A7), who see individuals as being differently ('multiply') positioned by a range of discourses at any given point of time, and who in turn are likely to articulate discourses consonant with those that are relatively dominant in their positioning at that point in time. For example, a child at a school in which an equal opportunities policy is frequently invoked may well articulate an equal opportunities discourse on occasion, especially if this same discourse is available at home too. Another child, however, perhaps one for whom this discourse is contested at home, may regularly produce traces of a different set of discourses.

Discursive psychology is increasingly utilised in gender and language study (for example, Wetherell et al. 1987, Weatherall 2002, Edley 2001 [see Unit B9.1]). Edley compares discursive psychology with 'traditional psychological' approaches as follows:

> Whereas in the past, psychologists have typically seen language as a resource, providing clues as to what is going on inside people's minds or brains, discursive psychology takes language as its topic, examining the ways in which people talk about – or construct – things like attitudes, memories and emotions.

> (2001: 190)

This contrasts with the idea that elicited data is about 'understandings'. The 'ways in which people talk about – or construct – things like attitudes, memories and emotions', relate much more closely to discourse (see Unit 7). In Unit B9.1, Edley uses discursive psychology to look at the epistemological site of 'masculinity'. (Masculinity was earlier somewhat neglected by gender and language study, but see Johnson and Meinhof's [1997] collection, *Language and Masculinity*, especially Sally Johnson's introductory chapter; see also Coates's *Men Talk* [2003]).

As discursive psychology acknowledges, elicited data is co-constructed by the researcher and the respondent. A simple example is an interview question which prompts the respondent to think in new ways, and express – for the first time – a certain idea. Less dramatically, interviewers' backchannel noises such as 'mm', and 'oh yes' may be seen as approval, and the interviewee may embellish or even exaggerate what he or she was saying in response. To return to Trudgill's and Cameron's different possible explanations about why women use more prestige forms (in terms of syntax and pronunciation) than men (see Cameron 1992b, also Unit A1.2), these could in principle be explored further by asking women about their use of prestige forms. However, their answers would only go so far, given that we cannot see these straightforwardly as 'factual information', waiting to be 'extracted'.

To summarise, gender and language study has drawn on both naturally occurring and elicited spoken data, though more on the former. For some examples from edited collections, see Table A9.3.

Note that, as in the last of these, it is possible to combine naturally occurring and elicited data. Either type may be seen as 'shedding light' on the other, that data-type then being 'secondary', and the other 'primary'. (Note that this is not the same as the traditional 'positivist' meaning of 'triangulation': from a social science paradigm in general, and certainly from a post-structuralist one, the findings of the two sets of

Table A9.3

Title of collection and editor(s)	Naturally occurring spoken data	Elicited spoken data
Feminism and Discourse (eds Sue Wilkinson and Celia Kitzinger)		'The bleeding body: adolescents. talk about menstruation' (Kathyryn Matthews Lovering) 'Sexual harassment: a discursive approach' (Celia Kitzinger and Alison Thomas) 'Feminist discourses and women's heterosexual desire' (Wendy Hollway)
Communicating Gender in Context (eds Helga Kotthoff and Ruth Wodak)	'Is Spain different? Observations on male-female communicative styles in Spanish group discussion' (Christine Bierbach) 'Complaint stories: constructing emotional reciprocity among women' (Susanne Gunthner)	
Language, Gender and Society (eds Barrie Thorne, Cheris Kramarae and Nancy Henley)	'Interaction: the work women do' (Pamela Fishman) 'Small insults: a study of interruptions in cross-sex conversations between unacquainted persons' (Candace West and Don Zimmerman)	
Gender Identity and Discourse Analysis (eds Lia Litosseliti and Jane Sunderland)	'Erotic discourse strategies in powerless women: Analysing psychiatric interviews' (Branca Telles Ribeiro) 'From representation towards discursive practices: Gender in the foreign language textbook revisited' (Jane Sunderland, Maire Cowley, Fauziah Abdul Rahim, Christina Leontzakou and Julie Shattuck)	

data would not be expected to correspond, and even apparent 'contradictions' [for example, someone saying they never say a certain word, whereas when they are audio-recorded they produce it frequently] would be a starting point, something to take on board and address, rather than a problem for the research.)

Task A9.3.2: Reflection task

➤ Consider the gender and language work with which you are familiar.

➤ Which used naturally occurring data, and which elicited?

A9.4 EPISTEMOLOGICAL SITES

All empirical data is selected from a particular epistemological site, any study of gender involving the broad 'site' of humans. The epistemological site for a given research study might be a literal site in the sense of a specific physical setting – a Starbucks coffee shop to investigate the naturally occurring production of complex noun phrases, for example – but the notion of epistemological site is broader than this. Depending on his or her RQ, the researcher might be conceptually concerned with a phenomenon, speech act, topic or concept, or more materially with a genre, domain, institution, group of people, event or setting, which he or she feels is revealing and fruitful in some way.

In *Gendered Discourses* (2004), I identified the classroom as one epistemological site (a setting), along with 'fatherhood' (an institution) and 'prize-winning children's literature' (another institution). I also suggested that these were 'fruitful episte-mological site[s] for the study of gendered discourses' (2004: 73). The identification of fruitful sites is shaped by theoretical understandings of the gender–language relationship. These have changed and developed over the past few decades. In the 1970s, the dominant paradigm for studying gender and language use was the '(male) dominance' model, and researchers working within this framework accordingly needed as data talk between women and men (or girls and boys), enabling exam-ination of 'gender differences' in verbosity, interruptions, tag questions, and so on. The dominant, paradigmatic epistemological site was thus private, mixed-sex conversation (see Units A.2 and A.3). (Studies of public talk, single-sex talk and written texts, were accordingly less frequently encountered.) In the 1980s, when the '(male) dominance' model gave way to the '(cultural) difference' model, data included the talk of single-sex groups (mainly women) (see Coates 1989). Now that both models have been largely left behind because of their unproductive focus on 'gender differences', and replaced with a focus on discourse(s), gender identity, representation, construction and performance of gender, epistemological sites are diverse and wide ranging. Written texts are frequently studied, and public contexts are of considerable interest for the talk that goes on there (see, for example, Baxter 2006). Similarly, Pavlenko and Piller (2001) note how the 'primary unit' where language and gender research is conducted has shifted from interpersonal encounters (for example, mixed-sex dyads) and speech communities to CofPs (for example, Eckert and McConnell-Ginet 1992a, 1992b, 1999).

The diversity of epistemological sites is evident in the many edited collections on gender and language. In *Reinventing Identities: the gendered self in discourse* (Bucholtz, Liang and Sutton 1999), epistemological sites include the language of women from a diversity of ethnic backgrounds (African American, Native American, Latina, Lakhota, Tunisia), deaf and hearing lesbian women, as well as the office, the TV-shopping channel, children's games, alternative publishing, and *News at 6.*

Using the distinction between material (genre-related) epistemological sites and those which can be seen as conceptual (usually focusing on some aspect of language itself), we can consult the programme of the 2004 IGALA3 Conference. Material epistemological sites for gender and language research reported on in presentations included:

- Internet chats
- call-in radio programmes
- ESOL classrooms
- business meetings
- a gender-identity clinic
- reality TV
- teenage romance fiction
- English academic discourse
- friendship group play
- dinnertime conversations
- singing games
- public arguments.

Conceptual sites included:

- ideologies of language and gender
- tag questions
- homophobia
- compliments
- silence
- collaborative narration
- humour
- gender-stereotypical speech
- intonation patterns
- language planning
- narrative
- contradictions.

The 'material' and the 'conceptual' frequently overlap and combine – in the topic of 'Gendered humour in ESOL classroom talk', for example. When deciding where best to collect or generate data in relation to one's RQs, it is worth considering both 'types' of site. The best RQ may be one to which an answer will enable the study to contribute theoretically to the field more widely. A conceptual site may achieve this better than a material one – doing research in a new geographical area for example is in itself unlikely to advance the field greatly.

Task A9.4.1: Reflection task

➤ Using Table A9.3 on p. 68, identify those epistemological sites that can be considered as material (genre-related), and those which can be considered as conceptual.

West and Fenstermaker (2002), investigating how gender, race and class are 'accomplished in social interaction', explicitly ask of their chosen epistemological site (a University of California Board of Regents on affirmative action policies): 'In what sense . . . does this meeting constitute a logical place to explore the ongoing accomplishment of gender, race and class in social interaction?' (They then provide a three-part answer in a very substantial paragraph [2002: 542].) Data selection (as opposed to collection) is, however, not always documented thus fully: though we are normally told where data came from, we are not always provided with a rationale for why. Yet the writer (including the postgraduate writer) who wishes to be accountable to her readers (and indeed her participants), would be well advised to do just this. In a discussion of discourse analytic research, Stephanie Taylor writes, 'For every project, the researcher must establish the justification for the data being used' (2001: 28). Establishing this justification may include acquainting the reader with the range of potential sites considered and rejected.

It is also useful to consider what might constitute 'ideal' data, i.e. what data from what site could be expected to provide the best answer to a given RQ? Sadly, this does not mean that the question of 'Which data?' is then answered, given the inevitable constraints, for example, on availability or access. In the real world, the researcher must consider the best data she or he can reasonably get. This requires epistemological consideration of to what extent the 'actual' data obtained represents a compromise, and in what way it might rhetorically limit claims that can be made about the status, generalisability or relevance of the findings. What is not acceptable is 'any old data'. There should always be a principled reason for the data in question, meaning that data choice, like choice of the epistemological site, should be motivated.

A9.5 'TRADITIONAL GENDER' AND 'NON-TRADITIONAL GENDER' SITES

A further distinction can be made between epistemological sites in which we might expect gender to be represented and constructed in a traditional way, and those in which we might expect non-traditional representation and construction. Predictable as traditional, for example, is the written discourse of 'Wedding Album' pages of local mainstream UK newspapers, which tend to report in a highly formulaic way who married whom, where, their occupations, who gave the bride away, what she wore, who the bridesmaids were, who the best man was, and the location of the reception and honeymoon. Such sites can however also be explored for traces of less traditional gendered discourses – perhaps, in a diachronic study, as evidence of change.

Potentially fruitful sites for the study of non-traditional gendered practices include those in which women and men 'transgress' culture-specific traditional gender norms: when men become pre-school teachers or 'escorts' for women (Taylor and Sunderland 2003), for example, or when women become combatants in the army, professional golfers in what were hitherto men's tournaments, or police officers with traditionally masculine responsibilities (McIlhenny 1995). Here, while traces of non-traditional gendered discourses may be evident (depending on its purpose and the affinities of the producer of the text[s] in question), it would not be surprising to find traces of thoroughly traditional gendered discourses as well.

Of course, any conceptual epistemological site may be associated with a range of genres. For example, the site of 'women's role in conflict' may be manifest in both official government documentation and 'Letters to the Editor'. The latter genre is likely to be characterised by a greater diversity of gendered discourses, identifiable through arguments against the desirability of women being in the army at all, and arguments for women and men having the 'right' to identical professional roles, challenges and opportunities.

 Task A9.5.1: Reflection task

➤ Identify some other possible 'traditional gender' and 'non-traditional gender' epistemological sites for gender and language study.

In her (1999c) contribution to the collection *Reinventing Identities: the gendered self in discourse* (Bucholtz et al. 1999), Mary Bucholtz provides an example of good practice in her indication of why a particular epistemological site is chosen. Bucholtz's immediate site is the material one of the 'shopping channel'. She justifies this epistemologically in two ways. First, popular culture (a conceptual site) is important for the role it plays as a resource for women's identity construction:

> Viewed as a set of discourses, popular culture splinters into multiple and sometimes conflicting representations that offer similarly conflicting

resources for women's identity construction. New cultural forms that blend or transcend conventional boundaries of genre or register present special challenges to analysts, for they facilitate new identity formations that may contradict traditional feminist analyses . . . or even traditional analyses of gender itself.

(Bucholtz 1999c: 349)

To oversimplify somewhat, shopping channels may, for example, construct women as preoccupied with the home and their appearance (two very traditional representations), and as autonomous in terms of having unlimited purchasing power (a non-traditional representation). Second, the shopping channel itself, a 'pastiche of public and private, entertainment and consumption' is '*an especially rich example of* . . . *discursive instability*' (Bucholtz 1999c: 349, my italics), hence of interest for the understanding of discourse more broadly.

A9.6 MORE JUSTIFICATIONS FOR SITES

Below I reproduce my own (co-written) justification for the three epistemological sites of the classroom, award-winning children's literature and fatherhood, which I identified as 'epistemologically fruitful'. The first two are justifications for material sites:

> The classroom . . . provides learning opportunities and constitutes a continuous and lengthy social experience, characterised by a vast range of practices . . . It is also a domain replete with concerns about and tensions surrounding gender . . . The study of discoursal contradictions is particularly well served by this epistemological site, where the critical '(Male) dominance discourse' on classroom interaction may compete with the 'Poor boys discourse'
>
> (Taylor and Sunderland 2003: 77)

> Children's literature . . . can be seen as an important epistemological site for discourse analysis in relation to gender since books are part of many young children's lives. Stephens (1992: 5) writes: 'it is through language that the subject and the world are represented in literature, and through language that literature seeks to define the relationships between child and culture'. In particular, children's literature is often written with the intention that it has something to *teach*. The discourses flowing through what children read, or have read to them, position them in particular ways which they may enjoy or resist (or both!). Children's books may then be experienced widely by young children during a possibly important period of 'early discourse production' (Francis 2000) . . . As regards gender, like media texts, children's literature needs to acknowledge in some way social change and challenges – though the desiderata here have gone beyond the provision of 'positive role models' for women and girls advocated by some feminist literary critics in the 1970s (see for example, Register 1975). As

regards *award-winning* children's books, these are reviewed and get a great deal of publicity, often their covers are embossed, sometimes they have a special status in children's libraries . . . They may also be systematically selected for purchase by parents and school librarians. Because of their special status they may be dramatized or filmed (as has *Holes*, a Newbery winner). Presumably all this exposure enhances their chances of being read, by children, and by parents and teachers to and with children.

(Sunderland 2004: 77)

The third is a justification for a material epistemological site ('parenting' magazines) in relation to the conceptual site of 'fatherhood':

Fatherhood . . . is an interesting epistemological site in that in a climate of continually changing gender relations, and indeed what might be called one of post-feminism, parenthood more generally may interdiscursively produce new gendered discourses and discoursal tensions. In many contexts, parenthood is now expected not only to be a responsibility of, but also a source of pleasure for, fathers as well as mothers (though not necessarily in equal measure). Fatherhood texts produced for consumption in this climate are thus likely to constitute interesting data. Several parenting magazines now have titles such as *Parents* rather than *M and M (the magazine for the mum-to-be and new mother)*. These materials beg the question of whether they really are for parents – or mainly for mothers.

(Sunderland 2004: 77)

The notion of epistemological site has a hierarchical dimension, as the 'children's literature' example suggests – a hierarchy that extends downwards from site to data and data-sampling. Children's literature was the broad (material) epistemological site, contemporary American award-winning children's literature a 'sub-epistemological site'. The actual 'data sources' (recent Newbery and Caldecott medal winners) were two sets of award-winners. Certain passages from each book – 'telling' or representative cases (see below) – were 'samples' for analysis or principled illustration. These 'samples' constituted the actual data.

There is, of course, no 'list' or hierarchy of fruitful epistemological sites for gender and language research. Identifying, 'carving out', and linguistically analysing and documenting data from such sites is part of the research endeavour. However, two broad topical categories of fruitful sites, already hinted at, are sex, and 'boundary crossing'.

The broad epistemological site of sex can be seen as both material and conceptual. Sites include 'sex education' sessions for school children, and magazine texts on male 'escorts' (see Taylor and Sunderland 2003). All texts about sex (academic, self-help, educational, popular, jokes, fiction, narratives) will almost without exception simultaneously be about gender too, including references to gender relations.

Boundary-crossing as a conceptual site refers to the talk of, but also about, women and men who 'cross boundaries' and enter arenas which are traditionally the province of the 'opposite' sex (for example, male pre-school teachers, female boxers or airline pilots; in some contexts, sprinters and cross-country runners). Here, gendered discourses (see Unit B7.1) – are likely to come to the fore. Work includes Bonnie McElhinny's (1995) study of women police officers, and Susan Speer's (2002) study of talk about women boxers and rugby players.

A9.7 'EVENTS' AS EPISTEMOLOGICAL SITES AND 'TELLING CASES'

Lastly, we can consider a whole 'event' as an epistemological site. An example is Clare Walsh's (2001) study of the campaign to allow women to be ordained as priests in the UK Anglican church. An 'event' may be brief or relatively lengthy. A 'long event' might be the talk of one specific individual, on the grounds of wider significance or ramifications (Taylor 2001) – for example, Fairclough's (2000) *New Labour, New Language?* which focuses on the rhetoric of (as I write) UK Prime Minister Tony Blair.

The researcher may know a certain event is coming, and can prepare for it, for example, a televised set of exchanges between two people with very divergent views about women. Alternatively, the event may be unexpected but identified as a seren-dipitous fruitful epistemological site, appreciated for its value, interest and relevance to gender and language study. The deaths of Princess Diana and Pope John Paul II and the talk surrounding them are good examples, as is Celia Kitzinger's 'coming out' study (Unit B8.3): Kitzinger was not intentionally looking for 'coming out' references when she made the recordings, but recognised several when listening for other things.

Associated with the 'event' type of epistemological site is the distinction between 'representative' and 'telling' data. Often there is merit in choosing 'representative' or 'typical' data: what seems like a 'typical' physics classroom or work-setting, for example, or a regular magazine feature that is read weekly by hundreds of thousands of people. A choice of this sort may aid claims about the generalisability of findings.

There is, however, at times, an argument for choosing 'unrepresentative' or 'atypical' data, and studying what might be described as a 'telling case' (Mitchell 1984) – again, the death of Princess Diana or of the Pope. This is basically an unusual event (or written text) which, because of its very unusualness, casts some aspect of Gender and Language in sharp relief. 'Telling cases' will probably be 'one-off' events.

Task A9.7.1: Reflection task

➤ Can you think of a particular 'event' of wide social significance that might constitute an interesting epistemological site for gender and language study?

➤ Can you think of a small, unusual event that can be seen as a 'telling case?

Unit A10
Written texts

Task A10.1: Reflection task

➤ What written text types would you consider particularly valuable 'epistemo-logical sites' (see Unit A9) for the study of gender and language, and why?

➤ Do you know of any studies of whole texts that have been analysed from a gender and language perspective?

With exceptions, whole written texts became of interest to gender and language study some time after spoken texts. In the 1970s, only 'snippets' of written texts tended to be cited, for example to show cases of sexist language in the media. This did not indicate a lack of concern with whole written texts. However, the early focus on whole texts could be seen as 'content analysis' rather than linguistic analysis: looking at what a text was broadly 'about', and carrying out related frequency counts, rather than how what it was about was expressed linguistically. For example, foreign-language textbooks (especially those for English as a foreign language) were regularly critiqued for their representation of female characters (see Cincotta 1978, Freudenstein 1978, Hartman and Judd 1978, Porecca 1984), and textbooks more widely were analysed for the number of their female and male characters. Later work supplemented content analysis with linguistic analysis, for example of the language used by the textbook characters in dialogues intended for classroom practice (for example, Poulou 1997, Jones et al. 1997).

Additionally, literary texts have always been seen as important. Writing on 'Women's fiction' in the late 1920s, Virginia Woolf produced the controversial – but symbolically interesting – claim that 'the very form of the sentence does not fit [a woman]. It is a sentence made by men, it is too loose, too heavy, too pompous for a woman's use' (see also Mills 1995a). In our own time, the journal *Language and Literature* features gender issues frequently. Sara Mills' edited collection *Gendering the Reader* (1994), which has a strong literary slant, looks at written texts (along with painting, film and song); two of these texts are given specifically linguistic 'readings'.

Literary texts extend to children's fiction (for example, Petersen and Lach 1990, Stones 1983, Sunderland 2004, also Unit A9). Bronwyn Davies' (1989a) critique here was written from a feminist perspective:

The texts through which children are taught to read are usually based on a 'realistic' rather than a fantastical version of the world. Within this realistic world the man is presented as active agent in the outside world, and the woman as passive, supportive other. As well, a sickly sweet and middle-class version of the nuclear family is presented as the norm. Freebody and Baker (1987) show how children in beginning readers are usually male–female pairs and that the patterns of interaction between them constitute 'correct' maleness and femaleness. Some examples they give are as follows:

> 'We have to jump this,' says Peter. 'Come after me. I know how to do it. Come after me, but keep out of the water,' Jane says, 'Mummy said that we must keep out of the water.' 'I know she said so,' says Peter, 'but we are not going in the water. I know how to do this,' Peter jumps again. 'You can do it, Jane,' he says. Then Jane jumps. She says, 'Yes, I can do it. Look at me, Peter, I can do it.' . . .

How apparently innocently the male is constituted as the one who knows, the one who reasons and the one who leads, and the female as obedient, mindless, passive, rule-follower. The mother is the authority, left behind in the domestic space, and in this non-domestic space the boy's authority is greater. The girl is constituted as achieving in the non-domestic space only through the encouragement of the boy, and the boy is constituted as adult male through the supportive work of the girl. The boy is the one who plays, who has fun, and the girl empowers him through her nurturing behaviour which facilitates his fun.

(1989a: 45)

Davies also took issue with the form earlier feminist critique had taken, which:

> is fairly superficial and adopts what Walkerdine calls a limited 'rationalist' stance. On a simple content analysis, the solution to Peter and Jane would appear to present a problem only if Mummy is always left at home and if Peter is always the leader. More subtle questions such as Mummy's presumed responsibility for the moral order, Peter's right (even obligation) to challenge that, the consistent male–female coupling, are generally left unquestioned in such analyses.

(1989a: 46)

Unit B10.2 includes another extract from Davies, in which she moves to an exploration of feminist fairy tales, and girls' and boys' interpretations of these.

Other epistemological sites in which whole written texts (together with associated visuals) provide data for gender and language study are journalism, in particular the representation of women in newspapers, and advertising. Judith Williamson's (1978) *Decoding Advertisements*, with its clear focus on gender, has become something of a classic, but in 1976 the UK group 'Women in Media' also produced a booklet called *The Packaging of Women*, and a 1978 issue of the UK Women's Liberation Movement magazine *Spare Rib* carried an article by Jill Nicholls and Pat Moan on the Advertising Standards Authority's responses to complaints of sexism (more recently, this was the topic of Deborah Cameron's Plenary talk at the 2004 International Gender and Language Conference; see Cameron 2006).

In Units 1 to 9, the only written texts considered as data are Alma's Graham's *American Heritage Dictionary* (Unit B5.1) and the language textbooks in Sunderland et al.'s (2002) 'talk around the textbook text' study (Unit B6.1). Within the Gender and Language field more widely, however, a range of written text types are the foci of investigation. Those cited in the *Gender and Genre Bibliography* (2006) (<http://www.ling.lancs.ac.uk/groups/clsl/current.htm>) include:

academic writing	erotic texts	narratives
advertisements (goods/services)	fiction	news reports
	graffiti	personal ads
autobiography	grammar books	play scripts
cartoons	greetings cards	poetry
children's literature	horoscopes	posters
comics	legal documents	problem pages
computer-mediated communication (CMC)	letters	religious texts
	magazines	tests (educational)
diaries	manuals	textbooks
dictionaries	medical/psychiatric texts	travel guides

All these genres are further divisible. For example, at the 2004 International Gender and Language Association Conference (IGALA3), magazine studies reported on included those of both teenage and consumer magazines.

 Task A10.2: Reflection task

➤ Can you add further genres which you think would be epistemologically fruitful, to this list?

➤ If so, and if you can find actual examples of work, please send the references to the address given in the *Gender and Genre Bibliography* (above).

A concern with gender and written texts can be seen as a concern with representation. Cosslett (1996: 6) writes: 'it is . . . important to distinguish between our experiences and the images we meet of these in the arts, media and other cultural texts'. Representation is, of course, those images. Representation has however tended not to be understood in terms of constitutiveness, and may therefore imply a mediated version of a pre-existing, material reality. (In this sense, it is not compatible with a full-blown post-structuralism.) Recently, the term 'construction' (of women and men, boys and girls), with reference to a given text, has come to be used. This may mean traditionally or newly constructed (for example, of someone in a way she or he has not been represented in a text before); it may also mean construction beyond the text. (See Unit A7 for Fairclough's distinction between *construal* and *construction*.)

Task A10.3: Reflection task

➤ In what sense might construction take place 'beyond' a written text? Consider some different possibilities here.

In addition to representation and construction is the question of interpretation by the 'consumer' (Stephens 1992: 162): there may be different views of what a particular representation or construction actually *is* (see, for example, Widdowson's (1995) critique of Fairclough's (1989, 1992a) analysis of medical discourse). Is a prostitute in (say) a short story or newspaper report read as exploited or as making rational and independent choices about the way she earns her living?

Investigating written texts does not mean studying only written words. We can also look at talk and writing together, as in Sunderland et al.'s study of teacher talk around gendered textbook texts (2000, 2002, see Unit B6.1 for an extract from the 2002 version). Further, multi-modality is evident – for example, written texts and visuals – in advertisements and, again, children's books. It is impossible to make full sense of some written texts without their accompanying visuals. Of particular interest is the creative tension between written text and visuals which do not correspond. John Stephens (1992) has analysed the children's book *Come Away from the Water Shirley* (John Burningham), in which what is illustrated, the adventures in the empowered Shirley's mind as she stands by the sea, bears no resemblance to the reality articulated by her father and mother in their deckchairs. Henrietta Dombey (1992) has similarly analysed *Rosie's Walk* (Pat Hutchins). She shows how, whereas in the book we read words and sentences about Rosie's calm and dignified walk around the farmyard, the illustrations are of a fox who is pursuing her, but who suffers one mishap after another. Neither of these books were analysed from a specific gender perspective, but both could be, and the multi-modal nature of each would be key to the analysis.

Written texts are frequently used in CDA (see also Unit A7). Critical work in Wodak's (1997) collection *Gender and Discourse* includes that on women's magazines (Suzanne Eggins and Rick Iedema), and Litosseliti and Sunderland's (2002) collection *Gender Identity and Discourse Analysis* texts includes work on 'moral arguments' in a UK newspaper (Lia Litosseliti) and men's 'lifestyle' magazines (Bethan Benwell) (see also Lazar 2005).

One relatively new form of written text is computer-mediated communication (CMC), including e-mail communication, Internet discussion sites, synchronous chat rooms and Instant Messenger (see, for example, Spender 1995). CMC has many characteristics of spoken language, sometimes taking place in real time. This has led to two branches of study: the traditional 'gender differences' investigations into whether women and men use CMC differently (for example, Herring 1996), and the more contemporary concern with construction of identity (one's own, and that of others, present and absent), with its implications for gender and for the notion of performativity (Bucholtz 2002, Butler 1990). Unit B10.3 includes an extract from Mary Bucholtz's paper on 'Geek feminism' about the 'Geek' identity young women have constructed for themselves in a particular chat room.

In chat rooms, users can be seen as 'disembodied': whether they are male or female, gay or straight, is not evident from their messages, and users can, and do, convincingly 'perform' a range of gender and sexual identities (see, for example, Baker 2001). The play *Closer* illustrates this with a heterosexual man in a chat room 'communicating' in cyberspace to the point of orgasm with someone he thinks is a woman, but as the audience knows, and as he comes to realise, is not. Gender can thus be studied in CMC texts (what is said about women, men, gender relations and so on) alone, without regard for the (unknown) biology or genetic make-up of the text producers. A question for gender and language study prompted by this sort of work is to what extent this can be achieved when biology and genetic make-up are known.

SECTION B
Extension

Unit B1
Early work on gender and language

Unit B1 looks at early work on gender and language by Mary Haas and Lesley Milroy. Based at the University of California, Mary Haas studied women's and men's speech in Koasati, a Native American language, in the 1940s. Unlike Jespersen (1922), whose observations came largely from his own intuition, Haas empirically investigated Koasati (and other, related languages) by working with its speakers.

Lesley Milroy (1980), who was working with the benefit of the invention of the tape-recorder, audio-recorded Belfast speakers, and then analysed her findings in relation to the social networks of which they were part.

**Text B1.1
M. Haas**

Mary Haas (1944) 'Men's and women's speech in Koasati', *Language* **20: 142–9 (reprinted in Hymes 1964)**

Task B1.1.1: Before you read

Read or reread Unit A1, focusing on the following points:

➤ the impressionistic/intuitive approach to the study of language use adopted by Jespersen (note down some problems with such approaches);

➤ the notions of sex-exclusive language and sex-preferential language.

Task B1.1.2: While you read

As you read the extract, identify and make notes on:

➤ what forms the gender differences Haas identified take, in general;

➤ some of Haas's findings as regards the 'rules' governing gendered language use in Koasati;

➤ any explanations offered for those findings of gender differences;

➤ change in the gendered use of Koasati.

The extract below includes the first of the three sections of Haas's article (in the second and third sections, she describes some other languages, from Canada, South America and Asia, in which sex-exclusive language patterns have been found).

M. Haas

Koasati is a Muskogean language now spoken in southwestern Louisiana. One of the most interesting features of the language is the fact that the speech of women differs in certain well-defined respects from that of men. The differences may be described by means of a fairly simple set of rules, and the most concise way to formulate them is to set up the forms used by women as basic and to derive the forms used by men from these. While this procedure is preferred because of the greater expediency it offers in the formulation of the rules, it is in most instances arbitrary. In a few instances, however, the speech of women is seen to be somewhat more archaic than that of men and to this extent it is possible to justify the procedure on historical grounds.

The differences between the two types of speech are confined to certain indicative and imperative forms of verbal paradigms. In order to simplify the statement of the rules governing the forms which differ in these paradigms, the rules governing the identical forms are presented first. These are as follows:

(1) If the women's form ends in a vowel, the men's form is the same. Examples:

W or M	
lakawwilí	'I lifted it'
oktawhiská	'you stirred it'
iskó	'he drank'

(2) If the women's form ends in č, the men's form is the same. Examples:

W or M	
lakáwč	'you are lifting it'
hí·č	'he is looking at it'
ča·kháč	'you (pl.) are chopping it'

The remaining rules take care of the instances in which the forms used by men differ from those used by women. The first three of these provide for the cases in which the men's forms substitute an *s* for the nasalization of a final vowel or for certain final consonants of the women's forms.

(3) If the women's form ends in a nasalized vowel, the men's form substitutes an *s* for the nasalization. Examples:

W	M	
lakawtakkó	*lakawtakkós*	'I am not lifting it'
lakawwá	*lakawwá·s*	'he will lift it'
Ką̇·	*ká·s*	'he is saying'

(4) If the women's form has the falling pitch-stress on its final syllable and ends in a short vowel followed by *l*, the men's form substitutes the high pitch stress for the falling pitch-stress and an *s* for the *l*. Examples:

W	M	
lacawwîl	*lalcawwís*	'I am lifting it'
molhîl	*molhís*	'we are peeling it'
lakawhôl	*lakawhós*	'lift it!' (addressed to second person plural)

(5) If the women's form has the falling pitch-stress on its final syllable and ends in a short vowel followed by *n*, the men's form retains the falling pitch-stress but substitutes an *s* for the *n* and lengthens the preceding vowel. Examples:

W	M	
lakawčîn	*lakawčî·s*	'don't lift it!'
tačilwân	*tačilwâ·s*	'don't sing!'
iltočihnôn	*Iltočihnô·s*	'don't work!'

The last rule takes care of the instances in which the men's forms differ from the women's by the simple addition of an *s*.

(6) If the women's form ends in a short or long vowel plus one or two consonants, the men's form adds an *s* except under the following circumstances: when the women's form ends in *č*, rule 2; when the women's form has the falling pitch-stress on its final syllable and ends in a short vowel followed by *l*, rule 4; when the women's form has the falling pitch-stress on its final syllable and ends in a short vowel followed by *n*, rule 5. (It should also be noted that *t* + *s* regularly contracts to *č*.) Examples:

W	M	
lakáw	*lakáws*	'he is lifting it'
lakáwwitak	*lakáwwitaks*	'let me lift it'
mól	*móls*	'he is peeling it'
lakáwwilit	*lakáwwilič*	'I lifted it'
í·p	*í·ps*	'he is eating it'
ta·ł	*ta·ł s*	'he is weaving it'
tačílw	*tačílws*	'you are singing'
Iltolí·hn	*Iltolí·hns*	'we are working'
mí·sl	*mí·sls*	'he is blinking'

This completes the rules governing the difference between the speech of men and of women. The table below summarizes these rules by showing in condensed form the final part of the word. Note that *a* stands for any vowel, *k* for any consonant while other letters and diacritics have their proper phonetic value.

W	M	W	M
a	a	ân	â·s
č	č	ak	aks
ą	as	a·k	a·ks
ą·dot	a·s	akk	akks
âl	ás	a·kk	a·kks

It sometimes happens that several of these rules operate within the same paradigm and in such a case the differences between the speech of the two sexes is particularly striking. This is illustrated in the three singular paradigms given below:

W	M	
o·tîl	o·tîs	'I am building a fire'
ó·st	ó·sč	'you are building a fire'
ó·t	ó·č	'he is building a fire'
lakawwîl	lakawwís	'I am lifting it'
lakáwč	lakáwč	'you are lifting it'
lakáw	lakáws	'he is lifting it'
ka·hâl	ka·hás	'I am saying'
í·sk	í·sk	'you are saying'
ka·	ká·s	'he is saying'

As has been mentioned, in some instances the speech of women appears to be more archaic than that of men. In rule 4 it is pointed out that when the women's form has a falling pitch-stress on the final syllable and ends in a short vowel followed by *l*, the men's form substitutes a high pitch-stress for the falling pitch-stress and an *s* for the *l*. In the cases that fall under this rule the women's forms are more archaic than those of men. In a first person singular present progressive form like *lakawwîl* (w. sp.) the *-l* is the first person singular sign and is related to the suffix *-li* which is used in the aorist and certain other paradigms; compare *lakawwîl* (w. sp.) 'I am lifting it' with *lakawwilí* (w. or m. sp.) 'I lifted it'. The men's form corresponding to *lakawwîl*, however, is *lakawwís* and in it the personal sign is missing. The archaism of women's speech is further illustrated in a first person plural present progressive form like *lakawhîl* (w. sp.). Here the personal sign is *-hil*, related to the first person plural sign *-hilí* which is used in the aorist and certain other paradigms; compare *lakawhîl* (w. sp.) 'we are lifting it' with *lakawhilí* (w. or m. sp.) 'we lifted it'. The men's form corresponding to *lakawhîl* is *lakawhís*; the *l* of the ending *-hil* has been lost.

This concludes the technical discussion of the differences between men's and women's speech in Koasati.

 Task B1.1.3: Reflection task

➤ What does the reader miss out on (at least up to this point) by knowing only the 'technical' aspects of the study?

It is of interest to note that at the present time only middle-aged and elderly women use the women's forms, while younger women are now using the forms characteristic of men's speech. The attitude of older Indians toward the two forms of speech is also interesting. One of my men informants thinks that the speech of women is better than that of men, He said that women talk 'easy, slow, and soft. It sounds pretty. Men's speech has too much ssss.'

Members of each sex are quite familiar with both types of speech and can use either as occasion demands. Thus if a man is telling a tale he will use women's forms when quoting a female character; similarly, if a woman is telling a tale she will use men's forms when quoting a male character. Moreover, parents were formerly accustomed to correct the speech of children of either sex, since each child was trained to use the forms appropriate to his or her sex.

Task B1.1.4: After you've read

➤ Would you describe the gendered use of Koasati as sex-exclusive or sex-preferential? Would you qualify your answer, at all?

➤ Haas writes that 'parents were *formerly* accustomed to correct the speech of children of either sex, since each child was trained to use the forms appropriate to his or her sex' (see above; my italics). What, then, is a factor in change in the gendered use of Koasati? Who might be in the vanguard of change, here?

➤ What can we infer from the above about the methodological details of Haas's investigation?

➤ Reread Haas's explanation of why she is presenting women's forms as 'basic'. If to a contemporary ear this sounds 'over-justified', why might Haas have written this section in this way?

As you will have noted, the differences Haas documents concern the pronunciation of word endings for some 'verbal paradigms', such as the Koasati for 'he will lift it' and 'we are peeling it' (for the latter, women said *molhiil*, and men *molhís*). Haas notes however that the *young* women in fact use the same forms as the men, suggesting a process of current and ongoing linguistic change.

Haas concludes her paper with a survey of comparable sex differences in other languages. She notes the possibility (explored later by Anne Bodine, 1975b) that language may also vary not with *speaker* sex but with sex of *addressee* (or 'hearer sex') – for example Tunica, in Louisiana – and cites instances in which this is precisely what occurs. This is something that is also often overlooked today, but see Cameron (1992), McConnell-Ginet (1988) for cases where it is acknowledged and explored. Anne Bodine (1975b) goes further, adding that differentiation also occurs with the sex of who is being spoken *about* (so that in English, for example, we have the nouns 'girl' and 'boy'). This may seem obvious. However, the distribution of such forms varies interestingly with languages, and the point is worth making as an antidote to the common perception that 'gender and language' study is all about 'how women and men speak differently'.

You will probably have noticed that there is very little in this extract (in fact, there is very little in the paper as a whole) on the participants in the study. We do not really know to what extent we are dealing with a linguistically heterogeneous speech community here (beyond the male/female and age differences). You will also have realised how little we are told about Haas's data collection methodology, how she actually collected her data in order to arrive at her findings. It is thus an odd experience reading the paper today, against a background of familiarity with 'Data and data collection' sections in more modern academic articles. (The relative lack of information about data collection was not, however, unusual for research papers of the time: see Bodine 1975, also Swales 2004.) We can, however, infer that Haas understood and spoke Koasati (and related languages) herself very well, since she records that she distinguished 'strange forms' from 'ordinary speech', and it is likely that she interviewed her informants in Koasati and documented their answers and detailed speech samples in fieldwork notebooks.

Haas does, however, as noted in Task B1.1.4, comment reflexively on the *presentation* of her findings (and, in effect, her analysis), right at the start of her paper. This somewhat defensive explanation may suggest not only that it was apparently unusual for investigators of the time to present women's language use as 'basic' (cf. Bodine 1975: 149), but also that to do otherwise without a very good reason indeed (i.e., here, the relative archaism) was to court controversy.

Lesley Milroy (1980) *Language and Social Networks*. Oxford: Basil Blackwell

Text B1.2
L. Milroy

Lesley Milroy in her Belfast study looked at the relevance and importance of social networks in linguistic (phonetic) variation. She gathered data in three areas of Belfast: Ballymacarratt, Hammer and the Clonard. Like Trudgill (1972a, 1972b, 1974) and Labov (1966), she took 'sex' as an unproblematic and 'given' sociolinguistic variable, like 'age'. She was thus not concerned with the later and more complex understanding of 'gender' as something that can be constructed through language use, which is thus not just a reflection of gender-differential tendencies in language use. Milroy however gave the lie to the essentialist myth that 'women' speak differently from 'men'. More specifically, her study was ground-breaking in its empirical demonstration that women as a group do not necessarily produce more 'standard' speech than men (as suggested by Labov [1966] and Trudgill [1972a, b]). This in turn challenged the stereotype of women's greater 'status consciousness'. She achieved this by identifying how social networks functioned in the speech of members of communities, demonstrating their predictive and explanatory potential (which was more relevant here than the predictive and explanatory potential of gender). The extracts below come from Chapter 6 of *Language and Social Networks* (1980).

 Task B1.2.1: While you read

Make notes on how Milroy 'measures' an individual's 'social network'.

➤ Make sure that you understand the distinction between 'density' and 'multiplexity'. Density concerns the number of social links an individual has (for example, with school friends, workmates, colleagues, family). Multiplexity builds on density, in that it concerns the number of roles within links, for example if someone knows someone else both as a colleague and a member of a political group.

➤ Look out for relationships between sex and age, sex and social network, sex and area (of Belfast), and sex and different linguistic variables (here, the phonemes (a) and (th)), and make notes on these as you read.

L. Milroy

The language of the individual speaker: patterns of variation and network structure

The objective in this chapter will be to go some way towards accounting for patterns of variability at the level of the individual speaker by making further use of the concept of social network. Since a quantitative approach is required, in order to allow a direct comparison between the language of speaker A and of speaker B, we also need to find a means of measuring the network patterns of A and B so that we can examine possible links with linguistic patterns.

This in fact, as might be expected, is a complicated matter; but it is possible to construct a measure which we shall call a network strength scale. This measure consists of a six-point scale going from zero to five, and functions rather like a social class index . . . in that each individual is assigned a score at some point on the scale. The scale is constructed with reference to the key notions of relative multiplexity and density of personal networks, and makes use of several indicators of these two network attributes.

. . . [D]ensity and multiplexity are excellent indicators of the pressures on a person to adopt the norms and values—including linguistic norms and values—of the 'local team'. Several other structural and content characteristics of a personal network may also be good indicators of the strength of pressures towards normative consensus. For example, degree of connection (number of contacts within a given time), centrality of position, intensity (affective value placed on relationships) are all apposite to any attempt to explain individual behaviour and are discussed by Mitchell (1969) and Boissevain (1974) in some detail.

However, most studies utilising the network concept have in practice found that either density . . . or relative multiplexity, offers powerful means of accounting for various behaviours. For example, problems as diverse as why individuals take one side in preference to another in a fight on the factory floor (Kapferer, 1969) and why patterns of gift exchange in an African community are variable (Trouwborst, 1973) are illuminated by analysis based on these two concepts. . . .

. . . we calculate an informant's network score by assigning him [sic] one point for each of the following conditions he fulfils:

1. Membership of a high-density, territorially based cluster.
2. Having substantial ties of kinship in the neighbourhood. (More than one house-hold, in addition to his own nuclear family.)
3. Working at the same place as at least *two* others from the same area.
4. The same place of work as at least two others of the same sex from the area.
5. Voluntary association with workmates in leisure hours. This applies in practice only when conditions three and four are satisfied.

Condition one is designed as an indicator of density, and reflects Cubitt's insistence on the importance of taking account of the density of specific *clusters* in considering networks as norm enforcement mechanisms. (A cluster is defined as a portion of a personal network where relationships are denser internally than externally.) The Jets, Cobras and T-Birds described by Labov form clusters; many of the young men in the Belfast communities belong to similar clusters; some of the middle-aged women belong to clusters of six or seven individuals who meet frequently to drink tea, play cards and chat. Some individuals, on the other hand, avoid association with any group of this kind.

Conditions two, three, four and five are all indicators of multiplexity; if they are all satisfied, the proportion of the individual's interactions which are with members of the local community is inevitably very high. Three and four are intended to reflect the particular capacity of an area of homogeneous employment to encourage the development of dense, multiplex networks; four also reflects the fact that polarization of the sexes usually occurs when there is a large number of solidary relationships in a specific neighbourhood.

Task B1.2.2: Reflection task

➤ Think about your own 'social networks'. To what extent are they dense, and to what extent multiplex?

➤ If you are currently living and/or studying away from where you normally live, or live at other times, compare your two sets of social networks.

➤ Consider the social networks of your mother and of your father. Do they differ? If so, what has brought this about?

The scale is capable of differentiating individuals quite sharply . . . Scores range from zero for someone who fulfils none of the conditions (although a zero score is rare), to five for several informants who fulfil them all. Such individuals must be considered extremely closely integrated into the community, in the sense that their kin, work and friendship ties are all contracted within it; additionally, they have formed particularly close ties with a corporate group (such as a football fans' club) or a less formal group based in the area. The defined territorial base associated with the kind of network structure which interests us is reflected in conditions one and two. This is very important, for . . . geographical mobility has the capacity to destroy the structure of long-established networks . . .

THE DISTRIBUTION OF NETWORK SCORES BY AGE, SEX AND AREA

. . . In applying an analysis of variance technique to look at the links between network score on the one hand, and age, sex and area on the other, we do not utilise the full range of the network strength scale. For statistical reasons, only *high* and *low* network scores are considered. High scores are those falling above the median, low scores are those falling below (the median is considered to be 3.0 here) and median scores are omitted from this part of the analysis.

The ratio statistic F indicates whether there is a significant difference in network scores between sex, age and area groups, and also whether there are significant interactions between any of these independent variables (network is considered as the dependent variable here). The results of this analysis are discussed briefly below. It will become clear shortly that this information is a necessary preliminary to a more direct investigation of the relationship between language and network.

Sex and network: interactions with other variables

As we might suspect, there is a significant difference between male and female network scores (F = 9.964, p < 0.01). The men score significantly higher than the women (means = 2.944: 2.0278). The sex by age interaction is not significant: that is, the sex difference in network scores is much the same for both age groups. However, there is a significant *sex* by area interaction (F = 8.025, p < 0.01). An examination of the male and female means for the three areas tells us where this difference lies. There is in effect very *little* difference between male and female means in two of the areas. In the Hammer, the men score only slightly higher than the women (means = 2.125: 1.875), while in the Clonard, the women actually score slightly higher than the men (means = 2.75: 2.875). However, these differences are very small in comparison with the very substantial differences between male and female scores in Ballymacarrett, where the men score very much higher than the women (means = 3.9583: 1.3333). Only in Ballymacarrett, in fact, are network scores significantly different for men and women.

There is also a significant sex by age by area interaction (F = 6.154, p < 0.01), which can tell us more about the distribution of network scores across these various subgroups. If we are focusing mainly on the relationship between *sex* and network structure, as we are at the moment, this means that male and female network scores vary between different areas with each age group in an extremely complicated manner. Again, if we compare the various subgroup means, we can see where this difference lies. The young *Ballymacarrett* women have the *lowest* network scores of any subgroup (mean = 0.667) while the young *Clonard* women have the *highest* of any subgroup (mean = 4.75). Clearly, this is a very high score as the maximum is 5.0. The young Clonard women are in fact the only female group who have substantially higher scores than the men in the same age group. (The mean for the young Clonard men = 3.0.) Since the *older* Clonard age group shows the expected pattern with men scoring higher than women (means = 2.5: 1.0), we can now see that the overall similarity between male and female scores in the Clonard is the result of the interaction effect of the variables of age and sex in this particular community.

It is already clear that these differences in the distribution of *network* scores co-vary, to some extent, with differences in the distribution of *linguistic* scores. Particularly, sharp and consistent sex differences in language score are associated with Ballymacarrett; the same area now emerges as showing sharp sex differences in network score . . .

Area and network; age and network

. . . Although the differences between area means are not quite statistically significant (B = 2.6458: C = 2.8125: H = 2.0), it is worth noting the substantial difference between the score for the Hammer, and those for the other two areas, which are more nearly comparable. However, there is a significant interaction between *age* and *area* (F = 6.5592: p < 0.01) with the younger age groups scoring higher in Clonard and the Hammer, and the older age group scoring slightly higher in Ballymacarrett. The subgroup means are given in Table [B1.2.1].

Table [B1.2.1] Mean network scores for two age groups in three areas

Age	40–55	18–25
Ballymacarrett	2.8333	2.4583
Clonard	1.7500	3.8750
Hammer	1.1250	2.8750

Although B*allymacarrett* shows very little difference between the network scores of the two age groups, the younger group considered overall (for all three areas together) scores significantly higher (means = 3.069: 1.903). This difference is very substantial, and similar in size to the difference between the sexes.

It is possible to relate some of these sex, age and area differences in network scores to different social conditions in the three communities . . .

Note first that only in Ballymacarrett are traditional *sex roles* retained in the form familiar from descriptions in the literature on working-class communities. The men are employed locally in a traditional and homogeneous form of employment (the shipyard) and contract solidary relationships associated with their work. The women are employed more diffusely, have fewer solidary relationships associated with work, but may contract multiplex relationships with kin and neighbours. The Clonard area, on the other hand, was experiencing severe male unemployment at the time of the interviews: both the Clonard and the Hammer had once been dependent on the now receding linen industry. Although unemployment was not quite as severe in the Hammer as in the Clonard, there was no local homogeneous form of employment.

These contrasting social conditions are reflected clearly in the big difference between male and female network scores in Ballymacarrett, a difference not found consistently in either of the other areas.

In the Clonard, the young women emerged as the only group who worked together and spent their leisure time together, contracting the kind of solidary relationships usually associated with working-class men. This socialization pattern is reflected clearly in the higher network scores of the young Clonard women—higher than those of the men—and it is also reflected in the complicated age by sex by area interaction effects, which level out the expected sex difference in network scores.

Although the Hammer area suffered similar but slightly less severe unemployment, no group emerged as having contracted particularly strong solidary relationships. The Hammer was notable principally for the geographical mobility of its residents: as a consequence of urban redevelopment, many had been allocated housing several miles from the Hammer. Although much social interaction was focused there in pubs, clubs, bingo sessions and corner-hanging groups, the residents had suffered a severe disruption of all the important sectors of their personal networks. This instability is reflected in generally low scores for the Hammer, and in very small differences between the sexes. For as we have seen, a clear pattern of men scoring high and women scoring low seems to be linked to a traditional working-class area with a homogeneous form of employment like Ballymacarrett, or like the mining community described by Dennis et al. (1957).

★ Task B1.2.3: Reflection task

> Take time to visualise each of the three communities, and sketch out a profile for each in terms of social networks, considering both age and sex.

> Does it make sense to you to see different social networks being associated with different patterns of language use?

We may begin to suspect at this point that there is a fairly clear relationship between language scores and network scores: for the distributional patterns are remarkably similar in many important respects. [. . . T]he sharpest sex grading in language *also* was to be found in Ballymacarrett; this is true for several linguistic variables. Second, in respect of the variable (a), we find particularly striking parallels. The Hammer score shows very little difference between male and female scores . . . Even more strikingly, the same interaction effect which influences the Clonard network scores . . . also influences the distribution of (a) scores in the younger Clonard age group. The young Clonard women emerge with unexpectedly high *linguistic* scores, in exactly the same way as they emerge with unexpectedly high *network* scores. We should note, however, that other linguistic variables do *not* necessarily reflect network structure in this way. For example (th) shows clear sex grading in much the same way for both age groups in all three areas. Nevertheless, we may suggest tentatively at this point that the distribution of the variable (a), at least, is more closely related to the network structure than to the sex of the speaker . . .

Task B1.2.4: After you've read

➤ Summarise Milroy's main findings about gender and language use, especially in Clonard and Ballymacarrett.

➤ What do you see as the significance of Milroy's findings for gender and language study?

Milroy summarises her explanation of these findings in terms of the fact that the young Clonard women 'hung about in a close-knit group during their time away from work' (1980: 84) and, unlike the young Clonard men, many also worked together. This made them a very 'dense and multiplex' social network, and their resultant high 'social network score' correlated with a high score on at least one non-standard linguistic variable (a). We can speculate that a similar situation might obtain in communities in which network density and employment patterns are similarly gendered.

Cameron (1992b) points to the usefulness of such studies, which both reveal and can deal with exceptions to the overall pattern of men using more non-standard speech than women (Labov 1966, Trudgill 1972a, 1972b). She warns, however, against seeing community ties only in paid work, work unrelated to the home (domestic work may also be done communally), and indeed work at all. She cites Beth Thomas's study of women in a Welsh-speaking community who 'preserved a vernacular Welsh feature that men had lost [and who] had strong community ties *through their membership of the local chapels*' (1992: 69; my italics). Cameron concludes:

> Sociolinguistics is most successful in explaining sex differences when it looks very carefully at the conditions of particular communities' lives . . . It is least successful when it makes stereotypical assumptions about women: that they behave in certain ways because they are mothers . . . for example. Stereotypes like these flatten out important details: they disguise the exceptions to the 'women speak more standard' rule, or else are unable to account for them. Whereas by looking at the exceptions we are able to perceive that the pattern itself is complex and produced by multiple factors. It is not just an automatic reflection of gender.
>
> (1992: 69)

In this, Cameron (like Milroy) was anticipating the CofP concept which would later prove valuable to the study of gender and language (see Unit A6 and Unit B6.2).

Unit B2
The influence of feminism and feminist linguistics (a)

Unit B2 is the first of two extension units on 'Feminism and feminist linguistics'. Here we look at the work of three writers who can be considered pioneers in the field: Robin Lakoff, Dale Spender and Pamela Fishman. While the work of each has been subject to considerable critique, Lakoff, Spender and Fishman all played a key role in laying the foundations of gender and language study as regards the early twin 'prongs' of 'sexist language' and 'gender differences in language use'.

Text B2.1
R. Lakoff

Robin Lakoff (1975) *Language and Woman's Place*. New York: Colophon Books

Robin Lakoff's *Language and Woman's Place* (1975) was a crucial early work in the study of language and gender. It has been hugely influential, both in the popular and the academic sphere. Though she does not use the word, Lakoff was in many ways writing as a feminist (she refers to 'sexism', to 'male chauvinism' and to women experiencing linguistic discrimination). Lakoff's work can be seen in part as an example of the '(male) dominance' current of gender and language study (see Cameron 1992: 71).

'Pioneer' works such as *Language and Woman's Place* are frequently evaluated negatively. Partly this is due to the inevitable wisdom of hindsight, but in Lakoff's case it was also in part because of her research methodology. In her 'Introduction', she writes (and I quote at length because this is important for her work and the studies that followed):

> The data on which I am basing my claims have been gathered mainly by introspection: I have examined my own speech, and that of my acquaintances, and have used my own intuitions in analyzing it . . . The sociologist, anthropologist or ethnomethodologist familiar with what seem to him [sic] more error-proof data-gathering techniques, such as the recording of random conversation, may object that these introspective techniques may produce dubious results. But first, it should be noted that any procedure is at some point introspective: the gatherer must analyze his data, after all. Then, one necessarily selects a subgroup of the population to work with: is the educated, white, middle-class group that the writer of the book identifies with less

worthy of study than any other? And finally, there is the purely pragmatic issue: random conversation must go on for quite some time, and the recorder must be exceedingly lucky anyway, in order to produce evidence of any particular hypothesis, for example, that there is sexism in language, that there is not sexism in language. If we are to have a good sample of data to analyze, this will have to be elicited artificially from someone; I submit I am as good an artificial source of data as anyone.

(Lakoff 1975: 4–5)

Lakoff was not being obtuse: she was writing at a time when introspection, part of the Chomskyan tradition (and Lakoff had been an associate of Chomsky), was more usual than it is now. Further, she had learned introspective procedures in the course of her training in syntax, in which naturally occurring spoken data were not collected or analysed. Introspection is, however, arguably more suitable to a study of *langue* ('Can X be said?') than of *parole* ('Is X said, and under what conditions?') – and it is *parole* (rather than 'sexism in language') which constitutes the focus of much of *Language and Woman's Place*. Lakoff's *claims* about women's and men's use of language were nevertheless new, interesting, challenging and timely, striking a chord with the feminist movement of the time, and showing that the new field of Gender and Language had much to contribute both to Feminist Studies and to Applied Linguistics.

Task B2.1.1: Reflection task

➤   What do you feel that audio-recorded data can achieve, that data from introspection cannot, in gender and language study? What *can* introspection achieve?

In some ways paradoxically, *Language and Woman's Place* spawned a range of empirical studies, many aiming to put Lakoff's claims to the test. These included work on women's and men's possible differential use of various linguistic features, for example, interruptions, verbosity, questions, topic initiation, minimal responses (or 'back-channelling') and, in particular, tag questions (see, for example, Dubois and Crouch 1975, Holmes 1984, Cameron et al. 1988). Tag-question studies resulted in a diversity of findings, simultaneously raising questions about the form–function relationship in language: Lakoff had associated women's use of tag questions with lack of confidence, but lack of confidence is just one of several possible meanings of a tag question.

Many of Lakoff's claims (and their generalisability) have now been challenged. However her work is still quoted uncritically in some academic work (often by non-linguists, or linguists outside the field of Gender and Language). This is a matter for concern, since this use of her findings *now* entails a theoretically dated essentialist representation of gender: women talk like this, men like that. This leaves little room for questions of power, individual nuancing, social and linguistic development and change, or the complexity of the gender–language relationship.

In the sections of *Language and Woman's Place* concerned with *langue*, Lakoff discusses at length the asymmetry of the 'pairs' 'bachelor'/'spinster' and 'widow'/ 'widower' as English semantic categories available for women and for men (1975: 32–5), as well as the phrase 'man and wife'.

 Task B2.1.2: Reflection task

Consider the terms 'bachelor'/'spinster', and 'widow'/'widower':

➤ In what senses can each be seen as a pair, and in what sense not?

➤ Do you use one item of each 'pair' more than the other? Do you use the two items of each pair in different ways?

➤ Can you think of a more modern equivalent for 'spinster' than 'bachelor girl', in English? What are the possibilities in other languages?

➤ How are the phrases 'widow' and 'widower' used now? What about in languages other than English?

Lakoff also discusses the 'generic *he*'. Interestingly, while taking exception to the semantic asymmetries in the connotative meanings of 'widower'/'widow', 'bachelor'/'spinster' and 'man and wife', Lakoff did not feel the same way about this other linguistic target of feminist critique (for example, Martyna 1978, 1980, Stanley 1978). She refers to this 'generic he' as 'mere grammatical nonparallelism' (1975: 48), and indeed uses it throughout the book. In this extract she makes two strong points: first, that some linguistic features are more appropriate targets of feminist reform than others, and, second, that social change precedes language change.

 Task B2.1.3: Before you read

➤ What is your position on the first of these two points? If you agree, what do you see as an 'appropriate' target of feminist reform?

➤ What is your position on the second? Do you feel that linguistic reform can help to bring about social change? If so, how might this happen?

Task B2.1.4: While you read

➤ Identify Lakoff's different arguments here supporting her two points.

➤ Consider the possibility that you agree with some of her arguments but not others.

On the 'generic' *he*

R. Lakoff

Linguistic imbalances are worthy of study because they bring into sharper focus real-world imbalances and inequities. They are clues that some external situation needs changing, rather than items that one *should* seek to change directly. A competent doctor tries to eliminate the germs that cause measles, rather than trying to bleach the red out with peroxide. I emphasize this point because it seems to be currently fashionable to try, first, to attack the disease by attempting to obliterate the external symptoms; and, second, to attack every instance of linguistic sexual inequity, rather than selecting those that reflect a real disparity in social treatment, not mere grammatical nonparallelism. We should be attempting to single out those linguistic uses that, by implication and innuendo, demean the members of one group or another, and should be seeking to make speakers of English aware of the psychological damage such forms do. The problem, of course, lies in deciding which forms are really damaging to the ego, and then in determining what to put in their stead.

A good example, which troubles me a lot at present, is that of pronominal neutral-ization. In English, as indeed in the great majority of the world's languages, when reference is made individually to members of a sexually mixed group, the normal solution is to resolve the indecision as to pronoun choice in favor of the masculine: the masculine, then, is "unmarked" or "neutral," and therefore will be found referring to men and women both in sentences like the following:

(25) (*a*) Everyone take his seat.
(*b*) If a person wants to ingratiate himself with Harry, he
                            *herself   *she
should cook him moo-shu pork.

In (25) (*a*), *her* could of course be used in an all-female group; the point is that in a mixed group, even one predominantly female, *his* will normally be the "correct" form. Many speakers, feeling this is awkward and perhaps even discriminatory, attempt a neutralization with *their*, a usage frowned upon by most authorities as inconsistent or illogical. In (25) (*b*), *herself* and *she* might conceivably replace *himself* and *he*, but the effect of the sentence would be changed, not too surprisingly: the ingratiation would be understood as an attempt at (sexual) seduction, or an attempt to persuade Henry to marry the "person."

That is, although semantically both men and women are included in the groups referred to by the pronouns in these sentences, only *he* and related masculine forms are commonly possible. An analogous situation occurs in many languages with the words for *human being*: in English, we find *man* and *mankind*, which of course refer to women members of the species as well. This of course permits us innumerable jokes involving "man-eating sharks," and the widespread existence of these jokes perhaps

97

points up the problem that these forms create for a woman who speaks a language like English.

I feel that the emphasis upon this point, to the exclusion of most other linguistic points, by writers within the women's movement is misguided. While this lexical and grammatical neutralization is related to the fact that men have been the writers and the doers, I don't think it by itself specifies a particular and demeaning role for women, as the special uses of *mistress* or *professional*, to give a few examples, do. It is not insidious in the same way: it does not indicate to little girls how they are expected to behave. Even if it did, surely other aspects of linguistic imbalance should receive equal attention. But more seriously, I think one should force oneself to be realistic: certain aspects of language are available to the native speakers' conscious analysis, and others are too common, too thoroughly mixed throughout the language, for the speaker to be aware each time he uses them. It is realistic to hope to change only those linguistic uses of which speakers themselves can be made aware, as they use them. One chooses, in speaking or writing, more or less consciously and purposefully among nouns, adjectives, and verbs; one does not choose among pronouns in the same way. My feeling is that this area of pronominal neutralization is both less in need of changing and less open to change than many of the other disparities that have been discussed earlier, and we should perhaps concentrate our efforts where they will be most fruitful.

But many nonlinguists disagree. I have read and heard dissenting views from too many anguished women to suppose that this use of *he* is really a triviality. The claim is that the use of the neutral *he* with such frequency makes women feel shut out, not a part of what is being described, an inferior species, or a nonexistent one. Perhaps linguistic training has dulled my perception, and this really is a troublesome question. If so, I don't know what to advise, since I feel in any case that an attempt to change pronominal usage will be futile. My recommendation then would be based purely on pragmatic considerations: attempt to change only what can be changed, since this is hard enough.

I think in any case that linguists should be consulted before any more fanciful plans are made public for reforming the inequities of English.

Task B2.1.5: After you've read

➤ From a feminist point of view, what do you think is it (a) most important to attempt to change, linguistically, and (b) realistic to attempt to change?

➤ Do you agree that 'attempting to obliterate the external symptoms' (i.e. language), since these are merely symptoms of 'real-world imbalances and inequities', is misguided?

➤ Do you agree that 'generics' like 'he' and 'mankind' are 'not insidious' in the same way as 'mistress' and 'professional' are, since they do not indicate 'to little girls how they are expected to behave'?

➤ Do you agree that whereas 'certain aspects of language are available to the native speakers' conscious analysis' (for example, 'spinster', 'man and wife'), others, like 'generic he', are 'too common, too thoroughly mixed throughout the language, for the speaker to be aware each time he [of course!] uses them'?

➤ What different models of language, of language and thought, of language and society, and of language change are evident in this passage?

The last extract, 'Talking like a lady', on tag questions, is one for which Lakoff is particularly famous. This is a question of *parole* (the book's main concern), rather than one of *langue*.

Task B2.1.6: Before you read

➤ Consider your own use, and that of people you know, of 'tag questions' (for example, 'Didn't she?', 'Can't you?', 'Isn't it?'). What different impressions might these convey to a hearer?

'Talking like a lady'

R. Lakoff

When we leave the lexicon and venture into syntax, we find that syntactically too women's speech is peculiar. To my knowledge, there is no syntactic rule in English that only women may use. But there is at least one rule that a woman will use in more conversational situations than a man. (This fact indicates, of course, that the applicability of syntactic rules is governed partly by social context—the positions in society of the speaker and addressee, with respect to each other, and the impression one seeks to make on the other.) This is the rule of tag-question formation.

A tag, in its usage as well as its syntactic shape (in English) is midway between an outright statement and a yes-no question: it is less assertive than the former, but more confident than the latter. Therefore it is usable under certain contextual situations: not those in which a statement would be appropriate, nor those in which a yes-no question is generally used, but in situations intermediate between these.

One makes a statement when one has confidence in his knowledge and is pretty certain that his statement will be believed; one asks a question when one lacks knowledge on some point and has reason to believe that this gap can and will be remedied by an answer by the addressee. A tag question, being intermediate between these, is used when the speaker is stating a claim, but lacks full confidence in the truth of that claim. So if I say

(7) Is John here?

I will probably not be surprised if my respondent answers "no"; but if I say

(8) John is here, isn't he?

instead, chances are I am already biased in favor of a positive answer, wanting only confirmation by the addressee. I still want a response from him, as I do with a yes-no question; but I have enough knowledge (or think I have) to predict that response, much as with a declarative statement. A tag question, then, might be thought of as a declarative statement without the assumption that the statement is to be believed by the addressee: one has an out, as with a question. A tag gives the addressee leeway, not forcing him to go along with the views of the speaker.

There are situations in which a tag is legitimate, in fact the only legitimate sentence form. So, for example, if I have seen something only indistinctly, and have reason to believe my addressee had a better view, I can say:

(9) I had my glasses off. He was out at third, wasn't he?

Sometimes we find a tag question used in cases in which the speaker knows as well as the addressee what the answer must be, and doesn't need confirmation. One such situation is when the speaker is making "small talk," trying to elicit conversation from the addressee:

(10) Sure is hot here, isn't it?

In discussing personal feelings or opinions, only the speaker normally has any way of knowing the correct answer. Strictly speaking, questioning one's own opinions is futile. Sentences like (11) are usually ridiculous.

(11) *I have a headache, don't I?

But similar cases do, apparently, exist, in which it is the speaker's opinions, rather than perceptions, for which corroboration is sought, as in (12):

(12) The way prices are rising is horrendous, isn't it?

While there are of course other possible interpretations of a sentence like this, one possibility is that the speaker has a particular answer in mind—"yes" or "no"—but is reluctant to state it baldly. It is my impression, though I do not have precise statistical evidence, that this sort of tag question is much more apt to be used by women than by men. If this is indeed true, why is it true?

These sentence types provide a means where by a speaker can avoid committing himself, and thereby avoid coming into conflict with the addressee. The problem is that, by so doing, a speaker may also give the impression of not being really sure of himself, of looking to the addressee for confirmation, even of having no views of his own. This last criticism is, of course, one often leveled at women. One wonders how much of it reflects a use of language that has been imposed on women from their earliest years.

One reading of question tags, Lakoff claims in her Example 12, is that the speaker is not bold enough to express what they believe, and that this is associated primarily with women. This seems to impute a degree of 'deficiency' to women's talk (and indeed *Language and Woman's Place* is often seen as drawing on a 'deficit' rather than '(male) dominance' model of language use).

This last extract is thus problematic in that, although Lakoff acknowledges the range of possibilities for meaning in relation to tag questions, she chooses not to explore it. Rather, she emphasises the 'wanting confirmation' meaning at the expense of the 'co-operative', trying-to-elicit-conversation meaning. Given the complexity and potential of human creativity, and of social and linguistic interaction, it is in any case hard to identify a single 'form–function' relationship: rather, a tag may be capable of several readings simultaneously.

Task B2.1.7: Reflection task

➤ To what extent is it legitimate, do you think, to critique a pioneer work, with the benefit of hindsight? Given that we cannot expect Lakoff to have anticipated and addressed all the critiques levelled at *Language and Woman's Place*, what could reasonably have been expected? Is it inevitable that 'trail-blazers' will overstate and oversimplify?

Dale Spender (1980) *Man Made Language*. London: Routledge & Kegan Paul

Text B2.2
D. Spender

In the next, short extract from *Man Made Language*, Spender summarises the findings of studies that suggest that 'generic he' and 'generic man' may not be interpreted generically.

Task B2.2.1: Before you read

➤ Read or reread the section on Dale Spender and *Man Made Language* in Unit A2.

➤ Consider your own use of the English 'generic he' and 'generic man'. Do you use them? If so, in speech, writing or both? What do you feel when you hear them? when you read them?

J. Schneider and Sally Hacker (1973) found that college students . . . thought male when confronted with such titles as Political Man and Urban Man. Unless students are unrepresentative of our society – an unlikely possibility – there seems to be considerable empirical evidence to suggest that the use of the symbol man is accompanied, not surprisingly, by an image of male . . .

D. Spender

. . . according to Linda Harrison [1975] and Wendy Martyna [1978] – who went slightly further in their research than other investigators who were exploring the links between male symbols and images – females understand that they are not represented in *he/man* usage; both Harrison and Martyna found that males used *man* more often than females and Martyna attempted to discover the basis for this choice.

When Wendy Martyna asked people in her sample what they thought of when they used the symbol *man*, the males stated that they thought of themselves. This was not the case for females. The females said they did not think of themselves, they did not use the term in relation to themselves, hence they used *he/man* less frequently than males. There is irony in the acknowledgment of females that they only used the terms *he/man* at all because they had been taught that it was grammatically correct! From this, Martyna concludes that 'Males may be generating a sex specific use of *he*, one based on male imagery, while females are generating a truly generic *he*, one based on grammatical standards of correctness' (Martyna, 1978). How convenient if this is the case! . . .

When the symbol *he/man* disposes us to think male, women who are required to use those symbols are required to think again. This is an extra activity, one which males are not called upon to perform. As members of the dominant group, having ascertained that their male identity is constant, males are not required to modify their understandings: they are never referred to as *she/woman*. But having ascertained their female identity women must constantly be available – again – for clues as to whether or not they are encompassed in a reference, for sometimes they are included in the symbol *he/man*, and sometimes they are not. What the dominant group can take for granted is problematic to the muted group and this could be another means whereby they are kept muted.

 Task B2.2.2: Reflection task

➤ To what extent do you feel that findings such as these challenge Lakoff's view of the unimportance of these 'masculine' generics?

➤ If you are female, do you feel that you 'search for clues' as to whether you are included in a *he/man* reference?

➤ If you are male, do you think of yourself, or of 'people as a whole', here?

Pamela Fishman (1983) 'Interaction: the work women do', in Barrie Thorne et al. (eds) *Language, Gender and Society*. Rowley, Mass.: Newbury House, pp. 89–101

Written in the early days of the 'western' Women's Movement, Pamela Fishman's chapter 'Interaction: the work women do' appeared in its original form in the journal *Social Problems* in 1978, and later, revised, in the collection edited by Barrie Thorne, Cheris Kramarae and Nancy Henley, *Language, Gender and Society* (1983). It is frequently cited, along with work by other '(male) dominance' theorists such as Fishman's contemporaries Pamela Edelsky, Candace West and Don Zimmerman, and Betty Lou Dubois and Isobel Crouch (for a summary of work in this current, see 'Women's features' and 'Men's features' in the Maltz and Borker chapter, an extract from which appears in Unit B3.1: these are also listed on p. 112). It was particularly important in that at this time there was still more focus on issues of *langue* ('sexist language') than of *parole* ('gender differences in language use').

Fishman was concerned not just with difference but with empirical findings about masculine power, and her paper is based on the micro-sociological premise that 'verbal interaction helps to construct and maintain the hierarchical relations between men and women' (1983: 89). Fishman's model of language was thus a constitutive one, in that she saw language as able to 'construct and maintain', as well as reflect. As with some work of her contemporaries, the nuances of gender and the gender–language relationship inherent in Fishman's work tend to have been unappreciated and even subsequently misrepresented.

As regards linguistic analysis, Fishman draws in part from conversation analysis (CA). Garfinkel, Sacks and Schegloff are all cited, and linguistic features characteristic of CA, such as topic initiation, question–answer 'adjacency pairs' (though the term is not used) and questions as 'interactionally powerful utterances' all examined. Fishman writes: 'a psychological analysis is unnecessary to explain why women ask more questions than men. Since questions are produced in conversations, we should look first to how questions function there' (1983: 94). By looking at the language of intimates, she claims, she is legitimately expanding the territory open to CA. CA however conventionally focuses on participants' orientations in talk, and because of Fishman's concern with male dominance, and because she identifies power and gender *a priori* as being relevant, a retrospective reading of this study as CA is problematic (see Schegloff 1998, Wetherell 1998; but see also Unit A8 and Units B8.1 and B8.2).

Task B2.3.1: While you read

➤ Note how Pamela Fishman justifies her 'epistemological site' of 'the talk of intimates'.

➤ Bearing in mind that this paper was written around twenty-five years ago, make a note of what sounds (a) dated; (b) as if it could have been written today, suggesting Fishman to have been in some ways ahead of her time.

➤ How does Fishman convey her own 'researcher commitment' here? To what extent do you feel that she is writing 'as a feminist'?

Interaction: the work women do

P. Fishman

. . . Recent work on gender and the English language shows that the male-female hierarchy is inherent in the words we use to perceive and name our world . . . Much less attention has been directed toward how male-female power relations are expressed through the dynamics of conversation. To complement other language and gender studies, we need more analyses of the interactional production of a particular reality through people's talk.

Conversational activity is significant for intimates. Berger and Kellner (1970) have argued that at present, with the increasing separation of public and private spheres of life, intimate relationships are among the most important reality-maintaining settings. They apply this argument specifically to marriage. The process of daily interaction in the marital relationship is ideally . . . one in which reality is crystallized, narrowed, and stabilized. Ambivalences are converted into certainties. Typifications of self and other become settled. Most generally, possibilities become facticities (1970: 64).

In these relationships, in these mundane interactions, much of the essential work of sustaining the reality of the world goes on. Intimates often reconstruct their separate experiences, past and present, with one another. Specifically, the couple sustain and produce the reality of their own relationship, and more generally, of the world.

Although Berger and Kellner have analyzed marriage as a reality-producing setting, they have not analyzed the interaction of marriage partners nor the differences and inequalities which may be involved in the reality-construction process. I shall focus here on the interactional activities that constitute the everyday work done by intimates and the different activities of the partners which emerge. It is through this work that people produce their relationship to one another, their relationship to the world, and those patterns normally referred to as social structure.

Work in interaction

Sometimes we think of interaction as work. At a party or meeting where silence lies heavy, we recognize the burden of interaction and respond to it as work. The many books written on "the art of conversation" call attention to the tasks involved in interaction. It is not simply an analogy to think of interaction as work. Rather, it is an intuitive recognition of what must be accomplished for interaction to occur.

Interaction requires at least two people. Conversation is produced not simply by their presence, but also by the display of their continuing agreement to pay attention to one another. That is, all interactions are potentially problematic and occur only through the continual, turn-by-turn, efforts of the participants.

Sacks and his followers (Sacks et al., 1974; Schegloff & Sacks, 1974; Schegloff, 1972) have sought to specify how conversationalists accomplish such things as beginnings and endings. They have ignored, however, the interaction between intimates. Schegloff and Sacks (1974: 262) characterize intimates in home situations as "in continuing states of incipient talk." . . . [But i]n any setting in which conversation is possible, attempts at beginning, sustaining and stopping talk still must be made. And these attempts must be recognized and oriented to by both parties for them to move between states of 'incipient' and 'actual' conversation.

In a sense, every remark or turn at speaking should be seen as an *attempt* to interact. It may be an attempt to open or close a conversation. It may be a bid to continue interaction, to respond to what went before, and elicit a further remark from one's partner. Some attempts succeed; others fail. For an attempt to succeed, the other party must be willing to do further interactional work. That other person has the power to turn an attempt into a conversation or to stop it dead.

Data

The data for this study come from fifty-two hours of tape-recorded conversation between intimates in their homes. Three heterosexual couples agreed to place tape recorders in their apartments. They had the right to censor the material before I heard it. The apartments were small, so that the recorders picked up all conversation from the kitchen and living room as well as the louder portions of talk from the bedroom and bath. The tapes could run for a four-hour period without interruption. Though I had timers to switch the tapes on and off automatically, all three couples insisted on doing the switching manually. The segments of uninterrupted recording vary from one to four hours.

The three couples had been together for various amounts of time—three months, six months, and two years. All were white and professionally oriented, between the ages of twenty-five and thirty-five. One woman was a social worker and the other five people were in graduate school. Two of the women were avowed feminists and all three men as well as the other woman described themselves as sympathetic to the women's movement.

The tape recorders were present in the apartments from four to fourteen days. I am satisfied that the material represents natural conversation and that there was no undue awareness of the recorder. The tapes sounded natural to me, like conversations between my husband and myself. Others who read the transcripts agree. All six people reported that they soon began to ignore the tape recorder; they were apologetic about the material, calling it trivial and uninteresting, just the ordinary affairs of everyday life. Furthermore, one couple forgot the recorder sufficiently to begin making love in the living room while the recorder was on. That segment and two others were the only ones the participants deleted before handing the tapes over to me.

Method

I began the research in order to explore the ways in which power was reflected and maintained in daily interactions. I had some ideas of what to look for, but generally my categories and concepts developed out of the conversations on the tapes. For example, I did not start the analysis with the conception of interactional work, but as I noticed the frequency of questions on the tapes and began to think about how they functioned conversationally, I came to the notion of work.

The frequency counts reported in the body of the paper are from twelve and a half hours of transcribed tapes. Five hours of the transcripts were the first ones I did and these were selected for two reasons. First, when I started the research I was looking for examples of decision-making and references to Garfinkel's (1967) "essential features" of conversation. I transcribed segments which showed either of these. Second, I also had the sense while listening to the tapes that some of the conversations were "good" ones and others were "bad." I transcribed some of each in hope that I could find what was going on conversationally that led me to those vague evaluations. The identification of conversational strategies and the conception of conversational work came out of my analysis of these first five hours.

The remaining seven and a half hours were transcribed with no motive but that of transferring more of the tapes to paper. They represent all the talk on one side of tape from each of the three couples. I then used these to double-check the frequency counts of the strategies I had by then specified (the variation has not been significant). The analysis of topic initiations which comes later in this paper was based on all the transcripts.

Task B2.3.2: Reflection task

➤ Is there anything we have not been told about Fishman's methodology, that you would like to have known?

P. Fishman

Findings: interactional strategies

Textual analysis revealed how interactants do the work of conversation. There are a variety of strategies to insure, encourage, and subvert conversation. The differential use of these strategies by women and men suggests that there is inequality in talk between the sexes. Conversation is more problematic for women, who work harder to make it happen. Talk seems less problematic for men, who exert control over when and how it will occur. As these findings indicate, there are specific ways to see this inequality in action.

While there are problems with generalizing from three couples to male–female conversations overall, I do so for a number of reasons. First, this work suggests many areas for further study: Will other researchers find the same patterns among other heterosexual couples? Do these patterns appear in other hierarchical relations, like bosses and workers, teachers and students? Are there male-female conversational differences in larger groups and are the patterns similar or different? What will we find in video-taped interactions? Second, while the findings are based on the conversations of three couples, they have been confirmed many times by my own informal obser-vations and by reports from other people of their experience. Finally, the findings are helpful. Since the strategies are quite concrete, they can be noticed in conversation. They are cues by which people, and particularly women, can figure out what is happening in their own interactions.

Asking questions

There is an overwhelming difference between female and male use of questions as a resource in interaction. At times I felt that all women did was ask questions. In the transcripts the women asked two and a half times the questions that the men did.

Other research (Lakoff, 1975) suggests that women ask more questions than men. Lakoff has interpreted women's question-asking as an indication of their insecurity, a linguistic signal of an internal psychological state resulting from the oppression of women. But a psychological analysis is unnecessary to explain why women ask more questions than men. Since questions are produced in conversations, we should look first to how questions function there.

Questions are interactionally powerful utterances. They are among a class of utterances, like greetings, treated as standing in a paired relation; that is, they demand a next utterance. Questions are paired with answers (Sacks, 1972). They "deserve" answers. The absence of a response is noticeable and may be complained about. A question does work in conversation by opening a two-part (Q–A) sequence. It is a way to insure a minimal interaction—at least one utterance by each of the two participants. By asking questions, women strengthen the possibility of a response to what they have to say.

Once I had noted the phenomenon of questions on the tapes, I attended to my own speech and discovered the same pattern. I tried, and still do try, to break myself of the "habit" and found it very difficult. Remarks kept coming out as questions before I could rephrase them. When I did succeed in making a remark as a statement, I usually did not get a response. It became clear that I asked questions not merely out of habit nor from insecurity but because it was likely that my attempt at interaction would fail if I did not.

Task B2.3.3: Reflection task

➤ Do Fishman's findings about questions correspond to your own experience of talk in mixed-sex pairs?

Fishman then looks at use of 'D'ya know', which was used twice as much by the women. She compares this to Sacks' (1972) study of the way children use similar devices to initiate a Q-Q-A sequence.

Attention beginnings

P. Fishman

The phrase, "this is interesting," or a variation thereof, occurs throughout the tapes. Ideally, the work of establishing that a remark is interesting is accomplished by both interactants. The first person makes a remark; the second person orients to and responds to the remark, thus establishing its status as something worthy of joint interest or importance. All this occurs without the question of its interest ever becoming explicit. The use of "This is really interesting" as an introduction shows that the user cannot assume that the remark itself will be seen as worthy of attention. At the same time, the user tries single-handedly to establish the interest of their remarks. The user is saying, "Pay attention to what I have to say, I can't assume that you will." The women used twice as many attention beginnings as the men.

There are also many instances of "y'know" interspersed throughout the transcripts. While this phrase does not compel the attention of one's partner as forcefully as "this is interesting" does, it is an attempt to command the other person's attention. The women said "you know" five times as often as the men (for further analysis of this phrase, see Fishman, 1980).

Task B2.3.4: Reflection task

➤ Do Fishman's findings about 'Attention beginnings' correspond to your own experience of the talk of mixed-sex pairs?

Minimal response

P. Fishman

Another interaction strategy is the use of the minimal response, when the speaker takes a turn by saying "yeah," "umm," "huh," and only that. Women and men both do this, but they tend to use the minimal response in quite different ways. The male usages of the minimal response displayed lack of interest. The monosyllabic response merely filled a turn at a point when it needed to be filled. For example, a woman would make a lengthy remark, after which the man responded with "yeah," doing nothing to encourage her, nor to elaborate. Such minimal responses operate to discourage interaction.

The women also made this type of minimal response at times, but their most frequent use of the minimal response was as "support work." Throughout the tapes, when the men are talking, the women are particularly skilled at inserting "mm's," "yeah's," "oh's," and other such comments throughout streams of talk rather than at the end. These are signs from the inserter that she is constantly attending to what is said, that she is demonstrating her participation, her interest in the interaction and the speaker. How well the women do this is also striking—seldom do they mistime their insertions and cause even slight overlaps. These minimal responses occur between the breaths of a speaker, and there is nothing in tone or structure to suggest they are attempting to take over the talk.

★ Task B2.3.5: Reflection task

➤ Do Fishman's findings about 'minimal responses' correspond to your own experience of the talk of mixed-sex pairs?

Fishman then looks at 'Making statements' (men produced more; also, men's statements, but not women's, almost always received a response), and 'Topic initiation': 'while the women made 62% of the attempts to introduce topics, they only raised 38% of the topics which evolved into conversation' (1983: 96).

★ Task B2.3.6: Reflection task

➤ Consider to what extent Fishman has analysed her data in a way that 'maps' one meaning onto one type of utterance (that is, implying 'form-function equivalence'). Can you think of other ways of interpreting this same data?

Conclusions

. . . These data suggest several general patterns of female–male interactional work. Compared with the men, the women tried more often and succeeded less often in getting conversations going, whereas the men tried less often and seldom failed in their attempts. Both men and women regarded topics introduced by women as tentative; many of these were quickly dropped. In contrast, topics introduced by the men were treated as topics to be pursued; they were seldom rejected. The women worked harder than the men in conversation because they had less certainty of success with the topics they raised. The women did much of the necessary work of interaction, starting conversations and then working to maintain them.

The failure of the women's attempts at interaction is not due to anything inherent in their talk, but to the failure of the men to respond, to do interactional work. The success of the men's attempts is due to the women doing interactional work in response to remarks by the men. Thus, the definition of what is appropriate or inappropriate conversation becomes the man's choice. What part of the world the interactants

P. Fishman

orient to, construct, and maintain the reality of, is his choice, not hers. Yet the women labor hardest in making interactions go.

As with work in its usual sense, there appears to be a division of labor in conversation. The people who do the routine maintenance work, the women, are not the same people who either control or benefit from the process. Women are the "shitworkers" of routine interaction, and the "goods" being made are not only interactions, but, through them, realities.

This analysis of the detailed activity in everyday conversation suggests other dimensions of power and work. Two interrelated aspects concern women's availability and the maintenance of gender. While women have difficulty generating interactions, they are almost always available to do the conversational work required by men and which is necessary for interactions. Appearances may differ by case: sometimes women are required to sit and "be a good listener" because they are not otherwise needed. At other times women are required to fill silences and keep conversation moving, to talk a lot. Sometimes they are expected to develop others' topics, and at other times they are required to present and develop topics of their own.

Women are required to do their work in a very strong sense. Sometimes they are required in ways that can be seen in interaction, as when men use interactional strategies such as attention beginnings and questions, to which the women fully respond. There are also times when there is no direct situational evidence of "requirement" from the man, and the woman does so "naturally." "Naturally" means that it is morally required to do so and a highly sanctionable matter not to. If one does not act "naturally," then one can be seen as crazy and deprived of adult status. We can speculate on the quality of doing it "naturally" by considering what happens to women who are unwilling to be available for the various jobs that the situation requires. Women who successfully control interactions are often derided and doubt is cast on their femininity. They are often considered "abnormal"—terms like "castrating bitch," "domineering," "aggressive," and "witch" may be used to identify them. When they attempt to control conversations temporarily, women often "start" arguments. Etiquette books are filled with instructions to women on how to be available. Women who do not behave are punished by deprivation of full female status. One's identity as either male or female is the most crucial identity one has. It is the most "natural" differentiating characteristic there is.

Whereas sociologists generally treat sex as an "ascribed" rather than as an "achieved" characteristic, Garfinkel's (1967, ch. 5) study of a transsexual describes one's gender as a continual, routine accomplishment. He discusses what the transsexual Agnes has shown him, that one must continually give off the appearance of being female or male in order for your gender to be unproblematic in a given interaction. Agnes had to learn these appearances and her awareness of them was explicit. For "normally sexed" people, it is routine.

To be identified as female, women are required to look and act in particular ways. Talking is part of this complex of behavior. Women must talk like a female it is work is obscured. The work is not seen as what women do, but as part of what they are. Because this work is obscured, because it is too often seen as an aspect of gender identity rather than of gender activity, the maintenance and expression of male–female power relations in our everyday conversations are hidden as well. When we orient instead to the activities involved in maintaining gender, we are able to discern the reality of hierarchy in our daily lives . . .

Task B2.3.7: After you've read

➤ From your own experience of mixed-sex talk, would you add anything to Fishman's list of linguistic ways in which women carry out the 'shitwork' of conversation?

➤ How does Fishman extrapolate from her linguistic findings to their implications for the notions of gender and power?

➤ In what ways do you see Fishman's research as being ahead of its time?

Unit B3
The influence of feminism and feminist linguistics (b)

Daniel Maltz and Ruth Borker (1982) 'A cultural approach to male–female miscommunication', in John Gumperz (ed.) *Language and Social Identity*. **Cambridge: Cambridge University Press, pp. 196–216**

Text B3
D. Maltz and
R. Borker

'A cultural approach to male-female communication' was published first in John Gumperz's (1982) edited collection *Language and Social Identity*, Maltz and Borker's starting point being 'the nature of the different roles of male and female speakers in informal cross-sex conversations in American English'. It has been highly influential, particularly in its contribution to theory, and has been widely drawn on and cited in the language and gender field (for example, Coates 1993, Tannen 1991). In particular, it facilitated what came to be known as the '(cultural) difference' current of gender and language study, standing in large measure in opposition to the '(male) dominance' current, exemplified by the previous work of Pamela Fishman (see Unit B2.3), Carol Edelsky, Don Zimmerman and Candace West.

The paper is not based on new data. Rather, its intention is to explain the findings of existing studies, such as those of Fishman (1978, 1983). Inevitably, then, the focus is on the use of American English (a form of hegemony evident throughout the Gender and Language field). Maltz and Borker's basic thesis, influenced by John Gumperz, is that 'the general approach recently developed for the study of difficulties in cross-ethnic communication can be applied to cross-sex communication as well. We prefer to think of the difficulties in both cross-sex and cross-ethnic communication as two examples of the same larger phenomenon: cultural difference and miscommunication' (1982: 196).

For Maltz and Borker, linguistic differences and miscommunication between American women and men can come about because they 'come from different linguistic subcultures, having learned to do different things with words in a conversation' (1982: 200), this learning having occurred 'during precisely that time period, approximately age 5–15, when boys and girls interact socially primarily with members of their own sex' (1982: 203). In comparing this with 'interethnic communication', they charitably claim that this 'does not assume that problems are the result of bad faith, but rather . . . the result of individuals wrongly interpreting cues according to their own rules' (1982: 201).

Task B3.1: Before you read

➤ Consider whether, when you were between five and fifteen years old, you 'interacted socially primarily with members of [your] own sex'.

➤ Note down some examples and compare them with the findings reported by Maltz and Borker.

➤ In what ways did you interact socially with members of the opposite sex?

Maltz and Borker begin their paper by summarising empirical findings (including Pamela Fishman's) about women's and men's different language use in 'cross-sex' conversation, for example, that women are more likely to:

■ ask questions (Fishman 1978);
■ make use of positive minimal responses, throughout as well as at the end of an utterance (Hirschman 1973, Fishman 1978);
■ adopt a strategy of 'silent protest' after they have been interrupted or have received a delayed minimal response (Zimmerman and West 1975, West and Zimmerman 1977);
■ use the pronouns 'you' and 'we' (Hirschman 1973);

whereas men are more likely to:

■ interrupt the speech of their interlocutors (Zimmerman and West 1975, West and Zimmerman 1977, West 1979);
■ challenge or dispute their interlocutors' utterances (Hirschman 1973);
■ ignore the comments of the other speaker, that is, to offer no response or acknowledgment at all (Hirschman 1973), or to respond slowly or unenthusiastically (Fishman 1978, Zimmerman and West 1975);
■ use more mechanisms for controlling the topic of conversation, including both topic development and the introduction of new topics (Zimmerman and West 1975);
■ offer more direct declarations of fact or opinion (Fishman 1978).

Maltz and Borker cite explanations for such differences in terms of power and dominance, sex roles, and psychology, but claim that these:

> do not provide a means of explaining why these specific features appear as opposed to any number of others, nor do they allow us to differentiate between various types of male–female interaction. They do not really tell us why and how these specific interactional phenomena are linked to the general fact that men dominate within our social system.
>
> (1982: 199)

Task B3.2: Reflection task

➤ Do you think the above quote is a fair criticism of Fishman, for example?

Task B3.3: While you read

➤ Consider whether this account resonates with your own experience of language use in single-sex and mixed-sex groups, in childhood and now.

➤ Note the strength of Maltz and Borker's claims and generalisations.

A cultural approach to male–female miscommunication

An *alternative explanation*: *sociolinguistic subcultures*

D. Maltz and R. Borker

Our approach to cross-sex communication patterns is somewhat different from those that have been previously proposed. We place the stress not on psychological differences or power differentials, although these may make some contribution, but rather on a notion of cultural differences between men and women in their conceptions of friendly conversation, their rules for engaging in it, and, probably most important, their rules for interpreting it. We argue that American men and women come from different sociolinguistic subcultures, having learned to do different things with words in a conversation, so that when they attempt to carry on conversations with one another, even if both parties are attempting to treat one another as equals, cultural miscommunication results.

Task B3.4: Reflection task

➤ Maltz and Borker see power differentials as making 'some contribution' to what happens in talk between women and men. What is your own position on the significance of this contribution?

The idea of distinct male and female subcultures is not a new one for anthropology. It has been persuasively argued again and again for those parts of the world such as the Middle East and southern Europe in which men and women spend most of their lives spatially and interactionally segregated. The strongest case for sociolinguistic subcultures has been made by Susan Harding from her research in rural Spain (1975).

D. Maltz and R. Borker

   The major premise on which Harding builds her argument is that speech is a means for dealing with social and psychological situations. When men and women have different experiences and operate in different social contexts, they tend to develop different genres of speech and different skills for doing things with words. In the Spanish village in which she worked, the sexual division of labor was strong, with men involved in agricultural tasks and public politics while women were involved in a series of networks of personal relations with their children, their husbands, and their female neighbors. While men developed their verbal skills in economic negotiations and

D. Maltz and
R. Borker

public political argument, women became more verbally adept at a quite different mode of interactional manipulation with words: gossip, social analysis, subtle information gathering through a carefully developed technique of verbal prying, and a kind of second-guessing the thoughts of others (commonly known as 'women's intuition') through a skillful monitoring of the speech of others. The different social needs of men and women, she argues, have led them to sexually differentiated communicative cultures, with each sex learning a different set of skills for manipulating words effectively.

The question that Harding does not ask, however, is, if men and women possess different subcultural rules for speaking, what happens if and when they try to interact with each other? It is here that we turn to the research on interethnic miscommunication.

Interethnic communication

Recent research (Gumperz 1977, 1978a, 1978b, 1979; Gumperz and Tannen 1978) has shown that systematic problems develop in communication when speakers of different speech cultures interact and that these problems are the result of differences in systems of conversational inference and the cues for signalling speech acts and speaker's intent. Conversation is a negotiated activity. It progresses in large part because of shared assumptions about what is going on.

Examining interactions between English-English and Indian-English speakers in Britain (Gumperz 1977, 1978a, 1979; Gumperz et al. 1977), Gumperz found that differences in cues resulted in systematic miscommunication over whether a question was being asked, whether an argument was being made, whether a person was being rude or polite, whether a speaker was relinquishing the floor or interrupting, whether and what a speaker was emphasizing, whether interactants were angry, concerned, or indifferent. Rather than being seen as problems in communication, the frustrating encounters that resulted were usually chalked up as personality clashes or interpreted in the light of racial stereotypes which tended to exacerbate already bad relations.

To take a simple case, Gumperz (1977) reports that Indian women working at a cafeteria, when offering food, used a falling intonation, e.g. "gravy," which to them indicated a question, something like "do you want gravy?" Both Indian and English workers saw a question as an appropriate polite form, but to English-English speakers a falling intonation signalled not a question, which for them is signalled by a rising intonation such as "gravy," but a declarative statement, which was both inappropriate and extremely rude.

A major advantage of Gumperz's framework is that it does not assume that problems are the result of bad faith, but rather sees them as the result of individuals wrongly interpreting cues according to their own rules.

 ### Task B3.5: While you read

➤ Can you think of examples of male–female (mis)communication which are less innocent than a case of 'individuals wrongly interpreting cues according to their own rules'?

The interpretation of minimal responses

D. Maltz and
R. Borker

How might Gumperz's approach to the study of conflicting rules for interpreting conversation be applied to the communication between men and women? A simple example will illustrate our basic approach: the case of positive minimal responses. Minimal responses such as nods and comments like "yes" and "mm hmm" are common features of conversational interaction. Our claim, based on our attempts to understand personal experience, is that these minimal responses have significantly different meanings for men and women, leading to occasionally serious miscommunication.

We hypothesize that for women a minimal response of this type means simply something like "I'm listening to you; please continue," and that for men it has a some-what stronger meaning such as "I agree with you" or at least "I follow your argument so far." The fact that women use these responses more often than men is in part simply that women are listening more often than men are agreeing.

But our hypothesis explains more than simple differential frequency of usage. Different rules can lead to repeated misunderstanding. Imagine a male speaker who is receiving repeated nods or "mm hmm"s from the woman he is speaking to. She is merely indicating that she is listening, but he thinks she is agreeing with everything he says. Now imagine a female speaker who is receiving only occasional nods and "mm hmm"s from the man she is speaking to. He is indicating that he doesn't always agree; she thinks he isn't always listening.

What is appealing about this short example is that it seems to explain two of the most common complaints in male–female interaction: (1) men who think that women are always agreeing with them and then conclude that it's impossible to tell what a women really thinks, and (2) women who get upset with men who never seem to be listening. What we think we have here are two separate rules for conversational maintenance which come into conflict and cause massive miscommunication.

Task B3.6: Reflection task

➤ To what extent does it seem reasonable to you to compare communication between women and men with inter-ethnic communication?

Sources of different cultures

D. Maltz and
R. Borker

A probable objection that many people will have to our discussion so far is that American men and women interact with one another far too often to possess different subcultures. What we need to explain is how it is that men and women can come to possess different cultural assumptions about friendly conversation.

Our explanation is really quite simple. It is based on the idea that by the time we have become adults we possess a wide variety of rules for interacting in different situations. Different sets of these rules were learned at different times and in different contexts. We have rules for dealing with people in dominant or subordinate social positions, rules which we first learned as young children interacting with our parents and teachers. We have rules for flirting and other sexual encounters which we probably started learning at or near adolescence. We have rules for dealing with service personnel and bureaucrats, rules we began learning when we first ventured into the public domain. Finally, we have rules for friendly interaction, for carrying on friendly conversation. What is striking about these last rules is that they were learned not from adults but from peers, and that they were learned during precisely that time period, approximately age 5 to 15, when boys and girls interact socially primarily with members of their own sex.

The idea that girls and boys in contemporary America learn different ways of speaking by the age of five or earlier has been postulated by Robin Lakoff (1975), demonstrated by Andrea Meditch (1975), and more fully explored by Adelaide Haas (1979). Haas's research on school-age children shows the early appearance of important male–female differences in patterns of language use, including a male tendency toward direct requests and information giving and a female tendency toward compliance (1979: 107).

But the process of acquiring gender-specific speech and behavior patterns by school-age children is more complex than the simple copying of adult "genderlects" by preschoolers. Psychologists Brooks-Gunn and Matthews (1979) have labelled this process the "consolidation of sex roles"; we call it learning of gender-specific "cultures."

Among school-age children, patterns of friendly social interaction are learned not so much from adults as from members of one's peer group, and a major feature of most middle-childhood peer groups is homogeneity; "they are either all-boy or all-girl" (Brooks-Gunn and Matthews 1979). Members of each sex are learning self-consciously to differentiate their behavior from that of the other sex and to exaggerate these differences. The process can be profitably compared to accent divergence in which members of two groups that wish to become clearly distinguished from one another socially acquire increasingly divergent ways of speaking.

Because they learn these gender-specific cultures from their age-mates, children tend to develop stereotypes and extreme versions of adult behavior patterns. For a boy learning to behave in a masculine way, for example, Ruth Hartley (1959, quoted in Brooks-Gunn and Matthews 1979: 203) argues that:

> both the information and the practice he gets are distorted. Since his peers have no better sources of information than he has, all they can do is pool the impressions and anxieties they derived from their early training. Thus, the picture they draw is oversimplified and overemphasized. It is a picture drawn in black and white, with little or no modulation and it is incomplete, including a few of the many elements that go to make up the role of the mature male.

What we hope to argue is that boys and girls learn to use language in different ways because of the very different social contexts in which they learn how to carry on friendly conversation. Almost anyone who remembers being a child, has worked with school-age children, or has had an opportunity to observe school-age children can vouch for the fact that groups of girls and groups of boys interact and play in different ways. Systematic observations of children's play have tended to confirm these well-known differences in the ways girls and boys learn to interact with their friends.

 Task B3.7: Reflection task

➤ Consider how and where boys and girls spend their days, both in your own and other cultural contexts.

➤ Do you find the description of different 'cultures' for boys and girls accurate, or overstated?

In a major study of sex differences in the play of school-age children, for example, sociologist Janet Lever (1976) observed the following six differences between the play of boys and that of girls: (1) girls more often play indoors; (2) boys tend to play in larger groups; (3) boys' play groups tend to include a wider age range of participants; (4) girls play in predominantly male games more often than vice versa; (5) boys more often play competitive games, and (6) girls' games tend to last a shorter period of time than boys' games.

D. Maltz and R. Borker

Task B3.8: Reflection task

➤ How many of these differences apply in a non-American cultural context with which you are familiar?

It is by examining these differences in the social organization of play and the accompanying differences in the patterns of social interaction they entail, we argue, that we can learn about the sources of male–female differences in patterns of language use. And it is these same patterns, learned in childhood and carried over into adulthood as the bases for patterns of single-sex friendship relations, we contend, that are potential sources of miscommunication in cross-sex interaction.

D. Maltz and R. Borker

Maltz and Borker go on to detail 'The world of girls' and 'The world of boys'. They note that:

Basically girls learn to do three things with words: (1) to create and maintain relationships of closeness and equality, (2) to criticize others in acceptable ways, and (3) to interpret accurately the speech of other girls.
 To a large extent friendships among girls are formed through talk. Girls need to learn to give support, to recognize the speech rights of others, to let others speak, and to acknowledge what they say in order to establish and maintain relationships of equality and closeness. In activities they need to learn to create cooperation through speech.

D. Maltz and R. Borker

For boys, however:

speech is used in three major ways: (1) to assert one's position of dominance, (2) to attract and maintain an audience, and (3) to assert oneself when other speakers have the floor . . .

D. Maltz and R. Borker

Maltz and Borker then trace the continuity between the talk of girls and of women, and the talk of boys and of men . . .

Task B3.9: While you read

➤ Again, consider how much of each of these descriptions is true of your own experience.

➤ If you are female, consider the 'Men's speech' section from your experience of being an 'overhearer' of men's talk (and vice versa).

D. Maltz and R. Borker

Women's speech

The structures and strategies in women's conversation show a marked continuity with the talk of girls. The key logic suggested by Kalčik's (1975) study of women's rap groups, Hirschman's (1973) study of students and Abrahams's (1975) work on black women is that women's conversation is interactional. In friendly talk, women are negotiating and expressing a relationship, one that should be in the form of support and closeness, but which may also involve criticism and distance. Women orient themselves to the person they are talking to and expect such orientation in return. As interaction, conversation requires participation from those involved and back-and-forth movement between participants. Getting the floor is not seen as particularly problematic; that should come about automatically. What is problematic is getting people engaged and keeping them engaged – maintaining the conversation and the interaction.

This conception of conversation leads to a number of characteristic speech strategies and gives a particular dynamic to women's talk. First, women tend to use personal and inclusive pronouns, such as 'you' and 'we' (Hirschman 1973). Second, women give off and look for signs of engagement such as nods and minimal response (Kalčik 1975; Hirschman 1973). Third, women give more extended signs of interest and attention, such as interjecting comments or questions during a speaker's discourse . . . Fourth, women at the beginning of their utterances explicitly acknowledge and respond to what has been said by others. Fifth, women attempt to link their utterance to the one preceding it by building on the previous utterance or talking about something parallel or related to it. Kalčik (1975) talks about strategies of tying together, filling in, and serializing as signs of women's desire to create continuity in conversation . . .

These strategies and the interactional orientation of women's talk give their conversation a particular dynamic. While there is often an unfinished quality to particular utterances (Kalčik 1975), there is a progressive development to the overall conversation. The conversation grows out of the interaction of its participants, rather than being directed by a single individual or series of individuals. In her very stimulating discussion, Kalčik (1975) argues that this is true as well for many of the narratives women tell in conversation. She shows how narrative "kernels" serve as conversational resources for individual women and the group as a whole. How and if a "kernel story" is developed by the narrator and/or audience on a particular occasion is a function of the conversational context from which it emerges (Kalčik 1975: 8), and it takes very different forms at different tellings. Not only is the dynamic of women's conversation one of elaboration and continuity, but the idiom of support can give it a distinctive tone as well. Hannerz (1969: 96), for example, contrasts the "tone of relaxed sweetness, sometimes bordering on the saccharine," that characterizes approving talk between women, to the heated argument found among men. Kalčik (1975: 6) even goes so far as to suggest that there is an "underlying esthetic or organizing principle" of "harmony" being expressed in women's friendly talk.

Men's speech

D. Maltz and
R. Borker

The speaking patterns of men, and of women for that matter, vary greatly from one North American subculture to another. As Gerry Philipsen (1975: 13) summarizes it, "talk is not everywhere valued equally; nor is it anywhere valued equally in all social contexts." There are striking cultural variations between subcultures in whether men consider certain modes of speech appropriate for dealing with women, children, authority figures, or strangers; there are differences in performance rules for story-telling and joke telling; there are differences in the context of men's speech; and there are differences in the rules for distinguishing aggressive joking from true aggression.

But more surprising than these differences are the apparent similarities across subcultures in the patterns of friendly interaction between men and the resemblances between these patterns and those observed for boys. Research reports on the speaking patterns of men among urban blacks (Abrahams 1976; Hannerz 1969), rural Newfoundlanders (Faris 1966; Bauman 1972), and urban blue-collar whites (Philipsen 1975; LeMasters 1975) point again and again to the same three features: storytelling, arguing and verbal posturing.

Narratives such as jokes and stories are highly valued, especially when they are well performed for an audience. In Newfoundland, for example, Faris (1966: 242) comments that "the reason 'news' is rarely passed between two men meeting in the road – it is simply not to one's advantage to relay information to such a small audience." Loud and aggressive argument is a second common feature of male–male speech. Such arguments, which may include shouting, wagering, name-calling, and verbal threats (Faris 1966: 245), are often, as Hannerz (1969: 86) describes them, "debates over minor questions of little direct import to anyone," enjoyed for their own sake and not taken as signs of real conflict. Practical jokes, challenges, put-downs, insults, and other forms of verbal aggression are a third feature of men's speech, accepted as normal among friends. LeMasters (1975: 140), for example, describes life in a working-class tavern in the Midwest as follows:

> It seems clear that status at the Oasis is related to the ability to "dish it out" in the rapid-fire exchange called "joshing": you have to have a quick retort, and preferably one that puts you "one up" on your opponent. People who can't compete in the game lose status.

Thus challenges rather than statements of support are a typical way for men to respond to the speech of other men.

Task B3.10: While you read

➤ If, in a given context, women and men do communicate differently in mixed-sex interaction, does this difference, in your experience, extend to miscommunication, for example in ways suggested below?

D. Maltz and
R. Borker

What is happening in cross-sex conversation

What we are suggesting is that women and men have different cultural rules for friendly conversation and that these rules come into conflict when women and men attempt to talk to each other as friends and equals in casual conversation. We can think of at least five areas, in addition to that of minimal responses already discussed, in which men and women probably possess different conversational rules, so that miscommunication is likely to occur in cross-sex interaction.

There are two interpretations of the meaning of questions. Women seem to see questions as a part of conversational maintenance, while men seem to view them primarily as requests for information.

There are two conventions for beginning an utterance and linking it to the preceding utterance. Women's rules seem to call for an explicit acknowledgment of what has been said and making a connection to it. Men seem to have no such rule and in fact some male strategies call for ignoring the preceding comments.

There are different interpretations of displays of verbal aggressiveness. Women seem to interpret overt aggressiveness as personally directed, negative, and disruptive. Men seem to view it as one conventional organizing structure for conversational flow.

There are two understandings of topic flow and topic shift. The literature on storytelling in particular seems to indicate that men operate with a system in which topic is fairly narrowly defined and adhered to until finished and in which shifts between topics are abrupt, while women have a system in which topic is developed progressively and shifts gradually. These two systems imply very different rules for and interpretations of side comments, with major potential for miscommunication.

There appear to be two different attitudes towards problem sharing and advice giving. Women tend to discuss problems with one another, sharing experiences and offering reassurances. Men, in contrast, tend to hear women, and other men, who present them with problems as making explicit requests for solutions. They respond by giving advice, by acting as experts, lecturing to their audiences . . .

 ### Task B3.11: After you've read

➤ Maltz and Borker's focus is very much the 'how' of talk. Do you think that the 'what' of talk may also play a role in male–female miscommunication? If so, how would this fit into the overall picture?

➤ To what extent is 'communication success' in the 'what' of talk likely to compensate for (any) miscommunication arising from the 'how'?

➤ How helpful is the evidence from the studies cited by Maltz and Borker?

➤ To what extent is this paper about 'women and men'?

➤ If you were a member of the editorial review board of a journal to which Maltz and Borker had submitted this paper, would you accept it, and, if so, what revisions, if any, would you suggest?

Unit B4
Developing understandings
of gender

The extracts in this unit come from work by Deborah Cameron, Mary Bucholtz and Cynthia Nelson, all of whom have drawn on feminist perspectives to challenge – and thus develop – notions of gender.

Deborah Cameron (1992) *Feminism and Linguistic Theory*. London: Palgrave

Text B4.1
D. Cameron

The extracts in Unit B4.1 come from the second edition of Deborah Cameron's *Feminism and Linguistic Theory*. Originally published in 1985, this second edition appeared in 1992, pointing to the importance of this book, and its author, to the field. Cameron was one of the first to substantially critique the very notion of exploring 'sex differences' in language in use. This was an important and provocative contribution to the Gender and Language field, given the concern with differences not only of pre-feminist writers (Jespersen, Trudgill, Labov), for whom gender (if they used the word) and sex were equivalents, but also of feminist linguists, many of whom in well-intentioned but over-straightforward ways equated the identification of differences with the exposure of girls' and women's disadvantage and oppression (for example, in the classroom). Similarly, different analytical interpretations of given utterances and possibilities of linguistic resistance tended to be under-explored. These feminist linguists were not only drawing on a model of gender as a binary opposition, and an opposition which was 'already there', but inadvertently perpetuating these. Cameron refers to this focus as the 'endless ferreting out of differences' (1992: 37). The debate is still relevant today, the prototypical meaning of 'gender' for most people (including, in my experience, postgraduate students of gender and language) still being 'gender differences' – in talk, or elsewhere. (A student of mine recently asked if the study of language and gender extended to phonetics, for example.)

In Unit B4.1, we look at two extracts from *Feminism and Linguistic Theory* (1992). In the first, Cameron explores *why* feminists and others have been so preoccupied with the way women and men talk differently (and the preoccupation with gender differences in general), and the problems this entails for feminism. In her book, Cameron looks at what she calls 'the sexism of linguistic science, as expressed in various assumptions and practices' (1992: 36); our main concern here, however, is what she writes about 'the political significance of sex difference itself'.

 Task B4.1.1: Before you read

➤ What do you think are some attractions of investigating 'gender differences', both inside and outside academia?

➤ What might be some alternative research foci for gender and language researchers who wish to go beyond looking at 'gender differences' in language use?

D. Cameron

Chapter 3 The politics of variation (1): sex differences in language

. . . Throughout this discussion I will be emphasising the idea that the study of sex differences cannot help having a political dimension, because the male/female difference is so important for the organisation of the societies in which studies of difference are done. This was true even before the current wave of feminism (Virginia Woolf in 1929 and Simone de Beauvoir in 1949 both marvelled at the huge volume of material on the subject); contemporary feminism has just made the political implications easier to see.

Historically, a lot of sex difference research was done specifically in order to provide a scientific account of an already-assumed female inferiority – taking comparative measurements of male and female brains, for instance, as a way of explaining why women were weaker intellectually than men. Even when this was not the overt purpose, research results have been used to justify particular aspects of women's subordination: thus even today it is sometimes said that girls don't become engineers because they lack spatial ability, or that their relative lack of aggression makes them less effective leaders.

Of course we can contest this kind of sexism by arguing about the accuracy of particular scientific findings. If a finding is incorrect, then the conclusions drawn from it are discredited at once. For instance, the generalisation that women are physically weaker than men has been qualified; in some areas, like endurance, they may be much stronger than was thought and capable of outperforming men in certain tasks.

But this is to allow the opponent to set the terms for debate, accepting assumptions that feminists ought perhaps to question (for example, that women should be treated equally only to the extent that they resemble men) and thus conceding a vital part of the argument. Inaccurate or biased research deserves our criticism, but it is just as important to ask the prior questions of why researchers have chosen to study sex differences so intensively in the first place (why does no-one study 'sex similarity'? There is plenty of it, after all) and why they have interpreted their findings in particular (and sexist) ways.

It is because of these broader questions that an honourable feminist tradition has arisen, especially in the social sciences, of directing attention to the way sex difference has been described and explained, rather than to the content of difference itself. This feminist critique is aimed at exposing the hidden political agenda of social science, its underlying motivation for the endless ferreting out of differences.

Curiously enough, though, this has not been the major concern of feminist work in the social science disciplines of linguistics and speech communication. Feminists studying language have in general been more interested in furthering the study of sex difference than in criticising it, and though it is acceptable to sneer at long-dead commentators like Jespersen . . . a thorough critique of modern sociolinguistics has been very slow to emerge.

Why should this be so? I would suggest that feminist linguists have two main motives for studying sex differences. One is *positive*: the quest for an authentic female language, whether this is taken to reflect some deep-seated cognitive difference, or the existence in many societies of a distinctive female subculture. The other is more *negative*: to identify the sexual power dynamic in language use, the conventions and behaviours through which speech reflects and perpetuates gender inequality. Both motives can be discerned in today's feminist linguistics; they are not necessarily totally opposed, though it must be said, at times their coexistence is rather uneasy.

Whichever motive is uppermost for them, feminist linguists engaged in sex difference research do not seem to find the idea of studying difference problematic in itself. They agree, too, that the differences they study are social rather than innate. They are products of, on one hand, women's own activities and values, or on the other, their oppression by men. By studying the differences and the ways in which they arise we can arrive at an understanding of how language relates to gender.

This is all very well. But it needs to be acknowledged here that the feminist concerns just mentioned have something in common with nonfeminist and even anti-feminist concerns in studying sex difference. Although they favour differing explanations, the feminist and the sexist share a belief that linguistic behaviour is one of the keys to understanding the nature and status of women. While this agreement is not altogether surprising – feminists cannot entirely avoid fighting on already established ground, and the cultural importance of sex difference is deeply entrenched – its consequences have sometimes been regrettable . . .

[Chapters 3 and 4 of *Feminism and Linguistic Theory*] constitute an attempt to address the question I consider to be of overriding importance, which is not whether male/female differences exist (they do), what they are or what causes them, but *what they mean*: what significant social uses are made of them, or more accurately of discourse about them. This is an important and also a difficult point, so let me try to make it clearer. It goes back to the question I posed above: what motivates people to study sex differences and to place such emphasis upon them?

In an article called 'Woman's Time', the philosopher and critic Julia Kristeva once put forward a three-stage model of feminism. The first stage was for women to demand equality with men ('liberal' feminism). The second stage was to reinterpret difference so that women's own activities would gain social value even though they were different from men's ('radical' feminism). The third stage – Utopian at this point – was to transcend gender divisions altogether. The male/female difference would not necessarily disappear, but it would become socially insignificant, as many human variations (height, blood group) are now.

Task B4.1.2: Reflection task

➤ Consider which stage of Kristeva's model of feminism you have most sympathy with.

> Have you been involved with any social or political activities related to one or more of these three stages? Are you familiar with individuals or groups who affiliate themselves to any of the stages?

> What is your own response to the desirability of Kristeva's 'third stage'? Is 'transcending gender divisions altogether' something you would welcome?

D. Cameron

Kristeva's model is not intended either as a concise account of feminism's recent history nor as an orderly, linear chronology for feminists to follow (though she does seem to think that each of her stages represents an improvement over the one before). The best way to understand it, in my view, is as a way of separating out the different impulses represented in today's highly varied feminist thinking. This is not to say that all the stages are equally well-represented and well-understood. Most contemporary feminist politics is somewhere between the first and second stages, that is, it oscillates between deploring and celebrating difference, between the negative and positive motivations I outlined above, without realistically expecting – yet – to transcend current gender divisions.

At this stage, as Kristeva implies, an interest in, even a fascination with sex difference is very much a fact of our lives; and it is certainly not a neutral fact. One way a visiting alien would be able to tell that the male/female difference is not just an insignificant human variation is by observing how obsessively, how incessantly we talk about it. As long as Kristeva's third stage is present in our thinking only as a Utopian dream, feminists cannot simply refuse to get involved in this endless discourse of difference; people who claim that this is a postfeminist era are living in a dream world. But we do have to face the paradox implicit in our contributing to the discourse, which is that every word we say on the subject of difference just underlines the salience and the importance of a division we are ultimately striving to end.

If we want studies of sex difference to work towards our liberation rather than perpetuating our subordination, we have to take this problem very seriously. What that means, among other things, is that feminists who engage in this kind of research must refuse easy answers, answers that can easily be accommodated within the system as it is now.

We must criticise explanations of difference that treat gender as something obvious, static and monolithic, ignoring the forces that shape it and the varied forms they take in different times and places. Such explanations are simplistic and pernicious, because whatever their intentions, they tend to end up just like non-feminist research, by giving an academic gloss to commonplace stereotypes and so reinforcing the status quo.

What I am trying to say is that merely paying attention to sex difference – affirming that women exist and are different from men – is not in and of itself a feminist gesture. It can just as easily fall back into anti-feminism. Even to celebrate what is distinctive about women does not, in my opinion, automatically qualify as feminist. Feminism begins when we approach sex differences as constructs, show how they are constructed and in whose interests. We underestimate at our peril the difficulty and danger with which the 'politics of variation' are fraught.

Task B4.1.3: After you've read

➤ Where do 'non-sexist language' practices and interventions best fit in Kristeva's model of feminism? (See Unit A2; see also Sunderland 2004, Chapter 9).

➤ How might feminists at each of Kristeva's stages address the question of (non-)sexist language?

➤ Can you think of an example of studies motivated in the two different ways identified by Cameron on page 123? A good place to start would be Jennifer Coates's edited collection *Language and Gender: a reader* (1998).

Cameron concludes Chapter 4 with a section called 'The politics of variation: a reprise':

Chapter 4 Sex differences in language (ii): empirical sociolinguistics

D. Cameron

The title of Chapter 3, 'The politics of variation', was intended to underscore the central point about sex difference research: that it is always undertaken for political reasons, and has traditionally been used to justify sex discrimination and exclusionary practices, making them seem natural and inevitable. Thus it would be perfectly possible for a sexist to argue . . . that women make poor leaders and high-pressure salespersons because of their lack of assertiveness, whereas they make good carers (nurses, home helps and so on) because of their sensitivity to the needs of other people in conversation.

The use of feminist linguistic research for such overtly sexist purposes may seem unlikely; but even now there are indications that something more subtly worrying is happening. The May 1990 issue of *Glamour*, a widely-read US women's magazine, has an article called 'Girl talk, boy talk' about a book on male/female communication by the linguist Deborah Tannen. In the article, Tannen's findings are presented as advice to women on how best to communicate with men: for example, 'Speak in a straight-forward way to male subordinates. Women shy away from blatant orders but men find the indirect approach manipulative and confusing'.

This is a fairly obvious gloss of Maltz and Borker's discussion of Goodwin's findings on directives [see Unit B3], but the *Glamour* presentation of it does two things the linguists do not do, or at least not to anything like the same extent. First, it makes the differences seem natural and inevitable – rather than questioning where they come from and what social functions they serve, readers are urged to accept and adjust to them. Secondly, it treats male/female differences as a problem *for women*. Women become responsible, as usual, for the 'interactional shitwork' of facilitating effective communication. (I doubt that men are reading magazines which counsel them to modify their style in order 'to communicate better with all the women in your life'!)

A recent issue of American *Cosmopolitan* had an even more blatant example: an article (patronisingly titled 'Why not speak like a grown-up?') listed various things for women to avoid when speaking in work settings, including tag questions, rising intonation and high pitch, because these things undermine a speaker's perceived authority. Readers will doubtless be able to identify the source of this advice as the

D. Cameron

work of Robin Lakoff: work which is highly contentious because of its speculativeness, lack of supporting evidence and hostility to nonaggressive speech styles [see Unit B2.1]. The effect of repeating Lakoff's observations as *prescriptions* is to endorse them as true (which they may not be) and to reinforce the value Lakoff places on particular features (which is disputed, and arguably sexist). Linguistic research which was meant to help women understand and change their reality is being used here to hurt them, if only by creating in the mind of the female reader one more problem, a linguistic inadequacy for which she must blame herself.

It is perhaps even more worrying that this kind of advice also turns up in assertiveness training texts and manuals used to train women in business. A typical American text called *Leadership Skills for Women* counsels: 'Use strong, direct language and stand firm when you are interrupted. Statistics show that women allow themselves to be interrupted 50 per cent more often than men. Don't contribute to those statistics'. Apparently, the authors have concluded from published research that women get interrupted because they 'allow themselves' to be (does this 'contributory negligence' argument remind us of anything?) and if they want to succeed they must emulate male speech.

★ Task B4.1.4: Reflection task

➤ What *does* the 'contributory negligence' argument remind us of? Reread the previous sentence (up to the second bracket) carefully and consider possible substitutions for 'interrupted'.

D. Cameron

This is the dominance approach carried to an extreme even Lakoff might shy away from. And though this manual, *Glamour* and *Cosmopolitan* are moderately 'feminist' publications and clearly mean well, in the end I see little difference between the kind of advice they peddle and the more obviously sexist 1950s books of advice to brides or wives on how to talk to their husbands.

It is surely nothing to celebrate when sociolinguistic descriptions of behaviour are turned into folklinguistic prescriptions about (women's) behaviour; but given the realities of history and power it is also nothing to be surprised about. Unfortunately all studies of sex difference in every field whatsoever carry this kind of danger. And I want to conclude by examining various ways for feminists to respond to it, apart from simply recommending that women eliminate difference by learning to behave more like men.

One possible response is to deny that the purported differences apply to all women, or to all situations. Just because Ms Average is a cooperative rather than competitive speaker, we cannot assume that Jane Smith who is sitting in front of you will not deliver the goods. In any case, Ms Average is a product of her sexist society. Since sexism is unjust you should make it a point to put women in positions where they have a chance to overcome their historic powerlessness. In terms of Julia Kristeva's model, which I introduced in the last chapter, this would be a first stage, liberal equal-rights-and-opportunities response.

Or alternatively we can accept the differences and reject the conclusions drawn from them, stressing instead the value of women's ways of doing things. Someone sensitive and caring might make a better leader or salesperson than someone more competitive. This would be a second stage response.

Finally, we can reverse the terms of the argument, insisting that women's difference from men is not the cause of sexism but an effect of sexism; social practices like not hiring women in certain positions or allowing them to become leaders have the effect, over time, of producing the very differences which are then used to justify the original discrimination.

While a feminist linguistics will probably want to make strategic use of all these responses, it is this last one, in my opinion, that is most radical theoretically, and most resistant to the danger that research into male/female differences will be co-opted to serve the existing sexist system.

Task B4.1.5: After you've read

➤ If you can, borrow a copy of the first, 1985 edition of *Feminism and Linguistic Theory*. Compare the two (1992) extracts above with their equivalents in this edition. In what ways does the second edition represent an advance on the first, here?

➤ Identify as many reasons as you can from the Cameron extracts (and from your own experience) 'why researchers have chosen to study sex-differences so intensively in the first place' and 'why does no-one study "sex similarity"?'

➤ Can you think of some good (actual or possible) social or political reasons for studying sex differences in language? Think of a particular context or situation which might justify this. What might be a political price to pay for such a study?

➤ Cameron's argument presents a challenge to the slogan 'Different but Equal' (or 'Different and Equal'). This can of course be used of groups other than women and men. Under what conditions might we, and might we not, be able to achieve a situation of 'Different and Equal'?

Mary Bucholtz (1999) 'Bad examples: transgression and progress in language and gender studies', in Mary Bucholtz, A. C. Liang and Laurel Sutton (eds) *Reinventing Identities: the gendered self in discourse.* Oxford: Oxford University Press, pp. 3–24

Text B4.2
M. Bucholtz

Unit B4.2 comes from Mary Bucholtz's introductory chapter to the collection *Reinventing Identities: the gendered self in discourse* (1999). The title of the collection is indicative of developments in the Gender and Language field more widely. 'Discourse' points to a construction which is social, constitutive and ongoing as well as linguistic. 'Gendered' (a relatively recent adjective) allows for both *ascription* (to the self, by others) and *achievement* (by the self). The plurality of 'Identities' collocates well not just with 'invention' but 'Reinvention'. One reading of this is that there is nothing natural or inevitable about identities; another is that if an identity has been invented *for* us, it can still be re-invented *by* us, allowing an additional reading of agency.

In her introductory chapter, 'Bad examples: transgression and progress in language and gender studies', Bucholtz deals in turn with identity as 'invention', 'ideology', 'ingenuity' and 'improvisation'. The extract reproduced below looks historically at the Gender and Language field in relation to feminist theory then moves on to: 'Bad habits', 'Bad girls' and 'Bad subjects'. Below is reproduced 'Bad girls', and the conclusion to the chapter. Since this is from the Introduction to the whole collection, it includes references to contributions that follow. I have retained several of these since they point to current topics and offer useful suggestions for further reading.

Task B4.2.1: Before you read

➤ What do you think Mary Bucholtz might mean by 'Bad habits', 'Bad girls' and 'Bad subjects'? Consider some different possibilities for each.

➤ Consider different meanings of 'practice' and how these may (differently) relate to language.

M. Bucholtz

Bad girls: transgressive identities

As the new focus on the margins of community membership may imply, another way that innovative language and gender researchers have set a "bad example" in their research is by using "bad examples" of speakers and linguistic phenomena. Much of the scholarship in language and gender has been what might be called "good-girl research": studies of "good" (that is, normatively female—white, straight, middle-class) women being "good" (that is, normatively feminine). Such research has been a necessary starting point. Yet this definition of what counts as a "good" example excludes many groups and practices. In fact, as Marjorie Orellana's research suggests, how girls use language to experiment with "badness" is itself a crucial question for feminist linguists. Being "good" is not a natural attribute but one constructed through the interplay of language and social expectation. "Bad" girls and women may pose problems for neat theories and hence be eliminated from research as atypical. What research does exist often succumbs to the urge to pathologize or exoticize such speakers. Conversely, speakers who conform precisely to cultural stereotypes of femininity, such as the drag queens in Rusty Barrett's study (chapter 16), are nevertheless almost entirely overlooked in language and gender research, not because of their anomalous femininity but because of their anomalous femaleness (but for examples of the growing scholarship on language and gender transgression, see Gaudio 1997; Hall & O'Donovan 1996; Kulick 1996). Barrett's chapter demonstrates the limitations of traditional definitions of the speech community as the locus of language and identity, for as developed in sociolinguistics by William Labov (1972a, [1972c]), membership in the speech community is a measure of cultural and linguistic authenticity as determined by gender, class, ethnicity, and other social factors. The artifice of many linguistic performances and practices cannot be accounted for in the Labovian framework. My study (chapter 18) of the shopping channel as an artificial community that constructs its own authenticity from consumers' linguistic practices indicates that authenticity is itself a production, not an objective measure of community membership and identity.

To display a transgressive identity is to risk not only exclusion but also retribution. Thus as A. C. Liang (chapter 15) shows, gay and lesbian speakers whose identities may put them in danger develop self-protective linguistic practices that allow them to reveal their identities only to those who are likely to be sympathetic. In a world where simply *being* can count as being bad, identities are often constructed in opposition to dominant cultural ideologies.

. . . As women change the shape of cultural discourse, the contours of intellectual discourse are changing as well . . . Many chapters in this book also contribute implicitly or explicitly to the recent project to interrogate previously invisible hegemonic categories such as whiteness, masculinity, heterosexuality, and the middle class . . . New approaches to power in language and gender scholarship likewise require that linguists recognize their own complicity in the reproduction of inequities based on gender, race, class, and other factors. Marcyliena Morgan (chapter 1) describes the social and cultural censure that many African Americans level against the act of "breaking bad," or pretending to a level of knowledge that one does not in fact have. Unlike the other forms of researcher "badness" delineated above, "breaking bad" cannot be recuperated for feminist use, for it results in acts of scholarly negligence and harm ranging from wrongful omission to misrepresentation to out-and-out inaccuracies. Both Morgan and Sara Trechter point out instances in which linguists represent dominated social groups as exotic "others" who are portrayed as fundamentally different from the normative, dominant group. Their work reminds language and gender scholars that reflexivity must always be a part of research and that as we move further from the confines of "good-girl" research we have an increasingly heavy obligation to describe speakers and the worlds in which they move without the distorting effects of our own cultural and intellectual ideologies about how such speakers "should" or "must" be. Considering how linguistics itself has contributed to the promotion of such ideologies will help ensure that as we strive to be "bad examples," we do not produce bad research.

Task B4.2.2: After you've read

➤ Make a list of some of the topics covered in *Reinventing Identities*, as well as important theoretical concepts flagged here. Make notes for yourself about the meanings of these different concepts.

Cynthia Nelson (2002) 'Why queer theory is useful in teaching: a perspective from English as a Second Language teaching', in K. Robinson, J. Irwin and T. Ferfolja (eds) *From Here to Diversity: the social impact of lesbian and gay issues in education in Australia and New Zealand*. Binghampton, NY: Haworth Press, pp. 43–53

This last extract in Unit B4 is from an article by Cynthia Nelson on 'queer theory'. Queer theory is a relatively new field, prompted by but going beyond and indeed critiquing Lesbian and Gay Studies. Shaped by post-structuralism in general and the work of Judith Butler (for example, 1990, 1999, 2004) in particular, it has great theoretical relevance to current gender and language study, entailing the need for continual problematisation and (as we saw in the extract from Mary Bucholtz) a vigilant reflexivity. Queer theory's influence on current thinking in gender and language study remains both profound and radical, and its influence on the discourses circulating around gender and language study is evident. The literature on it is growing (for example, Cameron and Kulick 2003, Jagose 1996).

Queer theory may also have professional applications: in her paper Nelson establishes its relevance to the teaching of English as a second language, for example in the way it addresses the notions of diversity and possible miscommunication in multicultural settings. Nelson has thus been a forerunner in the field in applying queer theory to language education. Queer theory's value for political activism and intervention is, however, less evident: 'The point is not so much to debate as to analyse' (2002: 50).

The following sections from Nelson's article look first at what queer theory is, and second at its applications to teaching in general and language education in particular.

 ### Task B4.3.1: Before you read

➤ What do you already know about queer theory? Make notes to remind yourself.

➤ Can you think of some political or theoretical limitations (or problems) associated with not going beyond promoting tolerance of minority groups, and inclusion of their members?

➤ In what ways can assigning a group to a category be helpful or a hindrance? For whom?

C. Nelson

Why queer theory originated

. . . As the gay/lesbian movement and community gained visibility and political clout, the focus began to shift from what its "members" had in common to what they did not. Gathered together under the political/cultural umbrella of a gay movement were people who identified as lesbian, gay, bisexual, and transgendered. Their sexual practices, sexual values, relationship styles, multiple identities, and political affiliations were not only diverse but in some cases conflicting. Meanwhile, critical theorists and linguists were theorizing identities not as socially constructed facts but as cultural and discursive acts (e.g., Gumperz & Cook-Gumperz, 1982; Le Page & Tabouret-Keller, 1985).

Task B4.3.2: Reflection task

➤ To what extent, intellectually, do you think identities can be theorised as 'discursive acts'?

➤ To what extent are you *comfortable* with the idea that identities are 'discursive acts'? For example, do you feel that you have an 'identity' which is in some sense independent of your discourse and that of those around you?

As a result of practical and theoretical challenges to identity-based social movements, in the mid-1980s queer theory and activism were developed. Whereas sexual identity formed the very basis of the lesbian/gay movement and community, queer theory makes sexual identity the subject of critique. The word "queer" is used to encompass "lesbian," "gay," "bisexual," and "transgender," but "queer" is also used to challenge clear-cut notions of sexual identity, purposely blurring the boundaries between identity categories (Warner, 1993). The paradoxical tension between the two meanings of queer – on the one hand including all "minority" sexual identities and on the other protesting the very notion of sexual identity – is central to queer theory.

C. Nelson

Why queer theory is useful in teaching

Theorizing sexual identities as acts rather than facts

According to queer theory, gay identity is not discovered and then expressed, but is actually produced through repeated discursive acts. In other words, sexual identities are not descriptive but performative – not what people are but what they do (Butler, 1990, drawing on Austin's [1962] notion of linguistic performativity). In this view, sexual identities are not personal attributes or individual constructions but culturally readable acts that are being created or "performed" during social interactions.

From a teaching or training perspective, there are several advantages to theorizing sexual identities as culturally readable acts rather than inner, universal essences. For one, this situates sexual identities within the realm of the ordinary – negotiating day-to-day interactions routinely involves "performing" and interpreting sexual identities. Secondly, it keeps the focus on observable behavior – what people say and do rather than who they feel they are. This is useful in those teaching contexts (such as ESL) where a major objective is to demystify social interactions unfamiliar to those who are new to, or outside of, a particular culture or subculture. With queer theory, it becomes possible to examine the linguistic and cultural patterns through which sexual identities are communicated, even constituted. Finally, the notion of "performativity" makes it clear that sexual identities are not universally accomplished but may be produced or "read" in different ways in different cultural contexts (see Livia & Hall, 1997). Acknowledging this diversity, and being able to examine it, are crucial to achieving intercultural understanding.

Extension

Problematizing all sexual identities rather than legitimizing subordinate ones

Lesbian/gay activism has sought to ensure that people who do not identify as hetero-sexual are not denied the same rights and privileges that are automatically accorded to those who do identify as heterosexual. Implicit to such efforts is the notion that it is possible, even desirable, to categorize people according to sexual identities. But queer theorists caution that sexual identities can be limiting as well as liberating, for they rely on exclusion as well as inclusion (Butler, 1991; Fuss, 1991; see also Foucault, 1990). In this view, affirming subordinate sexual identities has the (unintended) effect of reinforcing a hierarchical system, one that insists on solidifying sexualities into sexual identities, which can then be divided into those that are considered socially "acceptable" and those that are not. Rather than affirming sexual identity categories, queer theory questions the need for them. Rather than legitimizing minority sexual identities, queer theory problematizes all sexual identities.

In terms of teaching and learning, problematizing sexual identities does not mean presenting them in negative ways. On the contrary, it makes it possible to explore how acts of identity are not necessarily straightforward or transparent but can be complex, changing, and contested. It also acknowledges that, for a myriad of reasons, not everyone relates to a clear-cut identity category. To put it another way, acknowledging that identities are not truths, facts or things, but theoretical constructs that "arise at specific times, in specific places, to do specific work" (Poynton, 1997, p. 17) does not dismiss the need for identities nor their limitations. Instead, this approach makes it possible to ask what purpose identities serve, how they work, and also what constraints, dilemmas, or contradictions may be associated with them. In the end, problematizing all sexual identities may actually be more "inclusive" than simply validating subordinate sexual identities, because it allows for a wider range of experiences and perspectives to be considered. It may also be more practicable, since teachers or trainers are not expected to transmit knowledge (which they may or may not have) but to frame tasks that encourage investigation and inquiry.

Considering sexual identities potentially significant to anyone

Queer theorists discuss a "heterosexual/homosexual binary" by which sexual identities are defined. The argument is that questions of definition are meaningful not just to "a small, distinct, relatively fixed homosexual minority" ("a minoritizing view") but to "people across the spectrum of sexualities" ("a universalizing view") (Sedgwick, 1990, p. 1). One reason for this is that the hetero/homosexual binary shapes the production of all sexual identities – not just gay ones. That is, "heterosexuality" has meaning only in relation to "homosexuality," and vice versa, since the two terms are necessarily relational and interdependent (Fuss, 1991; Sedgwick, 1990; see also Weedon, 1987, p. 23 on Saussure's "sign theory"). In other words, straightness does not exist sepa-rately from gayness but is in fact defined by it (and vice versa). Furthermore, sexual identity is experienced or accomplished "in a particular class-, race-, or gender-mediated way, and only so" (Seidman, 1993, pp. 136–137); likewise, cultural identity is "done" differently depending on one's sexual identity (see Mac An Ghaill, 1994). When identities are understood to be not just multiple but mutually inflecting (see Pallotta-Chiarolli, 1996; Phelan, 1994), it becomes clear that to understand the workings of any domain of identity (e.g., gender) it is necessary to consider that domain as part of, or in relation to, the domain of sexual identity. Lastly, according to queer theorists the significance of the hetero/homosexual binary extends far beyond identities. This binary is a pervasive, shaping force throughout "Western" knowledges and discourses. Its cultural significance is as great as other powerful binaries such as masculine/feminine or bourgeois/proletariat (Sedgwick, 1990). Thus, classifying sexual identities involves more than just sexualities but extends to cultural patterns of thinking and living.

The application of queer theory to teaching or training contexts allows for acknowledgment that issues pertaining to sexual identities might be relevant to anyone, not just gay people, and for a range of reasons. This wider focus allows everyone, whatever their own positioning with regard to sexual identity, to participate in and contribute to the discussion. This may also help to counter any tendency to reductively construct people as either toler*ated* or toler*ant* (see Britzman, 1995, pp. 159–160). Also, considering sexual identity and other "acts of identity" as interconnected, even mutually constitutive, underscores the broad relevance of matters pertaining to sexual identities. Furthermore, learning opportunities are opened up when the hetero/homosexual binary is seen as working on and in a wide range of social and cultural practices, not just sexualities.

Looking at how certain sexual identities are (or are not) made to seem normal

Of primary concern within lesbian/gay identity-based theory and politics has been the promotion of tolerance and social justice in order to challenge and transform prejudicial attitudes (homophobia) and discriminatory systems and actions (heterosexism). Queer theorists, however, are concerned with analyzing cultural knowledges and discourses: "The roots of heterosexism are not socialization, prejudice, tradition, or scapegoating, but a basic way of organizing knowledges and fields of daily life which are deeply articulated in the core social practices of Western societies" (Seidman, 1995, p. 135). Queer theorists have therefore coined the term "heteronormativity," which refers to making heterosexuality – and only heterosexuality – seem normal or natural (Warner, 1993).

Identifying norms and analyzing how they operate may prove useful educationally for several reasons. First of all, the focus is not on whether a particular sexual identity is normal or natural, or even whether it *should* be considered natural, but on what makes it *seem* natural (or unnatural). (This follows Foucault's [1980, p. 118] interest not in discovering "truth" but in analyzing how "the effects of truth" are produced.) The point is not so much to debate as to analyze. Secondly, attempting to identify cultural and linguistic norms makes it possible to recognize not only prevailing norms but also competing norms. In linguistically and/or culturally heterogeneous groups it may be especially important to underscore the fact that norms are not static or universal but context-specific, changing, and contested. Lastly, and perhaps most importantly, making norms explicit enables people to make choices that are more informed and therefore more strategic as they position themselves in relation to those norms.

A focus on inquiry

An emphasis on inclusion, which adds subordinate sexual identities and aims to validate them, may be less effective than an emphasis on inquiry, which seeks to understand how language, culture, and social interactions operate with respect to all sexual identities. An inquiry approach follows queer theory in theorizing sexual identities as acts rather than facts, problematizing all sexual identities rather than legitimizing subordinate ones, recognizing the broad significance of sexual identities, and looking at how certain sexual identities are (or are not) made to seem normal. In culturally and linguistically diverse groups, a focus on investigating sexual identities as socially situated practices may be more useful than a focus on promoting "tolerance" of those who identify as gay. Educationally, the aim, as Burbules (1997, p. 111) puts it, should not be "[t]olerance of difference, or for that matter celebrations of difference," but "the critical re-examination of difference, the questioning of our own systems of difference, and what they mean for ourselves and for other people." It is this sort of inquiry that a queer theory approach invites.

 Task B4.3.3: After you've read

➤ In what way(s) can queer theory be seen as an advance on the promotion of lesbian and gay rights and on inclusion?

➤ On a political level, what can and do notions of inclusion and tolerance of minority groups and their members achieve? Can they ever work completely, for example in terms of removing prejudice and discrimination? If not, why not?

➤ What do you see as the advantages, theoretical and political, of problematising all sexual identities?

Unit B5
Developing understandings of language: Language change

Unit B5 consists of extracts from an article, a chapter and a specially commissioned piece which all point to the importance of language change: a topic important to early feminist linguistics (and indeed linguistic activism), but one which has proved problematic, unpredictable and theoretically exciting.

Alma Graham (1975) 'The making of a non-sexist dictionary', in Barrie Thorne and Nancy Henley (eds) *Language and Sex: difference and dominance.* **Rowley, Mass.: Newbury House, pp. 57–63**

Text B5.1
A. Graham

Alma Graham's 1975 article 'The making of a non-sexist dictionary', first appeared in *Ms.* magazine in 1973, a time when questions of linguistic sexism were being newly and hotly debated and fought over. The *American Heritage School Dictionary* project however had begun in 1969 – right at the start of the 'second wave' of the (western) Women's Movement (then the 'Women's Liberation Movement').

Graham's article falls into three parts: a description of the diversity of masculine bias in reading material schoolchildren encounter; an exemplification of sexism in English; and a description of the new, non-sexist *American Heritage School Dictionary*, for which the reading material data provided inverse guidelines. This extract largely comes from the first and third parts.

Task B5.1.1: Before you read

A. Dictionary study

➤ Have a look at any 'standard' dictionary.

➤ How is each 'entry' organised?

➤ How might a non-sexist dictionary actively use these conventions of the dictionary 'genre'?

➤ Write a complete dictionary entry for a progressive item to be included in an explicitly non-sexist dictionary.

B. Teachers and issues of sexist and non-sexist language

➤ How do you think teachers of English as a foreign or second language should deal with questions of language change in relation to gender?

A. Graham

The first dictionary to define *sexism*, to include the phrase *liberated women*, and to recognize Ms. was a wordbook for children published in 1972 by American Heritage Publishing Company.

The American Heritage School Dictionary contains 35,000 entries, which were selected after an unprecedented analysis of 5 million words encountered by American children in their schoolbooks.

When the task of compilation began in 1969, we could not predict that the dictionary would be the first ever published in which lexicographers made a conscious effort to correct the sex biases that exist in English as it is commonly used. But the computer revealed a pattern that we who were editing the dictionary could not ignore: in schoolbooks, whether the subject is reading, mathematics, social studies, art, or science, males command center stage . . .

Peter Davies, the editor in chief of the school dictionary, was the first to recognize what else the computer had delivered. To Davies, the vast body of words was a reflection of the culture talking to its children. He suspected that if imaginatively used, the computer could also supply a profile of what was being said between the lines.

For example, Davies noticed that when adults write for one another, they refer to young people as *children*, almost as often as they call them *boys* and *girls*. When writing books and stories for children, however, adults use the gender words boy and girl twice as often as the neutral words *child* and *children*. When the culture talks to its children, it is careful to distinguish them by sex. Moreover, no matter what the subject being taught, girls and women are always in a minority. Overall, the ratio in schoolbooks of *he* to *she*, *him* to *her*, and *his* to *hers* was almost four to one. Even in home economics, the traditional preserve of the female, the pronoun *he* predominated by nearly two to one.

It was suggested that some of those excess *he*'s might apply not to boys and men but to the unspecified singular subject, as in: a person . . . he; a student . . . his; someone . . . him. To check this out I made a survey of pronoun citations from an earlier, experimental sampling of 100,000 words. Out of 940 citations for *he*, 744 were applied to male human beings, 128 to male animals, and 36 to persons such as farmers and sailors who were assumed to be male. Only 32 referred to the unspecified singular subject. The conclusion was inescapable: the reason most of the pronouns in schoolbooks were male in gender was because most of the subjects being written about were men and boys.

In the real world, there are 100 women for every 95 men. Yet in the books read by schoolchildren, there are over seven times as many men as women and over twice as many boys as girls.

Then another oddity came to light. Despite the preponderance of the words *man* and *boy* in textbooks, the word *mother* occurs more frequently than the word *father*, and the word *wife* is used three times as often as the word *husband*. Women, it would seem, are typecast in the supporting roles that refer to their relationships to men and children.

Might this fact simply imply that in the world of the elementary school the mother is seen as the chief parent? The situation changes when the subject words analyzed are not *mother* and *father* but *daughter* and *son*. An examination of citation slips showed

A. Graham

that four times as many sons and daughters are referred to as the children of a male parent (Jim's son; the landlord's daughter) as of a female parent (her son; Mrs. Greenwood's daughter).

Other kinship-term citations revealed still more about this schoolbook never-never land. Two out of every three mothers are mentioned in relation to male children. Father references are even more extreme: four out of every five fathers are fathers of a male. And there's more bald bias: twice as many uncles as aunts, and of those aunts, four times as many have nephews (Charley's aunt) as have nieces (Nelly's aunt); sons outnumber daughters by better than two to one, and every single firstborn child is a son.

Where have all the young girls gone?

It seems clear that they have grown up and have been given (or taken) in marriage—because in schoolbooks wives are three times as numerous as husbands, showing that the speakers or main characters are males . . . Farmers' wives and farm wives (but no farm husbands) appear in citations, as do diplomats' wives and Cabinet wives.

Obviously, the basic imbalance in male/female pairs was far more than simply a numbers game. The 700,000 computer citation slips contained the evidence that boys and girls were also being taught separate sets of values, different expectations, and divergent goals. Boys in the schoolbooks ran races, rode bicycles, drove fast cars, and took off in spaceships for Mars. Girls, on the other hand, were less concerned with doing than with being. After reading, "He was the manliest of his sex and she was the loveliest of hers," a child would say that the word comparable to *manly* was *lovely*, not *womanly*. In the sentence, "The men are strong, virile, and graceful, and the girls often beauties," we note that girls, not women, are paired with men and that *virile* is parallel to *beautiful*. A feminine figure, a feminine voice, and a feminine laugh are no match for masculine prerogatives, masculine egos, and masculine drives. The "mannish uniform" of a female general in the Chinese Army is condemned by the very adjective that describes it, but three modifiers commend "a very feminine dream gown."

Task B5.1.2: Reflection task

➤ Does any of the above ring true of your own education, or of schoolbooks that you have seen but which are not used any more?

➤ Does any of it explicitly contrast with modern schoolbooks with which you are familiar?

A. Graham

If this new dictionary were to serve elementary students without showing favoritism to one sex or the other, an effort would have to be made to restore the gender balance. We would need more examples featuring females, and the examples would have to ascribe to girls and women the active, inventive, and adventurous human traits traditionally reserved for men and boys.

Our new archetypal woman took form gradually. Each of the dozen editors writing and reviewing word entries had special moments of insight and decision when we recognized her presence among us. Mine came at the word *brain*, where a computer citation asserted "he has *brains* and courage." In what seemed at the time an act of audacity, I changed the pronoun. "She has *brains* and courage."

A. Graham

As the number of word entries grew, the new woman made her way from example to example, establishing her priorities, aspirations, and tastes. She was "a woman of dedicated political principles." She "made a *name* for herself" and "everyone *praised* her good sense and learning." When she "*plunged* into her work, her mind began to *percolate*" (not her coffee), and "she *prided* herself on her eloquence" (not on the sheen of her freshly waxed floors).

Her appearances in the dictionary were widely separated, of course. Her brothers and traditional sisters continued to surround and outnumber her, example for example. But she had arrived, and from A, where at *abridge* she quoted the 19th Amendment, to Z, when "she *zipped* down the hill on her sled," her spirit, character, and credentials were never in doubt.

As the feminists—male and female—who had brought her into the lexicon cheered her on, "her *determination* to win" was bolstered by our "*devout* wish for her success."

Men in the dictionary examples continued to be active and daring, competitive and combative; but the liberated man could be vulnerable, too. He might be "striving to attain *mastery* over his emotions," but he was not disgraced if "his resolve began to *waver*" or if "tears *welled* up in his eyes." Like the new woman, he had a freer choice of careers than heretofore: 'He *teaches* kindergarten" and "he *studies* typing at night."

Ms. was the new word we watched with the greatest degree of interest. Some of us favored adopting it right away, but a problem arose over its pronunciation: it was an abbreviation that anyone could write but that no one could say. Arguments over "miz" or "mis" or "em es" continued through the summer. Then, in October, Bruce Bohle, our usage editor, urged that we enter Ms. in the dictionary as an abbreviation whether or not the title could be pronounced with ease. Thus supported, I wrote the definition . . .

Ms. or Ms An abbreviation used as a title of courtesy before a woman's last name or before her given name and last name, whether she is married or not.

Alma Graham continues by exemplifying further forms of linguistic sexism, including labelling the 'exception to the rule' (*woman* doctor, *male* nurse, career *girl*).

A. Graham

To fight these sexist habits of language, the school dictionary had to avoid gender assumptions that other dictionaries imposed more through custom than necessity. *Youth*, one dictionary said, is "the part of life between childhood and manhood." *Youth*, we said, is "the time of life before one is an adult." *Sex*, itself, we defined straightforwardly, with impersonal examples, avoiding a rival dictionary's use of "the fair, gentle, or weaker sex" and "the sterner or stronger sex" dichotomy.

While we were working our way through the alphabet, other word watchers were already speaking out. In Venice, California, Varda One (formerly Varda Murrell) was analyzing and commenting on a phenomenon she called "Manglish." We could not counter her criticism that dictionaries give less space to *woman* than to *man*. This is not the fault of the dictionary makers, but of a language in which the same word denotes both the human species as a whole and those of its members who are male. In English, contradictory propositions are true: a woman is a man; a woman is not a man . . . .

The American Heritage School Dictionary defines sexism as "discrimination by members of one sex against the other, especially by males against females." In order to avoid sexism in language that has come to sound "natural," we devised logical sex-blind substitutes. When referring to the human species, the dictionary employs the term *human beings*, not *man* or *men*.

In our efforts to reduce the superabundance of words referring to the male, we found it was possible to use the word *person* or a more specific substitute instead of *man*. The best man for the job is the best person or candidate; a 12-man jury is a 12-member jury; a real-estate man is a real-estate agent; and machines are used for work formerly done by people or by human beings—not by men.

To avoid unnecessary use of the pronoun *he*, we frequently shifted from the singular to the plural. Instead of saying "insofar as he can, the scientist excludes bias from his thinking," it is easy to change to *they*, *scientists*, and *their*. Plural pronouns desex themselves. The use of *one* is also convenient. A breadwinner, for example, can be "one who supports a family or household by his or her earnings."

Because of our conscious efforts, the nonsexist dictionary is as free of discrimination against either sex as the reformist editors could make it. But as proud as we are of our lexicographers' revolution, writing a nonsexist school dictionary is only the barest beginning. Most schoolbooks still reflect the assumptions of our sexist society. As writers and teachers and parents, we have an obligation now to weigh our words, to examine them, and to use them with greater care. Children of both sexes deserve equal treatment, in life and in language, and we should not offer them anything less.

Task B5.1.3: After you've read

➤ List and categorise the linguistic problems identified in the schoolbooks.

➤ List and categorise the linguistic solutions and strategies adopted in the creation of the *American Heritage School Dictionary*.

➤ From what we read here, has the dictionary addressed all the problems identified? Have any problems of 'sexist language' been neither identified nor addressed?

Sara Mills (2006) 'Changes in sexist language use'

Text B5.2
S. Mills

What counts as a 'sexist' language item, and how it might best be responded to, are, with the benefit of hindsight, far less straightforward now than Graham's early, upbeat piece suggested. In the next (specially commissioned) piece, Sara Mills exemplifies how, several decades later, feminist linguists face a different set of challenges.

Task B5.2.1: Before you read

➤ Consider how you would analyse these two short texts:

■ this advertising text for Yorkie chocolate bars (which Mills discusses): 'NOT FOR GIRLS: YOU DON'T WANT TO BREAK YOUR NAILS!'
■ the byline of the (heterosexual) UK men's 'lifestyle' magazine *Loaded*, which is *for men who should know better*.

In the 1970s and 1980s it seemed very clear to many feminists what sexism was. Sexism was defined as language that discriminated against women by representing them negatively or that seemed to implicitly assume that activities primarily associated with women were necessarily trivial (Vetterling-Braggin 1981). The aim of feminists therefore was to call attention to the way in which certain language items seemed to systematically discriminate against and cause offence to women, by compiling lists of such language items in dictionaries and to call for people and institutions to avoid using them (Kramarae and Treichler 1985, Doyle 1994, Miller and Swift 1982, Mills 1989, Mills 1995, Schultz 1990). These language items ranged from the use of 'girl' to refer to grown women, as in 'weathergirl', to the use of demeaning titles for jobs where women workers were in the majority, for example 'lollipop lady' and 'school-marm'. Many feminists enthusiastically adopted this cause and lobbied within their workplaces for changes to be made to the way language was used in official documents and discussed the messages which this usage seemed to be giving to their employees. Feminists often compiled lists of alternative terms that could be used, for example, 'chairperson' or 'convenor' could be used instead of 'chairman'; and 'Ms' could be used to refer to women so that the woman's marital status was not referred to. Pauwels (1998) charts the changes which have been brought about in a large number of European languages because of the campaigns of feminists to change language use – changes that are sometimes simply a matter of vocabulary choice and sometimes questions of grammatical features such as pronouns and word endings. These changes to the language have made a vital difference to many women who felt under-represented in the language. For example, when the so-called generic pronoun is used to refer to groups of people (e.g. *When the student has finished his exam he should hand in his paper to the invigilator*), many women felt that this usage was confusing since it was unclear whether it referred only to males or was in fact being used to refer to students in general. Such sentences using the generic pronoun had the additional effect of affirming the markedness of female reference (i.e. male is the norm and female is the marked form) and contributed to the general invisibility of females within the language. Feminist campaigns to use pronouns that are genuinely generic has led to a radical change in the usage of generic pronouns, so that it is rare now to encounter 'he' used generically, since publishers advise authors not to use them and generally edit out such usage, and institutions such as trades unions have produced guidelines for usage.

However, other feminists, such as Cameron in her work on 'verbal hygiene', have sounded a note of caution that this proposed reform of language seems very like conservative and perhaps reactionary reforming movements which had very problematic views about the nature of language (Cameron 1995[a]). Furthermore, Cameron suggests that the 'gender-free language' policies that institutions adopted seemed to her like 'the symbolic concession you can make to feminism without ruining your dominant status' (Cameron 1998: 155). Thus, for her, although it was necessary to draw people's attention to the way that certain language items might be considered to entail negative attitudes to women, suggesting alternative terms that might be used did not tackle the sexist attitudes of speakers, but merely enabled them to mask their sexist attitudes behind more 'politically correct' terminology (see also Dunant 1994). Many feminists noted the problems that had developed within campaigns around language use because of the development of the term 'political correctness', which was used initially by feminists and other language campaigners as an ironic term, but which was taken up largely by the media to mock the efforts of language campaigners. Those who were critical of 'political correctness' suggested that language campaigners had a sense of a 'correct' term which should be used and hence an over-punctilious approach to language, and also were obsessing needlessly over trivial language issues whilst more important political issues were being neglected (Mills 2003|a|). Thus, it became very difficult to discuss sexism without being accused of a concern with 'political correctness', and 'sexism' itself as a term started to feel very anachronistic.

Alongside these developments, changes seem to be occurring within sexism itself. Instead of overt sexism, a new more indirect form of sexism seems to have developed. Thus, it has started to be possible for people to make overtly sexist statements in a very knowing 'postmodern' way, drawing attention to the ludicrous nature of such attitudes, but at the same time keeping those sexist attitudes in play. For example, on BBC's Radio 1 in the UK, DJ Chris Moyles often uses overtly sexist terms such as 'tart' and 'dippy' to his female colleagues, but he does so by framing these remarks within an ironic, playful mode. When challenged about the use of such terms, the BBC generally responds by suggesting that Moyles is adopting a persona and his use of these terms should be seen to be making fun of such sexist usage. For many feminists, there is thus little possibility of contesting this usage without appearing puritanical and humourless. Another example is the advertising campaign for Yorkie bars, where the chocolate bar is advertised as 'Not for girls', and the advertisement suggests that women are not 'man' enough to eat such large bars of chocolate. However, this advert seems to mock sexist attitudes at the same time that it keeps them in play; for example, it seems to be taking stereotypes of masculinity and femininity to the limit, representing them humorously and ironically (the image of a woman that is used on the advertisement is of a silhouette of a woman with a handbag) and it is therefore difficult for its sexism to be pinned down or challenged. This type of ironising of one's position seems also to be very common in conversation; for example, in a recent meeting, one of my male colleagues received a phone call on his mobile and he said 'It's OK; it's just the wife'. When several female staff laughed and objected to this usage, he said that he assumed that we would know that he was being ironic, taking on board feminist concerns about language usage, and being playful.

A further difficulty encountered in language and gender research in relation to the analysis of sexism, is that very often there will no longer be agreement on what constitutes sexism. For example, a male colleague used the phrase 'you guys', a phrase that seems on the surface to refer to males, to refer to a mixed-sex group of researchers he was addressing; when some of the female members of the group objected to this usage, another of the females present stated that she herself used 'you guys' to address mixed-sex groups, and that she felt that this did not in fact seem to her to be sexist at all; she argued that although it may have started as a term that referred to males, because of its usage in American surfing culture especially, it had begun to be used as a generic term that could refer equally to males and females.

Thus, linguistic sexism can no longer be viewed as a set of lexical items where the meaning somehow resides within the words themselves, and, although it is necessary to bring people's attention to the offence that using discriminatory language can cause, there is a sense in which feminists have begun to recognise that there is a lack of agreement on what exactly constitutes sexism, particularly since, as I have shown above, sexism is now being used in playful and ironising ways. If one decides that a particular usage of a word is sexist, it may be judged to be so only in that particular context, rather than across the board, in every context of its usage. Furthermore, it has to be recognised that if someone is determined to be sexist, they will use different means to do so. Thus, for example, in a meeting that I chaired within a primary school, I asked if it would be possible not to refer to me as a 'chairman', which one of the older male members of the committee insisted on doing. The meeting agreed to this measure; however, whenever this member of the committee had to refer to me, he always used 'chairperson' with an exaggerated pronunciation, pronouncing it louder than the rest of his utterance and always prefacing it with an intake of breath and a pause. On the face of it, he had gone along with my insistence that we use a form of language that could be seen as anti-sexist, but he made his discomfort with such terminology evident by his pronunciation and pacing. On my part, this made it very difficult to challenge his marked usage, as it is impossible to label as sexist someone's pausing and pronunciation, although it was clear to everyone at the meeting that this was what his language usage meant. Thus, feminists now need to maintain a careful balance between analysing those usages that seem to be more generally sexist (for example, the generic pronoun, and insulting and degrading terms), but at the same time investigating those usages which contextually might be considered to be sexist but which are so indirectly rather than overtly.

 Task B5.2.2: After you've read

➤ Is Cameron right to suggest that use of non-sexist language can simply mask sexist attitudes?

➤ Have you had the experience of reading a 'gendered' text, yet not knowing quite how to take it? Or, have you interpreted a text as being, for example, sexist, while someone else sees it otherwise?

Juliane Schwarz (2003) 'Quantifying non-sexist language: the case of Ms', in Srikant Sarangi and Theo van Leeuwen (eds) *Applied Linguistics and Communities of Practice*. London: BAAL/Continuum, pp. 169–83

Drawing on ethnography, one approach to the study of sexist language is to interview users about their practices and understandings. An early example is Barbara Bate, who found that men reported that they were more likely to change their language use given 'the presence of significant females who are sufficiently credible . . . to be listened to when they propose changing a language habit' (1978: 148). More recently, Juliane Schwarz (2003) was concerned with the way women of different ages understand ('conceptualise') and evaluate non-sexist language items. She writes:

> The aim of my research is to look for metalinguistic awareness of my participants, i.e. how they report on their own practice, how they evaluate non-sexist language reforms and what concepts they associate with them. This kind of qualitative method places me [within] an approach which does not assume that attitudes are cognitive processes which are fixed but

seen as being negotiated locally as discussed in Discursive Psychology (Potter, 1996; Potter and Wetherell, 1987 [see also Unit B9]).

(Schwarz 2003: 171)

Such an approach takes us beyond sociolinguistic description. Schwarz's premise being that some choices are better in a feminist sense than others, it also entails *commitment*.

Schwarz's data came from focus group discussions. Here she draws on data from three groups of female undergraduate students from various disciplines, native speakers of British English but different ages. These were:

- Late teen group (18–19): Kelly, Emma, Abi, Lisa
- Mid-thirties group (35–7): Rebecca, Louise, Kate, Gemma
- Over-fifties group (52–64): Anne, Helen, Elizabeth, Chris.

The extract below looks at Schwarz's findings as regards 'Ms'.

Task B5.3.1: Before you read

★

➤ Consider your own use, or non-use, of 'Ms'. Complete the second column of Table B5.3.1 below (men can and should do this too). Then ask women in two age groups other than your own what they think. Indicate (approximate) age groups in the table.

Conceptualisation

In the three groups, Ms is discussed in relation to the following concepts: Ms as an alternative choice, certain marital statuses and non-disclosure of marital status; Ms as indication of being a feminist or being a lesbian; and Ms as a indication of age.

Ms *as an alternative choice*

Ms as an alternative choice is discussed by Deborah Cameron as a positive outcome of non-sexist language reforms (of which she is otherwise rather critical): 'Choice has altered the value of the terms and removed the options of political neutrality' (Cameron, 1995[a]: 119).

The concept of having an alternative to Mrs and Miss is spontaneously brought up in all three groups. The idea of having a choice itself is seen to be important and rather positive for the participants, e.g. in Helen's (Over 50s Group) and Emma's (Late Teen Group) arguments as discussed above. However, the more political idea of 'not only having a choice but it being non-neutral' is not found directly in my data.

In the Mid 30s Group, Louise makes a slightly different point. Whereas Helen and Emma discuss the title as an alternative which is good to have, Louise points out that

Table B5.3.1

	Use of Ms		
	You Age Group	Woman 1 Age Group	Woman 2 Age Group
Do you use *Ms*, ever?			
If yes, in what spoken or written context(s)?			
With whom?			
To/Of whom?			
Who do you know who *typically* uses it?			
What is your attitude to the term? What do you see as its value today, if any?			

a woman using Ms might be perceived as somebody making an active choice and therefore sees Ms as a tool to convey agency and strength:

'I think Ms (..) gives (..) the idea that **you choose** (.) to be that. . . if you choose to be Ms (.) then you've decided that (.) and that's what **you** want to be' (Louise, Mid 30s Group, 154).

She compares Ms to Miss:

'. . . whereas Miss (.) you don't choose (.) because you just haven't been saved by a man (.) do you know (.) it's that (.) isn't it (.) it's like (.) if you stay at Miss (.) then (..) you're lacking something (.) because somebody else hadn't come and changed you (.) your name . . .' (Louise, Mid 30s Group, 154).

Another participant in the Mid 30s Group describes how she has to defend herself when she introduces herself as a Ms. She makes it, however, quite clear that she has the right to choose the title which she thinks best:

'when I (.) when I do say Ms (.) to some (.) some different groups (.) it's particularly older men (.) they (.) they normally go off on one . . . and I have to defend (.) why I'm saying Ms (.) and I have to explain to them the whole history behind it (.) and than eventually (.) they'll say (.) oh right (.) yeah (.) I guess you have a right to call yourself that of course (.) I've got a right to call myself anything I bloody want [laughs] but they have the attitude (.) that I have to really defend it' (Rebecca, Mid 30s Group, 160).

Ms *as indication of certain marital statuses and non-disclosure of marital status*

In the Over 50s Group and the Late Teen Group, the first reaction to the question about Ms is that the title is used by divorcees: 'because there are so many (.) erm (.) divorced ladies now (..) who prefer that . . .' (Anne, Over 50s Group, 206) and 'for me (..) em (..) the people who I know who use that are usually divorced women' (Kelly, Late Teen Group, 121).

Anne's idea that Ms is used mainly by divorced women is immediately challenged by Elizabeth in the Over 50s Group. Elizabeth does not seem to believe that Ms is a title for divorced women but that 'it was a symbol of (.) er (.) somebody who (.) refused to say (.) whether they were married or not' (Elizabeth, Over 50s Group, 209). Anne justifies her assumption by referring to her own experiences. Her daughter is divorced and uses the title.

The participants of the Late Teen Group suggest four more groups of people who might use Ms, in addition to those given above:

Women who are not married but cohabiting;
Women who do not want people to know whether they are relying on men;
Women who feel too old not to be married (and who are embarrassed about it);
Women who might think that they would be regarded differently whether they
    are married or not.

Ms *as indication of being a feminist or being a lesbian*

Some studies suggest that the new title Ms is associated by hearers with certain social identities of its user. As shown above, one such could be that Ms users are identified as being divorced. There are, however, other concepts which the title may convey in different CoPs [communities of practice], e.g. being a feminist or being a lesbian (Ehrlich and King, 1992; Pauwels, 1998, 1987).

The concept that Ms is an indicator of a feminist can be found in the utterance of just one of the participants. She makes it clear, however, that this is not the opinion of the participant herself, but of certain groups of people who construct Ms users negatively:

> but if you use Ms as well (.) I mean sometimes as you say that (..) especially to men (..) they did (.) sometimes it's like (.) you know (.) they've got that knowing look like (.) you know (.) bra-burning (.) feminist (.) bolshy (..) you know (.) manic-type person (Kate, Mid 30s Group, 157)

The association between Ms use and feminists is not made anywhere else in the discussion groups. Feminism itself, however, is brought up in the Late Teen Group in relation to Ms. One of the participants refers to feminism and Ms in three different turns. None of the others mention it but do seem to support Emma (yeah) when she argues that Ms is 'like a feminist thing'.

> I think (.) that's **like a feminist thing** [some: **yeah**] (..) to me (.) I don't know (.) that's like (.) a couple of teachers were like Ms so and so and (.) that was (.) I think (.) that was (.) **a feminist thing** (.) because they don't wanna (..) [sb yeah] they didn't want people to know whether they were married or not (.) because the fact that whether or not (.) they were (.) like (.) relying on their man (..) [J laughs] it's irrelevant (.) and it's like that (..) to me (.) that's **like a feminist thing** (Emma, Late Teen Group, 124)

Not disclosing one's marital status seems to be a 'feminist thing' for Emma because overtly married women might be seen as relying on their men. Feminism is brought up again by Emma when I ask the group whether 'there might be any point abolishing Mrs and Miss altogether'. After a pause, Emma indicates that 'there is a feminist argument for that'; for her, however, it is not necessary to abolish Miss and Mrs since neither of these titles seem to be negative.

> 147 E yeah (.) I could see (.) that there's **like a feminist argument for that** . . . but in (.) in reality I don't (..) think that that's necessary
> 148 J you don't think (.) it's (.) it's important
> 149 E no (.) cause I don't think either of them are negative (.) are they . . . I don't think either of (..) either of the Miss or Mrs are negative terms (..) if they were (.) then yeah (.) maybe that should he abolished (.) cause (.) but I (..) like I say (.) there is (.) **there is a feminist argument for it** (.) but in reality (.) I don't think it's necessary (.) that's my opinion

Emma constructs herself as aware of a feminist argument which supports the substitution of Ms for Mrs and Miss. She makes it clear, however, that this is not her own personal opinion. She distances herself from this argument by claiming that the two older titles are not negative. She constructs the 'feminist argument' as unrealistic by inserting a contrastive structure **'there is** a feminist argument for it (.) **but** in reality' (Atkinson, 1984), which indicates that the abolishing of the two older terms is not an endeavour corresponding with reality.

Unlike findings of other studies (Pauwels, 1987), Ms in this study is associated more with feminism and feminist ideas, than as an indicator of being a feminist. Similar observations can he made in relation to the concept 'Ms as indicator of being a lesbian'.

Ms as indicator of being a lesbian is mentioned only once but, as in 'Ms being a feminist', it is not the participant's own opinion but rather a hypothetical position against which she has to defend herself. In the Mid 30s Group, Rebecca lists some assumptions associated with the title by some different groups (particularly older men): 'is it because I'm a **lesbian** (.) and stuff like that (.) and there is a whole assumption that I'm a man hater' (Rebecca, Mid 30s Group, 160). Neither Rebecca nor the other participants themselves seem to associate the use of Ms with being a lesbian. There seems to be some metalinguistic awareness, however, that some groups of people do make this connection.

Ms *as an indication of age*

As indicated above, age is identified as an important factor of Ms usage by Pauwels (2003, 2001, 1998). Age is conceptualised in relation to the title in the Mid 30s Group and the Late Teen Group. In the Mid 30s Group, Rebecca explains why she prefers using Ms instead of Miss by identifying the second title as one for younger women 'I'm not a Miss (.) I'm not a girl anymore' (Rebecca, Mid 30s Group, 108).

In the Late Teen Group, age seem to be a bigger issue. It is mentioned three times and mainly in connection of being old and not married.

> some people I know (.) they use it (.) cause like (.) they feel they're quite old not to be married (..) but if (.) if they call themselves Miss (.) they think of elderly (.) spinster type (Abi, Late Teen Group, 125)

> yeah (.) you more (.) not want people to know if you weren't married (.) so you might use Ms (.) but (.) **our age** obviously (..) you not gonna be married (.) or something (Emma, Late Teen Group, 141)

> it's good that there is a choice (.) cause if women like (..) are embarrassed about the fact that they are **older and still not married** (Emma, Late Teen Group, 143)

Age thus seems to be an important concept in the choice of a female title in the youngest discussion group along with marital status. The title is seen mainly in relation to these two concepts. It is worthwhile remembering that the whole group agreed that they were non-Ms users. This implies that their present title choice, Miss, is as a temporary option which might change in the case of marriage and/or when they get older.

Task B5.3.2: After you've read

➤ Reread the sections about the focus group members whose age most nearly approximates your own. Do you share some of their conceptualisations?

➤ If you are male, do you think these conceptualisations correspond to those of women you know?

➤ Why might age make a difference to conceptualisations of non-sexist language, do you think? Is it more likely to do with maturity, the age one was at the time 'non-sexist-language' was first implemented, or both? Make speculative notes for yourself on both these possibilities, and indicate how you would investigate this empirically. Note: do not carry out the study!

Unit B6
Developing understandings of language: Context

The three sets of extracts in this unit go sequentially from the relatively micro- to the relatively macro-contextual. The first concerns the talk surrounding a written text. The second concerns the necessarily local (though not necessarily geographically constrained) idea of the CofP. The third concerns a 'cultural con-text', which spreads over a geographical region (but is not defined by national boundaries).

J. Sunderland, M. Cowley, F. Abdul Rahim, C. Leontzakou and J. Shattuck (2002) 'From representation towards discursive practices: gender in the foreign language textbook revisited', in L. Litosseliti and J. Sunderland (eds) *Gender Identity and Discourse Analysis.* **Amsterdam: John Benjamins, pp. 223–55**

Text B6.1
J. Sunderland
et al.

This extract comes from a report of a study carried out by a team. Such an approach means that more data can be collected from more sites than if one researcher works alone, and works particularly well for empirical studies in which the research question is along the exploratory lines of 'What possible range of things happens when . . . ?', and the possibilities really are unknown. Here, the research team wanted to identify as many ways as possible in which teachers dealt with 'gendered' texts – texts in which gender is salient in some way – regardless of whether the gender representation in those texts was broadly 'progressive' or 'traditional'. The challenge for the team was then to put the findings together and to theorise a 'working model' of this range of ways.

The paper was originally published in *Linguistics and Education* (2000); the following extract comes from a later (2002) version.

Task B6.1.1: Before you read

➤ Imagine that a teacher is faced with a rather traditional, conservative textbook text. In principle, in what different ways might she approach this?

➤ What are her options if she is faced with a very progressive text?

> ➤ As a student (or perhaps teacher trainer or mentor), have you ever had an experience of seeing a text being treated in class in a surprising (perhaps disappointing, perhaps enlightening) way?

> ➤ Have you ever, yourself, deliberately used a text in a way the writer most probably did not intend?

J. Sunderland et al.

Can *actual* treatment of language textbooks . . . ever be predicted? Experience suggests that different teachers will always implement a textbook differently, depending in part on the amount and kind of autonomy their teaching situation allows and expects. Even if a group of teachers intended to teach the textbook in the same way, the different behavioural responses of students, and the fact that all lessons must be 'co-productions' between teacher and learners (Swann and Graddol 1988; Allwright and Bailey 1991), mean they could never really do so.

Let us take as an example a gender-stereotypical textbook dialogue between 'Susan' and 'Pete', in which Pete speaks more, first, last, and gives Susan the information she requests. The teacher may *not* teach the dialogue in the way it is written. She may, for example, give Pete's part to Susan and Susan's to Pete, or get male students to play Pete and female students Susan, and encourage discussion of either approach, or she may turn the lesson into a (perhaps critical) discussion of some aspect of gender relations. Because of the range of pedagogic strategies and discourses which can be used in relation to a given text, then, rather than predicting, it is surely necessary to look empirically at what is done with the text in practice.

A little work has been done on teacher use of textbooks. Stodolsky, for example, working in mathematics classrooms, "found little evidence in the literature or our case studies to support the idea that teachers teach strictly by the book" (1989: 180). She identified "a real need for more study of textbook use, particularly in subjects other than the basic areas of reading and math" (1989: 181). Correspondingly, Alderson observes that "Research into aspects of the use that is actually made in class of textbooks is rare in language education" (1997: 12). As an exception, he cites Bonkowski, who found that "teachers either ignore the teachers' guides to textbooks, or make selections from the text and the teachers' guides and distort the authors' intentions" (1997: 12; see also Hutchinson 1996). Teachers do this, Bonkowski claims, because they interpret the intentions of the author through their own models of language, language learning and language teaching – to which we could add their models of gender relations and identities, and of the role of the teacher in *mediating* gender relations and identities as represented in the textbook . . .

Dendrinos in an interview with Chouliaraki cites one relevant *instance* she observed of an EFL teacher in Greece, who was teaching 'Making Predictions' through the future perfect tense. The teacher was using Dendrinos's own *Task Way English* (1988), one aim of which is to systematically question sexist stereotypes (Chouliaraki 1994). Before the teacher started on the unit, Dendrinos notes that she provided her own examples, "most of which were tremendously sex biased" ([Chouliaraki] 1994: 126). She describes how, using a photograph, the teacher says: "Now, this . . . eh . . . this poor man is having trouble with his au . . . authoritarian wife". The lesson continues:

> T: She is . . . you know, she is . . . em . . . very . . ., what is . . . very bossy and he is very weak, eh? Tell me, what will have happened . . . in five years time? Yes?

P:　Em . . . he will have had a divorce . . . ah . . . in ten years time . . . eh . . . he will have had a divorce

T:　He will . . . have divorced her, or . . . or he will have suffered more by her, OK, do you agree? (Dendrinos, 1992: 194).

Though an account of only one event, this is a telling illustration of how a non-sexist text or a whole non-sexist textbook is no guarantee that the teacher's discourse will follow suit . . .

This study: investigating gender identity and teacher talk around language textbook texts

This study thus takes as its theoretical and methodological approach the concept of 'talk around the text', as realised in teacher discourse. From a *critical* discourse perspective (Fairclough 1992[a, 1992b]), this 'talk around the text' can be seen as 'consumption' of the text, as the 'discursive practice' which may be realised, or instantiated, in different discourses, and which occurs in relation to social practices which are gendered in a variety of (often patriarchal) ways. The 'discursive practice' concept is essential – it is only when the text is unused, for example when the textbook it is in remains in the storecupboard, that there is no associated discursive practice (or practices). As soon as a text is 'consumed', it ceases to be text alone . . .

The study took the form of a project undertaken by members of the 'Language and Gender in the Classroom' (LAGIC) research group, based in the Department of Linguistics and Modern English Language, Lancaster University . . . As well as apparently gender-biased texts, we were also concerned with those that were apparently 'egalitarian' or 'progressive', which had not been a concern of the earlier text-based studies. This was because we recognised not only that such texts did exist, but also that there was no guarantee that progressive texts would be taught in the spirit their authors intended: "The most non-sexist textbook can become sexist in the hands of a teacher with sexist attitudes" (Sunderland 1994: 64).

. . . Our main research question . . . was the exploratory and relatively open one of: 'What are some different ways language teachers talk about gendered texts in the classroom?' . . . [G]iven the usual constraints of time and a need for efficiency, we decided that the best strategy would be to observe teacher talk around *already gendered texts*, when those texts were the focus of the lesson. . . . Beyond this stipulation, we agreed that, given our intention to conduct the research in *naturalistic* classroom settings, it was not possible to pre-select a text with a view to investigating the teacher's treatment of this. Having identified a suitable educational institution as a research site, we would rather find out in advance what textbook and textbook units would be taught (if any) during the data collection period, and, if one or more texts in those units were gendered, to observe those lessons. We accepted this might mean missing gendered talk around non-gendered texts.

We decided to refer to those gendered texts to be taught in the lessons we would observe as 'gender critical points' (to the best of our knowledge, our term). The gender representation might appear to maintain or exaggerate traditional gender roles (with or without irony), or might appear 'progressive', representing gender roles saliently broadened so as to extend the range of activities normally available to men or women, boys or girls. All these make available to the student representations of gender identities; all we saw as thus potentially (but only potentially) constitutive of identity.

J. Sunderland
et al.

The points were 'critical' in the sense that, having reached such a point in the textbook, the teacher *would then have to do something about the particular gender representation* (even if that something was 'playing it by the book', or ignoring it). . .

When observing the lessons, the researcher would concentrate particularly on what the teacher said when a given 'gender critical point' was reached and would take fieldnotes on the classroom discourse surrounding this. She would also audiorecord the whole lesson, with a view to transcribing the parts of the lesson(s) which included teacher talk around the 'gender critical points' . . .

Research project 1: Julie Shattuck (Portugal)

Shattuck collected her data from adult EFL classes in a British Council language school in Portugal. Her study is the only one reported in detail here, and within this her study of the teaching of the same text by two different teachers, Clive and Alison.

J. Sunderland
et al.

The textbook used by both Clive and Alison was *Upper Intermediate Matters* (1992), written by Jan Bell and Roger Gower. Shattuck identified two 'gender-critical points' in the unit to be taught: Unit 13, 'Wedding Customs'. The gender-critical points were two short texts called 'Just a piece of paper?' and 'The mayor has nine wives' [not reported here].

'Just a piece of paper'?

This text centres around a wedding between an Indian man and a Swedish woman.

J. Sunderland
et al.

The two teachers dealt with the text very differently. Alison, who taught Unit 13 in two different lessons, uses 'Just a piece of paper?' in only one, explaining in her interview that "the students were a lot younger (.) and I don't think that weddings are something they are particularly interested in talking about". In the lesson in which she did teach it, she used it, Shattuck notes, "as suggested in the TG [Teacher's Guide] as an introduction to the listening activity and the idea of arranged marriages [but] does not talk about wedding customs in any great detail" (1996:24). Shattuck observes that the other teacher, Clive, however

> uses the text as a springboard into a whole class comparison of English, Portuguese and Spanish wedding customs. He has only three students in his class, and he commented to me after the lesson (unrecorded) that he knew the topic would generate a good discussion because his students are all married women.

She then claims that Clive "confuses his students about the role of the women in an English wedding ceremony by his use of 'humour' ". He tells them that:

> the bride (.) usually (.) if it's especially for the church wedding will wear white (.) and (.) the bridesmaids (.) she will often choose the (.) the outfit for them (.) usually she chooses something horrible so they (.) don't look as good as her

Unfortunately, because of the timing of her observation of this lesson, Shattuck was not able to interview Clive. However, in retrospect, Clive is articulating what might be called a 'women beware women' discourse – arguably a discourse which is still legitimised in some contexts. Shattuck observes critically that:

> He is positioning the women as in competition with each other: the bride feels threatened by the physical appearance of her bridesmaids. . . . This fore-grounds the idea that appearance is of the utmost importance for women. In contrast, the best man's clothing is not discussed and he is described as helping the groom, not being in competition with him (1996: 27).

There may have been a measure of irony in Clive's words, which may or may not have been picked up by the students. However, no-one could blame the textbook writer for Clive's folk-stereotypical representation of brides (and, by extension, of women). Traditional representations of femininity were actually being exaggerated in Clive's chosen commentary.

In Shattuck's study of the second text, 'The mayor has nine wives', Alison ignores the text's presuppositions and remains gender-blind throughout the lesson.

Like 'Just a piece of paper?', then, Shattuck's second example of the discourse around a text in the classroom also illustrates convincingly how studies of the text as product alone must be limited. In particular, it illustrates how discourses which are widely available, at least in most Western contexts – in this case, feminist or legitimised 'Equal Opportunities' discourses – are not always taken up. However, this lack of take-up on Alison's part may not be monolithic: one reading . . . is, as Shattuck words it, that Alison can be seen as 'indirectly challenging' the superficially positive representation of polygamy, and her gender-neutral stance can (if with difficulty) be read similarly. Alison is thus not in any straightforward way endorsing traditional representations of gender roles; however, she can be seen as missing an opportunity for class discussion which could have interestingly challenged such representations, and, in addition, have been pedagogically useful . . .

Reports of the other studies follow.

Developing a working analytical framework

. . . we could now draw up the following chart to represent our empirical findings in relation to the 'gender critical points' of the relevant textbook texts. It is, of course, a highly interpretive analysis, as well as one which comes from a particular (broadly feminist) standpoint. The question mark under 'Alison' functions as a reminder that it may not always be possible even to interpret. Table [B6.1.1] is thus a representation of the different empirically-observed forms of teacher discourse around the various texts.

We can conceptually add to this Angela's [French teacher's] observation [in an interview] that she made fun of stereotypical representations, and Jonathan's [German teacher's, also in an interview] that he would comment on them, which can both be seen as potential forms of *subversion of traditional gender representation*. What was now needed was a working *model* of analysis of teachers' discourse around gender in textbooks, one that took account of both the text itself, and of what is said about it. Such a model could then be used for analysis of other gendered texts in conjunction

J. Sunderland et al.

J. Sunderland et al.

J. Sunderland et al.

Table [B6.1.1] Discursive practices as perceived by the researchers from the 'Teacher talk around the texts'

Text	*'Just a piece of paper?'*	*The mayor has nine wives*	*Babysitting*	*It takes all sorts*		*Dear Markus*
Teacher	Clive	Alison	Nancy	Anna	Martha	Jonathan
Discursive practices/ 'Teacher talk around the text'	Exaggerates traditional gender representation	?	Ignores non-traditional gender representation	Subverts non-traditional gender representation	Endorses non-traditional gender representation	Ignores traditional gender representation

J. Sunderland et al.

with the way in which they are talked about by teachers. We will now outline such a model [see Figure [B6.1.1]], informed both by the findings and by the group's subsequent discussion of these.

The model is in the form of a classification system which can accommodate the different *discursive practices* accorded to different *text types* ... We ... decided to retain as working descriptors of gendered texts *as they stand* the dichotomy we had learned to use: 'going beyond a traditional representation of gender roles' and 'maintaining a traditional representation of gender roles'. Operationalising these requires a relatively high level of inference and sensitivity on the part of the analyst but simultaneously takes account of her/his understandings and perceptions as valid and useful. The dichotomy alone may not allow for irony, or for 'non-approving' reasons for traditional gendered behaviour represented in texts. However, if inference and

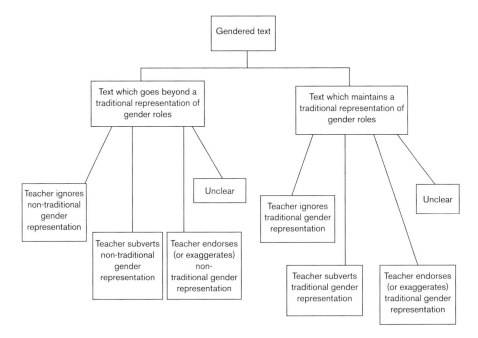

Figure [B6.1.1] A working model of gendered discursive practices in relation to textbook texts

interpretation on the part of the (sensitive) analyst are seen as productive, these can be accommodated.

Moving from this 'text descriptor' part of the model to the 'discursive practice' level, the model can now be informed by the empirical findings of the study as presented in Table |B6.1.1|. The categories here are essentially data-related rather than an expression of a philosophy of text. The chart uses four performative verbs to describe teacher talk: *exaggerates/endorses /ignores/subverts*. However, since it may not always be meaningful to distinguish between 'endorsement' and 'exaggeration' (the latter sometimes being one realisation of the former), we decided that these two categories should be conflated. Gender issues in the 'traditional' texts |including| 'Weddings' |and| 'The mayor has nine wives' . . . were in different ways 'exaggerated' and 'ignored'; those in the non-traditional |texts| . . . were 'ignored', 'subverted' and 'endorsed'. This gives five categories. However, subversion can logically also be applied to texts which 'maintain a traditional representation of gender roles', and indeed Jonathan and Angela . . . indicated this to be precisely what they *did* do with such texts – giving a total of six categories.

There will, however, always be discourse which resists characterisation (in this case, Alison's treatment of 'Just a piece of paper?' and 'The mayor has nine wives'). This meant two further, 'Unclear' categories.

The resultant working model is represented in Figure |B6.1.1|. It can be seen either as a working and developing *description* of the range of ways teachers can deal with gendered textbook texts (acknowledging that these ways are likely to be context-related if not *highly* situated, with particular local meanings), or, more tentatively, as *hypotheses* regarding the range.

Task B6.1.2: After you've read

➤ Consider the possibility of the research team being increased further in size. You would be able to get more data on the same teachers, more on the same texts, or more on different teachers using different texts. The objective of this extended study would be to develop an even richer understanding of the range of ways language teachers treat gender in textbooks. List some new *research questions* you might ask here.

Penelope Eckert and Sally McConnell-Ginet (1992) 'Communities of practice: where language, gender, and power all live', in Kira Hall et al. (eds) *Locating Power: proceedings of the Second Berkeley Women and Language Conference*. Berkeley, Calif.: Women and Language Group, pp. 89–99

The article can be divided into three parts. In the first, 'Too much abstraction spoils the broth', Eckert and McConnell-Ginet warn against abstracting gender 'from other aspects of social identity', language 'from social action', interactions and events 'from community and personal history', and linguistic and social behaviour 'from the communities in which they occur' (1992[a]: 90). Rather, what is needed is 'a view of the interaction of gender and language that roots each in the everyday social practices of particular local communities' (1992[a]: 91). Accordingly, gender does not 'mean' the same across communities.

In the second section, 'Language, power and gender viewed locally', Eckert and McConnell-Ginet exemplify how language, gender and power can be explored ethnographically and viewed in 'local' terms: dinner-time dramas, police reports. Epistemologically, these are 'fruitful research sites'. They stress the importance of the (tremendous) variability – of women, of men – for an understanding of gender. Why the gender category of 'tomboy', for example? And when there are correlations between linguistic behaviour and gender (sex?), these 'point us towards areas where further investigation might shed light on the linguistic and other practices that enter into gender dynamics *in a community*' (1992[a]: 93, my italics). Methodologically, Eckert and McConnell-Ginet challenge Labov's assertion that ethnography needs to answer to 'survey studies', arguing that 'ethnographic studies must answer to each other, and that survey and experimental studies in turn must answer to them' (1992[a]: 94; see also Labov 1991).

In the third section, reproduced in part below, Eckert and McConnell-Ginet discuss the relevance of the CofP notion (from Lave and Wenger) for gender and language study, showing how the 'practice' element arguably represents an advance on the notion of the 'speech community'.

 Task B6.2.1: While you read

➤ Which CofPs do you feel that you are you part of? Given that these defined by social engagement, what is the role of 'place' here?

P. Eckert and S. McConnell-Ginet

Language, gender, and communities of practice

A community of practice is an aggregate of people who come together around mutual engagement in some common endeavor. Ways of doing things, ways of talking, beliefs, values, power relations—in short, practices—emerge in the course of their joint activity around that endeavor. A community of practice is different as a social construct from the traditional notion of community, primarily because it is defined simultaneously by its membership and by the practice in which that membership engages. Indeed, it is the practices of the community and members' differentiated participation in them that structures the community socially.

A community of practice might be people working together in a factory, regulars in a bar, a neighborhood play group, a nuclear family, police partners and their ethnographer, the Supreme Court. Communities of practice may be large or small, intensive or diffuse; they are born and they die, they may persist through many changes of membership, and they may be closely articulated with other communities. Individuals participate in multiple communities of practice, and individual identity is based in the multiplicity of this participation. Rather than seeing the individual as some disconnected entity floating around in social space, or as a location in a network, or as a member of a particular group or set of groups, or as a bundle of social

P. Eckert and
S. McConnell-
Ginet

characteristics, we need to focus on communities of practice. Such a focus allows us to see the individual as an actor articulating a range of forms of participation in multiple communities of practice.

Gender is produced (and often reproduced) in differential membership in communities of practice. People's access and exposure to, need for, and interest in different communities of practice are related to such things as their class, age, and ethnicity, as well as their sex. Working-class people are more likely on the whole than middle-class people to be members of unions, bowling teams, close-knit neighbourhoods. Upper-middle-class people, on the other hand, are more likely than working-class people to be members of tennis clubs, orchestras, professional organizations. Men are more likely than women to be members of football teams, armies, and boards of directors. Women, on the other hand, are more likely to be members of secretarial pools, aerobics classes, and consciousness-raising groups.

And associated with differences in age, class, and ethnicity are differences in the extent to which the sexes belong to different communities of practice. Different people, for a variety of reasons, will articulate their multiple memberships differently. A female executive living in a male-dominated household will have difficulty articulating her membership in her domestic and professional communities of practice, unlike a traditional male executive "head of household." A lesbian lawyer "closeted" within the legal community may also belong to a women's community whose membership defines itself in opposition to the larger heterosexual world. And the woman who scrubs toilets in the household "managed" by the female executive for her husband and also in the home of the lesbian lawyer and her artist lover may be a respected lay leader in her local church, facing a different set of tensions than either of her employers does in negotiating multiple memberships.

Gender is also produced and reproduced in differential forms of participation in particular communities of practice. Women tend to be subordinate to men in the workplace, women in the military do not engage in combat, and in the academy, most theoretical disciplines are overwhelmingly male with women concentrated in descriptive and applied work that "supports" theorizing. Women and men may also have very different forms of participation available to them in single-sex communities of practice. For example, if all-women groups do in fact tend to be more egalitarian than all-men groups, as some current literature claims (e.g., Aries 1976), then women's and men's forms of participation will be quite different. Such relations within same-sex groups will, of course, be related in turn to the place of such groups in the larger society.

The relations among communities of practice when they come together in over-arching communities of practice also produce gender arrangements. Only recently, for example, have female competitive sports begun to receive significant recognition, and male sports continue to bring far greater visibility, power, and authority both to the teams and to the individual participants in those teams. The (male) final four is the focus of attention in the NCAA basketball world every spring, with the women's final four receiving only perfunctory mention. Many a school has its Bulldogs and Lady Bulldogs, its Rangers and Rangerettes. This articulation with power and stature outside the team in turn translates into different possibilities for relations within. The relation between male varsity sports teams and female cheerleading squads illustrates a more general pattern of men's organizations and women's auxiliaries. Umbrella communities of this kind do not offer neutral membership status. And when several families get together for a meal prepared by the women who then team up to do the serving and clearing away while the men watch football, gender differentiation (including differentiation in language use) is being reproduced on an institutional level.

P. Eckert and
S. McConnell-
Ginet

The community of practice is where the rubber meets the road—it is where observable action and interaction do the work of producing, reproducing, and resisting the organization of power in society and in societal discourses of gender, age, race, etc. Speakers develop linguistic patterns as they engage in activity in the various communities in which they participate. Sociolinguists have tended to see this process as one of acquisition of something relatively "fixed"—the linguistic resources, the community, and the individual's relation to the two are all viewed as fixed. The symbolic value of a linguistic form is taken as given, and the speaker simply learns it and uses it, either mechanically or strategically. But in actual practice, social meaning, social identity, community membership, forms of participation, the full range of community practices, and the symbolic value of linguistic form are being constantly and mutually constructed.

And so although the identity of both the individual and the individual community of practice is experienced as persistent, in fact they both change constantly. We continue to adopt new ways of talking and discard some old ways, to adopt new ways of being women and men, gays and lesbians and heterosexuals, even changing our ways of being feminists or being lovers or being mothers or being sisters. In becoming police officers or psychiatrists or physicists or professors of linguistics, we may change our ways of being women and perhaps of being wives or lovers or mothers. In so doing, however, we are not negating our earlier gendered sociolinguistic identities; we are transforming them, changing and expanding forms of femininity, masculinity, and gender relations. And there are many more unnamed ways of thinking, being, relating, and doing that we adopt and adapt as we participate in different ways in the various communities of practice to which we belong.

What sociolinguists call the linguistic repertoire is a set of resources for the articulation of multiple memberships and forms of participation. And an individual's ways of speaking in a particular community of practice are not simply a function of membership or participation in that community. A way of speaking in a community does not simply constitute a turning on of a community-specific linguistic switch, or the symbolic laying of claim to membership in that community, but a complex articulation of the individual's forms of participation in that community with participation in other communities that are salient at the time. In turn, the linguistic practices of any given community of practice will be continually changing as a result of the many saliencies that come into play through its multiple members.

The overwhelming tendency in language and gender research on power has been to emphasize either speakers and their social relations (e.g., women's disadvantage in ordinary conversations with men) or the meanings and norms encoded in the linguistic systems and practices historically available to them (e.g., such sexist patterns as conflating generic human with masculine in forms like *he* or *man*). But linguistic forms have no power except as given in people's mouths and ears; to talk about meaning without talking about the people who mean and the community practices through which they give meaning to their words is at best limited.

 Task B6.2.2: After you've read

➤ Reread the paragraph beginning 'And associated with differences' (page 157). Do you experience any particular tensions in the way you 'balance' or 'negotiate' such 'multiple memberships'?

➤ Explain to yourself what Eckert and McConnell-Ginet mean by the metaphorical claim that: 'The community of practice is where the rubber meets the road' (page 157).

➤ Eckert and McConnell-Ginet write: 'But if gender resides in difference [an idea they are concerned to problematise], what is the status of the tremendous variability we see in actual behaviour within sex categories?' (1992: 93). They provide an interesting answer to this interesting question. Can you add some more categories (including some 'dichotomous' ones) to their list?

Puleng Hanong Thetela (2006) ' "Sex discourses" in Southern Africa'

Text B6.3
P. Hanong
Thetela

This paper is an invited 'expanded abstract' developed by Puleng Hanong Thetela (School of Literature and Language Studies, University of the Witwatersrand, South Africa) from her original 2002 paper, 'Sex differences and gender constructions in Southern Sotho', which appeared in the journal *South African Linguistics and Applied Language Studies*, 20: 177–89. A special half issue of this, edited by Elizabeth de Kadt, was devoted to gender and language studies relevant to the region. The abstracts can be viewed at <http://www.nisc.co.za/journals>.

Hanong Thetela brings to our attention the practice of *hlonipha*, a little-known linguistic phenomenon of southern Africa which is of considerable interest to gender and language study (see Swann 2000). *Hlonipha* is about respect, including for women, but is also associated with women's politeness and associated use of sexual euphemism in their use of language (here, Sesotho). Hanong Thetela shows how this sex-exclusive requirement works for women when reporting sexual assault.

Very sadly, Puleng Hanong Thetela died in June 2005, not long after writing this piece. An obituary by Teun van Dijk can be found in *Discourse and Society* (2005) 16 (6): 807.

The analysis of discourse and gender in this study is based broadly within the post-structuralist approach in which gender is seen as constructed and negotiated in actual social interactions in discourse (for example, Coates 1993, Sunderland 1995, Cameron 1996, Eckert and McConnell-Ginet 2003). Many feminist linguistic studies working within this tradition overwhelmingly emphasise 'the gendered nature of linguistic representations of discourse' (Erhlich 2001: 14). It is from this perspective that the analysis of police interviews of rape victims in this paper is approached. Using transcripts of police interviews of rape victims, I argue that the gender identities and power relations in the legal system (in this case police interviews) cannot be divorced from the ideological basis on which the very nature of the legal process is based (for example, Philips 1998, Van Dijk 1998). Taking police interviews as a discourse, I examine how these can function to normalise certain socially held values, in this case asymmetrical power relations between men and women through different degrees of accessibility to discourse. In this manner, police interviews as a discourse can be seen as 'engendered'.

P. Hanong
Thetela

P. Hanong
Thetela

Despite extensive research on discourse and gender, much of this has focused on Western cultures, with very little work done on non-Western cultures such as southern Africa. The main contribution of this study, therefore, is to bring a non-Western perspective to the study of discourse and gender. The study focuses on the discursive constructions of gender in southern Africa, using Southern Sotho (hereafter referred to as Sesotho) – a dialect of the Sotho language spoken by the Basotho (singular, Mosotho) in Lesotho and the Free State Province of South Africa, and one of the eleven official languages of South Africa – as a case study. Primary data are transcripts of recorded police interviews of rape victims (collected in Lesotho and the Free State between 1997 and 1999) in which all participants are native speakers of Sesotho. The study focuses on the notion of 'sex discourses': text and talk about human sexuality, sexual behaviour and sex practices in the Sesotho culture.

Based very broadly within the critical discourse analytical (CDA) approach espoused in the works of, for example, Van Dijk (1997), and also drawing on sociolinguistics and cultural studies, the research employs the concepts of discourse, ideology and gender, whose origins, definitions, and analyses vary from one discipline to another. Starting from the premise of (sex) discourses as social action/practice, I examine how different discourse choices from Sesotho potentially 'do', construct or reproduce gender and gendered identities. In particular, I examine the discursive role of the culturally derived hlonipha in Sesotho (see Moeketsi 1999), the equivalent of *isihlonipho sabafazi* in Xhosa (for example, Finlayson 1995) – language connoting respect for women. In sex discourses, *hlonipha* is realised through politeness indexicals such as euphemistic expressions, avoidance of profanities (for example, Moeketsi 1999), and vagueness (for example, Channell 1994).

In Sesotho (and I believe in other African cultures), sex is regarded as private, secretive, and as such it is a taboo subject. This is linguistically manifested by a vast range of euphemistic and vague references – what I call the *hlonipha* repertoire – used to communicate and negotiate sexual meanings. The traditional roles of women in society – raising, nurturing and socialising young people into the Sesotho culture – require women to find the appropriate discourses to carry out these roles; and the acquisition of hlonipha is crucial, particularly in dealing with culturally sensitive matters such as sexuality and cultural taboos. It is through *hlonipha* that such culturally sensitive matters are communicated and negotiated. Below are some of the common euphemistic references to sex discourses in Sesotho:

penis: *kwae* (tobacco or snuff), *peipi* (clay pipe), *bonna* (manhood) *botho* (humanity), ntho (thing),[1]

bokapele (the front)[2]

testicles: *ditapole* (potatoes)

vagina: *kuku* (cake), *bosadi* (womanhood), *Lesotho*[3] (the country of the Basotho)

sexual intercourse: *ho robala mmoho* (to sleep together), *ho arolelana dikobo* (to share blankets), *ho bapala* (to play),[4] *ho etsa diketso tsa motabo* (to engage in acts of *motabo*[5])

to get pregnant: *ho boela morao* (to go back), *ho ithwala* (to carry oneself), *ho ba mmeleng*[6] (to be in the body)

Note: The use of *ho* is the equivalent of the *to*-infinitive preceding verb phrases.

Even though *hlonipha* is, in the main, a characteristic feature of women's speech, it is also worth noting that women's speech patterns are a part of the politeness repertoire of the Sesotho culture. It is not surprising therefore to find this code in the language of other social groups, particularly in public discourses such as the media. A good illustration is that of *Lesedi ka Sepolesa* (1997–9), a police newspaper in which sex crimes (for example, rape) are reported in euphemistic terms. Examples of such terms are: *ho apola dikobo ka sheshe/kgang* (to expose blankets by force), *ho fetola mosadi* (to turn into a woman), *ho etsa diketso tsa motabo* (to engage in *motabo* acts), *ho kena-kenana* (to interfere with), *ho hohla phatla ya tshwene* (to scrub the forehead of a monkey), as well as many other culturally unique (and anomalous) references for which English equivalents are non-existent. It is against the background of the *hlonipha* culture that the sex discourses of police interviews of rape victims should be analysed and understood.

The analysis of police interviews of rape victims indicate that the interviewers (mostly male police officers) focus more on the sexual than the criminal aspects. This view echoes other studies on rape reports and trials (for example, Lees 1997). In the interviews, my data shows that questions asked are mainly on sexual issues – torn panties, bodily fluids (for example, menstruation, vaginal discharge, semen, etc.), the victim's past sexual experiences, and penetrative aspects of rape – all of which are discussed in graphic detail. Due to *hlonipha* constraints on the language of women, the interview sessions are evidently extremely difficult for the female victims – and in some ways for the police officers too. The extract from an interview of a twenty-three-year-old woman (W) by two police officers (PO1 and PO2) below (translated from Sesotho) illustrates this difficulty.

2.1 PO1:		What did he then do? Tell us everything that happened.
2.2 W:		After he lay on top of me, he parted my legs, and *pushed his thing inside me*.
2.3 PO2:		*What thing did he push inside you*? I want to repeat that you have to tell us everything *and you should use adult and not childish language*; it is not my fault but the law requires that you tell us everything.
2.4: W:		um . . . [*silence*]
2.5 PO2:		Are you going to tell us what this man did to you or what? We cannot stay here the whole day. We have other important things to do.
2.6 W [*sobbing*]:		He pushed his pipe, his [*inaudible*] inside my cake . . .
2.7 PO2 [*interrupts*]:		What? [*laughs out loud*] You seem to be very stubborn. Being stubborn does not work in cases like these.
2.8 W:		He pushed his thing here [demonstrates by placing her hand between her thighs].
2.9 PO1:		I don't think you understand what I am saying. *You are a woman and not a girl*,[7] according to this medical report. The doctor clearly points out that you did not suffer any injuries *during the sexual intercourse*. Isn't it?
2.10 W:		[*silence*]

(For more, related data, see also Hanong Thetela, 2002)

The analysis of the interviews used for the study raises important issues. First, the study points to the cross-talk phenomenon (used in the sense of Connor-Linton [1999]

Extension

to refer to forms of communication clash) resulting from conflicting speech registers between the interviewer and the interviewee. While police officers mostly use the sexually explicit register (for example, the use of the term 'sexual intercourse' in 2.9), and demand that the victims do the same, the latter religiously stick to the *hlonipha* register (for example, euphemisms) throughout the interview. In the extract above, the victim refers to her assailant's penis as 'his thing' (2.2, 2.8), 'his pipe' (2.6) and to her vagina as 'my cake' (2.6) – using the culturally appropriate code for women. All the interview cases used show that, despite demand for sexual explicitness from police officers, all the women cling to euphemistic and vague expressions. In 2.3, for instance, PO2 attempts to force register shift from the victim by demanding what he terms 'adult' and not 'child' language, the latter referring to euphemisms. The victim, however, does not comply, and continues with the use of the *hlonipha* discourse. The non-compliance by the victim should be understood, not as an indication of stubbornness (as suggested by PO2 in 2.7) but as a result of the constraints put on women by the culture of *hlonipha*. To rape victims, the sexual explicitness of police interviews is a totally new kind of discourse, which is not part of their sociocultural and linguistic repertoire.

A second important feature of the interviews is the extensive use of pauses and hesitations, or complete silences in the speech of the victims. A closer look at this phenomenon (for example, 2.4, 2.6) further supports the view of limited access to sexually explicit discourse by women. For example, most occurrences of hesitations, pauses and silences mark stages of difficulty that the women come across in the interview – the narration of the rape event, problems with answering difficult and sensitive questions, reference to sexual terms, and many related issues. Hesitations are usually accompanied by mumbling and/or inaudible utterances. At times the lack of sensitivity in the police officers' questions, and words of ridicule (for example, 'you are a woman and not a girl' in 2.9), lead to frustration, silence, loss of composure and crying (for example, 2.6).

Third, the analysis points to asymmetrical power relations between the police officers and the victims. First, in the interview session, the police officer occupies a powerful position – he initiates the topic of the interview, selects the questions and questioning strategies, interrupts the interviewee, chooses the preferred register, has full access to the sex discourses, and also makes comments if and when he chooses to do so (for example, the comment on the sexual experience of the victim as exemplified by 2.9 above). All these are symbolic of his discursive power over the victim. Conversely, the lack of clarity and precision of the victim's responses, as seen in the constraints of the *hlonipha* above, place her at a disadvantaged position, as she cannot describe the events of her ordeal in precise terms required by the interview event.

In this paper I have examined how sex discourses in Southern Sotho draw upon cultural resources (i.e. the *hlonipha* repertoire) to reproduce gendered identities; and the linguistic representations of such gendered identities. Using police interviews as a sample of social interaction between men (i.e. male police officers) and women (i.e. women rape victims), I have suggested that while men enjoy unlimited access to sex discourses, women's access is constrained by the *hlonipha* culture to which to they are expected to adhere in their everyday discourse interaction. However, when they fall victim to a sex crime such as rape, they enter into a completely foreign discourse environment in which *hlonipha* is out of place. This conflict between cultural expectations of women's discourse, on the one hand, and that of the legal system (of explicitness for the sake of clarity and precision of evidence) on the other, is a phenomenon of which the police officers, who are Sesotho mother-tongue speakers,

P. Hanong
Thetela

are aware. They probably feel uneasy about this – for example, in the extract above, PO2 blames the demand for explicitness on the legal system (i.e. his statement in 2.6 that 'the law requires that you tell us everything') – but are not prepared to entertain euphemistic expressions as the alternative to the standard Sesotho ones. However, it is worth noting that had these women agreed to the use of sexual explicitness, the reaction of the same officers would have been that of contempt for the women, who would be seen as lacking a sense of modesty and self-respect. The demand for standard Sesotho expressions, we could speculate, is not intended to clarify any details of the rape events, but is intended to embarrass and ridicule rape victims. In this way, the demand for the use of sexual explicitness illustrates a lack of compassion and sensitivity on the part of the police.

From the analysis of the manner, the attitudes, and the language used by the police in interviewing rape victims, it could be argued that one important contributing factor to Basotho women's failure to help bring about the conviction of rapists is that of the sociocultural constraints on language use – their adherence to the *hlonipha* code prevents them from expressing themselves in the type of register required by the legal system, thus they fail to capture both the violent and criminal nature of the rape event. Their choice of *hlonipha* terms for rape (for example, 'blankets', 'sleep', etc.) reproduces rape as conventional sex; thus the central issue of non-consent, which is crucial in rape cases, is undermined by this linguistic code. The *hlonipha* culture thus arguably constrains women from engaging fully in the legal process, and from sharing the kind of freedom enjoyed by male interactants (for example, the police). This inequality of access to discourse potentially contributes to the legal system as 'engendered' (see also recent research in feminist jurisprudence, for example, Rumney 1999, Smith 1993).

The study has important implications for the legal system in southern Africa. First, there is a need for radical reforms in the legal system in order to address issues of gender asymmetry such as those raised here. One important area is that of the development of training programmes for all paralegal and medical personnel, including all who deal with rape issues. The present study has, for example, pointed to problems of lack of proper training of the police, in legal matters in order to be sensitive to the trauma that rape victim's experience. There is also a need for training in cultural awareness so that the linguistic constraints placed on women by the *hlonipha* culture can be understood and appreciated. This would go a long way to eliminating all kinds of misunderstanding between the police and the victims in that it would help the victims of rape successfully tell their stories in the language of their choice – be this *hlonipha* or standard Sesotho.

Notes

1. The term is synonymous with the term 'thing' in English. However, in sexual terms, it functions as an avoidance term for a penis. For example, the South African newspaper, the *Mail & Guardian* (12 September 1997) reports on the rape of a mentally retarded nine-year old girl who told her older sister, 'My teacher took his *thing* and put it in me'.
2. I suspect the term derives from the position of the male genitalia in relation to the other parts of the body. It is worth noting that the term can also be used with reference to female genitalia.
3. Although none of my respondents knew precisely why the name of the country (Lesotho) is used, there was some speculation that since a country is normally seen from motherhood terms (i.e. illustrated through the 'she' reference in English), and the term might have both femininity and fertility implications.

4. This expression is found in Sekese (1999: 6) in his account of the Sesotho marriage, and the first intercourse between the newly married couple: E*sale ka phirimana, mohlankana le morwetsana ba theha papadi* (Early in the night the young man and the young woman start playing).

5. In Sesotho, the lexical term *motabo* refers to some soft ash commonly from an aloe leaf, used as a mixture for ground tobacco leaves in order to produce snuff; without such a mixture, the snuff cannot have its needed potency.

6. Any English translation for such terms would result in complete loss of meaning for these terms.

7. Although in Sesotho 'woman' and 'girl' semantically distinguish between 'married' and 'unmarried', respectively, they also have the cultural meaning of sexual experience: a girl who has lost her virginity is derogatively dismissed as a 'woman', whereas a virgin retains the term 'girl'. Thus referring to a girl as a woman implies promiscuity, and is in this way highly offensive.

 Task B6.3.1: After you've read

➤ What do you think of Hanong Thetala's 'implications for the legal system' (last paragraph)? Do you think her optimism in the last sentence is justified?

Unit B7
Developing understandings of
language: Discourse and discourses

The extracts in Unit B7 come from two recent books. Both are on the topic of gender and discourse. The first two come from Jane Sunderland's *Gendered Discourses* (2004), the third from Judith Baxter's *Positioning Gender in Discourse* (2003).

Jane Sunderland (2004) 'Discourses, discourse identification and discourse naming', *Gendered Discourses.* **London: Palgrave Macmillan, pp. 27–50**

Text B7.1
J. Sunderland

Gendered Discourses is in part a theoretical and in part a data-centred work which brings together new data and existing work on gendered discourses, including 'classic' discourses such as Adrienne Rich's 'compulsory heterosexuality'. This first extract comes from Chapter 2, 'Discourses, discourse identification and discourse naming'. It focuses on 'discourse identification'. The aim of the extract (and the chapter) is to help enable those investigating discourse from a critical or post-structuralist perspective to interpretively identify, name and discuss the significance and workings of discourses in their own research.

Task B7.1.1: Before you read

➤ Are you aware in your reading of any discourses (gendered or otherwise) which have been identified and named to date?

My own starting point in identifying discourses . . . is to see a discourse provisionally as a 'way of seeing the world'.

J. Sunderland

For the analyst, this can be derived (and as a working definition can be operationalized) from the way people speak and write about things. While this starting point does not convey the crucial *ideologically constitutive potential* of a discourse, as in Fairclough's claim that discourse 'structures knowledge and social practice' (1992|a]: 3; see also Foucault, 1972), it is broadly operationalizable, can be checked against the understandings of readers or listeners, and thus has useful implications for empirical research, for gender and language pedagogy, and indeed for discoursal deconstruction and other linguistic intervention . . .

J. Sunderland

Discourse and linguistic features

Mills notes that we can 'detect a discursive structure' because of 'the systematicity of the ideas, opinions, concepts, ways of thinking and behaving which are formed within a particular context' (1997: 17). These may each be manifested – systematically – in language. But, given that discourses are interpretively identifiable in part through linguistic 'traces', we need to know what traces might be relevant. Critical discourse analysts typically draw on linguistic features such as nominalisation, passivisation and sequencing (Jaworski and Coupland, 1999; see also Halliday, 1985), but I will also refer to the more recent, related work of van Leeuwen (1995, 1996) on 'social actors' and 'social action'. These notions include ideas, knowledge, beliefs and practices (including linguistic practices). . .

As regards 'labelling' practices, I look at lexical choices, especially repeated lexical choices, in how social actors are referred to (e.g. in noun phrases). For 'social action' I look at verb types, verb phrases, activization/passivization and speech acts. For both I look at collocations, and at 'absences' as well as 'presences', i.e. at what possibilities do not appear, but could have done (van Leeuwen, 1995, 1996), and, from a feminist perspective, arguably should have done. (In other work, the focus is on modality and transitivity choices.) Such traces facilitate the text-based part of identification of discourses, in particular of *related discourses* within the same text (*intratextuality*) as well as in different texts. . . .

. . . After a little guided practice, discourse identification can be done independently by students through close reading of culturally familiar texts, if they are willing to think systematically and linguistically – (intra)textually, intertextually and interdiscursively, i.e. to bring to bear understandings from outside the text to the text itself – as well as critically.

[An example] of 'discourse spotting'

I start with [an example] from [a] 2002 British newspaper text . . . to show how gendered discourses can be provisionally and interpretively identified, or 'spotted', and named . . . I focus on some of the linguistic features referenced above. I hope to make the identification process as explicit and transparent as possible. This is partly in response to Potter, who observes that 'the relation of Foucault's notion of discourse to any particular instance of talk or writing is not always well specified' (1996: 87), and to Francis (2000), who has criticized writers for failing to explain how they categorize discourses . . .

It has to be said that the discourses are not only interpretive and provisional, but are also an effect of 'Western' co-construction. They are also partial, in that still others could have been identified. This is because discourses are not only not non-finite but also non-ubiquitous, rather produced within particular educational, social and political contexts. Different discourses are accordingly likely to be 'spotted' by different social groups of readers and analysts – for example those who favour a feminist perspective and those with a more traditionalist perspective – even when looking at exactly the same textual set of linguistic traces. This will depend on 'orientation', and in part on what seems self-evident, 'common sense' or simply salient to given readers/listeners. An anti-racist discourse may be spotted by anti-racist campaigners (and even by advocates of racist practices!) but not by those who simply don't care. Alternatively, members of different 'Communities of practice' (say) may 'spot' the same

J. Sunderland

discourse at the same time but evaluate it differently. A 'Discourse of fantasy', for example, can be viewed positively ('a dream come true!') or negatively (a cynical distraction, ideologically blinding individuals to what is really 'going on').

The text, [Figure B7.1.1] from my weekly local newspaper, the *Lancaster Guardian*, was found on the 'Wedding Album' page. Entitled: 'Tie the knot at Leighton Hall – A dream wedding', it tops the page. (Leighton Hall is a country house in Lancashire, UK, parts of which are open to the public.)

Contained in the three short columns of 'Tie the knot at Leighton Hall' I suggest are linguistic traces of a variety of discourses . . .

Some of these discourses are categorised as 'descriptive', others as 'interpretive'. Two 'descriptive ones (which most people would agree on) are an 'architectural' and a 'legal' discourse. The 'architectural' discourse is realised by 'semi-specialist lexical traces', such as *backdrop*, *Gothic towers*, *turrets* and *'flying' staircase*. The 'interpretive' discourses are divided into two sub-categories: 'general' and 'gendered'. The former include a 'promotional discourse', a 'consumerist discourse' and a 'discourse of late

Tie the knot at Leighton Hall

A dream wedding

by Gayle Rouncivell

FAIRYTALE dreams can soon come true for North Lancashire brides now Leighton Hall has been awarded permission to host civil wedding ceremonies.

The historic house with its spectacular backdrop and Gothic towers and turrets, has been a popular wedding reception venue for the last ten years but the increase in competing venues having wedding licenses has spurred the owners to apply for their own.

Couples can now exchange vows at Leighton, as well as cele-brating their special day within the most romantic and idyllic of settings.

Suzie Reynolds, owner of Leighton Hall, person-ally supervises the hall's weddings.

She said: "Modern cou-ples want to get married somewhere extra special and a bit unusual - his-toric settings, such as Leighton, are increasingly popular.

"More people are enjoy-ing the convenience of getting married, taking photographs and celebrat-ing their reception at the same venue so we decided it was time that we too were able to offer this full service.

"We are looking for-ward to giving couples the wedding days about which they have always dreamed!"

Brides can choose one of two rooms for their cer-emony - the music room, which overlooks the Victo-rian walled garden and enjoys spectacular views of the parkland, or the main hall with its 'flying' staircase, down which the bride can make a breath-taking entrance.

For more information contact Leighton Hall on 734474.

Figure B7.1.1 From *Lancaster Guardian*, 11 January 2002

modernity' (see Sunderland 2004 for a discussion of these). The 'gendered' discourses include the aforementioned 'discourse of fantasy', a 'biggest day of a woman's life' discourse, and a 'compulsory heterosexuality' discourse.

... readers may ... wish to return to the text to identify possible linguistic 'traces' of these (and perhaps reminders of – relationships with – other texts and discourses).

★ Task B7.1.2: Reflection task

➤ Now do just this! Then read on (or, where indicated, read Sunderland, 2004) to compare your responses.

J. Sunderland

Linguistic traces, intratextuality and intertextuality

We will now look more closely at the linguistic traces of the ['gendered'] discourses apparent in [this text]. Although most readers use the language of texts to co-construct discourses unsystematically and unconsciously, I suggest that it is possible for the discourse analyst to do so systematically and consciously. . . .

Gendered discourses

The three discourses in this category are interpretively named from a feminist perspective.

(i) a 'Discourse of fantasy'

This discourse is recognizable through several noun phrases: *fairytale dream*, *dream wedding*, and *most romantic and idyllic of settings*, which sit neatly alongside the *Gothic towers*. There are intertextual associations with the women waiting in their towers in *Rapunzel* and *Sleeping Beauty*. Members of [a] discussion group referred to a 'fairytale discourse' and a 'Hollywood discourse' – the latter not only because of the fantasy element, but also because Leighton Hall is represented almost as a theatre for the wedding (among other things, it has a *backdrop*). Interestingly, absent is any reference to the marriage of which the wedding is the beginning – like fairytales, the wedding here is all-important.

(ii) a 'Biggest/Best day of a woman's life' discourse

This idiomatically and ironically-named discourse is suggested by the idea of 'dreams coming true' for *North Lancashire brides*, who *make breath-taking entrances down the flying staircase* and choose the room for *their* ceremony. (This *their* could in principle refer to 'the couple', though this requires something of a 'reading against the grain', sandwiched between two occurrence of *bride*.) Interesting here is the lexical absence of *bridegroom* as an independent social actor – he could have been mentioned, since he is entailed in the recurring (thrice-mentioned) *couples*, but is not. *Brides* is the subject and agent of *can choose* and *the bride* is the actor in the final subordinate clause of the same sentence: *down which [staircase] the bride can make a breath-taking entrance.* (These are cases of the 'can of possibility' – rather than of ability – which dovetails with the overall consumerist stance of the text.) This *breath-taking entrance* entails being the object of gaze – traditionally, the *male* gaze (in particular, of the bridegroom, and her father) and the *envious* female gaze. The groom is subjected to nothing like the same visual evaluation. Interestingly, *bride* in the British National Corpus collocates mainly with content words (*blushing, prospective, dress*), *groom* with functional words (*like, then, would, as*). It is also syntagmatically and atypically first in the male/female 'pair' *bride and groom*, and unmarked (like *widow*). *Bride*, with its collocational 'load', can thus be seen as almost functionally reproducing certain discourses (Paul Baker, personal communication).

In this discourse two propositions are evident: (i) marriage (of which the wedding is the symbol) is more important for women than men (really, the only way to make sense of this text), and (ii) marriage is more important for women than anything else. Together, these constitute the implicit traditional representation of a woman as a (future) *wife*, the fairytale wedding the return for a future relatively circumscribed identity. 'Behind' this discourse, then, lies a *patriarchal* discourse. This is not explicit (there is nothing, for example, about the bride's father 'giving her away', or about the best man speaking 'on behalf of the bridesmaids', as traditionally happens in Anglican church weddings in the UK, and these *absences* may even be seen as faint traces of a competing 'Late modernity discourse'). A patriarchal discourse is however suggested by intertextually-linked *absences*: if the groom is backgrounded in this 'fairytale' text, his important, grounded, 'real life' concerns must be elsewhere.

(iii) 'Compulsory heterosexuality'

Adrienne Rich's 'compulsory heterosexuality' (1980) discourse . . . can be seen in 'Dream Wedding' in that there is no suggestion that couples who might be interested in 'exchanging vows' (with or without legally 'tying the knot') are anything other than heterosexual (*bride* entails *bridegroom*), despite three mentions of *couples*, and despite the fact that religious constraints would not obtain. This also resonates with 'fantasy/fairytale' discourses (again as enthusiastically endorsed by Hollywood), and fairytales are replete, as noted above, with heterosexual weddings, the couple then (we are often informed) unproblematically living happily ever after.

Jane Sunderland (2004) 'Celebrity fatherhood: the "Blair baby"', *Gendered Discourses*. London: Palgrave Macmillan, pp. 122–40

Text B7.2
J. Sunderland

The second extract from *Gendered Discourses* is a report of a study of a set of texts from UK newspapers: editorials on the birth of Leo Blair to (as I write) British Prime Minister Tony Blair and Cherie Booth, a barrister and judge. Various 'fatherhood discourses' are provisionally identified/co-constructed and named.

Task B7.2.1: Before you read

➤ Consider some different ways fatherhood might be represented in the media. You might begin by thinking of ways to complete the noun phrase 'Father as . . .'

Extension

. . . Celebrity fatherhood newspaper texts are . . . newsworthy for the coinciding of a lifestyle most of us do not share with experiences which many of us do, and for their novelty, since men in the news tend to be represented as speaking in public or professional roles (Caldas-Coulthard, 1995) . . . Media representation of the birth of Leo is interesting epistemologically here since Tony Blair was elected as a potentially dynamic and *modern* leader, the family man who already had three children, and no shortage of convictions and principles, who might be expected to promote (if not practice) 'shared parenting' more than most Prime Ministers. Additional interest comes from the fact that Cherie Booth had no intention of renouncing her own professional career for full-time motherhood.

Celebrity fatherhood often creates plenty of data, since much mileage is extracted by the media from such events (consider magazines such as *Hello!* and *OK*). The 'Blair baby' was no exception. Data for the study comes from almost all British national newspapers – the *Guardian*, *Times*, *Independent*, *Daily Telegraph*, *Sunday Telegraph*, *Observer* (broadsheets) and the *Express*, *Express on Sunday*, *Mirror*, *Sunday Mirror*, *Mail*, *Sunday Mail*, *Mail on Sunday*, *Sunday Post*, *Sun*, *News of the World*, *Sunday People* and *Sport* (tabloids), as well as from one regional paper, the *Daily Mail North West Edition*. Most newspapers carried 'Blair baby' features on several pages, just after the birth and the days following it. . . .

Fatherhood discourses in the editorials

. . . Caldas-Coulthard claims, rather dramatically, that 'In media discourse in general, evaluation is a crucial entrance point to the hidden discourse' (1996: 268). Newspaper editorials are particularly appropriate epistemological sites for the analyst to look for (and co-construct) discourses, since evaluation and opinion are the purpose of the genre. Evaluation and opinion can also be 'read off' in a relatively straightforward way – though with some allowance for irony and humour. Here, though the ostensible focus of these editorials was Leo's birth, this event was used as a springboard for discussion of many other topics. In the process, a variety of discourses of fatherhood discourses were produced . . .

[A] traditional backdrop is faintly visible in what we might refer to as the 'Triumphant father discourse'. Traces are evident in two editorials. The *Sunday People* refers to Blair as 'a proud and delighted new father who wanted to share his joy with the world'. And the *Sunday Telegraph* focuses on the role of 'any new father', i.e. announcing the birth (jocularly making the point that whereas 'most men . . . can use the traditional route for such announcements – a series of telephone calls to relations, followed by a notice in the *Daily Telegraph*', Tony Blair did it facing a battery of cameras). Other newspapers used Leo's birth to address a more Political (large P) agenda. Several produced a recognizably conservative, provisionally-named 'Traditional family fatherhood discourse'. The *Mail on Sunday* editorial is headed 'Blair as the family man we elected'. This refers to Blair as 'a man for whom the family was of fundamental importance', claims that '"married with children" is still, overwhelmingly, the lifestyle to which Britons aspire' and expresses disappointment about

> why the Prime Minister has allowed the Chancellor to skew the tax and benefits system even further against marriage by scrapping the Married Couple's Allowance. And why the Cabinet as a whole has seemed so strangely determined

to advance a social agenda whose outcome, if not avowed objective, would be to put homosexual relationships on a legal and moral par with marriage.

The *Mail on Sunday* also appears to be trying to use Blair's apparent principles against him, to suggest that he has sold out ideologically. Its editorial concludes

. . . it would be nice to think, as Mr Blair enjoys a well-earned two weeks with his expanded family, that when he again picks up the reins of power, he will be inspired to use them to advance the values he so clearly espouses himself.

A 'Traditional family fatherhood discourse' is evident too in the *Sunday Times*, though the linguistic traces are 'weaker'. This editorial rather oddly wishes Cherie 'a speedy recovery', very traditionally refers to Leo as being 'born to a serving prime minister and his wife', and notes 'the prime minister's position as the head of a conventional family – and, despite increasing rates of family breakdown, 70% of children are still brought up by their natural, married parents'. It critically raises the issue of 'benefit-dependent' couples with children and single parents whose income has been rising proportionately more than that of couples (one or both of whom are working) with children. It suggests that 'the pendulum may have swung far enough in the direction of greater liberalism and that society's conventional defences need shoring up' and concludes

Leo Blair is indeed fortunate to have been born into a happy, traditional family. His father should not hesitate to ensure that such families do not become a minority, and that they are encouraged as the best means of bringing up children.

Also political, but in a more progressive direction, were the editorials in the *Guardian* and the *Observer*, both broadly drawing on what we can call a 'Shared parenting discourse'. The *Guardian* commented:

Now, it is going to be very hard not to look to Blair family circumstances for evidence on a number of hot policy topics, especially the protection and support offered by the state to mothers and the obligations of employers to female (*and male*) staff with children (my italics).

and refers positively to the European Union parental leave directive.

The *Observer* editorial refers to babies' uncompromising demands and how 'sometimes their yells reverberate through their *parents'* offices, factories, county courts or schools' (my italics). The second paragraph reads

If, Leo, you one day read today's issue of this paper, you will find that we had barely begun to sort out how parents should raise children while earning money for their needs: the 'life-work balance' it was called. You may learn that as your mother went into hospital to give birth, another 'Blair babe', Tess Kingham, was forced to concede that she could no longer represent her constituents and answer the demands of her family within today's archaic parliamentary system.

This is presumably not intended to read that Kingham was incompetent, disorganised or poor in her time-management, or that she should not have tried to be a Member of Parliament in the first place (or that mothers should not thus try) – though it *could* be read as any of these. It *is* presumably intended to identify the *parliamentary system* (and, by extension, other organisational systems and places of work), described as *archaic*, as causative and at fault in leading Kingham to make this decision. This can be seen as drawing on an implicit discourse of 'Positive state intervention' in relation to parenthood (and indeed beyond), intervention which is needed if women like Kingham are to remain as MPs. There also however seems to be a trace of a *traditional* parenthood (and thus fatherhood) discourse here in that 'Positive state intervention' seems to start from the position that women are the 'main carers' and that it is this 'given' and the problems it causes which need to be addressed institutionally (e.g. with 'family friendly' hours of work, allowing breastfeeding in the House, and so on). It does not seem to start with a recognition of the possibility and value of 'shared parenting' (which would, after all, considerably reduce the onus on women, and bring demands for change from all MPs).

An explicit 'New Fatherhood discourse' (named by me; see below) was most apparent in *The Times*:

> . . . Tony Blair is now going to be woken by hungry cries. Old-fashioned fathers quickly learn to simulate sleep throughout the crying. But the Prime Minister takes pride in being a new man as well as New Labour. And he has gone on record with the statement that it takes a nuclear explosion to wake his wife after she has gone to sleep. So for at least half the night alarms, he is going to be the stumbler around in the dark.

> The washing machine has sanitised some of the smelly drudgery that a baby brings into a house, even in Downing Street. But Mr Blair is going to have to *re*learn other old parenting skills of testing bottles and baths for warmth, rocking the baby in his arms to bring up wind or stop him screaming, and keeping his voice down when Leo is asleep.

Unlike several of the newspaper reports, this goes well beyond nappy changing as the prototypical practice of the new father. And the editorial is paying Blair the complement of saying he will have to relearn these old parenting skills – implying he became competent at them well before the days when everything he does risks being seen as a publicity stunt. At first sight, this construction of Blair as a father who shares the childcare is surprising, since the *Times* is not by any means a left-wing paper. The editorial can however be read as mischievously trying to hoist Blair by his own petard and setting him up to fail – i.e. he believes in all the above, but will he do them in practice? I refer to this discourse somewhat ironically as 'New Fatherhood' since I suspect that the *Times* has its tongue at least partly in its cheek (and is satirising New Labour). I intentionally do not refer to it as a 'Shared parenting discourse' – not only because of its teasing nature, but also because of its individual, asocial focus, and because there is no explicit mention of either shared childcare or parental leave . . .

The *Independent* does not draw on a specific fatherhood discourse. It does, however, draw on what might be seen as a liberal discourse of (late-)modernity, and – to the extent that this is most definitely not a 'Traditional family discourse' – a wider 'Progressive discourse', which extends to fatherhood. The editorial (in its entirety) reads as follows:

> It is not very significant for the destiny of the nation that Tony Blair is the first serving prime minister to have a baby for 151 years. But it is a little, because politicians will keep pontificating on 'the family'.

There is something unmistakably modern about the balance between Mr Blair's tolerance of the forms families take and his insistence on the moral responsibilities they require.

As for form: his wife has kept her name; his press secretary, chief of staff and secretary of state for health have young children and are not married; and his is the first Cabinet to contain ministers who are open about being homosexual. As for responsibility: Mr Blair keeps the state out of it except to try to make fathers play a part in bringing up their children, and to increase child benefit, which rightly puts the child's welfare at the centre of public policy.

Of course, the new baby's privacy must be respected. But, to the extent that he strengthens Mr Blair's authority to speak on these matters, and prompts us to question the authority of the childless ideologues who demand that the state decree what kinds of family people ought to have, Leo Blair should be welcomed to the public stage.

This 'Discourse of diversity', implicit in the latter traces of paragraph 4 – in contrast to that of 'Traditional fatherhood' in the *Sunday Times*, whose traces included expressions of approval of the 'conventional family' – clearly embraces unmarried (presumably responsible) fatherhood, as well as adoption by gay male (and female) partners.

The newspaper editorial has proved here to be a fruitful genre and epistemological site for the investigation of fatherhood discourses, having enabled the interpretive identification of a 'Triumphant father discourse', an ironic 'New Fatherhood discourse', a 'Traditional family discourse', a 'Shared parenting discourse' and a 'Progressive discourse'. To have been thus recognizable (at least to this analyst), and, indeed, produced, these discourses must also (by definition) be circulating and their traces evident *outside* these editorials. The first and third we can see as being part of the same 'order of discourse', the fourth and fifth part of another, and we can see the two pairs as competing. 'New Fatherhood' on the surface shares the same order as 'Shared parenting' and the 'Progressive' discourses. Wider discursive practices (e.g. the political stance normally adopted in *Times* editorials) however enable us to see the discourse here being used largely ironically, so that 'New Fatherhood' may not 'comfortably' share this order of discourse with the 'Shared parenting' and 'Progressive fatherhood' discourses at all. However, for the irony to work, the *Times* editorial must be seen to be appropriating traces of these discourses, and, in drawing on them, it intertextually acknowledges them.

. . . Only the *Guardian* and the *Observer* . . . directly problematised fatherhood as institution, by raising the social and political question of how best to facilitate the combining of paid work and parenthood.

Task B7.2.2: After you've read

➤ Consider and note down other text types in which you might find examples of (i) fatherhood discourses, and (ii) gendered discourses more generally.

➤ Read the last two sections of Chapter 2 of *Gendered Discourses*, on 'Discourse naming' and 'Existing named discourses'.

> Read Chapter 6 of *Gendered Discourses*, on 'Celebrity fatherhood: the Blair baby', which looks at reports of the birth of Leo Blair as well as relevant editorials.

Judith Baxter (2003) *Positioning Gender in Discourse: a feminist methodology*. London: Palgrave Macmillan

This extract comes from Chapter 3 of Baxter's book: 'Getting to grips with FPDA'. FPDA, 'Feminist post-structuralist discourse analysis', developed out of her earlier 'PDA' ('Post-structuralist discourse analysis') (2002a). 'Within the post-structuralist spirit of encouraging interplay between different voices and perspectives', Baxter writes, 'there should never just be *one* version of FPDA, but a whole variety of versions or approaches' (2003: 58).

Task B7.3.1: Before you read

> Given your understandings of 'feminism', 'post-structuralism' and 'discourse analysis', do you see any contradictions and tensions in the name of this approach?

> Alternatively, do you see potentially fruitful synergies here?

Principles of FPDA

There are a number of principles constituting the practice of the discourse analyst, which clearly define the FPDA approach but nonetheless overlap with certain aspects of the methodologies associated with CA and CDA. These are: self-reflexivity, a deconstructionist approach and selecting a specific feminist focus.

Self-reflexivity

In Chapter 2, I discussed how different interpretations of the principle of self-reflexivity – or the need to be critical of our assumptions – form an important part of the research practice of CA, CDA and FPDA analysts. Here, I consider three roles for self-reflexivity within the specific context of FPDA research.

First of all, FPDA practitioners should aim to make their theoretical positions clear, and make explicit the epistemological assumptions that are to be applied to any act of discourse analysis. This is based on the way that both post-structuralist theory (Scott and Usher, 1996) and more recent feminist theory (e.g. Butler, 1990; Lather, 1991; Mills, 2002[a]) have challenged the positivist view that there is a determinate world that can be definitively known and explained (Elliott, 1996; Foucault, 1980; Lyotard, 1984). In contrast, both feminist and post-structuralist theories argue that any interpretation of data must explicitly acknowledge that it is constructed, provisional, perspectival and context-driven. A post-structuralist feminism must therefore accept its own status as context-specific, the product of particular sets of discursive relations. It has no more claim to speak the truth than any other discourse but must

J. Baxter

own up to its own points of view, specific aims, desires and political positions within power relations. Yet, . . . post-structuralist theory argues that researchers should only temporarily associate themselves with a particular stance for fear that a 'will to truth' will convert into a 'will to power'. Certainly FPDA practitioners should take care not to engage more than temporarily with any single agenda, in order to encourage a wider and richer interplay of ideas and viewpoints in the discursive arena. This is not to say that FPDA practitioners cannot identify with a feminist perspective or take on a particular cause – quite the opposite. FPDA, in keeping with post-structuralist theory (e.g. Elliott, 1996), *does* have a transformative quest; to represent the complexities and ambiguities of *female* experience, and within this to give space to *female* voices that are being silenced or marginalised by dominant discourses. If and when this specific quest is achieved, FPDA should seek to overturn its own dominant discourse by looking to other 'silenced' issues within the field of gender and discourse or cease to function. This in a sense is its particular declared bias; this *is* its *raison d'être*. Self-reflexivity is the principle which governs the business of declaring, monitoring and evaluating the FPDA quest, or any other theoretical/epistemological position, while conducting discourse analysis.

Secondly, an approach to FPDA involves being self-reflexive about the deployment of a specialist technical vocabulary or 'foundational rhetoric' (Billig, 1999: 552). This means an explicit awareness that technical terms cannot describe 'objective' realities in an unproblematic way. Of course, post-structuralist theory has anyway collapsed the distinction between a material reality and a language that describes it, preferring to view language or discourses as 'practices that systematically form the object of which they speak' (Foucault, 1972: 49).

Task B7.3.2: While you read

➤ What are some different ways of understanding this last sentence of Baxter's?

➤ What are some different ways of understanding Foucault's characterisation of discourses to which Baxter refers?

J. Baxter

From a post-structuralist viewpoint, a specialist rhetoric is always associated with a particular knowledge. As this knowledge becomes more defined, accepted and established, its specialist vocabulary becomes a 'technology' by which it can be transformed into a 'truth narrative'. For this reason, FPDA analysts need to be aware that its own 'foundational rhetoric' can operate as a form of arcane, scholastic discrimination, with the potential to exclude and marginalise uninitiated readers and researchers. Ironically but quite justifiably, post-structuralism has itself become a target for jokes and criticisms directed at the obfuscating nature of its jargon. For instance, McWilliam (1997: 201) has criticised what she calls the 'PMT' (post-modernist tension) of certain feminist post-structuralist writers. She cites Lather (1991) as an example of the kind of writer who argues for openness and self-reflexivity, yet seems quite obscure to other readers because of her use of highly verbose styles of writing. Thus, FPDA practitioners must be prepared to call attention to the assumptions and range of definitions implied in their use of key analytic terms. This is also important because all terms have the potential to be multi-accentual, to be read in plural if context-bound ways. This is why I have explained |earlier| apparently quite obvious terms such as 'feminism',

Extension

'post-structuralism', 'discourse', 'power', all of which are open to a wide range of possible readings and interpretations. I would suggest that it is a legitimate authorial practice for FPDA practitioners to 'close down' the range of readings of terms in this way, provided they are self-reflexive in foregrounding the range of meanings that they are potentially invoking or excluding.

Thirdly, FPDA involves the need to be overtly self-aware of the fictionality and textuality of the research process and the phenomenon that any act of research comprises a series of authorial choices and strategies. According to the post-structuralist view, all pursuits of knowledge are to do with creating a world (Usher, 1996), and hence research is itself a discursive construct and constitutive or 'world-making'. Post-structuralism sees any act of knowledge generation, such as discourse analysis, as a 'textualising' practice in that no form of knowledge can be separated from the structures, conventions and conceptuality of language as inscribed within discourses and texts. The business of textualising will constitute the researcher as literally an 'author', with a certain control over their own work of fiction. However, the researcher is in turn positioned by the limited range of scholastic discursive practices which legitimate particular ways of recording, analysing and interpreting discourse. Few researchers succeed if they work outside approved discursive practices, and this is a truism barely contested by the scholastic conventions adhered to in this book! However, one of the strengths of the FPDA approach is that it encourages researchers to use 'writerly' (Barthes, 1977) strategies in order to foreground the textualising process of conducting discourse analysis. In simpler terms, researchers need to draw attention to the choices they make in determining exactly how they are going to analyse texts, and then be prepared to justify or explain the effects of those choices. Arguably, the FPDA approach to self-reflexivity adds to and enriches other forms of analysis, such as CA and CDA, by the particular focus it places on the authorial role of the analyst and the 'fictionality' or constructed nature of all acts of research.

A deconstructionist approach

In this section, the first part of which is omitted, Baxter emphasises the principles and importance of 'textual interplay'.

I would therefore suggest that there are various strategies by which FPDA practitioners can develop an organised and focused approach to their work whilst simultaneously acknowledging the continual textual interplay of the data arising from their research, *without* being swallowed up by deconstructionist relativism. The *first* is by consciously not developing an overriding authorial argument at the expense of alternative points of view. Those 'alternative points of view' might be represented by the voices of other theorists in the field, the participants in the research study, and/or by different members of a research team in conducting the business of analysing texts. Partly implicated in this is the principle of self-reflexivity: the author/analyst must own up to his/her ideological motives, perspectives and short-comings within a given discursive context. But additionally there is the post-structuralist recognition of a kind of intellectual pluralism that the author/analyst has no more claim to speak 'the truth' and no better right to be heard than any other participant in the study. The purpose of supplementing the analyst's voice with the voices of other participants is different to its role in more traditional ethnographic terms (e.g. Hammersley, 1990: 606) where the cross-validation of multiple accounts are added to produce 'one true description'.

Instead, FPDA's purpose is to pre-empt the imperialism of the author's voice and bring a richer, potentially more imaginative range of ideas and viewpoints into play. In other words, the author/analyst should allow their own voice to be supplemented by voices from a variety of data sources, so that they do not privilege their own readings at the expense of those who may have contributed to, or constituted the data.

Secondly, aiming for textual interplay as a discourse analyst also means resisting the temptation to go for narrative closure, and allowing space for an open-ended verdict, or for alternative voices to comment on the data. From a deconstructive perspective, this inhibits the possibility of ossification or degradation into hierarchical structure, and opens up the recognition of the subtle, continuous shifts between terms, ideas and perspectives. The job of the FPDA analyst is effectively like that of a juggler who is striving to keep all the batons in the air simultaneously. However, this particular analogy not only implies multiple accounts (the batons) but also an author (the juggler). In self-reflexive spirit, I must therefore acknowledge that the post-structuralist advocacy of open-ended, endlessly deferred meaning goes against the grain for most researchers, trained as they are in the business of having something significant to say from which others might learn. My answer to this is that within an FPDA framework we should attempt to do both: provide opportunities for multiple, open-ended readings of a piece of analysis, but self-reflexively juxtapose our own supplementary accounts alongside those of other participants. Thirdly, we should be self-reflexively open to the incipient irony of what we say and do as authors and analysts: this book represents an attempt to fix meaning, however much it purports to be in the business of destabilising the meanings generated by 'authoritative discourses' (Bakhtin, 1981). Finally, despite the emphasis upon textual interplay and juggling on the part of the analyst, the methodology of FPDA involves a strictly pragmatic, focused, logical and organised process . . . This is because FPDA scholarship very much resides in system- atically highlighting the diverse voices constituting the data from the cacophony of any research setting. It would be counter-intuitive and frankly daft to expect discourse analysts or their readers to accept a kind of fuzzy, ever-questioning interpretation of spoken discourse where things have no pin-downable meanings.

Finding a feminist focus

|Earlier| I explored how 'third wave' or post-structuralist feminism works to defuse and dissolve the oppositions and tensions, which inscribed the emancipatory agenda of modernist feminism. I argued that current versions of feminism are in many ways compatible with, and supplement post-structuralist theory. For example, post- structuralist feminism has been concerned to critique many of the fundamental tenets of 'second wave' feminism, challenging constructs of gender dichotomy (e.g. Bing and Bergvall, 1998) and supplementing them with constructs of diversity and complexity. While it would be wrong to ignore or smooth away the potential contradictions between post-structuralism's advocacy of textual interplay on one hand, and femi- nism's commitment to privileging the female voice on the other, I have suggested that there is space for a partnership between the two perspectives since both support the quest to release the voices of those who have been silenced or suppressed.

As Mills (2002|a|) has argued, feminist research is no longer about exploring the effects of the 'big' sociolinguistic variable of gender on different social groups in a top-down, all-embracing way, nor is it about demonstrating that girls/women are universally subordinated or oppressed. Within a post-structuralist paradigm, a feminist focus is, among other things, 'a form of attention, a lens that brings into focus particular questions' (Fox-Keller, 1985: 6). It is concerned with feminist questions and issues that might arise in the study of specific communities of speakers, and is therefore ideally suited to small-scale, localised, short-term, strategically planned projects which intend to transform some aspects of cultural practice for girls/women. This focus may be preconceived and therefore self-reflexively imposed on the analysis of the data. For example, I applied a preconceived focus to the management study . . . where I chose to study the ways in which one female senior manager negotiated her competing subject positions within the context of a series of male-dominated business meetings. Alternatively, in ethnographic spirit, the feminist focus might arise 'naturally' from extended observations within a research setting. This occurred in the classroom study . . . where I gradually became aware that a dominant discourse of gender differentiation was interwoven with other discourses to position girls as generally more silent than boys in public classroom settings such as whole class discussion.

Thus, selecting a feminist focus to post-structuralist discourse analysis must inevitably move away from the old issues of the oppression and subordination of women, or the effects of gender upon the speech patterns of particular social groups. It involves highlighting key discourses on gender as they are negotiated and performed within specific, localised contexts. It also involves making sense of the ways in which these discourses position female speakers (in particular) as relatively powerful, powerless or a combination of both. It acknowledges the complexities, ambiguities and differences in the experiences of particular female speakers, as well as focusing on the possibilities for resistance and reinterpretation of social practices. It celebrates and foregrounds moments of *strength* in women's interactions with others, whilst self-reflexively pointing up the dangers of becoming complacent about privileging certain (female) voices over those of others.

Sources of data

A powerful source of data for the FPDA practitioner, apart from transcripts of talk or written texts, is that which is gained from a range of different voices: whether those of the research subjects themselves, other members of the research team, theorists in the field or, indeed, the author's own voice.

Baxter continues by exploring two interrelated constructs to do with these 'different voices': polyphony or 'multiple-voices', and heteroglossia or 'competing voices and accounts'.

★ Task B7.3.3: After you've read

➤ Read Baxter's Chapter 2 on polyphony and heteroglossia. While you read, consider similarities and differences between the two.

➤ Then read Baxter's exemplification of doing FPDA in terms of these principles in her 'classroom study' (Chapters 4–5) and 'management team study' (Chapters 6–7) in *Positioning Gender in Discourse.*

Unit B8
Approaches to gender and language research

In Unit B8 we look at examples of what might be seen as one methodology (or 'tool'), and one approach. The extracts come from three articles: one on corpus linguistics, the methodology; and two on conversation analysis (CA), the approach.

Paul Rayson, Geoff Leech and Mary Hodges (1997) 'Social differentiation in the use of English vocabulary: some analyses of the conversational component of the British National Corpus', *International Journal of Corpus Linguistics* **2 (1): 133–52**

Text B8.1
P. Rayson et al.

In this unit, Rayson et al. investigate 'social differentiation' in the use of English vocabulary through the spoken English sub-corpus of the British National Corpus. This differentiation includes 'gender' as a binary category, and it is the section of the article on gender which is reproduced here. Rayson et al. looked at words most characteristic of male and of female speech, use of family terms and parts of speech (common nouns, proper nouns, pronouns and verbs).

Task B8.1.1: Before you read

➤ If you were asked to suggest which words women tend to use more than men, and vice versa, could you do this? If so, note these down. Are you thinking of certain groups of women/men here?

➤ If you cannot do this, does this mean that you are not aware of any such tendencies? Or is there a different reason?

1. Introduction

P. Rayson et al.

. . . The British National Corpus (BNC) is a c. 100-million-word corpus of present-day British English, containing a c. 10-million-word subcorpus of spoken language recorded in the period 1991–1993. The spoken subcorpus, in its turn, is subdivided into a part sampled by demographic methods (the "Conversational Corpus") and a part sampled by context-governed methods.

P. Rayson et al.

The Conversational Corpus, consisting of 4,552,555 words, was collected by the following method. A market-research firm, the British Market Research Bureau, sampled the population of the UK (over the age of 15) using well-tried methods of social survey research. Individuals taking part in the project were equipped with a high-quality Walkman sound recorder, and recorded any linguistic transactions in which they engaged during a period of two days. These individuals, whom we will henceforth call "respondents", numbered 153 and were sampled in order to obtain a good representation of the population of the UK, given the unavoidable practical limitation in the number of respondents, according to:

Region: south, midland, north
Gender: male, female
Age: 15–24, 25–34, 35–44, 45–59, 60 and over
Social Group: A, B, C1, C2, D, E

In addition, respondents undertook to obtain the permission of other speakers with whom they engaged in conversation and to note for each speaker details of gender, age, social group, etc. Thus the Conversational Corpus provides an unparalleled resource for investigating, on a large scale, the conversational behavior of the British population in the 1990s . . .

2. Gender variation

Using the whole of the Conversational Corpus material for which gender of speaker is indicated, we find that female speakers have a larger share of the corpus than male speakers according to a number of different measures. Firstly, there is a small built-in bias in the corpus, in that 75 female respondents but only 73 male respondents were enlisted as volunteers to participate in the collection of data. In addition, female speakers overall took a larger share of the language collected, as shown in Table [B8.1.1].

Not only were there more female respondents, but also more female speakers, who on the whole took more turns and longer turns than the male speakers. All this led to a greater female than male representation in the Conversational Corpus. It should be borne in mind, therefore, in the following tables, that for every 100 word tokens spoken by men in the demographic corpus, 151 were spoken by women. Because of this disparity, the normalized frequency of each word is presented in the following tables in the form of a percentage of all word tokens (M% = percentage of the number of word tokens spoken by males; F% = percentage of the number of word tokens spoken by females). The χ^2 value is based on comparison of such normalized frequencies. The 25 most significant words showing overrepresentation in male and female speech are shown in Tables [B8.1.2 and B8.1.3], in order of significance.

Table [B8.1.1] Distribution of the Conversational Corpus between female and male speakers

	Female speakers	Male speakers
Number of speakers	561	536
Number of turns	250955	179844
Number of words spoken	2593452	1714443
Number of turns per speaker	447.33	335.53
Number of words per turn	10.33	9.53

Table [B8.1.2] Words most characteristic of male speech

Word	Males	M%	Females	F%	χ^2
fucking	1401	0.08	325	0.01	1233.1
er	9589	0.56	9307	0.36	945.4
the	44617	2.60	57128	2.20	698.0
yeah	22050	1.29	28485	1.10	310.3
aye	1214	0.07	876	0.03	291.8
right	6163	0.36	6945	0.27	276.0
hundred	1488	0.09	1234	0.05	251.1
fuck	335	0.02	107	0.00	239.0
is	13608	0.79	17283	0.67	233.3
of	13907	0.81	17907	0.69	203.6
two	4347	0.25	5022	0.19	170.3
three	2753	0.16	2959	0.11	168.2
a	28818	1.68	39631	1.53	151.6
four	2160	0.13	2279	0.09	145.5
ah	2395	0.14	2583	0.10	143.6
no	14942	0.87	19880	0.77	140.8
number	615	0.04	463	0.02	133.9
quid	484	0.03	339	0.01	124.2
one	9915	0.58	12932	0.50	123.6
mate	262	0.02	129	0.00	120.8
which	1477	0.09	1498	0.06	120.5
okay	1313	0.08	1298	0.05	119.9
that	31014	1.81	43331	1.67	114.2
guy	211	0.01	95	0.00	108.6
da	459	0.03	338	0.01	105.3
yes	7102	0.41	9167	0.35	101.0

Table [B8.1.3] Words most characteristic of female speech

Word	Males	M%	Females	F%	χ^2
she	7134	0.42	22623	0.87	3109.7
her	2333	0.14	7275	0.28	965.4
said	4965	0.29	12280	0.47	872.0
n't	24653	1.44	44087	1.70	443.9
I	55516	3.24	92945	3.58	357.9
and	29677	1.73	50342	1.94	245.3
to	23467	1.37	39861	1.54	198.6
cos	3369	0.20	6829	0.26	194.6
oh	13378	0.78	23310	0.90	170.2
Christmas	288	0.02	1001	0.04	163.9
thought	1573	0.09	3485	0.13	159.7
lovely	414	0.02	1214	0.05	140.3
nice	1279	0.07	2851	0.11	134.4
mm	7189	0.42	12891	0.50	133.8
had	4040	0.24	7600	0.29	125.9
did	6415	0.37	11424	0.44	109.6
going	3139	0.18	5974	0.23	109.0
because	1919	0.11	3861	0.15	105.0
him	2710	0.16	5188	0.20	99.2
really	2646	0.15	5070	0.20	97.6
school	501	0.03	1265	0.05	96.3

P. Rayson et al.

Table [B8.1.3] continued

Word	Males	M%	Females	F%	χ^2
he	15993	0.93	26607	1.03	90.4
think	4980	0.29	8899	0.34	88.8
home	734	0.04	1662	0.06	84.0
me	5182	0.30	9186	0.35	83.5

 Task B8.1.2: Reflection task

➤ What overall 'profile' of masculine and feminine speech do Tables B8.1.2 and B8.1.3 suggest? What do you think about the fact that pronouns tended to be used more by female speakers?

P. Rayson et al.

Perhaps the most notable (though predictable) finding illustrated in Table [B8.1.2] is the tendency for taboo words ("swear words") to be more characteristic of male speech than female speech. (This tendency is found not only with *fucking* but also with other "four-letter words" lower down the list: shit $\chi^2 = 37.4$, hell $\chi^2 = 22.8$, crap $\chi^2 = 44.3$.)

Task B8.1.3: Reflection task

➤ Do the (quite striking) gender tendencies in use of 'taboo' words correspond to your own experience?

P. Rayson et al.

Another tendency is for males to use number words: not only *hundred* ($\chi^2 = 251.1$), and *one* ($\chi^2 = 123.6$) but also, for example, *three* $\chi^2 = 168.2$, *two* $\chi^2 = 170.3$, *four* $\chi^2 = 145.5$. Females, on the other hand, make strikingly greater use of the feminine pronoun *she/her/hers* and also of the first-person pronoun *I/me/my/mine* (see Table [B8.1.4])

As Table [B8.1.2] shows, men are more likely to use the filled-pause marker *er* and certain informal interjections or word-isolates such as *yeah, aye, okay, ah* ($\chi^2 = 143.6$), *eh* ($\chi^2 = 77.5$), and *hmm* ($\chi^2 = 28.5$). Women, on the other hand, make more use of *yes* ($\chi^2 = 101.0$), *mm* ($\chi^2 = 133.8$), and *really* ($\chi^2 = 97.6$).

Table [B8.1.4] Use of some pronouns in female speech

Word	Males	M%	Females	F%	χ^2
she	7134	0.42	22626	0.87	3109.7
her	2333	0.14	7275	0.28	965.4
hers	26	0.00	110	0.00	24.3
I	55516	3.24	92945	3.58	357.9
me	51882	0.30	9186	0.35	8305
mine	505	0.03	818	0.03	1.5

Task B8.1.4: Reflection task

➤ Do any of these apparent gender tendencies in use of filled-pause markers, interjections and word-isolates correspond to your own experience?

➤ What might be some possible interpretations here?

The preference for *the* and *of* in male speech in Table [B8.1.2] may appear more puzzling, but accords with the stronger male preference for nouns (in particular common nouns) over verbs and pronouns (see Table [B8.1.5]. One would hypothesise, on the basis of figures presented in Table [B8.1.5] below, that male speech shows a stronger propensity to build noun phrases (including articles and common nouns) where female speech has a tendency to rely more on pronouns and proper nouns.

P. Rayson et al.

Table [B8.1.5] Parts of speech as percentage of all word tokens

	Males %	Females %	χ^2
Common Nouns	8.49	7.93	395.18
Proper Nouns	1.44	1.64	257.78
Pronouns	13.37	14.55	1016.27
Verbs	20.30	21.52	721.51

Many fascinating lexical patterns of gender preference could be followed up here, and their reasons explored, but we will content ourselves with mentioning one other area – that of family relationships – where the sexes are strongly differentiated in lexical preference. On the whole, women are more strongly oriented towards family terms, although there are some interesting exceptions (see Tables [B8.1.6 and B8.1.7]).

The provisional conclusion of this section is that the differences between male speech and female speech in the Conversational Corpus are pronounced (to judge from χ^2 values, they are greater than differences based on age or social group), but are matters of frequency, rather than of absolute choice. For example, although taboo words are much more frequent in male speech, they are by no means absent from female speech. A further investigation, which we have not been able to carry out, would be to find out how speech in the corpus varies according to the gender of the addressee as well as the gender of the speaker.

Table [B8.1.6] Some family terms used more by females

Word	Males	M%	Females	F%	χ^2
mother	272	0.02	627	0.02	34.2
father	115	0.01	307	0.01	27.7
sister	105	0.01	257	0.01	17.6
brother	136	0.01	229	0.01	1.0
daughter	70	0.00	171	0.01	11.6
daddy	353	0.02	624	0.02	5.5
grandma	58	0.00	207	0.01	35.5
aunty/auntie	74	0.00	179	0.01	11.8

Table [B8.1.7] Some family terms used more by males

Word	Males	M%	Females	F%	χ^2
mummy	742	0.04	755	0.03	59.6
mum	1647	0.10	1856	0.07	76.2
son	171	0.01	149	0.01	24.8
dad	941	0.05	1275	0.05	6.6

★ Task B8.1.5: After you've read

➤ To what extent does this article acknowledge that the findings reflect tendencies rather than differences?

➤ Identify the words and phrases that do this, as well as any that do not.

➤ How representative are the findings reported here, in terms of gender? (Or, rather, what are they representative of?)

➤ Is corpus linguistics simply a conservative return to the 'gender differences' paradigm?

Text B8.2
E. Stokoe and
J. Smithson

Elizabeth Stokoe and Janet Smithson (2001) 'Making gender relevant: conversation analysis and gender categories in discourse', *Discourse and Society* 12 (2): 217–44

In this extract, Elizabeth Stokoe and Janet Smithson engage theoretically with the ongoing debate in *Discourse and Society* about whether there can be a productive relationship between CA and feminism, without compromising either. Relatedly, and following, B8.3 is an extract from an article by Celia Kitzinger, which focuses on 'coming out talk' – an 'empirical demonstration', Kitzinger claims, 'of the value of conversation analysis (CA) for feminist research' (2000: 163).

Noting a 'culture of exaggeration in [past] sex difference research' (2001: 218), Stokoe and Smithson point to the more recent focus on gender being located in interactions, its 'performative nature', and the importance of 'gender's discursive articulation'. However, they also critique research which focuses on the 'doing' of gender, since this still entails there being 'two genders': 'Contrasting how speakers "do" one of masculinity or femininity involves the production of theories based on gender dualism'. They suggest CA as an alternative (this is where the extract starts), but also highlight the problematic nature of CA for feminist research. The final section of the extract looks at how the CA notion of 'participants' orientations' might be understood in relation to gender.

Task B8.2.1: While you read

➤ Carefully note down some differences between a CA approach, a critical discourse analysis (CDA) approach and an FPDA approach.

One solution is to interrogate the category of gender *as it appears in people's talk*, using ethnomethodological principles and the related methodology of conversation analysis (CA). CA constitutes an 'analytic mentality' that requires researchers to consider their data without pre-selecting concepts and theories to test or explore (Hester and Eglin, 1997). This means that rather than seeking to impose categories on to the analysis of discursive data (such as 'gender', 'power'), the focus is upon what participants, or *members*, orient to in their discussions. If one wants to make claims about sociological variables such as gender or class, such variables must be shown to be *relevant to the participants*. Conversation analysts argue this approach sets up a less interpretational basis for the analytic claims made because the basis is in 'people's own orientation to what's going on: what they take to be relevant and to be pertinent to the interaction as it proceeds' (Antaki, 1995: 23). Summarizing the fundamental assumption of this position, Schegloff (1992: 192; emphasis in original) writes:

> . . . showing that some orientation to context is demonstrably relevant to the participants is important . . . in order to ensure that what informs the analysis is what is relevant to *the participants in its target event*, and not what is relevant in the first instance to its academic analysts by virtue of the set of analytic and theoretical commitments which they bring to their work.

In his 1997 article, Schegloff challenges a critical discourse analytic (CDA) theorization of gender and interaction and sets out the CA alternative. Consistent with the ideas described above, Schegloff argues that in order to warrant a claim that gender is relevant in interaction, analysts must be able to demonstrate its *relevance for speakers*. There is a small body of work outside the rather inward-looking field of language and gender that adopts such a framework for explicating members' practices of gender categorization, providing a radically different approach to the study of gender and discourse (Edwards, 1998; Hopper and LeBaron, 1998; Philipsen, 1990/1; Stokoe, 1998; Stringer and Hopper, 1998). From this perspective, no commentary is produced about wider discourses or repertoires that may be drawn upon by the speakers, or the gendered styles of the speakers themselves. The analysis sticks closely to the local context in which the speaker makes gender pertinent.

. . . we argue that CA is a useful tool for making claims about the relevance of gender in talk-in-interaction because such claims are grounded in speakers' orientations . . . This is in sharp contrast to other work in the field, which imposes analysts' assumptions and categories on to the analysis. However, the application of CA to the study of gender and other social categories has recently generated heated debate, as evidenced in the pages of *Discourse & Society* (Bergvall and Remlinger, 1996; Billig, 1999; Hutchby, 1996; Schegloff, 1997, 1998, 1999a, 1999b; Speer and Potter, 2000; Stokoe, 1998; Van Dijk, 1999; Weatherall, 2000; Wetherell, 1998). We extend this debate by problematizing some of CA's claims and reflect on a number of related points. First, we consider the extent to which the 'analytic stances' of feminism and conversation analysis are compatible. Second, we question whether, as Schegloff (1997) suggests, it is fruitful (or even possible) to rely on descriptions of and orientations to gender

E. Stokoe and J. Smithson

solely in participants' terms. Linked to this, we ask what, precisely, counts as an orientation to gender? We suggest that the actual discursive practices of 'attending to', 'making relevant' or 'orienting to' gender remain unspecified in CA. This leads to our final point. While we propose CA is a useful tool for making claims about gender, and that such claims are grounded in speakers' orientations, we suggest that culture and common-sense knowledge, of both members and analysts, are largely unacknowledged and unexplicated resources in CA . . .

Feminist conversation analysis: an oxymoron?

Davis (1988) starts her feminist conversation analysis of doctor-patient interaction from the position that any interaction between women and men will involve power asymmetry and that this is a 'social fact'. In contrast, a central argument of CA is that analysts should adopt a stance of 'unmotivated looking' when analysing data and thus bring no assumptions, theories or categories to it (Psathas, 1995; Sacks, 1984). Categories should only be understood within the context that is built up by interactants as they display their understandings of emergent social actions. This position has stimulated responses from other analysts of discourse and conversational interaction. For example, Wetherell (1998) has argued that a complete scholarly analysis of data, as opposed to a solely technical analysis, must include a focus both on the argumentative trajectory of talk as displayed in participants' orientations and the broader interpretative resources that members draw upon.

For us, what is problematic about CA's stance is its potential incompatibility with a feminist approach to data analysis. We take the position that a key feature of feminist research is the investigation of sexism in society and the political location of the researcher as feminist within the research; as such, no method is *prima facie* incompatible with feminism (Brannen, 1992; Maynard and Purvis, 1994; Stanley and Wise, 1983). However, many feminists have generally eschewed CA as a possible method because of its perceived inability to advance political arguments (discussed by Wetherell, 1998) or for its perceived 'positivism' (Hollway, 1989). As Speer (1999) has shown, recent CA textbooks (for example, Hutchby and Wooffitt, 1998; ten Have, 1999) typically ignore feminist concerns and critiques, although she concludes that there is nothing intrinsic in the type of CA advanced in these texts that would prevent feminists with a critical agenda from using it to ask politically motivated questions. Indeed, feminists such as Davis (1988; see also Ainsworth-Vaughn, 1992; West, 1995) feel entitled to take a broadly critical perspective and combine this with authentic CA-based analyses, something that 'fundamentalist' commentators such as Schegloff might dispute.

A major problem for feminists with using CA is that making claims about approaching data with a 'clean gaze' is a stance within itself, rather than a 'neutral' stance, and imports its own theoretical assumptions (Billig, 1999; Buttny, 1993; Cameron, 1994). Feminist philosophy informs us that it is impossible to maintain an impartial position in any research because analysts inevitably bring their own experiences, cultural background and values to bear on the data (Hollway, 1989; Weatherall, 2000). Feminists also stress the importance of reflexivity and subjectivity in the research process and a political commitment to social change and transformation (Wilkinson, 1997). So whereas CA would argue that if gender is embedded in society then it should be observable in talk, feminists would maintain that it is not only impossible to come to the data 'without bringing any problems to it' (Sacks, 1992)

E. Stokoe and
J. Smithson

but not even desirable or valid to try. Much feminist work necessarily starts from a certain political perspective and with certain things as axiomatic. Most importantly, we suggest that despite claims to the contrary researchers do not come 'neutrally' to analysis, but bring their cultural (gendered) 'baggage'. At this point in our argument, it seems that CA and feminism are incompatible due to these opposing analytic positions.

Gender as a participants' category

We have established that, for conversation analysts, claims that gender is relevant to an interaction can only be made if speakers themselves attend to it. A second issue in the debate, therefore, and one which is largely ignored in the literature, is *what precisely counts* as an orientation to gender? Whereas many authors have written about 'participants' orientations', 'member's categories' and so on, the actual discursive practices involved in 'attending to', 'making relevant', 'indexing' or 'orienting to' gender remain unspecified. Conversation analysts describe both explicit and implicit ways that speakers might demonstrate their orientation to gender. But what mechanisms are involved in this process, for both speakers and analysts?

Schegloff sets out his position on this matter in the recent series of exchanges in *Discourse & Society*. For instance, in his analysis of 'Marsha and Tony' (1997: 173), he suggests how CDAs might describe the interaction 'along gender lines, in which the asymmetries of status and power along gender lines in this society are played out in the interactional arena of interruption and overlapping talk'. In other words, Schegloff objects to the assumption that gender can be read off interactional patterns, a criticism made of much language and gender research (for example, Cameron, 1992[b]). Consequently, he argues that CDA does not allow for 'the overtly displayed concerns of the participants themselves. . . . Such analyses insist instead on character-isations of the parties, the relevancies, and the context, to which the analyst is oriented' (1997: 174). This position is echoed in the comments of other conversation analysts. For example, LeBaron (participating in transcribed discussion in Tracy, 1998: 15) argues:

> . . . we should not . . . say 'oh, look, here's man and a woman talking; let's look at how they talk; oh, we can make these conclusions about gendered commu-nication'. But rather we should say, 'gender only becomes an issue when the participants themselves make it one and we can point to different things about that'.

Buttny (participating in the same discussion, Tracy, 1998) also argues against the omnirelevance of gender, claiming that a 'gender always matters' position is illogical. Finally, Hopper and LeBaron (1998: 61) claim that 'researchers may specify the relevance of a feature of context (for example, gender) mainly in moments of social interaction in which actors observably orient to that feature'.

The argument, then, is that speakers must show that gender is relevant to them. But *what counts* as an orientation to gender? For Schegloff, 'what counts' is demon-strated in his analysis of 'Chicken Dinner' in which explicit mention of the term 'ladies' during the course of interaction shows how 'gender is relevant here after all' (1997: 182). Other analysts have also described the content of and processes involved in attending to gender in interaction. For example, Stringer and Hopper (1998: 213)

E. Stokoe and
J. Smithson

explore instances in which speakers use the pseudo-generic *he* when referring to 'sex-unspecified incumbents of traditionally male social categories'. When another speaker problematizes the generic *he*, gender becomes the axis around which the conversation proceeds. Similarly, Hopper and LeBaron (1998) note that in their data, self- or other-repairs of gender references are oriented to the need for gender-inclusive language, promoting the salience of gender as part of the context. In an analysis of couples therapy, Edwards (1998) discusses how participants use different gender references, 'woman' and 'girl', at strategic points in their discussion of the husband's affair. Finally, Philipsen (1990/1) analyses the gender references in a film script in which a teacher is referred to as such, then as 'Mrs Ganin', 'she' and 'a lady'. The latter three references all index (female) gender as the salient thing about the teacher.

In all of these studies, attending to gender can be defined as the *explicit mention of a gender reference*, such as 'he', 'she', 'ladies', 'girl', or 'woman'. However, this definition seems rather restrictive for, as Ochs (1992) points out, very few words in the English language exclusively index gender. Kitzinger (2000: 171) complains that it would be 'unbearably limiting' if conversation analysts had to rely on such explicit orientations. Schegloff himself acknowledges the potential limitations of such a narrow definition. He writes: 'explicit mention of a category term . . . is by no means necessary to establish the relevant orientation by the participants . . . orientation to gender can be manifested without being explicitly named or mentioned' (1997: 182). This concession is problematic for, if something is implicit in conversation it is up to the analyst to reveal something that, logically, is not available directly . . .

Schegloff is not alone in suggesting that gender may be indexed implicitly although, so far, we are no closer to defining what this might mean practically. Weatherall (2000: 287–8) suggests that 'linguistic indexes of gender may occur at every level of language. So, even if gender is not explicitly privileged by participants as relevant to the conversation, it is an omnipresent feature of all interactions'. According to Hopper and LeBaron (1998), these features might include gender-marked names and terms of address and reference. They also argue that 'gender can be indexed as a relevant part of the context by ambiguous words with possible references to sexuality; reference to female appearance or male appearance; or references to female demeanor or male demeanor' (1998: 171). Hopper and LeBaron further suggest that gender-indexing resources might include references to gendered activities (they give the example of 'car mechanics') and conclude that, 'in fact, speakers would experience some difficulty not indexing gender in many utterances' (1998: 171). Finally, a number of authors claim that gender is indexed in English through high or low pitch of voice, intonational qualities, or by using particular vocabulary (Hopper and LeBaron, 1998; Kessler and McKenna, 1978).

What counts as orienting to or indexing gender has therefore shifted, from a restrictive definition comprising explicit gender references to much broader but contestable indexes such as the use of sexist language particles, pitch of voice and intonation, references to sexuality and gendered activities. Implicit indexes are potentially ambiguous, open to disagreement between analysts, and generally more difficult to make claims about. For example, Hopper and LeBaron argue that the activity 'car mechanic' indexes male gender. But there is nothing intrinsic in this term that indexes gender; this example can only be given (and any subsequent analysis performed on it) if the analyst imports something of their own background knowledge about gendered references and activities . . .

What can we conclude about this issue of indexing gender? First, we argue that the most straightforward answer to the question 'what counts?' is to restrict any claims about the relevance of gender to instances where speakers use explicit gender references: 'he', 'she', 'man', 'woman', and so on. Pitch and intonational cues might be omnipresent, but they have to be evidenced as relevant by speakers. To further complicate matters, perhaps there are two types of index or 'relevancies' – one where we can simply spot speakers using explicit gender references, but these do not appear relevant to speakers in the ensuing turns at talk, and a second where it is 'noticed' in the subsequent interaction. The first of these, as well as pointing to terms such as 'car mechanic', references to sexuality and demeanour, requires the import of cultural knowledge on behalf of the analyst. This is problematic for |those| conversation analysts who argue that explanations must be grounded in what participants do and say.

Stokoe and Smithson continue by looking at examples of how this indexing might work, using data from seminar discussions, and, interestingly (since CA conventionally uses naturally occurring data) focus groups. They also address the question of interpretation – noting that analysts always draw on their own 'interpretive resources'. They suggest that the analyst can also be seen as a 'member', sharing cultural understandings with speakers.

Task B8.2.2: After you've read

➤ How many different ways can you think of in which people might be seen as 'orienting to gender' in their talk?

➤ What do you see as the problems with (a) considering gender only as what is 'oriented to' in some ways by speakers?; (b) basing 'findings' on the analyst's 'imposed' interpretation?

➤ Reread and carefully consider the last paragraph of the extract, and think of examples of the 'two types of index'.

➤ Do you feel that some theoretical and methodological approaches are more appropriate than others for research into gender and language? If so, which, and why? (A useful reference here is Kroløkke and Sørensen [2006]).

Celia Kitzinger (2000) 'Doing feminist conversation analysis', *Feminism and Psychology* 10 (2): 163–93

Celia Kitzinger has written widely on gender, sexuality (particularly lesbian sexuality) and conversation analysis (CA). Currently she is a reader in Lesbian and Feminist Psychology. In the first part of her article, like Stokoe and Smithson, she argues in favour of the use of CA for feminist research, challenging the fundamental criticism that CA's social theory is incompatible with feminism. She notes how in CA people are understood as 'agents actively engaged in methodological and sanctioned procedures for producing or resisting, colluding with or transgressing, the taken-for-granted social world' (2000: 168) but that CA does not straight-forwardly and naïvely attribute more agency to women than is possible under heteropatriarchy. Kitzinger notes that CA is concerned with people's *own* interpretations, which is also a tenet of much feminist research (women as research 'subjects' rather than 'objects'), and, though it may be unsuitable for 'sex differences' research, can nevertheless serve feminist purposes.

Like Stokoe and Smithson, who propose that the analyst can be seen as a 'member', sharing cultural understandings, Kitzinger cites the value of the analyst's orientations. Her perspective is that (as referred to by Stokoe and Smithson):

> it would be unbearably limiting to use CA if it meant that I could only describe as 'sexist' or 'heterosexist' or 'racist' those forms of talk to which actors orient as such. Indeed, it is *precisely the fact that sexist, heterosexist and racist assumptions are routinely incorporated into everyday conversations* without anyone noticing or responding to them that way which is of interest to me.
>
> (2000: 171; Kitzinger's italics)

A feminist CA 'would use this focus on talk to uncover the practical reasoning through which the taken-for-granted world is accomplished (and resisted)' (2000: 173). This constitutes an imaginative bridging of a central concern of CA (the routine incorporation of assumptions into conversation) and the feminist concern that the analyst's interpretations are valuable – indeed, are necessary, to identify such assumptions.

Kitzinger also addresses the feminist concern that CA is 'too micro' by identifying the 'appropriate question' as 'what, if anything, CA's "micro" perspective has to offer us' as regards issues of power and oppression (2000: 173). She then illustrates what it offers with examples of how CA can be used to develop a feminist approach to date rape and to 'coming out' talk. The extract below includes just one case of 'coming out' talk, that of 'Linda'. It follows Kitzinger's identification of a research niche in the lesbian and gay psychology literature in the form of 'the act of disclosure itself' – rather than 'coming out stories'. The symbols used are conventional CA transcription symbols.

 Task B8.3.1: While you read

> ➤ Is it possible for the analyst to consider participants' orientations without drawing on her own?

C. Kitzinger | **Doing feminist conversation analysis**

By accident, I happen to have (so far) 12 instances of 'coming out' on audiotape. They come from a variety of sources including focus groups and training sessions, but most

. . . are taken from small group seminar sessions with undergraduate students, run as part of the 'Human Sexualities' module at Loughborough University, recorded, with students' signed permission and informed consent, for ongoing research by several members of the department on how sexuality is produced through talk. My interest, as a feminist, in this coming out data was initially promoted by what seemed to be a bewildering absence of response to the 'comings out' on the part of the audience (including, in four cases, me). In what I've come to think of as the mundane form of everyday coming out for people in relatively safe environments, nobody expresses disgust, talks about hell fire and damnation, or accuses anyone of being a disgusting pervert – but equally, nobody says 'congratulations!' or 'that's wonderful', or even gives any indication that they've registered the information. And yet I know from other discussions with the students who were coming out in these settings, or who had been the audiences for the comings out of others, that these were intensely important experiences. Coming out was extensively discussed beforehand, experienced as important and significant at the time, and considered newsworthy enough to report to other people afterwards – and yet, at the time the coming out was being done, nobody (me included) reacted to it in this way. There is virtually nothing in the lesbian and gay research literature which addresses the issue of lack of response, nor is there any consideration by feminist or critical psychologists about the political implications of these 'non-responses' to coming out. These, then, are the data extracts to which I am currently applying CA techniques in an attempt to gain a better understanding of how coming out is achieved and reacted to.

In this . . . example, I am leading a seminar discussion on intersexuality and the students are discussing how they would feel if they learned that someone they were attracted to was intersex, and the implications of that for their sexual identities. In this context, an undergraduate ('Linda') comes out as having found herself attracted to a woman a few years before. Other than a few 'mms' in response to this information, neither I nor any student in the group gives any re-action at all . . .

Linda comes out

01 *Kate:* I think it would change y- your concept of (0.2)
02 of (.) w- what it is that attracts you to somebody
03 (0.2) and i- their sex would n-not not be that feature,
04 perhaps ¿
05 (1.0)
06 *Kate:* Have I explained what I mean? I'm not sure whether I've
07 said what I me(hh)an.
08 CK: So y- (0.4) inst- (.) I mean, >I think a lot of lesbians
09 and gay people use that argument anyway which is that
10 it's not< (.)
11 *Kate:* [mmm]
12 CK: [the] <u>sex</u>, it's the <u>person</u> [I think]
13 *Kate:* [Yeah, I]
14 think my brain w'ld, it'd do it that way.=
15 *Linda:* = It *does*, it *does* have an effect on you because (0.2)
16 if you've thought of yourself as heterosexual (1.0)
17 and you (.) >suddenly find yourself attracted to a woman
18 °it happened to me, < (0.2) a few years ago°

19 it's <u>very</u> (0.8) dis<u>turb</u>ing, |in a| way it's=
20 CK: |mm|
21 *Linda*: =it's (0.2) makes you very <u>anx</u>ious (.).
22 because you then *don't* know how you're supposed to respond=
23 CK: —m|mm=
24 *Linda*: = |and (.) if you e- found out that your partner was an
25 <u>int</u>ersex you would wonder (.) >how do I respond to this
26 person sexually< I don't <u>know</u> (.) how to approach, how
27 to be romantic how to (.) wh<u>at</u> this person expects
28 from <u>me</u>, whereas if you (.) think of- you know of
29 yourself as <u>het</u>erosexual, then you <u>know</u> (0.2) the
30 responses you <u>know</u> how to interact.
31 |So it's those kind of|
32 CK: |There's a sort of set of| <u>guide</u>lines, aren't there,
33 ?: mmm
34 CK: for how to (.) how to <u>do</u> sexual interaction

In this extract, then, Linda tells us that she was sexually attracted to a woman a few years ago, and it creates barely a ripple on the surface of the conversation about intersex . . .

Many of Harvey Sacks's *Lectures on Conversation* |1995| are devoted to explorations of how people methodically achieve recognizable conversational actions without paying some negative price associated with them: how to avoid giving your name without refusing to give it; how to avoid giving help without refusing it; how to get help without requesting it; how to talk in a therapy session without revealing yourself. Part of what my analysis suggests is that many of us have developed a technique which could be called 'How to come out without anybody noticing'.

CA asks that we understand these 'coming out' utterances not only as a matter of information transfer from the person coming out to their co-conversationalists but also as actions in interactional sequence. Conveying new information is not the same thing as announcing news: not all new information conveyed is set up by speakers to be treated as news by the person to whom it is told. There is, for example, a substantial CA literature on breaking 'bad news' (for example, of serious diagnoses and deaths), which shows a range of devices used to avoid one person being heard to tell another bad news, while also ensuring that the information is imparted. In ordinary conversation, news telling can be organized so that the recipient, rather than the bearer of the news, ends up pronouncing it (Schegloff, 1988) and clinicians presenting parents with a diagnosis of mental retardation in their child use particular strategies to present the diagnosis as a simple 'confirmation' of something the parent already knows (Maynard, 1992). So, although the comings out I have collected do, as it happens, convey new information to the listeners about the speakers' sexuality, the first thing to observe, from a CA perspective, is that speakers are not doing 'news announcement'. Undoubtedly, there are some comings out which do news announcement, and which we can recognize as such: they begin with classic phrases (pre-announcements) like 'Mum, I've got something to tell you', or 'Guess what? I'm gay.' News announcement normatively makes relevant from the recipient an acknowledgement of news receipt and assessment of the information so conveyed. When 'comings out' are done as news announcement, then, they would make relevant assessments which can be anything from 'Oh no! it'll kill your father' to 'Oh, that's wonderful, I'm so pleased for you'. But Linda |and Kitzinger's other people coming out| are not doing news announcements. Instead, information about the speaker's sexuality is conveyed as an aside, as a list item or as a passing instance or illustration of some other point altogether. Not presenting information about one's sexuality as news has decisive consequences for shaping the course of the talk's development. If it is not announced as news, recipients have to work hard to receive it as such.

There's something else, though, about the construction of this coming out talk which makes audience response to it as news unlikely, and that's the location of the information in the turn-taking organization. Turn-taking organization is one of those classic areas of CA with which feminists and other radicals are often most impatient – but it offers a powerful tool for understanding why it is that these recipients of comings out do not react. Information about the speaker's sexuality is often deeply embedded within turn constructional units in ways that would render as interruptive any acknowledgement or assessment of this information from a co-conversationalist.

In Sacks et al.'s (1974) classic paper on turn-taking, they propose a model for conversation which seeks to explain the practices people use for ensuring – with systematic and orderly exceptions explainable by the theory itself – how it is that people in conversation overwhelmingly speak one at a time. The model proposes the existence of turn constructional units (TCUs), which can be whole sentences, phrases or sometimes just words, but which are recognizable (in context) as potentially constituting a complete turn. Each speaker is initially entitled to just *one* of these: after that, another speaker has the right (sometimes the obligation) to speak next. The model is complex and sophisticated and I have oversimplified it radically, but the key point of relevance here is that the turn-taking organization is not indifferent to the size of the turns parties take: rather, its 'underlying (though supercessable) organization is designed to minimize turn size' (Schegloff, 1982: 73) and consequently we need to understand long turns, with lengthy and/or multiple TCUs, as 'achievements and accomplishments' (Schegloff, 1982: 73) which have overcome the inherent bias of the system.

In the coming out episodes, the speaker, the one who is coming out, uses *long* TCUs, and *many* TCUs – and as CA shows us, that is something which has to be worked at: it does not just happen. Conversation analysts have documented some of the techniques people use when they want to keep speaking for a long time. Long TCUs can be accomplished by using particular sentence structures (such as 'if/then') which are hearably not complete until a second part of the sentence (such as the 'then' part) has been produced. People can project a long TCU simply by taking a big in-breath: studies show that in-breaths put hearers on the alert for a long (possibly multi-unit) turn. Multi-unit turns can be secured at the beginning of a speaker's turn by making a bid to tell a story ('did you hear about the time when . . .'); by using a list launcher ('four things . . .'); and by using 'markedly first verbs' (such as 'I thought . . .' or 'I tried . . .', which are regularly used to mark things incorrectly thought, or unsuccessfully tried, and therefore project accounts of what is now known, or an account of failure). Speakers may also employ methodical devices for achieving multi-unit turns during the course of their talk. They may 'rush through' a possible transition point – talking right through the intersection between one TCU and the next, not pausing to take a breath until a point of maximum grammatical control (that is, where it is obvious that the speaker is not complete). Even more radically, speakers sometimes prevent the end of a TCU (and hence possible speaker transition) from occurring simply by not uttering the last word or syllable of the TCU. (For all this, and more, see Schegloff, 1982.) Although critics have poured scorn on the turn-taking organization research as a tedious political irrelevance which . . . could only obscure the operation of power,

Schegloff (1999[a]: 563) has said that 'those committed to analyzing forms of inequality and oppression in interaction might do better to harness this account of turn-taking organization as a *resource* for their undertaking than to complain of it as an ideological distraction' (emphasis in original). And that is exactly what we can do here.

If we look back at Linda's coming out, we see that she embeds her coming out in the middle of an 'if/then' structure ('if you've thought of yourself as hetero-sexual . . .' [line 16]/ '[then] it's very disturbing' [line 19] – although the 'then' isn't actually spoken) which projects the first possible transition place to well after her coming out. In addition, at line 19, at exactly the point where the TCU is reaching possible completion, and speaker transition becomes relevant, she augments it with another unit which acts as a 'pivot' to get her across the transition place from the end of one TCU to the beginning of the next. The pivot ('in a way', line 19) is both the last part of the TCU and the beginning of the next TCU: 'it's very disturbing in a way'/'In a way it's it's makes you very anxious'. By using the pivot to get her across the possible transition space, Linda again postpones her co-conversationalists' opportunity to offer any acknowledgement or appraisal of the information she has imparted. After using an 'and' (line 24) to indicate 'still not finished', she then launches another TCU which again uses an if/then structure (and a listing device) to maximally extend the turn. By the time CK, who is leading the seminar group, comes in at the next possible transition place – and note that even here Linda keeps talking (lines 31 and 32 are in overlap) – it is far too late to respond to 'it happened to me a few years ago'. In sum, Linda actively uses the turn-taking organization of conversation to extend her turn beyond her coming out moment to decrease the likelihood of anyone offering an assessment of, or any other response to, it. And in fact no one does . . .

So, what political relevance can be derived from this conversation analysis of the turn-taking structure of coming out talk? Linda and Pat (and others in data not presented here) are coming out, but they are using the turn-taking organization to avoid their sexuality becoming topicalized, and they are conveying the information about their sexuality in a 'not news' format (as an instance or example of something else). The design of these comings out is attentive to, and hence can be used to explore, the conditions of our oppression in (at least) two ways.

First, they are attentive to the accusation of 'flaunting it' – to the complaint 'I don't mind gays but why must they be so blatant?'. Their construction as 'not news', as conversational asides, and their embeddedness in long turns, is designed precisely not to flaunt, not to draw attention to, not to make an issue of it – to slip it into the conversation so as to make it public, but in a way that is demonstrably relevant to the conversation, displayed as being an instance or piece of evidence in support of some other point. Another reason why coming out might be done in this way is to mark some kind of resistance to the whole idea of coming out, to the notion that it should be necessary; that unless we announce as newsworthy our difference from a presumed heterosexual norm, then we can legitimately be assumed to be hetero-sexual. As recent theorists have suggested, there is a sense in which coming out colludes with the notion that before we came out, we were hiding, and that in letting other people know our sexuality, we are revealing the past deception of the closet. By making lesbianism an aside, an instance, a deliberately casual exemplar of something else, these young women may be invoking and constructing the notion that that's indeed all it is (or all it should be), that – in fact – there is nothing of note to 'flaunt'. Coming out in a way that clearly avoids 'flaunting' sexuality as a newsworthy, commentable-on piece of information can be seen, then, both as collusion with the heterosexual imperative not to be public about our sexuality, and equally as a resistance to the whole notion that our sexuality can be assumed to be heterosexual unless we announce to the contrary.

Second, there's a protective element in these comings out: they are both protective of others and self-protective. By embedding information about the speaker's sexuality in the middle of turn construction units, or in following them with multiple TCUs, speakers protect the recipients from having to produce a response. Both the location of the information, and its structure as 'not news' (as an aside, or instance), provides for recipients to hear it and yet not to have to deal with it there and then. Hearers are insulated by subsequent talk against the potential shock value of the information they are receiving. It is a way in which speakers protect others from being potentially crass recipients of the delicate information conveyed – and, of course, protect themselves from having to deal with such potentially crass responses.

Task B8.3.2: After you've read

➤ Reread the last two paragraphs: would you 'read' what Linda said in one of these ways rather than the other? Do you think Linda might have had one (or both) of these ideas in mind?

➤ Read Kitzinger's article in its entirety. How does her discussion of feminist approaches to date rape address the question of the role of analysts' own interpretations of conversational data?

Unit B9
Data and data sites

Text B9
N. Edley

Nigel Edley (2001) 'Analysing masculinity: interpretative repertoires, ideological dilemmas and subject positions', in Margaret Wetherell, Stephanie Taylor and Simon Yates (eds) *Discourse as Data*. London: Sage/Open University, pp. 189–228

Unit B9 focuses on one particular broad conceptual epistemological site: masculinity. In relation to this, Nigel Edley uses discursive psychology to analyse interviews of young men – part of a wider project on middle-class masculinity in the UK – about their understandings of feminism. For discursive psychology, the focus is socially shaped language use – how people talk about things – rather than the 'inner self' or 'what is going on in people's minds' (see the box within the extract). This also contests the idea that elicited data (for example, interviews) are straightforwardly about 'understandings'.

★ **Task B9.1: Before you read**

➤ What different relationships do you see between language and masculinity?

➤ What do you feel are some 'normative' ways for men to behave, within a particular culture (or, if you prefer, CofP)?

N. Edley

Masculinity as discourse

In recent years there has been a high and sustained level of interest in issues to do with men and masculinity. As well as television programmes, newspapers and magazine articles, each year has seen the publication of a string of academic titles, spanning a wide array of disciplinary fields including anthropology (Cornwall and Lindisfarne, 1994), psychology (Scher *et al.*, 1993), sociology (Connell, 1995), linguistics (Johnson and Meinhof, 1997) and cultural studies (Berger *et al.*, 1995). Yet in amongst this diversity there is a growing consensus that language lies at the heart of understanding men and masculinity, with many writers now insisting that masculinity (and gender more generally) is something constructed in and through discourse.

However, because there are a number of different definitions of discourse or the 'discursive' in current circulation (see Jaworski and Coupland, 1999; Macdonell, 1987; Potter *et al.*, 1990) it becomes necessary to specify what one means by these concepts . . . I shall be using a . . . definition . . . which encompasses a whole range of different symbolic activities, including styles of dress, patterns of consumption, ways of moving, as well as talking. Within contemporary British culture, for example, I would see masculinity as being made up of things like watching football, drinking pints of beer at the pub and trying to get away from the traffic lights faster than the cars in the next lane. It is part and parcel of putting up shelves, fixing the toaster and digging over the vegetable patch. All of these things (and many more) are viewed as being typical of men within our culture. This does not mean, of course, that all men will do them or even that they are the sole preserve of men (after all, plenty of shelves are put up by women). Rather, they are understood as *normative* forms of behaviour, the sum total of the **practices** and characteristics which we conventionally associate with men.

Task B9.2: Reflection task

➤ Given that Edley describes these practices as normative, is it reasonable to see them as making up masculinity within 'contemporary British culture'?

Discursive psychology's challenge to more traditional understandings of men and masculinity lies in the status it accords activities such as beer drinking and brawling. In the past they have often been seen as *symptoms* of masculinity; the by-products of something that is both prior to and more fundamental than the activities themselves. Many people today remain convinced that gender is in some way rooted in biology, such that when men race off from the traffic lights, for example, it is often attributed to an aggressive and competitive *nature* inscribed at the level of genes or hormones. Of course, within the human and social sciences there is a long established challenge to this kind of biological reductionism (see Edley and Wetherell, 1995, for a review). Amongst others, psychoanalysts, sociologists and psychologists have argued that people are not born masculine or feminine, but *become* gendered as they grow up in society. They have suggested that, like the making of a jelly or blancmange, the characters of new-born infants are initially quite fluid such that they can take on the shape or form of whatever 'mould' they are poured into. Socialization theories imply that it is only gradually that people begin to solidify into particular sorts of personalities. Once formed, we might 'wobble' a bit if pushed but, generally speaking, it is assumed that we will resist attempts to alter what we have become.

In contrast, a discursive psychologist would insist that gender is neither something into which we are born nor something that we eventually become. In terms of the same metaphor, we would argue that the jelly never sets. We claim that people's gender identities remain relatively fluid, capable of adapting to the particular social settings or contexts in which people find themselves. At the heart of a discursive psychological analysis are the practices listed earlier (i.e. fixing the toaster, digging the vegetable patch, and so on), for here gender comes to be understood as something that is 'done' or **accomplished** in the course of social interaction. So where traditional psychological analyses have seen men's tinkering with cars and their repeated conversations about beer and football as *footprints* and set out to track the animal that produced them, the discursive psychologist insists that these words and deeds *are the beast itself.* Masculinity is viewed as a consequence rather than a cause of such activities.

Discourse versus practice

It has been traditional, within the social sciences, to make a distinction between words and deeds, or between discourse and social practice. In discursive psychology, however, this is often considered a false distinction (or dualism). In drawing upon the arguments of people like Wittgenstein and Austin, discursive psychologists point out that language is *itself* a form of practice. It is used to do things, like giving orders, making promises and sealing bets. Still, some constructionists want to draw a distinction between discursive and 'material' practices (for example, Parker, 1992; 1998). For example, they would see the theft of a car as consisting of two different orders of 'reality'; the car (and its removal) belonging to the material realm and the act of 'theft' belonging to the symbolic (i.e. it would be seen as a *constructed* reality – a consequence of viewing the event through a particular moral-judicial framework – see Foucault, 1977). Yet once again this distinction breaks down when it is put under pressure. For instance, the fact that a perpetrator's status as a 'thief' is constructed via a set of texts or discourses (for example, the magistrate's pronouncement and the resulting criminal 'record') does little to diminish the damaging material effects of being so described. Those texts alone could cost the offender a good deal of time and money. Likewise, a car is much more than just a physical hunk of machinery. For as Barthes (1973) has ably demonstrated, cars have a strong mythical quality; they are important symbols of status and power. Indeed, it is precisely this quality of cars, as objects of desire, that renders them so vulnerable to being stolen in the first place. We should see that discourse and practice are inextricably bound up with one another.

Task B9.3: Reflection task

➤ In what sense do you think masculinity might be 'discursively reproduced'?

The discursive reproduction of masculinity

There can be little doubt that the recent proliferation of discourse-based accounts of gender is due, in no small part, to the fact that it constitutes such a powerful challenge to the essentialism and reductionism of more traditional understandings. The fact that discursive psychologists see masculinity and femininity not as permanent or fixed, but as constantly remade on a moment-to-moment basis provides not just a radical destabilizing of the assumption that gender is something that is natural, inevitable or God-given, but also a much more positive sense of how change may be effected. Transforming the status quo becomes understood as a matter of challenging and changing discourses, encouraging people to tell different stories about themselves and others. No longer can people hide behind the defence that they are just 'doing what comes naturally'.

At the same time, however, we are wary of seeming to exaggerate the ease with which such changes can be made. Reconstructing identities is not a simple matter of voluntary action (Eagleton, 1991); being a man is not something that a person can accept one day and refuse the next . . .

There are restrictions that apply to the construction of gender identities. . . . the free-play of possibilities is certainly limited by what others will agree to or allow. People may be able to experiment with new versions or definitions of masculinity, but there is no guarantee that these will be accepted. Instead, men may rely upon much more tried and tested constructions; those versions of masculinity which they know from experience work. For many years men have learned, for example, that it pays for them to be forthright and assertive. They have discovered that society treats them better if they put a brave face on their hurts and disappointments (Cohen, 1990; Jackson, 1990; Seidler, 1989). In a sense, therefore, the historical reproduction of certain forms of masculinity is not so much a matter of 'doing what comes naturally' as doing what works best.

Yet the reproduction of more conventional forms of masculinity is not just a reflection of their functionality. And neither are the limits on identity construction always imposed from 'outside'. For instance, it has often been noted that, within Western cultures, men tend to avoid constructing themselves as emotional beings. Without doubt this has often been in their own best interests (see Seidler, 1989; 1994), but there is also evidence to suggest that men might find some difficulty in constructing themselves as emotional even when the situation 'demands' it. For example, Tannen (1991) tells a story of a man, who, having been advised by a marriage guidance counsellor to be more expressive of his feelings for his wife, took to washing her car! From the point of view of discursive psychology, it appears that when it comes to expressing certain feelings and emotions, many men are literally *out of practice*. In other words, 'emotion talk' represents a form of discursive activity which is not a part of many men's everyday, practical routine.

A critical discursive psychology recognizes that, as a way of being in the world, masculinity becomes something of a routine or habit (see Bourdieu's concept of *habitus* – 1977). Masculinity may well exist as a set of discursive practices which inform the way men speak, feel and think, but it is important to understand that many of these practices become so utterly familiar, so thoroughly routinized and automatic, that most men (and women) mistake history for nature. Men don't typically have to think about looking and sounding like men. When they spread themselves out on the sofa, for example, they don't have to concentrate upon the careful placement of their limbs (see Henley, 1986; Wex, 1979). They just plonk themselves down and make themselves comfortable. For most of the time the vast majority of men remain completely oblivious to the ways in which masculinity has inscribed itself upon their bodies. They fail to see how it has infiltrated their muscles and moulded their bones. And yet, even if they were to see the connection, it would be no easy matter to transform these bodily habits (Bourdieu, 1977).

Discursive psychologists (e.g. Edley, 1993; Edwards and Potter, 1992; Potter and Wetherell, 1987; Shotter and Gergen, 1989) and cultural anthropologists (Geertz, 1973; 1993) have tried to demonstrate that identities are more fleeting, incoherent and fragmented than many of us would have believed. They have identified the assumption that people are unique, self-contained motivational and cognitive universes as part of an 'Enlightenment myth'. At the same time, however, they acknowledge the productive (or constructive) power of that myth. They recognize that most people in the Western world are invested in a philosophical tradition which values personal integrity and the consistency of identity over time. Westerners are very keen to be seen, by themselves as well as others, as some one in particular. This explains why, when people are encouraged or forced to see the contradictions in their own identity 'projects', they often feel defensive or embarrassed. The ideology of the Cartesian subject works, as Foucault (1972) would say, to construct the object of which it speaks. It has become a socially or discursively constructed reality.

Summary

- Masculinity is a discursive accomplishment rather than a natural fact.
- It is something that is done collectively or jointly with others.
- Gender identities are typically negotiated and involve the operation of power.
- Men are not free to construct themselves as they wish. To some extent, it is their cultural history which determines the kinds of identities they can assume.
- Masculinity may be a performance, but it is one that often becomes habitual or routinized.

Implications

There are a number of implications that follow from this summary in terms of how we should go about a discursive psychology of men and masculinity. Firstly, we should be in no doubt about where to start, for if masculinity is reproduced and transformed in and through discourse then . . . we need to focus our analytic attention upon people's talk. Moreover . . . we need an approach that is capable of analysing conversations or dialogue, for it is precisely here that masculinities should be constructed and negotiated. Secondly, our approach needs to be sensitive to the cultural history of masculinity. It needs to be able to identify the various resources that society makes available for the construction of masculine identities. The beauty of being able to do this is that, in seeing what forms of masculinity are 'on offer', we start to get an insight into the kinds of choices that are being made. The third and final requirement is for an approach which is sensitive to the operation of power. We need to look at whose interests are best served by prevailing definitions of masculinity and to examine how they are maintained, resisted and transformed.

Discursive psychology meets these requirements via a number of key concepts; namely, **interpretative repertoires**, **ideological dilemmas** and **subject positions**. [In this extract, we look only at the first of these.] . . . I intend to show how they have been employed in an on-going research project which looks at the discursive construction of masculinity. Let me begin with some background information about this project.

Analytical materials

[The data] presented and analysed below come from a relatively large-scale project on the construction of masculine identities (Edley and Wetherell, 1996; 1997; 1999; Wetherell and Edley, 1998; 1999) based upon a number of different sources of empirical data gathered during 1992 and 1993. One branch of research involved an extensive period of 'field work' conducted in and around the sixth form common room of a UK-based, independent boys' school. Here small groups of 17–18 year old male students were interviewed (by myself) around eight times over the course of two school terms with the aim of gaining an insight into the construction of middle-class masculinities in one institutional site. A second source of data comes from a series of 'one off' small group discussions with a more heterogeneous collection of men who were all, at that time, in their first year of studying at the Open University. The aim here was to obtain a more general picture of the discursive and ideological climate in which masculinities come to be negotiated. Of the 60 men who took part in this branch of the study, most were white, aged between 20 and 64 years and came from a wide variety of occupations and social class backgrounds. Everyone who took part in these studies was a volunteer, and their anonymity was guaranteed through the use of pseudonyms.

The interviews were designed to explore a range of different issues central to men's lives, including work and family life, sexuality and friendships, and images of men in popular culture (see Wetherell, 1994, for full details). At all times the aim of the interviewer was to create an informal atmosphere in which, to a large extent, the participants themselves directed the flow of conversation. The meetings, which usually lasted for between 60 and 90 minutes, were tape-recorded and later transcribed . . .

Task B9.4: While you read

➤ If you have read Unit 7, or if you are familiar with the notion of 'discourses' from elsewhere, consider in what ways the concepts of discourses and interpretative repertoires might be similar, and in what ways they might be different. Edley addresses this directly at the end of his chapter (not included here).

Interpretative repertoires

The concept of interpretative repertoires first appeared in 1984 with the publication of Nigel Gilbert and Mike Mulkay's book *Opening Pandora's Box*. Gilbert and Mulkay were working within the sociology of scientific knowledge (or SSK for short) – a branch of sociology interested in examining the way that science itself gets done. Gilbert and Mulkay were particularly concerned to look at participants' own understandings of what was involved in scientific work. So they gathered together a wide variety of accounts, from laboratory reports and published articles through to recordings of both formal meetings and break-time conversations. When they analysed these different accounts they discovered that there was no single, consensual story about how science proceeded. Instead, there appeared to be two quite separate ways of talking about or constructing scientific activity. Gilbert and Mulkay called these different ways of talking, interpretative repertoires.

The concept was later imported into social psychology by Jonathan Potter and Margaret Wetherell. In their highly influential book, *Discourse and Social Psychology*, they defined interpretative repertoires as "basically a lexicon or register of terms and metaphors drawn upon to characterize and evaluate actions and events" (Potter and Wetherell, 1987: 138).

The main point about interpretative repertoires is that they are relatively coherent ways of talking about objects and events in the world. In discourse analytical terms, they are the 'building blocks of conversation', a range of linguistic resources that can be drawn upon and utilized in the course of everyday social interaction. Interpretative repertoires are part and parcel of any community's common sense, providing a basis for shared social understanding. They can be usefully thought of as books on the shelves of a public library, permanently available for borrowing. Indeed, this metaphor captures nicely the point made earlier, that when people talk (or think) about things, they invariably do so in terms already provided for them by history. Much of it is a rehearsal or recital. This is not to say, of course, that there can never be such a thing as an original or novel conversation. Indeed, there is often no telling how conversations will turn out. What it does mean, however, is that conversations are usually made up of a patchwork of 'quotations' from various interpretative repertoires. Or, in terms of a quite different metaphor, interpretative repertoires are like the pre-figured steps that can be flexibly and creatively strung together in the improvisation of a dance.

Whilst this might give us a reasonably good idea of what interpretative repertoires are in theoretical terms, it is possible that we are left with a somewhat vague sense of what they actually look like 'on the ground'. When it comes to doing some of our own analysis, how do we go about spotting them? How do we know which interpretative repertoires are being utilized and how do we decide where the boundaries lie between one interpretative repertoire and the next? Unfortunately, there are no easy answers to these questions. As Wetherell and Potter (1988: 177) themselves note: "Analysis is not a matter of following rules or recipes; it often involves following hunches and the development of tentative interpretative schemes which may need to be abandoned or revised".

Identifying interpretative repertoires turns out to be a 'craft skill' rather than being something that one can master from first principles. It is an ability that develops with practice. Of course, this makes it a daunting prospect for students new to discourse analysis. However, as a general rule, the trick to spotting interpretative repertoires is familiarity with one's data. From my own experience, I know that it helps to have been the person who collected the data in the first place. As an interviewer, for example, there usually comes a time when one begins to feel as though you've heard it all before. People seem to be taking similar lines or making the same kinds of arguments as others previously interviewed. The same kind of thing occurs with the repeated reading of transcripts. Gradually, one comes to recognize patterns across different people's talk, particular images, metaphors or figures of speech. This is a sure sign, as an analyst, that one is getting a feel for the 'discursive terrain' that makes up a particular topic or issue. In a very real sense, it is an indication that one has captured or encountered most of what there is to say about a particular object or event.

In order to provide a clear sense of how this is done in practice, I would like to look at some data that emerged from the research project described above, where the general topic of discussion was feminism and social change (see also Edley and Wetherell [e.g. 2001]). This issue was typically introduced using one of three standard questions:

1. What is a feminist (or feminism)?
2. What do you think of feminism?
3. What do feminists want?

As we might expect, these questions generated a variety of responses. However, as we will see, they also produced some highly regular patterns of talk.

Extract 1

    NIGEL: What are feminists (.) what are they after
    HARRY: Women (.) what do women want

NIGEL: What do *feminists* want (.) yeah
HARRY: Equality
NIGEL: Right (.) just that
HARRY: Just that (.) equality (.) they er (.) that's all they need

Extract 2

NIGEL: Give me an imaginary picture of a feminist
ADRIAN: I seem to think of a feminist woman as like ugly women (.) with like
        shaved hair (.) stuff like that you know (.) who can't get a chap and so
        they think "I'll become a feminist"
NIGEL: Right
ADRIAN: Lesbians (.) that sort of thing (.) I don't know

Extract 3

NIGEL: What do you think feminists want of men [laughter]
SIMON: Well (.) I think they want us all to jump in the river don't they really (.)
        kill ourselves (.) I dunno (.) slaves . . . I think at times they seem to have
        us under siege and always blaming us for some of the most ridiculous
        things and I think to myself "What the hell do these people want (.) do
        they want us dead or what" (.) I mean they don't want to find any
        common ground (.) they just hate men (.) regardless

Extract 4

NIGEL: What do you think feminism is
NATHAN: It depends what (.) we've got one teacher who's got very strong ideas
        on feminism . . .
NIGEL: Go on (.) tell me
NATHAN: He's (.) well seeing as we're (.) we're in my group doing a feminist
        novel in the French Lieutenant's Woman and he's giving us his
        opinions on feminism (.) how feminists (.) they don't want equality
        with men they want to be better than men and they want to destroy
        all tradition without having anything to put in it's place (.) and
        there's a kind of anarchy sort of thing but I don't know (.) *personally* I
        could take some of his arguments but I think it's more trying to be
        equal

Extract 5

NIGEL: What's your impression of feminists (.) have you got any sort of
        mental image of who they are and what they're like . . .
TIM: I used to think they were like (.) you know (.) used to wear men's
        clothes (.) boots and things (.) you know (.) I've met so many that (.)
        they come in all sorts of (.) (NIGEL: Hmm) I don't think they're easily
        recognisable (NIGEL: Right)

N. Edley

CHARLIE: I think er I think when feminism probably first came to the forefront er (.) I think the initial impressions would be (.) as you said that a lot are very strong minded women who hated men (.) who probably have short cropped hair erm (.)

TIM: Doctor Marten boots [laughs]

CHARLIE: Yeah (.) whose sexuality would probably relate to the sort of lesbians and things like that

TIM: Yeah the sort of Greenham Common type women

CHARLIE: Yeah (.) when it first came out I think the initial impressions of that would be there (NIGEL: Hmm) bearing in mind I was a lot younger then when it sort of first came to the foreground (.) but I think nowadays it's sort of erm (.) I think for me I probably look at it in a different light thinking it's (.) they're probably women that are just fighting for (.) to be looked on as being equal to their male counterparts

Extract 6

NIGEL: Okay (.) so what . . . do you think feminists are after

JASON: The way I see it is equality

GREG: I was gonna say in one word equality of opportunities put [inaudible] opportunities yes but equal rights in (.) in everything

When assembled in this way it becomes fairly clear that there is not just one but two quite different ways of talking about feminists. There are, in other words, two distinctive interpretative repertories in common circulation. In one, the image of the feminist is very simple and straightforward. She is portrayed as a woman who just wants equality with men (most evident in Extracts 1 and 6). By comparison, the second interpretative repertoire is much more rich and complex. It typically includes details of the feminist's physical appearance (invariably ugly and/or manly), sexual orientation (nearly always lesbian) and general demeanour (often aggressive men-haters). If we look at these few examples (of which there were many more in our data), we can see that these two repertoires are drawn upon in a number of different ways – to indicate what feminists are really like or what others say they are like or what people used to think they were like. However, there remained a high degree of consistency in terms of the content of these two constructions.

★ Task B9.5: Reflection task

➤ In what sense are these 'interpretative repertoires' relevant or identifiable beyond this particular group of young men?

➤ What might these two interpretative repertoires tell us about masculinity, society and/or different possibilities for gender relations?

Interpretative repertoires are an important concept within critical discursive psychology because, in the context of this project, it is here that we encounter what I have referred to as the cultural history of masculinity. By looking for the different ways that people can talk about men and masculinity, we begin to understand the kinds of limitations that exist for the construction of self and other. That is, we come to see what is possible to say about men and what, by implication, is not.

Task B9.6: After you've read

➤ Read the rest of Nigel Edley's chapter, in which he discusses the concepts of *subject position* and *ideological dilemma*, and presents some more data on middle-class masculinities in the UK.

➤ Note particularly his comparison between *interpretive repertoires* and *discourses*.

➤ At the end of his article, Edley suggests some 'further reading' in the area of discursive psychology (with comments). Some of this work you may already be familiar with (for example, Wetherell 1998). If you are working in a group, each person can read one article and present a summary to the group, perhaps together with a brief written review. (See Unit C8.10 for references.)

Unit B10
Written texts

The written texts discussed in Unit B10 are advertisements, feminist fairy tales, and computer-mediated communication (CMC) in the form of chat-room talk.

<table>
<tr><td>Text B10.1
J. Thornborrow</td><td>**Joanna Thornborrow (1994) 'The woman, the man and the Filofax: gender positions in advertising', in Sara Mills (ed.) *Gendering the Reader*. Hemel Hempstead: Harvester Wheatsheaf, pp. 128–51**</td></tr>
</table>

Gendering the Reader (1994), in which Thornborrow's paper first appeared, in the words of the blurb, 'explores the relationship between gender and reading/ interpretation' and 'the contributors . . . examine the way that gender does and does not make a difference'. In her chapter, Thornborrow compares two different advertisements for the same product, a Filofax: one ad aimed at women, one at men. She describes her theoretical framework, making reference to the notions of transitivity, modality and vocabulary, lexical collocation and address; her readings of these texts are thus thoroughly informed by linguistics. The extract below includes Thornborrow's section on transitivity.

J. Thornborrow	**The advertisements: first impressions**

The two Filofax advertisements in Figures [B10.1.1 and B10.1.2] appeared in Sunday newspaper supplement magazines in December 1989. While they both advertise the same product, and have some features of layout and text in common, the discursive style of each advertisement is very different. One is explicitly aimed at women readers, the other is implicitly aimed at men. In the one aimed at women, this targeting of the reader is achieved on an interpersonal level through features of direct address in the text. In the advertisement aimed at men, it is achieved on an inferential level through assumptions accessible to readers in making sense of the text . . .

Before going on to analyse these differences, and other stylistic features of the two advertisements, I look first at the similarities between them, henceforth to be referred to as advertisement A (Figure [B10.1.1], targeting women) and advertisement B (Figure [B10.1.2], targeting men).

Thornborrow here compares layout, shared textual elements, the photograph in (A) and the graphics in (B), and the gendered associations of the various visual elements and the predictions about the written texts readers might make from these.

busy mother seeks

SECRETARY ACCOUNTANT TRAVEL AGENT DIETICIAN & LINGUIST

to help organise successful family

*t*hings get hectic at times, don't they? All that professional help could keep control of the busiest life – no matter how complicated it gets. But let's be practical - a Filofax Personal Organiser, with its uniquely useful pages, is a more realistic answer. If you must ring that neighbour who's ferrying your eldest to school, you can find the number. If your husband wants that suit cleaned by Thursday, Filofax will help you remember to take it, *and* to find the receipt. Because Filofax produce special memory-jogging pages, and neat storage sleeves for fiddly bits such as tickets and stamps. Filofax is the most famous name in personal

organisers, and still the finest. The top-quality cover is made to last, because unlike a conventional diary, Filofax retains information such as birthdays and anniversaries, year after year. Only Filofax offers you such a wide choice of cover styles and finishes, plus the biggest range of insert pages. There are several types of diary layout to choose from, as well as

practical planners to show school holidays and other forthcoming events, at a glance. Our Home Entertainment pages help you arrange ideal combinations of guests, and record their favourite food and drink. With the unique Filofax shopping, budgeting and dietary pages, you can keep control of pennies or calories equally easily. The Travellers Checklist, another original from Filofax, simplifies holiday planning. And while you're there, foreign phrases are at your fingertips in Filofax Phrasefiles. Quality stationers everywhere can show you all the practical benefits of Filofax. The only name that means so much in personal organisers - for yourself, or as gifts that show you care.

THE ANSWER IS
ƒILOFAX.
PERSONAL ORGANISERS

Filofax plc, Filofax House, Forest Road, Ilford, Essex IG6 3HP

Figure B10.1.1

*i*t was to be a fortnight to remember: and one that my Filofax wouldn't let me forget...

WILL I BE STUMPED BETWEEN ONGAR AND OVAL?

Soon spotted an easy run, using the latest Filofax tube map, and just bowled over. Lunch: Lamb out for duck. England collapse. I slip quietly to the coast.

BRIGHTON TO BIRMINGHAM ON ONE TANK OF 4-STAR?

Phone Marina for latest news. She's sailed through her exams (it's not that she's a swot - my sister uses Filofax revision guides). Birmingham is the next port of call: we're seeing Clapton at the NEC. No problem, with the Filofax travel information and maps. I'm flying off to NYC later: my Data Set lets me verify flight times, and make an airline reservation.

WHAT DO I CHECK IN BEFORE I CHECK-IN?

Forgetfulness abolished by Filofax - even when you have to pack a lot in. It's my personalised databank, with all practical information to hand. Consult the Traveller's Checklist before packing. Imagine Manhattan without contact lens solution.

YOU CAN ƒIND IT ALL IN ƒILOFAX

BED FOR THE NIGHT, IN THE CITY THAT NEVER SLEEPS?

Arrive JFK, five hours late due to heavy weather. Body willing but spirits dampened. Decide New York's all-night chemist is indispensable. But the name, number and location? Fortunately I had this city in my pocket – another Filofax Guide.

OUT OF MILK, COFFEE AND TIME – AT 4.00 AM?

Six days later, back in London: wide-eyed and breadless. Tap into 24-hour cashpoint, then straight to the dusk-'til-dawn shopperama. "Late and All-night London Guide" saves day, and night.

IS L'ESCARGOT IN FRITH STREET OR GREEK STREET?

Consult Day Planner. "Suzi - 6pm, Freuds". Filofax also helps avoid anxiety neurosis, and assists me in booking a table for two in a recommended restaurant nearby. White Burgundy, 1978 a tasteful choice, according to vintages chart. Suzi impressed.

HOW DO I WORK OUT AND MAKE IT COUNT?

Need to resume the battle of the bulge. Filofax exercise and diet pages reduce excess bulk, in one slim volume. One hour's squash burns 600 calories. Fitness account moving into credit.

To thousands of everyday (and every year) questions that would defeat your diary: Filofax is the answer. Filofax is not only the most famous name in Personal Organisers - with its uniquely useful pages, it is also the most comprehensive.

And, with the widest choice of quality covers, Filofax can meet everyone's needs. For business or leisure, given or received. Quality stationers everywhere can show you all the practical benefits.

THE ANSWER IS ƒILOFAX.
PERSONAL ORGANISERS

Filofax plc, Filofax House, Forest Road, Ilford, Essex IG6 3HP

Figure B10.1.2

Task B10.1.1: While you read the advertisements

➤ What sort of points do you think Thornborrow analyses in her comparison of the advertisements?

➤ Can you imagine a similar pair of advertisements appearing today (i.e. more than fifteen years after they originally appeared?)

Thornborrow then analyses the advertisements from four different linguistic perspectives:

1. modes of address: constructing textual speakers and hearers;
2. patterns of transitivity: agents and actions;
3. contrasting 'discourse genres': i.e., here, the genres of informal chat (A) and a personal diary (B);
4. lexical collocation and semantic fields.

The section on transitivity is reproduced below.

Transitivity is the linguistic function which shows 'types of processes, participants and circumstances' (Halliday 1981: 330), or, more simply, 'the arrangement of lexical items into sentences' (Montgomery 1986[ ]: 184). For any given clause, there will be an agent, a process and possibly an affected entity. I want to focus in particular on the agent and affected entity positions for the textual addressee in advertisement A, and for the narrating subject in advertisement B.

J. Thornborrow

The second-person pronouns in the following verb phrases position the addressee of A as the agent of specific processes, or actions:

You ring that neighbour.
You find that number.
You remember to take [that suit to the cleaners].
You arrange ideal combinations of guests.
You keep control of calories.

However, these actions are mitigated through their embedding in conditional or modal structures, or by their embedding in a main clause. For example, in the following sentences, 'you' is in the affected position of the main clause in the sentence:

Filofax will help you remember to take it.

where the subject, or agent, of the main verb 'help' is 'Filofax'. Similarly, in the sentence:

Our home entertainment pages help you arrange ideal combinations of guests.

the subject of the main clause is 'our home entertainment pages', the main verb is 'help' and 'you' again occupies the affected object position. The same pattern is repeated in the sentence:

J. Thornborrow

Only Filofax offers you such a wide choice of cover styles.

where 'you' is in the affected position, while at the same time being the agent of the nominalised action: you choose cover styles. This structural embedding of clauses of which the agent is 'you' into main clauses of which the agent is 'Filofax', positions the addressee of the text as the agent of a set of actions. However, these actions are in some way initiated or enabled by 'Filofax', as the head noun phrase occupying the agent position of the main clause.

Another instance of mitigated action in advertisement A occurs in the conditional sentence:

If you must ring that neighbour who is ferrying your eldest to school.

where the necessity, or obligation, expressed by the modal 'must' is mitigated by the conditional structure 'if you must'. This structure often functions in talk to imply that the necessity for action is perceived by one participant in an exchange, but not by the other, such as in the example:

A: Can I open the window?
B: If you must.

It can be interpreted in this way here, that is, the necessity to ring the neighbour is not perceived equally by the speaker and hearer in the text. The difference can be demonstrated by substituting the verbs 'have to' or 'want', which do not produce the same interpretation:

If you have to ring that neighbour,
If you want to ring that neighbour.

Here, there is no marked difference in the perception of necessity by the participants. The use of 'if you must' contrasts with the obligation expressed in the other conditional sentence in advertisement A:

If your husband wants that suit cleaned.

where, as above, there is no difference in the degree of necessity perceived by the addresser and addressee. The effect of these conditional sentences in the discourse is to represent the woman's ringing the neighbour as not really necessary, and the man's wanting his suit cleaned as necessary.

These patterns of transitivity and embedded clauses contrast with those in advertisement B, where the narrating voice of the text is the agent of most of the main clauses. The first-person pronoun 'I' occupies the agent position of the following verb phrases:

I slip quietly to the coast.
I'm flying off to NYC later.
I had this city in my pocket.

and the first person is the elided agent in the abbreviated forms:

soon spotted an easy run
just bowled over
phone Marina
consult traveller's checklist
arrive JFK
consult day planner

The frequency of the first-person 'I' as the subject of main clauses in the narration contrasts with the mitigated actions of the textual addressee in A, where the second-person 'you' never occurs as the agent of a main clause unless it is embedded within a conditional or modal structure. Similarly to A, Filofax also occurs as the agent of the enabling verbs 'lets', 'help' and 'assist' in the following:

My data set lets me verify flight times.
Filofax helps avoid anxiety and neurosis and assists me in booking a table for
   two.

and in the agent position of the sentence:

Filofax exercise and diet pages reduce excess bulk.

The difference between the two advertisements is in the type of actions which are enabled in each case. In A, the types of processes represented are confined to the domestic domain: taking husband's suit to the cleaners, arranging dinner parties, remembering family anniversaries and keeping control of *pennies and calories*. In B, the processes of which the narrating subject is the agent represent unconstrained movement: *easy run*, *bowled over*, *slip to the coast*, *flying*, and the type of actions enabled by Filofax include booking tables in restaurants and making airline reservations
. . .

The patterns of transitivity discussed here seem to reinforce two behavioural stereo-types. On the one hand, the woman addressed by the text is represented only in activities which are limited to the home and family. Through the syntactic embedding of clauses where she is the agent, she is not the initiator of any action, but is involved in processes which are enabled by Filofax, and which are entirely domestic in nature. On the other, the narrating male subject of B is the unmitigated agent of the rapid succession of different actions, all related to high-status, executive travel and 'play' (going to concerts, restaurants, etc.). The domain of the woman is represented as the confined space of home and family, while the domain of the man is represented as the outside world . . .

Task B10.1.2: After you've read

➤ Follow up this analysis by reading the remainder of Thornborrow's analysis, on the other three linguistic dimensions.

➤ Which dimension do you consider the most interesting?

Text B10.2
B. Davies

Bronwyn Davies (1989) *Frogs and Snails and Feminist Tales*. Sydney: Allen & Unwin

This book is a detailed report of Davies' study of young children's understandings of gender, focusing on their understandings of 'feminist fairy tales'.

Task B10.2.1: Before you read

➤ Can you recall your own responses to traditional fairy tales, as a child?

➤ What might be some different responses to traditional fairy tales?

B. Davies

The sense children make of feminist stories

Children's stories present them not only with the mundane gendered world of women in kitchens but also the fantasy world in which women escape kitchens and are beautiful and loved, their reward for which, is, of course, their own kitchen. If a woman is active and powerful she can only be accepted as such if her agency is directed in a *selfless* way towards a man or child whom she loves (see, for example, Aiken's *The Kingdom Under the Sea*). Men, in contrast, have a much more complex array of possibilities—their power is admired and celebrated, their strength and cleverness can be associated with negative or positive powers, even both at the same time, and their right of access to safe domestic spaces by no means depends on their virtue. The text of the story is generally a subtle and complex mixture of events that might really happen, and of events or characters that no-one is expected to hold open as a genuine possibility. . . .

But as Walkerdine says, a critique of children's stories should not be based on attempts to insist that they should more accurately reflect the real or the ideal world. We need, rather, to analyse the way in which they provide a vehicle for children to discover ways of positioning themselves as a person: 'We need not point to some untainted reality outside the text, but to examine instead how those practices within the text itself have relational effects that define who and what we are' (Walkerdine, 1984: 64). She goes on to say that 'the positions and relations created in the text . . . provide a fantasy vehicle which inserts the reader into the text' (1984: 165).

Feminist analyses of stories, then, need to pay attention not only to the content, but also to the metaphors, the forms of relationship, the patterns of power and desire that are created in the text. How the child relates to the text, inserts her or himself into the text, and thus how she or he interprets and uses the text are also critical issues for a feminist reading of children's texts . . .

Feminist stories are themselves a critique of 'traditional' stories, but writers and analysts of these need to take the above on board. Davies looked in a two-stage study at pre-school children's responses to four feminist stories: 'Oliver Button is a Sissy', 'The Princess and the Dragon', 'Rita the Rescuer' and 'The Paper Bag Princess'. Here, we look at her study of 'The Paper Bag Princess'.

Feminist stories are about providing narrative structures in which new ways of resolving existing conflicts are presented. Because of the complexity of this task it is inevitable that some of them fall short of the mark. The feminist story is constrained by something of a double bind: if the primary focus is just on new images and the story fails to confront the issues and conflicts surrounding gender as it is experienced and understood, then it cannot adequately generate new possibilities. But to work from what is already known and apprehended inevitably means that the story is constructed out of, and thus potentially confirms, the very metaphors and attendant forms of relations that need to be worked beyond.

The Paper Bag Princess

The Paper Bag Princess . . . at first sight appears to be a simple reversal in which the female is given a typical male hero's role in which the hero displays public bravery and publicly fights against injustice, but it is a story with many subtle twists and an unexpected ending. This is by far the children's favourite story, though few of them understand its feminist message, at least on the first few readings.

In this story Princess Elizabeth is the hero who takes on the dragon in order to save Ronald. The intention here is to present a female hero who is not dependent on the prince in shining armour for her happiness nor for confirmation of who she is. It also casts serious doubt on the concept of the prince who can provide eternal happiness. In this story Elizabeth is not a unitary being. She experiences the multiple and contradictory subject positionings we each experience in our everyday lives. She is positioned at the beginning as the uncomplicated, happy and loving princess, living out the romantic narrative of love and happiness ever after. She is then positioned as the dragon's victim, but rejects this positioning and becomes the active, heroic agent who is in control of the flow of events. She is then positioned as victim again by Ronald and again refuses this positioning, skipping off into the sunset, a free agent.

When the dragon burns Elizabeth's castle and steals Prince Ronald, he also burns her clothes off and makes her very dirty . . .

Task B10.2.2: While you read

➤ Are you surprised by any of the children's responses? Disappointed?

The story from the boys' point of view

The perception of Ronald at the beginning by the boys is mixed, though on balance it is positive, despite the fact that he is depicted as a self-satisfied prig. Some commented on the fact that he was a king or handsome or brave or a medal-winner. Some commented that he was a tennis player and envied his tennis outfit. Some noted that he didn't love Elizabeth. Other isolated comments were that he was a bully, shy, silly and sad.

Their perception of Elizabeth at the outset is generally positive. She is described as loving Ronald, happy, a princess with a crown, nice, good-looking and wearing beautiful clothes. But when the dragon burns the castle and seizes Ronald there is almost universal dislike of Elizabeth; certainly when asked if they liked her, none said yes. She is primarily described as having no clothes and as angry. She is also seen as sad and dirty. The boys do not, for the most part, focus on Elizabeth's dirtiness until Ronald does at the end. Their attention is more on her nakedness and this is, for them, an unspoken theme throughout the story. When Ronald rejects her for being dirty, they go along with this, but there are many clues that it is the nakedness that is the central problem. Elizabeth has thus 'turned into' a paper bag princess and is no longer the same lovely princess that she was at the beginning. Ronald does not get much mention at this point as he sails away in the distance held by the dragon by the seat of his pants. Where he is mentioned he is described as sad, upside down, and cross, though Sebastian manages still to constitute him as an agent in control of his own fate: 'I'm glad he held onto his tennis racquet so hard. When you've done that, well, you just have to hold onto your racquet tight and the dragon holds you up.'

Most of the boys demonstrate a clear understanding that Elizabeth is going to trick the dragon, saying that she is doing it in order to get Ronald back (presumably because she needs him). Only two talk in terms of her saving him. Perception of her character is unclear at this point, many not knowing what they think of her, and only three saying she is brave, one saying she is not brave, one that she is nice, and one that she is 'yukky and nice'.

In light of the fact that the boys understand that Elizabeth is tricking the dragon, their response to the ending where Ronald rejects Elizabeth is intriguing. Very few think Ronald behaved badly. Some of them would have liked her to get cleaned up so they could be friends again (two envisaging marriage and two a love affair); some reject her without comment, and some reject her outright and turn Ronald into a hero who didn't want to marry her anyway or who found someone else.

Those who rejected her for her dirtiness and agreed that Ronald's rejection was right said that Ronald told her to go away 'because she was yuk', 'because she's very dirty, and he doesn't want to see all that' and 'she had ash all over her'. If they were Ronald they imagine they would say things like: 'You look dumb with your old paper bag on.' Only one envisages Elizabeth replying: 'Shut up you, go away.'

One boy who also rejected her for her nakedness, but focused on and identified with the dragon says: 'The dragon breaked her dress . . . the dragon ripped her dress.' Those who reject her for her dirtiness but who can envisage positive outcomes say that they would say, if they were Ronald, 'You're all dirty, you have to come another day and dress all nice', or, once she was clean, 'You're lovely and I adore you and you can come to my house forever', or simply, 'He'd smile, and she wouldn't be angry any more'. Of those who thought that Ronald behaved badly, three would simply ask her where her clothes were or suggest she get some, one would 'make love' to her when she cleaned up, and only one would not mention the clothes and would thank her for saving him. It is fascinating to see that the logic of gender relations and of the way one expects a story to be overrides any rational interpretation of the story. Within the logic of the story Elizabeth has not got and cannot get any clothes, and quite clearly Ronald is in danger and needs to get out quickly. It is also quite clear that Elizabeth has saved him. But what is heard is a story in which Elizabeth is in error for presenting herself to her prince dirty and naked. The story model is the frog prince (in this case princess), and she needs to get changed back into a real princess before she is acceptable. The story also has something of Little Red Riding Hood in it with the powerful dragon standing in for the wolf. With these narrative structures providing the basis for interpretation, the children will be anticipating that Elizabeth's actions are designed to demonstrate her goodness and virtue, and it is totally within Ronald's rights to tell her that her virtue is insufficient. In this model—which, incidentally, lies at the heart of romantic love—love is not rational but magic and uncontrollable—Elizabeth cannot be expected to use her reason to see that Ronald is not worth loving (cf. Davies, 1988b.)

The story from the girls' point of view

The girls who listened to *The Paper Bag Princess* were also mixed in their responses to the story. None of them turned Ronald into a hero, but some did manage to see him as a handsome, brave, nice prince who loves Elizabeth. The expectation that the central male will be attractive was sufficient to override the impression of Ronald as unpleasant, at least for some of them. However, some notice immediately that he does not love Elizabeth, some see him as naughty or mean, and one calls him a smarty pants. As for Elizabeth, like the boys, their image of her is positive. They see her as loving Ronald, as a beautiful, nice, happy princess. One believes that they are already married, one calls her a 'sleeping princess' and one predicts that he kisses her and she turns into a frog. When the dragon burns the castle and captures Ronald, the girls are not so obviously seized by dislike of her as were the boys. Many mention her anger, though they tend to associate anger with not feeling good. Some mention that she is burnt and some that she is sad or lost. Only a few mention her missing clothes or refer to her dirtiness. Two specifically dislike her, two mention that she no longer looks so good, and only one says she likes her. One expresses great disappointment that the clouds of smoke prevent her seeing Elizabeth's naked body. Again, none turn Ronald into a hero. He is seen as sad, angry or unlikeable, but for most he doesn't rate a mention.

Most of the girls demonstrate a clear understanding of Elizabeth's plan to save Ronald, seeing her as brave and nice, though, for some, still yukky. During the part of the story where she is tricking the dragon there is, for the girls, unlike the boys, an awareness of her anger, though only one mentions that she is clever and one says she is stupid. More girls than boys see her as saving Ronald and only two see her as 'getting him back', but some see her as having fun with the dragon, or being angry with the dragon because of her clothes, and some have no idea what she is doing or why.

At the end, some totally reject her for her dirtiness, and one for her nakedness. Some mention that they would have liked a happy ending, either marriage or friendship. Only a few think she was right to walk away, and one thinks she shouldn't have bothered to save him in the first place. Of those who think Ronald was right to reject her, the major focus is on her dirtiness. . . .

Clearly, for most of the girls Elizabeth is to blame for the state she is in, even perhaps being at risk of being raped for it. Of the girls who wanted a marriage ending, some wanted it despite the fact that Ronald is not altogether nice and some wanted a different ending. Jane from Moore St says, 'If I were Ronald, I'd say when you get back to your castle, put one of your expensive clothes on, and tell your mother and father about it'. Joanne thinks 'they should both get dressed up'.

But most think she should do as Ronald tells her and get cleaned up. Only three reject Ronald. Elise (Lothlorien) could not comprehend why Elizabeth wanted to save him in the first place.

(Would you like to be like the princess when she is being very clever and tricking the dragon?) I'd like to be that clever, but I wouldn't like to look like her. (What sort of a prince would you love?) None. (If you were Princess Elizabeth would you love that prince?) No. (If the dragon smashed your castle and snatched Prince Ronald off would you bother to save him?) No. (You wouldn't you'd just let him go?) Yeh.

Diana (Moore St) said she would not want to be a princess, since she was going to grow strong like a boy and play baseball and then grow up to be a teacher. Connie (St Michael's) said that although Elizabeth really loved Ronald, it was right to leave him. But most girls do not hear the story as a feminist story. Elizabeth is not acceptable in her dirty, naked state. Her bravery and cleverness are not powerful enough to override the romantic theme in which princesses are virtuous and clean and have no rights of their own. Nor is it comprehensible that Elizabeth does not want her prince whom she clearly loved at the outset and who could have been the key in turning her back into the beautiful princess she was at the beginning. Nor is it comprehensible that she does not accept his right to dictate her actions, and that she takes her life into her own hands. As Walkerdine notes of traditional romantic plots, 'any thought for self, any wanting, longing, desire or anger is bad' (1984: 172).

Davies then comments on these children's responses overall.

The story is set up at the beginning to evoke Elizabeth as a traditional princess. In light of that image, the twist at the end when she rejects Ronald is, for adults, very funny. Many of the children are highly amused by the fact that she calls him a 'bum' but the humour for them is in unexpectedly hearing rude words in a book. The humour which most of them cannot yet hear is from the clash between the romantic frame and the feminist frame. But unfortunately most four- and five-year-olds are simply puzzled and want a different, 'proper' ending. However, the children want to hear this story over and over again. The conflict between woman as active agent and woman as romantic love object is one that engages them, and though they prefer at this stage the romantic version which fits their fantasies about male–female relations, Elizabeth is clearly a salient character who chooses, at least for the moment, to break that connection. For those who bring a feminist interpretation to the story and who support Elizabeth's line of action, this is clearly an important narrative in which the female hero makes her own choices and does not depend on a man for her happiness. For these children it is a narrative in which the female copes with her contradictory positionings and in which the usual power relations are undermined and with it the dualism that hangs on and supports those relations.

It would seem, then, that it is possible to shift the metaphors through which narratives are constructed, and to provide alternative relations of power and desire, and at the same time to relate these shifting images ages to the narrative structures that the children already understand. The power of the pre-existing structure of the traditional narrative to prevent a new form of narrative from being heard is ever-present, however, and there is no single solution to this for the feminist writer or for the adults who are interacting with and reading stories to children.

 Task B10.2.3: After you've read

➤ Read the complete *Frogs and Snails and Feminist Tales*, and its sequel, *Shards of Glass* (1993). Are reasons for optimism suggested in the latter?

Mary Bucholtz (2002) 'Geek feminism', in Sarah Benor et al. (eds) *Gendered Practices in Language: proceedings of the First IGALA Conference*. Stanford, Calif.: CSLI Publications, pp. 277–307

Text B10.3
M. Bucholtz

This extract combines a study of a relatively new epistemological site – a CMC discussion thread – with an analysis of the constructed identity of one particular group of users, who are practising what Bucholtz calls 'geek feminism'. Mary Bucholtz's article is as much a study of gender and feminism as of gender and written discourse.

Task B10.3.1: Before you read

➤ Make a list of different attitudes towards computer use which you have heard expressed by women.

M. Bucholtz

Building on [Kira] Hall's [1996] work, I present another form of feminism on the Internet: *geek feminism*, a variety of cyberfeminism that acknowledges the concerns of feminism but preserves the commitment to a geek identity as resistant and oppositional to mainstream gender norms (cf. Bucholtz 1998, 1999[a, 1999b]). Rooted in the practices and issues of serious computer users who happen to be women, geek feminism presents an alternative . . . manifested in both ideology and discursive practice. The cyberfeminism of female hackers advocates neither the erasure of gender espoused by postmodern cyberfeminists nor the gender separatism of radical cyberfeminists. Neither of these versions of feminism adequately captures the realities of female geek experience. On the one hand, as participants in the overwhelmingly male domain of hacking, most female geeks cannot afford and do not want to separate themselves entirely from their male colleagues as some radical cyberfeminists urge. On the other hand, the challenges they face as female hackers, as well as their pride in bucking the gender odds and succeeding in the world of computers and technology, have made them skeptical of the postmodern cyberfeminist ideal of gender fluidity, an ideal that in any case is not attainable for most female geeks in their professional lives. Yet geek feminism is not liberal feminism: female geeks may be highly critical of normative gender arrangements and male hegemony both on- and offline, and their goal is not simply to fit into a male milieu. In any case, women, including geeks, may espouse positions in line with more than one of these theoretical perspectives, for geek feminism, like all political affiliations and identities, is not a category with which to classify individuals but a stance that shapes and is shaped by social practice.

Indeed, in some ways, geek feminism is akin to the forms of radical and postmodern cyberfeminism promoted by Webgrrls, Cybergrrlz, Old Boys Network, and similar websites. However, geek feminism differs from these perspectives in at least two ways. First, geek feminism is not primarily centered on gender difference, whether to reduce it, emphasize it, or subvert it, as these other forms of technology-oriented feminism are; instead, it emphasizes the shared project of geeks of both genders. Unlike some strands of liberal, radical, and postmodern cyberfeminism, geek feminism does not usually focus on the particular strengths and skills of women, and when this perspective is offered it is frequently challenged, as illustrated below. Second, whereas for most of the cyberfeminists described in studies of gender and technology, their feminism motivates their computer use, for geek feminists, their computer use motivates their feminism. That is, in other forms of cyberfeminism, computers provide a new medium in which to promote gender equality, feminist political activism, or gender fluidity, but for geek feminists computer use raises gender issues that they must address simply in order to assert their place in the technological domain. For this reason, although geek feminism may have its theorists, I am more interested in the on-the-ground practices whereby technically proficient women negotiate gender and digital technology . . .

Do female geeks exist?: geek feminism on Slashdot

I take up these issues in the context of a series of online discussions on Slashdot, a web-based news service for computer specialists that bills itself as 'News for Nerds'. In addition to headlines from the computer industry, the site provides editorial columns, reviews, and moderated discussion threads on a variety of topics . . . Slashdot . . . promotes the anticorporate ethos of many serious computer users, who proudly label themselves *hackers* or *geeks*. It is difficult to know the number and gender of Slashdot users, although it may be some indication of the scope of Slashdot's readership that the site receives between 600,000 and 800,000 hits a day and that the tendency of its enthusiastic readers to overwhelm and crash servers by following links posted on the site is so legendary that the phenomenon has come to be known as 'the Slashdot effect' or 'slashdotting'. As in other computer-related domains, it is likely that among Slashdot readers, men outnumber women, although there is no way to be certain. Most discussions on Slashdot are not concerned with gender, but every few months a Slashdot feature article on female geeks generates an animated discussion of the status of women in the computer industry . . .

The . . . discussion thread that I analyze developed in response to a Slashdot column entitled 'Female geeks: do they exist?' that appeared on the site in November 1998. The author of the column, Kirrily Robert, whose online nickname is Skud, is a self-identified female geek based in Australia. In a number of ways, Skud's column is overtly oppositional to traditional feminist discourse about women and technology. She begins her remarks by stating:

> (1) Everyone's heard that girls aren't encouraged to take technical subjects at school, that all the computer games around are violent and only appeal to boys, that somehow women's brains are built differently and just aren't cut out for logic and technical detail. Well, whether it's true or not, I'm not going to go into it. You can read it in the mainstream press if you want to; it's been done to death. I'm bored with it.

By contrast with these conventional concerns, the focus of Skud's own discussion is 'some random interesting facts about female geeks'. One of the 'facts' Skud goes on to enumerate extends her critique of traditional feminism: 'We're mostly apolitical', a statement that appears to mean that female hackers do not adhere to many of the tenets of earlier forms of feminism. She writes, 'Most hardcore geek girls are sick to death of hearing well-meaning "feminists" make statements like "Computers are inherently male and exclude women" when it's obviously grossly inaccurate'. She goes on to offer some reconstructed dialogue from a 'really awful' forum she attended on 'Women and the Web':

M. Bucholtz

(2) Them: "Women find computers really hard to use."

Me: "I don't, and I think your statement marginalises and degrades women in technical fields."

Them: "Uh, duh . . . "

Them: "And there's, like, all this pornography and stuff . . . "

Me: "Yeah, it's great that the technology can be used for all forms of communication, isn't it?"

Them: "Uh, duh . . . "

Whereas the us/them dichotomy in radical cyberfeminism divides women from men, in Skud's discourse it divides female geeks from traditional feminists. The column thus locates tensions between many feminist discourses and the discourse of the technogeek; as Skud puts it, 'This is why feminist theories on technology are mostly the domain of humanities types, and us geeks just get on with our coding'. But despite such arguments for the apolitical nature of female hackers, the discourse of many female geeks, I maintain, participates not in anti-feminism—which involves opposition to the goal of gender equity—but in geek feminism.

The thread that developed in response to Skud's Slashdot column comprised 407 messages, most of them written within forty-eight hours of the original posting (discussion threads are quickly archived due to the high e-mail volume at the site). Discussion participants are of two types: registered users, whose name or nickname and e-mail address appear in the header at the beginning of their posts; and users who do not send postings under their own names or nicknames. Those in the latter category are known as 'Anonymous Cowards', and this name appears in the header of all unregistered postings. In the thread under analysis, almost half the messages—180—were sent by Anonymous Cowards. It is impossible to know how many messages were sent by the same person, since very few Anonymous Cowards sign their posts, and only occasionally does a user refer to a previous message that she or he sent . . .

Task B10.3.2: While you read

➤ Consider carefully your own position in relation to some of the views expressed in this discussion thread. Do you share Bucholtz's characterisation of these views as (a form of) feminism?

Challenging normative femininity and feminism

M. Bucholtz

Many female [i.e. self-identified as female] geeks who participated in the 1998 Slashdot thread in response to Skud's column mentioned gender-based assumptions from customers or clients as central frustrations:

(6) I work as a techie at an ISP and am the only female techie (the other female in the office does the front desk duties). I deal with customers all day who don't believe I know what I'm talking about and some will even go so far as to ask to speak to one of the 'guys'. This gets old. There ARE women who know what we're doing.

Such customers may be female as well as male. However, complaints about the sexism of male geeks are not uncommon:

(7) I love Radio Shack's stuff, but I cannot ABIDE their staff—99% male and 100% sexist. As soon as they see you're a woman, they drop into "Mr. Rogers" mode: "Can I sell you a nice computer? Look—it does fun things like get on the Internet and send electronic mail. You can send some recipes to your Mom!" "No, I'm just looking for [insert piece of hardware here] . . . " "Oh, it's over there. Now are you sure you know what it's used for?"

(8) I use the name < . . . > which can be male, save and except when I am no a site I 'need' to appear male so use < . . . >. This is to avoid the 'aren't you cute' crap which still crops up, along with, 'who needs a WOMAN'S views' as if possessing a penis is mandatory for computer literacy.

The patronizing and denigrating attitudes described in these comments are predominantly, but not entirely, attributed to men: the author of (7), for example, implies that Radio Shack's female employees, despite their small numbers, share the sexist assumptions of their male counterparts.

For some female geeks, the recognition of male geek sexism has led to separatist initiatives, such as Grrl Net, an IRC (Internet Relay Chat) support group for female hackers:

(9) People always say that we (grrl net) have something to prove, and that is true. We are proving that we are just as good if not BETTER than all the guy geeks out there.

In this sense, geek feminism and radical cyberfeminism are overlapping enterprises. It is worth noting, however, that members of such separatist groups often continue to participate in mixed-gender hacker groups like Slashdot and that many female geeks are critical of such separatist efforts (e.g., Anderson 1996).

More generally, many female hackers do not embrace traditional feminist positions on harassment, particularly those which may be viewed as casting women as victims or as lacking competence. While acknowledging the reality of sexual harassment, for example, one female user rejects the traditional definition of this concept:

(10) I'm perfectly capable of saying no. This has always been my position on sexual advances: I don't want anyone else telling me when I may or when I may not receive them (the old "unwanted sexual advances" being part of the litmus test for harassment). I'd like them all (at least the first time from any given person), thank you very much, so that I may pick and choose between them:)

Although the author quickly moves from sexual harassment to the much narrower arena of sexual advances, thus effacing the wide range of overtly hostile acts that also fall under the rubric of harassment, the point she makes is not that harassment does not exist but that she does not want her agency in this (or any other) realm to be slighted. Likewise, following Skud's attack on traditional feminist perspectives on women and technology, female geeks on the thread offered their own criticisms of such views:

(11) I agree with <Skud's critique of> the whole tiresome gender blah-blah. Personally, I don't have time for it, and you'd have to drag me kicking and screaming to one of those women-in-technology seminars.

Similarly, another female user writes:

(12) and frankly, those women from that "women and the web" forum Kirrily/you spoke of sound like they're making excuses for not getting out there and *trying.*

This position leads to a general critique of the helplessness of nongeek women around technology:

(13) I think a willingness to admit your lack of knowledge is a good thing . . . some women, unfortunately, take it overboard:)

It may be tempting to read some of these critiques of nontechnically oriented women as antifeminist or even misogynistic; example (12) in particular tends to set off alarm bells for nongeek feminists. But it is important to remember that feminism has been enriched throughout its history by challenges issued by women who were marginalized or excluded by mainstream feminism: lesbians, women of color, working-class women, and many others have made feminism more inclusive. Geek feminism contributes to this project by reminding feminists that not all women are uncomfortable in the male-dominated world of computers. Such a perspective should be seen less as an attack on women and more as an affirmation of the geek outlook, as indicated in the following posting:

(14) < . . . > I certainly don't begin to approach the two attitudes most seen by non-geeks, which are 1) computers are scary; I don't want accidentally destroy something! and 2) computers are just tools; show me what I need to know to get my job done. Both of those points of view are almost incomprehensible to me.

However, and this may be why these examples are troubling to some feminists, rejecting traditional feminist principles may also mean rejecting traditional feminist practices, including traditional discourse practices. Thus some messages from female geeks are hardly "sisterly" in their form:

(15) As a female geek/nerd whatever the fuck, i find it annoying how whenever any nerd chick has anything to say, all the guys are all "good work! wicked article" just because a female happened to write it. when in actuality, the article was garbage. My 9 year old sister who plays mindsweeper and sets up hotmail accounts could write the same thing. Skud, that article sucked ass. maybe if i have the time one day I'll sit down and write a good article to post, until then, i hope all you male geeks have fun ranting and raving over shit articles written by code bitches. =)

While this position may not appear feminist by usual standards (to say the least), it does uphold two basic geek feminist principles: women and girls can be competent computer users; and female geeks should not be treated differently from male geeks . . . Despite the fact that this flaming may be more akin to the stereotypical male than

M. Bucholtz

female online style . . . or indeed even because of this aggressive oppositional style, such women deserve a more central place in the study of language, gender, and technology. After all, the notion of 'cooperative' discourse as characteristic of female interactional style is itself a reified construct that has been challenged by numerous language and gender scholars from Goodwin (1980) on. Indeed, one important insight from Hall's study is that even in the separatist space of radical cyberfeminism, supportive interactions are not a natural outcome of women's different communicative style but rather are the result of a deliberately maintained political experiment. Conflict and hostility are still in evidence, though negatively sanctioned, on the list she studied. Thus, we should not be surprised to find women as well as men engaged in oppositional discourse practices online. However, this example, which concludes its stream of personal invective with a mitigating smiley-face emoticon, is more accurately classified as manifesting a 'mixed' stance (i.e., one that includes elements of both opposition and alignment). . .

Task B10.3.3: After you've read

➤ Read Mary Bucholtz's article in its entirety. Then search the World Wide Web for an Internet discussion group which deals with similar issues. Start with Webgrrls, Cybergrrl and 'radical cyberfeminism'.

➤ Use the web to find out about 'postmodern cyberfeminists', identified at the beginning of Bucholtz's extract.

➤ Look for other academic work on women's *uncooperativeness* in language use, starting with Goodwin (1980).

SECTION C
Exploration

Unit C1
Early work on gender and language

 Task C1.1: Reviewing historical work

➤ Follow up one of the references provided by Otto Jespersen (1922), Mary Haas (1944) or Anne Bodine (1975b) on cases of sex-exclusive or sex-preferential language use in a particular language.

➤ Read the work carefully, then write a critique of it from a twenty-first century perspective.

➤ Address the following questions:

  ■ To what extent is men's language seen as 'basic' or 'the norm'?
  ■ Are there any indications of evaluation (either from the writer, or his/her informants) of male vis-à-vis female forms, and, if so, how are these evaluations expressed?
  ■ Are the issues of exceptions, particular speech events, children's acquisition of the sex-preferential forms and transgression dealt with, and, if so, how?

➤ Post your critique on your Gender and Language web site.

References

Adam, Lucien and Henry, Victor (1980) *Arte y vocabulario de la lingua chiquita.* Paris: Maisonneuve.

Boas, Franz (ed.) (1911–38) (2 vols) *Handbook of American Indian Languages.* Bureau of American Ethnology Bulletin 40. Washington, DC: Government Printing Office.

Bogoras, Waldemar (1922) 'Chukchee', in Franz Boas (ed.) *Handbook of American Indian Languages.* Bureau of American Ethnology Bulletin 40. Washington, DC: Government Printing Office.

Bunzel, Ruth (1933–8) 'Zuni', in Franz Boas (ed.) *Handbook of American Indian Languages.* Bureau of American Ethnology Bulletin 40. Washington, DC: Government Printing Office.

Chamberlain, Alexander (1912) 'Women's languages', *American Anthropologist* 14: 579–81.

Chatterji, Suniti Kumar (1921) 'Bengali phonetics', *Bulletin of the School of Oriental Studies* 2 (1): 1–25.

Dixon, Roland and Kroeber, Alfred (1903) 'The native languages of California', *American Anthropologist* 5: 1–26.

Dorsey, James O. and Swanton, John R. (1912) *A Dictionary of the Biloxi and Ofo Languages*. Bureau of American Ethnology, Bull. 47. Washington.

Flannery, Regina (1946) 'Men's and women's speech in Gros Ventre', *International Journal of American Linguistics* 12: 133–5.

Frazer, James G. (1900) 'A suggestion as to the origin of gender in language', *Fortnightly Review* 73: 79–90.

Furfey, Paul Hanly (1944) 'Men's and women's language', *American Catholic Sociological Review* 5: 218–23.

Gashchet, Albert S. (1884) *A Migration Legend of the Creek Indians*. Philadelphia, Pa.

Jenness, Diamond (1932) *The Indians of Canada*, Bull. 65. National Museum of Canada.

Sapir, Edward (1929) 'Male and female forms of speech in Yana', in St. W. J. Teeuwen (ed.) *Donum Natalicium Schrijnen* 79–85. Reprinted in Mandelbaum, David (ed.) (1949) *Selected Writings of Edward Sapir*. Berkeley, Calif.: University of California Press.

Wagner, Gunter (1933–8) 'Yuchi', in Franz Boas (ed.) *Handbook of American Indian Languages*. Bureau of American Ethnology Bulletin 40. Washington, DC: Government Printing Office.

Task C1.2: Mary Haas

➤ Using the World Wide Web, plus any other relevant non-electronic sources, find out as much as you can about Mary Haas, and write a two-page biography of her life.

➤ Indicate whether her work on Koasati was representative of her work as a whole.

➤ Can you detect any issues in her life or work that might be described as 'feminist'?

➤ What do you see as her (unintended!) contribution to feminist linguistics?

➤ Post your biography on your Gender and Language web site.

Task C1.3: 'Speaker sex', 'hearer sex' and the 'sex of the spoken about'

Step 1
➤ Read the following: Bodine 1975b, Cameron 1992b, McConnell-Ginet 1988.

Step 2
➤ Think of and make a list of cases in which people you know vary their language use (of any language) with the sex of the person (or people) they are talking to. In what ways do they do this?

Step 3
Of course, both speaker sex *and* hearer sex might come into play.

➤ Imagine the same topic being discussed, or 'speech event' being conducted, between (a) two male speakers, (b) two female speakers, and (c) a female speaker and a male speaker. (The speakers should be of the same age and educational background.)

➤ Write three different (imaginary) dialogues to show how you think both speaker sex *and* hearer sex might come into play.

- Possible topics: favourite films, organising one's study time, how best to relax.
- Possible 'speech events': asking for/giving directions, asking for/giving advice.

Step 4
➤ Arrange for six friends or fellow students (three female, three male) to 'role play' conversations (a), (b) and (c). All three conversations should be on the same topic or should enact the same speech event (chosen from those above). The conversations should last no more than five minutes.

➤ Audio-record each conversation.

Step 5
➤ Transcribe the conversations. See below for an example of a transcription system (slightly adapted). This one was designed by Sue Garton for foreign-language classroom discourse. Whether or not you are interested in this area, it illustrates how your system should be designed to suit your own research purposes.

S. Garton

An example of a transcription system

As far as possible, the system used is that of van Lier (1988: 243–4), although for word-processing reasons some adaptations were necessary.

Identified learners have been given pseudonyms

T indicates the teacher

F indicates an unidentified female learner

M indicates an unidentified male learner

(where an unidentified learner takes more than one turn in a sequence or more than one unidentified learner of the same sex speaks in a sequence, then numbering is used)

. , .. , . . . give a notional idea of the relative length pauses up to one second

((10)) indicates the approximate length of pauses longer than one second

{yes} indicates overlapping utterances

{okay}

( ) indicates uncertain transcription

(=) indicates translation of Italian text. An approximate English translation is given, not a literal one.

(( )) is used for glosses

// is used for phonetic spelling of non-standard pronunciation

? indicates questioning intonation

A indicates the pronunciation of the letter 'a'

So indicates a word pronounced particularly forcefully or non-standard word stress

ye:s indicates a drawn-out syllable

= indicates run-on turns, either by the same or different speakers

As transcriptions were done on somewhat unsophisticated equipment, long pauses above one second are indicated extremely approximately and the decision as to how many periods to use for short pauses is entirely intuitive. Pauses above 1 second are considered as gaps and indicated on a separate line. Shorter pauses are considered hesitations and included within a turn or at the beginning (indicating a hesitation by next speaker before starting a turn).

Step 6

➤ Compare your transcripts with your fictional dialogues.

➤ Then compare the conversations with each other. Clearly, these are not representative of 'speaker sex' and 'hearer sex' in general. However, do you feel that the differences between them are related to speaker/hearer sex in any way?

➤ Discuss this with the six speakers, as a group.

Step 7

➤ Reread Anne Bodine's (1975b) article; in particular, highlight her observations about the 'spoken about'.

Step 8

➤ Write a review of Bodine's article, referring to your own findings where relevant.

➤ Highlight Bodine's contribution to feminist linguistics.

➤ Post this on your Gender and Language web site.

Key reference

Bodine, Anne (1975b) 'Sex differentiation in language', in B. Thorne and N. Henley (eds) *Language and Sex: difference and dominance.* Rowley, Mass.: Newbury House, pp. 130–51.

 Task C1.4: Fictional social networks

➤ Choose a community from a particular television or radio soap opera with which you are familiar. This can be one produced or shown in any country, about speakers of any language (or languages).

➤ Chart the density and multiplexity of the community in question by considering the various ways in which the same people relate, e.g.

- family (nuclear and extended)
- shared employment situation
- shared living accommodation
- friendship or romantic relationship

➤ Draw a labelled diagram to chart this density and multiplexity.

➤ If the relationships in this community were actual, what might we *predict* about gender and vernacular usage, extrapolating from Milroy's study (Unit B1.2)?

 Task C1.5: Actual social networks

Step 1
➤ Carefully read Lesley Milroy's five conditions for calculating an individual's 'network score' (Unit B1.2, p. 89), and the paragraphs that follow. Calculate your *own* network score for where you live now and, if this is different, for where you lived before starting at this educational institution.

Step 2
➤ Did Milroy's 'network score' method work perfectly satisfactorily for you? Adapt and/or reword it, for example for full-time or part-time students.

Step 3

➤ Read Chapters 1–5 and Chapter 7 of Lesley Milroy's *Language and Social Networks* (the extract in Unit B1.2 came from Chapter 6), as well as Chapter 6 in full.

Step 4

➤ Consider how you would use Milroy's approach to investigate phonological variation by gender within a monolingual or multilingual community with which *you* are familiar. Plan and outline the study, as follows:

- Decide on the community to be studied.
- Decide which phonemes you would investigate, and why.
- Decide which members of the community you would study, and why.
- Decide what data you would need.
- Identify your data collection methods (Observation? Interviews? Asking participants to read word lists, tell a story, etc.?).
- How would you analyse your data (i.e. what would you do with it?) in order to come up with your findings?

Step 5

➤ On your Gender and Language web site, post:

- the adapted method of network scoring, illustrated with your own case;
- your plan for your investigation of phonological variation by gender within a monolingual or multilingual community.

Task C1.6: Quotations

Step 1

➤ Using a dictionary of quotations, identify and list quotations about the talk of women and of men (not quotations written by women and by men). See also Dee 1999, Ehrlich 1996, Platt 1989.

References

(2003) *The New Penguin Dictionary of Modern Quotations*. London: Penguin.

Bartlett, John (2000) *Bartlett's Familiar Quotations*. First published 1919. Boston, Mass.: Little, Brown.

Knowles, Elizabeth (1999) *The Oxford Dictionary of Quotations*. Oxford: Oxford University Press.

The Online Dictionary of Quotations <http://www.quotationreference.com/author_index.php>.

Step 2

➤ Which type of quotations (about the talk of women, or of men) are the more numerous? What might be some different reasons for this?

➤ How would you characterise the various quotations? How would you group them? What sort of 'profile' of women's talk and men's talk results?

Step 3

➤ Think of some different reasons why this sort of 'folk-linguistics' (see Cameron 1992b) is of interest to gender and language study.

 Task C1.7: Proverbs and proverb use

Step 1

➤ Read the list of proverbs about women and language use in Unit A1.

Step 2

➤ If you can, collect more such proverbs, asking speakers of as many different languages as you can.

Step 3

Put all these together.

➤ What aspects of women's use of language feature in proverbs?

➤ What 'profile' emerges?

➤ How homogeneous is this and how much variability is there?

➤ Are there some interesting exceptions?

➤ Is your list entirely conservative and predictable?

➤ If you have also done Task C1.6, ask yourself whether the profile shown by the proverbs is comparable with that shown by the quotations.

Step 4

➤ Write some new, positive proverbs about women's talk! You might adapt some existing ones, or develop some from scratch. Post these on your Gender and Language web site.

References

Schipper, Mineke (1991) *Source of All Evil: African proverbs and sayings on women.* Chicago, Ill. and London: Ivan Dee.

—— (2003) *Never Marry a Woman with Big Feet: women in proverbs from around the world*. New Haven, Conn.: Yale University Press.

Step 5
A proverb may exist, but this tells us nothing about how it is used (and even less about any 'effect' it might have on language users).

➤ Consider how a given proverb *might* actually be actually used in talk (or writing). (Start by thinking how *you* use it.) Note down some possibilities.

➤ You may be aware of a particular 'speech event' in which familiar proverbs are regularly quoted – for example, a traditional African court hearing, marriage rite, marriage song or birth ceremony. Can you think of other such speech events?

➤ Audio-recording most talk is unlikely to be fruitful in terms of proverb use. Why?

Step 6
➤ Identify a particular proverb about gender and language use known to speakers of a particular language (not necessarily one you knew already).

➤ Ask two or more speakers of that language about their *practices* here: do they ever use this proverb? in what context? to whom? how? (for example, they might use it ironically, they might say 'As the proverb says,' or refer to 'the proverbial . . .', they might use it in certain written genres).

➤ Ask how they think *others* use the proverb.

Step 7
➤ Follow this up by reading the 'Prologue' of Mineke Schipper's (2003) *Never Marry a Woman with Big Feet: women in proverbs from around the world*.

Task C1.8: Language use, gender and the notion of 'accommodation'

Step 1
➤ Investigate the sociolinguistic notion of 'accommodation', developed by Howard Giles and Nikolas Coupland (1991). Given that 'hearer sex' (as well as 'speaker sex') may be related to the way a person speaks, think about whether the notion of 'accommodation' may be utilised in gender and language study.

➤ Read the sociolinguistics literature for documented examples of accommodation (for example, Giles and Coupland 1991, Giles et al. 1992, Holmes 1992b, Robertson and Murachver 2003). Does gender figure at all here? Consider how you might introduce a gender perspective into a particular documented discussion of this notion, or into a particular study which uses the notion.

Step 2
➤ Write a 500-word paper on 'Gender and language study and the sociolinguistic notion of *accommodation*', and post it on your Gender and Language web site.

 Task C1.9: Linguistic variation, sex and 'prestige'

Having found that women in Norwich tended to use more prestigious forms than men in their pronunciation, Peter Trudgill (1972a: 182) suggested that this pointed to their greater status consciousness. He offered two possible reasons for this apparent status consciousness:

> (i) The social position of women in our society is less secure than that of men, and, usually, subordinate to that of men. It may be, therefore, that it is more necessary for women to secure and signal their social status linguistically and in other ways, and they may for this reason be more aware of the importance of this type of signal. (This will be particularly true of women who are not working.)

> (ii) Men in our society can be rated socially by their occupation, their earning power, and perhaps by their other abilities – in other words by what they *do*. For the most part, however, this is not possible for women. It may be, therefore, that they have instead to be rated on how they *appear*. Since they are not rated by their occupation or by their occupational success, other signals of status, including speech, are correspondingly more important.

To be fair, Trudgill describes these reasons as 'necessarily speculative'. In Chapter 4 of *Feminism and Linguistic Theory* (1992b), Deborah Cameron takes issue with Trudgill on various fronts.

Step 1
➤ Before you read Cameron's critique, formulate and make notes on your own response to Trudgill's two possible reasons.

➤ Consider (a) demographic factors (including the proportion of women who may have been working outside the home) and (b) methodological factors (including social classification).

Step 2
➤ Read Trudgill's (1972a) article and Cameron's (1992b) chapter in their entirety.

➤ Consider the different fronts of Cameron's critique.

➤ Is each reasonable, do you think?

➤ Can you cite cases in which you, Cameron, or Trudgill need more information before making a judgement?

Key references

Cameron, Deborah (1992b) *Feminism and Linguistic Theory*, 2nd edn. London: Macmillan.

Trudgill, Peter (1972a) 'Sex, covert prestige and linguistic change in the urban British English of Norwich', *Language in Society* 1: 179–95.

Task C1.10: Etiquette books

Step 1

➤ Find an old (pre-twentieth-century) etiquette book in any language which features the way a woman should talk in public, for example as the 'hostess' of a dinner party. If you cannot find one in your library, try a second-hand bookshop, or track one down from the World Wide Web. The references in Eble (1975, 1976), Newton (1994) or Cameron (1995a) should help you here.

Step 2

➤ Make notes on some of the ways in which women have been advised to talk, and not to talk.

➤ What evidence of 'prescriptive language' is there here?

➤ Note down assumptions about gender, gender roles and gender relations.

➤ To what extent were these assumptions made explicit?

Step 3

➤ Follow this up by reading the relevant sections of Eble (1976) and Cameron (1995a). See also <http://courses.lib.odu.edu/engl/jbing/delosh.html> for a 1993 paper by Shelley DeLosh on 'Etiquette books as vehicles for gender stereotypes'.

Step 4

➤ Write sample dialogues between men and women in which some of this advice is followed.

➤ With a friend, act out the dialogues.

➤ Does the advice make sense, linguistically?

➤ What might women who follow(ed) this advice feel or have felt like, do you think? What about their male interlocutors?

Step 5

➤ Repeat the exercise with a modern etiquette book published within the past decade. One possibility is *Debrett's New Guide to Etiquette and Modern Manners* (Morgan 1999).

Step 6

➤ Prepare a Powerpoint presentation on the above tasks, and present the results to friends or fellow students. (You might like to do this with a friend or fellow student, acting out the dialogues you produced in Step 4.)

Unit C2
The influence of feminism and feminist linguistics (a)

Task C2.1: '-*person*' words

Step 1

➤ Using 'Situations Vacant' columns of English language newspapers (both local and national), what examples of -*person* words can you find? Start by looking for 'barperson' and 'spokesperson', but there may be others.

➤ What conclusions can you come to about the relative frequency of these?

Step 2

➤ 'Test' the words you have found on a corpus of written or spoken English, for example:

- MICASE (Michigan Corpus of Academic Spoken English): <http://www.hti.umich.edu/m/micase>
- British National Corpus: <http://www-dev.natcorp.ox.ac.uk>
- Santa Barbara Corpus of Spoken American English: <http://projects.ldc.upenn.edu/SBCSAE>

➤ What conclusions can you reach about the contexts of use, robustness and possible future of each of these -*person* words?

Task C2.2: 'Singular *they*'

Though welcoming it, Dale Spender also describes the common usage of 'they' for sex-indeterminate reference (e.g. 'Anyone can play if they learn'), as technically '"grammatically incorrect"' (1980: 149). Is it grammatically incorrect?

Step 1

➤ Carry out a survey of recent grammar books to see what is said about such sex-indeterminate references, including whether a distinction is made between spoken and written English.

➤ Include learners' grammars (used in schools), 'pedagogic' grammars (for learners of a second or foreign language) and grammars of both American English and British English.

Step 2
➤ Where these exist, compare older and newer editions of the same grammar.

Step 3
➤ Carry out a corpus study (e.g. BNC, MICASE, Santa Barbara) of *written* occurrences of 'anyone/everyone . . . they/their' phrases.

➤ Alternatively, try an Internet search engine (but remember that you are looking for 'naturally occurring' instances of these phrases, not discussions *of* them).

➤ To what extent is this usage restricted to informal genres? Is it associated with some social practices rather than others?

Task C2.3: 'Generic *he*' and 'generic *man*'

Step 1
➤ What objections to masculine 'generics' such as 'man' and 'he' have been raised? Follow up the references in Thorne, Kramarae and Henley's bibliography (1983) in the section on 'Generics', pp. 174–82.

Step 2
➤ Investigate occurrences of 'generic he' in written texts, for example in books on education, anthropology, children's science books.

➤ Identify as many instances as you can.

Step 3
➤ Ask various people: 'What do you visualise when you hear this sentence?: "If a student learns Latin, he is also learning history and literature"'.

➤ Note down their responses.

➤ Only ask directly about the sex of the student of Latin if this is not forthcoming.

Step 4
➤ Carry out a corpus study (e.g. BNC, MICASE, Santa Barbara) of spoken English to find out

- the frequency of use of 'generic he' compared with 'sex-specific he';
- whether men are indeed more likely than women to use 'generic he'.

Step 5

➤ Look in the non-fiction section of a library for books about people (e.g. psychology, education, anthropology, child development, sociology, social research) which were written since 1970.

➤ Find and note down as many examples as you can of: explanations (e.g. in a footnote, or at the start of a book) for the use of 'generic he' (or its equivalent in other languages); actual uses of 'generic she' (and are these commented on?). You may need to ask around for such examples.

➤ Can you identify any patterns or principles?

Step 6

➤ Produce a report of your findings about use of 'generic he' and 'generic she' and post it on your Gender and Language web site.

Task C2.4: 'Deficit' approaches to gender and language

Some early (pre-feminist) work as well as feminist work on gender and language has been retrospectively characterised as following a 'deficit' model or approach (i.e. taking as given that women's language is in some way deficient relative to that of men). This is a 'gender dichotomy' approach: 'women speak like this, men like that'.

Step 1

➤ Read Otto Jespersen's (1922) chapter, 'The woman', in his book *Language: its nature, origins and development*, and Peter Trudgill's work on 'language and sex' in *Sociolinguistics* (1974, 1983) and the journal *Language in Society* (1972a). Both Jespersen's and Trudgill's positions on women's language have been described as 'deficit' models (but not by them, of course).

➤ Make notes on what aspects of women's language use are being represented as somehow 'deficient', and how, linguistically, this is done.

➤ Is it fair to describe Jespersen's and Trudgill's representations of women's language as following a 'deficit' model?

Step 2

Robin Lakoff's model of women's language use in *Language and Woman's Place* (1975) is also often described as, at least in part, 'deficit' – somewhat paradoxically, given that Lakoff was writing from a feminist perspective.

➤ Read or reread *Language and Woman's Place*, and try and identify elements of a 'deficit' approach here (exclude Chapter 3 in Part 1, which is about the representation of women in the English language).

Step 3

A new edition of *Language and Woman's Place* has recently been published (Lakoff 2004). This includes a new introduction by Lakoff herself with annotations on her original text, as well as 'commentaries' by other writers in the field on the book's contribution to feminist linguistics.

➤ Read Lakoff's annotations and introduction carefully to see whether or not she addresses the question of women's 'deficient' language use, to what extent, and how.

➤ Finally, use the index to see how some of the contributors to this new edition address the question of 'deficit'.

Step 4

➤ Write a report on ' "Deficit" approaches to gender and language use' and post it on your Gender and Language web site.

 Task C2.5: Investigating 'damaging' sexist language

Step 1

In relation to her discussion of the 'generic he', Robin Lakoff notes that 'the problem, of course, lies in deciding which forms are really damaging to the ego' (1975: 43).

➤ Read how she addresses this question in both editions of *Language and Woman's Place* (1975, 2004).

Step 2

➤ Read the following three early studies, which have investigated possible 'effects' of sexist language, and a recent chapter, which looks at the question of 'damaging discourse' more generally: Bem and Bem 1973, Martyna 1980, Schneider and Hacker 1973, Sunderland 2004.

➤ Note down your own conclusions about 'damaging' language.

Step 3

➤ Write (but do not send) a letter to Robin Lakoff, saying whether and to what extent we should be concerned about 'androcentric' forms such as the 'generic he', giving reasons. Acknowledge any changes in her position indicated in *Language and Woman's Place* (2004).

➤ Post your letter on your Gender and Language web site.

Task C2.6: Men's linguistic agency

Step 1

➤ Read the whole of Dale Spender's chapter 'Language and reality: who made the world?' in *Man Made Language* (1980).

➤ Identify as many of her claims about men's (in general) linguistic agency as you can find.

➤ How convincing do you find these claims about the power of patriarchy?

➤ Is it possible to read these claims in different (e.g. non-literal) ways?

Step 2

Maria Black and Ros Coward (1981) critiqued both Spender's notion of 'patriarchy' and the 'unreclaimed version of Marxism' to which they saw it as related (1981: 72). They took Spender to task for her emphasis on 'pre-given groups' (such as 'males'), since these 'give . . . us no real purchase on how ideologies participate in the production of groups and secure identification with the subject positions produced there' (1981: 72). Meanings are produced in ideologies, so that, for example, it is not only men who may define childbirth as an 'ultimately satisfying' experience for women (as Spender claims), rather both men and women are capable of claiming this, as well as of emphasising the attendant pain. Different men's and women's positions here will depend on the gendered discourses on which they draw (see Sunderland 2004).

➤ Read and make notes on Black and Coward's (1981) critique of *Man Made Language*.

Step 3

➤ Write a review of *Man Made Language*, giving Spender credit where appropriate, and identifying the strengths of this work, but taking on board Black and Coward's now classic critique.

Key references

Spender, Dale (1980) *Man Made Language*. London: Routledge.

Black, Maria and Coward, Ros (1981) 'Linguistic, social and sexual relations: a review of Dale Spender's *Man-Made Language*', *Screen Education* 39: 69–85.

Sunderland, Jane (2004) *Gendered Discourses*. London: Palgrave Macmillan.

Task C2.7: The encoding of gender in early English grammars

Step 1
➤ Find the sixteenth-, seventeenth- and eighteenth-century English grammars which Dale Spender identifies in Chapter 5 of *Man Made Language* (1980) in the section entitled '*He/man* language' (e.g. the grammars written by Wilson, Poole and Kirkby).

➤ Check Bodine (1975a) for other references.

Step 2
➤ Make notes on what aspects of language in relation to gender were of concern to each of these early grammarians, i.e. what is each concerned to change, or to maintain?

➤ What reasons, if any, are given?

Step 3
➤ Produce a chart, summarising this aspect of the work of these early grammarians, and post it on your Gender and Language web site.

 ### Task C2.8: Conversational interaction and conversation analysis

Conversation analysis (CA) is not simply the analysis of naturally occurring conversation.

Step 1
➤ Reread the extract from Pamela Fishman's chapter (Unit B2.3), focusing on her references to CA.

Step 2
➤ Read an introductory text on CA, for example, Hutchby and Wooffitt (1998).

Step 3
➤ In the light of this, make notes on the sense in which Fishman can be seen to be using CA in her study, and in which sense not.

Step 4
➤ If you wish to familiarise yourself further with the value of CA for gender and language study, read the debate between Emanuel Schegloff and Margaret Wetherell in *Discourse and Society* (1997, 1998), as well as the subsequent contributions to this debate in later issues of *Discourse and Society*. (These include an article by Stokoe and Smithson [2001], an extract from which appears in

Unit 8. Data actually analysed by Celia Kitzinger using CA is described in another extract [Unit B8.3].)

Task C2.9: Single-sex and mixed-sex talk

Step 1
➤ Audio-record a few minutes of discussion on a particular (assigned) topic (e.g. 'Tipping in restaurants') between three dyads (pairs): one woman–man, one man–man and one woman–woman dyad. The speakers should be a similar age, and from similar social, ethnic and educational backgrounds. The discussion should be in the same language, but this language need not be English.

Step 2
➤ Transcribe the three discussions, including minimal responses and indicating overlaps and approximate pause lengths. (See Task C1.3 for an example of a transcription system.)

Step 3
➤ For each *single-sex* transcript, identify differences and similarities in communication style between the participants.

➤ Based on this data from this small sample of speakers, which would you say is the *most striking*? Similarities 'within' women, similarities 'within' men, differences 'between' women or differences 'between' men?

➤ Rank these from 1–4.

Step 4
➤ For your *mixed-sex* transcript, identify differences and similarities in communication style between the woman and the man.

➤ Consider how these relate (if at all) to the women's/men's *single-sex* communication styles.

Step 5
➤ Add 'differences and similarities between women and men' to the profiles.

➤ How do these fit in?

➤ Add these to the ranking (which will then be 1–6).

Step 6
➤ Given more data, decide whether it would be possible, in principle, to create a profile for 'men's communication style' and 'women's communication style', at least for people of similar age, and social, educational and ethnic background.

Step 7

➤ Write up the study and post it on your Gender and Language web site.

 Task C2.10: Slippage towards the masculine . . .

Step 1

➤ Focusing on the section 'There's many a slip' in the chapter entitled 'Language and reality: who made the world?' in Dale Spender's *Man Made Language* (1980), locate Spender's several 'giveaway' examples. One is the often-quoted 'Man needs food, water and access to females' (Erich Fromm). Two examples from other sources are:

- ■ 'The commons were popular with Newburians and other locals. People took picnics, "walked out" with their girls, picked bluebells and primroses in season' (Adams 1990, in *The Guardian*, 5 January 1990).
- ■ 'A coloured man subjected to racial abuse went berserk and murdered his next door neighbour's wife with a machete, Birmingham Crown Court heard today' (*The Guardian*, cited in Cameron 1994).

Step 2

➤ For each of the above, identify the grammatically 'common gender' noun which is actually being used as a masculine noun.

➤ In what sense do such examples illustrate not only the 'think male' phenomenon, but also the limitations of the value of 'non-sexist language'?

Step 3

➤ Find and list some more examples like these. They can be in any language, and preferably not just English. If possible, they should be original, rather than those cited in books on gender and language!

 Task C2.11: Wedding discourse

Step 1

Early editions of *Book of Common Prayer* of the (Anglican) Church of England, in the section on the 'Solemnization of matrimony', includes the utterance: 'I pronounce that they be man and wife together'.

➤ How many variations on this can you find? Look for texts used in:

- ■ revised versions of the Anglican *Book of Common Prayer*
- ■ wedding ceremonies in other languages
- ■ wedding ceremonies from other religions
- ■ non-religious wedding ceremonies
- ■ weddings or civil ceremonies of gay or lesbian couples.

Step 2

➤ List and categorise these 'pronouncements'. Post the results on your Gender and Language web site.

Task C2.12: Arguing against arguments against non-sexist language items

Step 1

➤ Make notes on how you might argue for and against the following claims:

- ■ 'But all this chairperson stuff is just about language, I'm interested in really serious problems.'
- ■ 'Changing language can't change society.'
- ■ 'I often say "he" to mean "he or she" – and I really do mean he or she.'

Step 2

➤ With a friend or fellow student, role-play these arguments and the opposing arguments here.

Step 3

➤ In writing, summarise the two sides of this debate.

Step 4

➤ Read the following article and chapter:

- ■ 'An analysis of classic arguments against changing sexist language' (Blaubergs 1980).
- ■ 'This new species that seeks a new language: on sexism in language and language change' (Henley 1987).

Step 5

➤ Amend your summary (of both sides of the debate) accordingly.

Task C2.13: Gender as 'achieved' and 'ascribed'

Step 1

Pamela Fishman in her article 'Interaction: the work women do' (Unit B2.3) refers to Garfinkel's (1967) study of the 'achieved sex' of a transsexual.

➤ Follow up this reference.

➤ Make notes on Garfinkel's study, and on its relevance to Fishman's.

Step 2

➤ Think of three examples (imagined or actual) of how gender (which may better describe what Garfinkel was referring to) may be similarly said to be 'achieved' rather than 'ascribed'.

➤ Focus on the possible and/or partial achievement of gender through the use of language and linguistic interaction in a range of contexts.

 Task C2.14: 'Degrading' language

One of the early claims about the sexist nature of the English language was that it entailed women being linguistically and referentially 'degraded' as a result of the process of 'semantic derogation' (e.g. Schultz 1975, 1990). This process, Schultz claimed, affected terms for women, but not for men.

Step 1

➤ Consider the rather traditional masculine–feminine English 'pairs' in Table C2.14.1, which are often cited as evidence of the 'semantic derogation of women'.

➤ In each case the female term has acquired particular additional connotations – including of negativity, inferiority or a socially disapproved-of sexuality – but the male term has not.

Step 2

➤ Find more modern examples of this sort of 'asymmetry', in English.

Table C2.14.1

Male term	Connotation	Female term	Connotation
Wizard Bachelor	Positive	Witch Spinster	Negative
Manager Governor Lord	Superior	Mistress Governess Madam	Inferior
Master King Sir	No sexual connotation	Manageress Queen Lady	Sexual connotation

➤ Find examples in languages other than English (if you are only familiar with English, ask speakers of a range of languages).

Step 3

➤ Write these new examples in Table C2.14.2 (revise it if you wish).

Table C2.14.2

Language	Male term	Connotation	Female term	Connotation
		Positive		Negative
		Superior		Inferior
		No sexual connotation		Sexual connotation

Reference

Hines, Caitlin (1999) 'Rebaking the pie: the woman as dessert metaphor', in Mary Bucholtz et al. (eds) *Reinventing Identities: the gendered self in discourse.* New York: Oxford University Press. (This is a more recent study of contemporary derogatory terms for women.)

Task C2.15: Tag questions

Step 1
➤ Carry out a literature review of empirical studies of gender tendencies in the use of tag questions in English. Start with the following: Cameron et al. 1989, Dubois and Crouch 1975, Holmes 1984, McMillan et al. 1977.

Step 2
➤ Make a list of the different functions of tag questions that have been identified.

Step 3
➤ Carry out your own study of use of tag questions, as follows:

➤ Audiotape a mixed-sex group of four or five people in an informal setting talking for about 30 minutes.

➤ Transcribe the talk (see Task C1.3).

➤ Identify all the tag questions.

Step 4
➤ Analyse the transcript for:

  ■ frequency of tag questions,
  ■ different functions of tag questions,

in relation to gender, using your list from Step 2.

Step 5
➤ Compare your findings with those in the studies documented in Step 1.

Step 6
➤ Write up your study and post it on your Gender and Language web site.

Step 7
➤ If possible, replicate this study with speakers of another language but one which also has a form of tag questions (for example, the French *n'est-ce pas*).

Key reference

Dubois, Betty Lou and Crouch, Isobel (1975) 'The question of tag questions in women's speech: they don't really use more of them, do they?' *Language in Society* 4: 289–94.

Task C2.16: Interactional strategies and topic initiation

Replicate Fishman's study, but on a smaller scale, as follows:

Step 1
➤ Audio-record a conversation (as naturally occurring as possible) between a male/female couple, of approximately 15 minutes.

Step 2
➤ Transcribe the conversation, including any pauses and minimal responses. (See also Task C1.3.)

Step 3
➤ Analyse one or two of the features that Fishman looked for.

Step 4
➤ Compare your findings with those of Fishman. Any surprises?

➤ Think of some possible reasons for variation here.

Step 5
➤ Write up your study and post it on your Gender and Language web site. Set your study explicitly against the background of Fishman's.

Task C2.17: Use of 'non-sexist language'

Step 1
➤ Choose one or two of the following English items:

➤ 'Ms' (remember that this can also be used by men of women)

➤ 'chairperson'

➤ 's/he' or 'she or he' or 'generic she'

➤ 'singular they' (e.g. *Everyone should bring their lunch*).

Step 2
➤ Devise a chart to record people's use/non-use of your item, with reason(s), and context.

Step 3
➤ Ask friends and/or colleagues about their use of the item(s) and record their responses on your chart.

Step 4
➤ Summarise your findings.

➤ What can you conclude about the current use of this/these non-sexist language item(s) (at least as far as this mini-study is concerned)?

Step 5
➤ Post your findings on your Gender and Language web site.

Unit C3
The influence of feminism and feminist linguistics (b)

Task C3.1: Miscommunication between women and men?

Step 1
If you have done Task C2.9, use your transcripts to identify any apparent instances of miscommunication. Consider:

➤ possible explanations for these instances;

➤ whether the data suggests arguments for '(male) dominance', '(cultural) difference', or other interpretations of what is happening.

Step 2
'There may be more than one way of understanding what is happening in a particular conversation' (Maltz and Borker 1982: 215). This is as true for analysts as for language users.

Maltz and Borker are talking about American women and men, presumably from the same ethnic groups.

➤ Find and read their chapter in full.

➤ What do you think Maltz and Borker would say about communication between women and men who are *also* from different ethnic groups?

Task C3.2: Can gendered adult conversational styles be traced back to childhood?

> American men and women come from different sociolinguistic sub-cultures, having learned to do different things with words in a conversation, so that when they attempt to carry on conversations with one another, even if both parties are attempting to treat one another as equals, cultural miscommunication results.
>
> (Maltz and Borker 1982: 200)

Step 1
➤ Read Maltz and Borker's (1982) chapter in its entirety.

Step 2
➤ Choose two of the five 'areas' in which they say that men and women may have different conversational rules (in the section 'What is happening in cross-sex communication?').

➤ Trace each of these two areas back to the previous four sections to find its apparent 'origin'.

➤ Do you feel there is valid theoretical, if speculative, support here for Maltz and Borker's claim?

Step 3
➤ Write a 500-word argument either in favour of or against Maltz and Borker's position, and post it on your Gender and Language web site.

Task C3.3: *You Just Don't Understand!*

Step 1
➤ Read at least part of *You Just Don't Understand!* (Tannen 1991).

Step 2
➤ Use the World Wide Web to track down some popular reviews (i.e. not from academic publications) of Deborah Tannen's *You Just Don't Understand!*, written when or soon after it first came out in 1990.

➤ What do these suggest about the reasons for its commercial success?

Step 3
➤ Read and summarise some academic critiques of the book from the Gender and Language field (for example, Cameron 1992a, Troemel-Ploetz 1991, Uchida 1992).

➤ Now read Tannen's (1992) response to Troemel-Ploetz (1991).

Step 4
➤ Summarise the debate, finally indicating your own position. Post this on your Gender and Language web site.

Task C3.4: Gender and miscommunication

Deborah Tannen's *You Just Don't Understand!* (1991) was heavily influenced by Maltz and Borker's (1982) important paper.

➤ Trace Tannen's understanding of male–female miscommunication back to this paper.

➤ Identify similarities and any differences of emphasis and focus.

 Task C3.5: Self-help books

Since Deborah Tannen's *You Just Don't Understand!*, a range of popular self-help books has been published, based on similar 'gender differences' premises. These include the well-known *Men are from Mars, Women are from Venus* (John Gray) and *Men Can't Cry, Women Can't Read Maps* (Allan Pease and Barbara Pease).

Step 1
➤ Use web sites or visit a large bookshop to find books with similar premises.

➤ Note down their titles.

➤ What do these suggest about current understandings of gender and gender relations?

Step 2
➤ Choose one of these books and identify any sections/claims about alleged communication differences between women and men.

➤ To what extent are these claims qualified (e.g. as varying with cultural context)?

➤ To what extent are these claims mitigated (e.g. through modalisation)?

➤ What reasons (if any) are given for these alleged differences, in terms of their origin and/or maintenance?

➤ How would you judge the adequacy of these reasons?

➤ Note whether or not the apparent communication differences are evaluated as beneficial, overall.

➤ Note whether change is seen as achievable, and, if so, who is expected to change, and how.

Step 3

➤ Looking at web sites for these books, how (and to whom) do you think they are marketed?

Step 4

➤ What does this additionally tell us about popular understandings of gender?

➤ In particular, why do you think books such as these, which start from a premise of 'gender differences', are so popular?

➤ Is this surprising, or not, at the start of the twenty-first century?

Step 5

➤ Write up and post this study on your Gender and Language web site.

Task C3.6: Overlapping speech

Step 1

Maltz and Borker (1982) cite a range of work on overlapping speech and interruptions (e.g. West 1979, West and Zimmerman 1977, Zimmerman and West 1975).

➤ Read this early work and document how the field developed during this period, in terms of methodological approaches and understandings. In particular, indicate developments in the understanding of how 'overlapping speech' may not constitute an 'interruption'.

Step 2

➤ Then read some later studies of gender and overlapping speech, for example Beattie 1981, Talbot 1992.

Step 3

➤ Audio-record ten minutes of talk between a man and a woman. This can be in any language.

Step 4

➤ Transcribe it, considering the question of transcription of overlapping speech. (Jennifer Coates' *Women Talk* [1996] might give you some additional ideas here, see also Task C1.3.) Your transcript should show *all* occurrences of overlapping speech in a clear and systematic way.

Step 5

➤ Carefully study and then apply Beattie's (1981) framework for analysing 'successful speaker switches' to this stretch of data.

➤ Do you have examples of each type?

> What are your findings in terms of (a) frequency, and (b) distribution of types across the two speakers?

Step 6
> As a result of this exercise, can you suggest any refinements to (or even simplifications of) Beattie's framework?

Step 7
> Write up a report of this study and post it on your Gender and Language web site.

 Task C3.7: Gossip

Step 1
> Read Jennifer Coates's paper 'Gossip revisited' (1989).

Step 2
Coates adopts a very broad perspective on gossip, noting that topics of gossip are personal-experience-related (see also Jones 1990). Such topics, she claims, are more characteristic of women's than of men's groups.

> Consider your own experience and make notes on this claim.

References

Johnson, Sally and Finlay, Frank (1997) 'Do men gossip? An analysis of football talk on television', in Sally Johnson and Ulrike Hanna Meinhof (eds) *Language and Masculinity*. Oxford: Blackwell, pp. 130–343.

Jones, Deborah (1990) 'Gossip: notes on women's oral culture', in Deborah Cameron (ed.) *The Feminist Critique of Language*, 1st edn. London: Routledge, pp. 242–50.

Pilkington, Jane (1998) ' "Don't try and make out that I'm nice": the different strategies women and men use when gossiping', in Jennifer Coates (ed.) *Language and Gender: a reader*. Oxford: Blackwell, pp. 254–69.

For additional references, use library search tools (e.g. 'Linguistics and language behaviour abstracts').

 Task C3.8: You can('t) tell an approach by a book cover

Step 1
> Borrow a selection of books on gender and language.

> Compare (a) the titles, and (b) the visuals and text on the front covers.

➤ What focus is suggested?

➤ What different models of gender, of language, and of gender and language does each book suggest?

Step 2
➤ Now arrange the books chronologically.

➤ Are the theoretical changes undergone by gender and language study reflected in the changing titles and covers?

(This task was inspired by Victoria Bergvall, see <http://www.linguistics.ucsb.edu/faculty/bucholtz/conference/bergvall.html>.)

Step 3
➤ Post the results of this study on your Gender and Language web site.

Unit C4
Developing understandings of gender

 Task C4.1: Gender differences

Step 1
➤ Write a research proposal for a project investigating gender differences (or tendencies) in language use, motivated by and based on an intention to expose disadvantage of some sort. Draw on your own professional experience here.

➤ Consider:

- why the research needs to be done (academic and/or political reasons);
- the research questions you want to explore;
- the language(s) in use here;
- the data you need (for each research question);
- the data collection process;
- the analysis of the data;
- how you will disseminate the findings.

➤ Relate these carefully, e.g. show:

- how your data will allow you to address your research questions;
- how you will address your research questions in your analysis.

Step 2
➤ Write a final section, anticipating and addressing potential criticisms that in the process of carrying out this research, you may risk hardening unproductive gender divisions.

 Task C4.2: 'Warrants' for gender

Step 1
➤ Read Julian Edge and Keith Richards' (1998) paper 'May I see your warrant, please?' and any other work in which 'warrants' are mentioned. (Such work often falls within CA.)

Step 2
In her article 'Yes, but is it gender?' (2002), Joan Swann identifies seven 'warrants' that have been used to claim that gender is (or at least may be) relevant in a particular stretch or set of data in language and gender research. These warrants are:

- quantitative and/or general patterns;
- indirect reliance on quantitative and/or general patterns;
- 'participants' orientations';
- speakers'/participants' solicited interpretations;
- analysts' theoretical positions;
- analysts' intuitions;
- the fact that speakers/participants are male/female.

➤ Carefully read Swann's article. Make sure that you understand what each of the 'warrants' is referring to.

Step 3
➤ Identify five reports of empirical gender and language studies. Start with studies of gender and language with which you are familiar, and look in edited collections on gender and language for others.

➤ Which warrant(s) for gender were used most frequently? Were some warrants not found at all in your search?

The list of edited collections on language and gender (at the start of the Bibliography), may be useful here. See also the review essay by Janet Holmes (1992a).

Step 4
➤ Repeat the exercise with a piece of your own empirical work on gender and language, or work of another student or colleague with which you are familiar.

➤ What warrant(s) for gender were used?

Step 5
➤ Post the results of the study on your Gender and Language web site.

References

Edge, Julian and Richards, Keith (1998) 'May I see your warrant, please? Justifying claims in qualitative research', *Applied Linguistics* 19 (3): 334–56.
Swann, Joan (2002) 'Yes, but is it gender?', in Lia Litosseliti and Jane Sunderland (eds) *Gender Identity and Discourse Analysis*. Amsterdam: John Benjamins, pp. 43–67.
See also Katz 1997, Toulmin 1969.

Task C4.3: Changing models of gender

Step 1
➤ Read three contributions of your choice in the edited collection *Reinventing Identities* (Bucholtz et al. 1999).

Step 2
➤ For each, identify (a) how gender is conceptualised (find actual quotations if you can); and (b) the theoretical approach and/or methodology used.

Step 3
➤ Repeat the exercise with two earlier edited collections, selected from the following (ideally, include one of the 1995 collections): Cameron 1998a, Coates 1998, Hall and Bucholtz 1995, Johnson and Meinhof 1997, Kotthof and Wodak 1998, Mills 1995b, Wodak 1997.

Step 4
➤ Identify some changes in understandings of gender that have taken place in the field of gender and language during these few years.

➤ In particular, is it true to say that published 'gender differences' studies are on the wane?

Step 5
➤ Post your conclusions on your Gender and Language web site.

 Task C4.4: Creating an annotated bibliography of gender and language collections

Step 1
➤ Create an annotated bibliography of edited collections of work on gender and language study (see the start of the bibliography of this book).

➤ Identify what makes each collection *distinctive* (both in terms of claims, and actual contents). To do this, you will need to read at least the introductory chapter to each.

Step 2
➤ Arrange your annotated bibliography chronologically.

➤ Add an introduction and a conclusion (this last should include a summary of the changes that have taken place over time (e.g. in theoretical approach, in type of data). The contents pages of each work may also help you do this.

Step 3
➤ Post the final version of your annotated bibliography on your Gender and
Language web site.

Task C4.5: The textual mediation and construction
of gender difference

How are 'gender-differentiated practices' (i.e. women doing one thing or being
treated in one way, men doing or being treated in another) (a) described and (b)
justified in texts?

Step 1
➤ Consider carefully what might be some good 'epistemological sites' here: sports
science texts, for example, or texts on religious practices, military roles . . .
anything that might (need to) address the question of gender-differentiated
practices.

Step 2
➤ Name and list these sites, and the practices they may have to justify.

Step 3
➤ Find two examples (e.g. on the World Wide Web) of one of the text types you
have identified.

➤ Check to what extent this is indeed a good epistemological site for the study of
textually mediated gender-differentiated practices.

Step 4
➤ Consider in what sense these texts exemplify both the 'construction' and
'mediation' of gender difference.

➤ Make notes on the meaning of both concepts.

Task C4.6: The distribution of studies on the language
of gay women/gay men

Is it fair to say that there has been more work on the language of (and about) gay
men than on the language of (and about) gay women?

Step 1
➤ Look on the World Wide Web and check bibliographies for an answer to this
question.

➤ Document your methodology for doing this.

Step 2

➤ If you find that there is indeed more work on gay men's language, what might be some possible explanations for this?

Step 3

➤ Does the work on gay women, or gay men, tend to encompass any other identities in particular, for example ethnicity, or deafness?

Step 4

➤ Identify and interview (face to face or by e-mail) a 'gender, sexuality and language' or queer theory scholar who researches in this area to find out more about these questions.

Step 5

➤ Post a report of this study on your Gender and Language web site.

★ Task C4.7: Reading and writing academic reviews

Step 1

➤ Read two academic book reviews published in a journal. These can be of any book related to language.

Step 2

➤ Search the World Wide Web for reviews (including very brief ones) of *Language and Sexuality* by Deborah Cameron and Don Kulick (2003).

➤ Read these reviews carefully, noting particularly (a) how much is descriptive, how much evaluative, and (b) how negative comments are phrased.

Step 3

➤ Now, read *Language and Sexuality* yourself, making notes throughout for your *own* review.

Step 4
Either:

➤ Search the World Wide Web for publishing companies or distributors promoting this book who are also soliciting reviews of it. Write your review and send it to one such company.

Or:

➤ Write a review of the book for a local publication such as a social sciences or postgraduate student newsletter.

Task C4.8: 'Identity'

Step 1
➤ Consider the notion of identity in relation to language.

➤ For how long has this concept been current?

➤ Extend this to the notion of 'gender identity'.

Step 2
➤ Explore the notion of identity in the work of Deborah Cameron, Mary Bucholtz and Cynthia Nelson (Unit B4), but this time read the complete articles/chapters.

Step 3
The concept of 'identity' has not been embraced with enthusiasm in all parts of the gender and language field, and has been subject to considerable re-evaluation.

➤ Explore the position taken by discursive psychologists on identity (e.g. Edley 2001, Weatherall 2002).

➤ Explore why Judith Butler's book *Gender Trouble* (1990, 1999) is subtitled 'Gender and the Subversion of Identity'. (Refer particularly to the Bucholtz extract in Unit B4.2.)

➤ Are Butler's and Bucholtz's views of identity entirely in opposition? You may wish to do Task C4.9 before completing this.

Step 4
➤ Write a paper on the range and diversity of understandings of 'identity', and 'gender identity', highlighting different ways these are of relevance to gender and language study. In what different ways does the concept of *identity* represent an advance on that of *role*?

➤ Consider also how the study of gender and language has, in turn, contributed to understandings of identity.

Task C4.9: Judith Butler

Step 1
➤ Read or reread the comments on Butler in Unit A4.

Step 2
➤ Read pp. 1–9 of either edition of *Gender Trouble* (1990, 1999) – if the latter, do not read the new Preface yet.

Step 3

➤ Make notes on the following questions:

- What exactly is the problem when the category of 'woman' is taken as 'a coherent and stable subject'?
- Do you think that it is possible (Butler suggests it is not), to invoke the concept of 'woman' for strategic purposes?
- Given sexual dimorphism, meaning that (most) women share a common biology, different from men, is it possible to suggest that women do, in fact, share a few universal *other* commonalities – even though these will be radically mediated and situated? If so, what might these be? If not, is a shared biology sufficient to warrant the category 'woman'?
- To what extent do you agree with Butler that *performativity* is a more relevant concept than *identity* for the study of language, gender and sexuality?

Step 4

➤ Read Butler's new preface to the 1999 edition of *Gender Trouble*.

In this Preface, Butler stresses the destabilisation of gender (through, for example, a range of non-normative sexual practices: homosexuality, transsexuality, drag). (Hence *Gender Trouble*: the conventional notion of gender is in trouble, the notion of gender can also itself usefully cause trouble.) She also returns to her 1990 notion of performativity. This is an alternative to the idea of gender as some sort of 'internal essence': rather, any apparent 'essence' is in fact 'manufactured through a sustained set of acts, posited through the gendered stylisation of the body' (1999: xv). Butler carefully makes the additional point that performativity entails neither 'voluntarism' nor a rejection of agency.

Step 5

➤ Consider and make notes on the following questions:

- Butler raises the question of whether the role of language in performativity is 'linguistic' or 'theatrical' (1999: xxv). For her, the speech act is both, and speech itself 'a bodily act with specific linguistic consequences . . . its status as word and deed is necessarily ambiguous'. In what different ways might performativity in relation to gender be linguistic?
- Butler's position is that gender is produced and consolidated by 'heterosexual normativity' (1999: xii). How might this work?

 Task C4.10: Understandings of sex and gender

Step 1

➤ Read Cameron's chapter 'Theoretical debates in feminist linguistics' (1997b). In this chapter, Cameron cites the French sociologist Nicole-Claude Mathieu's three different understandings of gender in relation to sex.

Step 2
➤ Read and make notes on Mathieu's original chapter, 'Sexual, sexed and sex-class identities' (1996).

Step 3
➤ Consider how Mathieu's three understandings relate to 'popular' understandings of sex and gender (if at all).

➤ How do they relate to more scholarly understandings?

➤ Document for yourself your own personal 'take' on the gender–sex relationship.

Key references

Cameron, Deborah (1997b) 'Theoretical debates in feminist linguistics: questions of sex and gender', in Ruth Wodak (ed.) *Gender and Discourse.* London: Sage, pp. 21–36.
Mathieu, Nicole-Claude (1996) 'Sexual, sexed and sex-class identities', in Diana Leonard and Lisa Adkins (eds) *Sex in Question: French materialist feminism*, first published in French, 1989. London: Taylor & Francis, pp. 42–71.

Task C4.11: Language and sexual identity: The case of Polari

Step 1
➤ Find out as much as you can about 'Polari', a language that was spoken in the UK in the twentieth century by some gay men.

Step 2
➤ Make notes on its origin and decline and its various possible functions in relation to sexual identity. Start with Baker 2002. Web sites on Polari will also help you with this project.

Task C4.12: How is 'sex difference' described?

Unit B4.1 included the following quotation from Deborah Cameron: 'an honourable feminist tradition has arisen, especially in the social sciences, of directing attention to the way sex difference has been described and explained, rather than to the *content* of difference itself' (p. 122, my italics). Cameron points out that this sort of analysis is less prevalent in linguistics than in other social sciences.

➤ Look at examples of sociolinguistic work (for example, by William Labov, Peter Trudgill, Jenny Cheshire, Susan Gal, Lesley Milroy), and at sociolinguistics textbooks.

➤ How is sex difference described and explained?

➤ Is there any reflexive comment on this?

➤ How is 'sex similarity' treated (if at all)?

⭐ Task C4.13: Philosophy and the 'gender binary'

➤ If you are interested in the philosophical underpinnings of what has been called 'the hierarchical female/male duality', read Moira Gatens's chapter 'Modern rationalism' (1990), and follow up the references.

⭐ Task C4.14: 'Sex differences' in the popular media

Step 1
➤ Go to several bookshops/newsagents and list all the titles of magazines for women and magazines for men you can find.

Step 2
➤ Note down all the feature titles on the magazine covers that focus on 'sex differences' in some way.

➤ Compare women's/men's magazine covers in this respect.

Step 3
➤ Identify feature titles that focus on women and men not being able to understand each other (e.g. what they say/mean/want/think).

➤ Carefully read two articles with such titles.

➤ What is said about the reason for this mutual lack of comprehension?

➤ Is advice given to overcome this, and, if so, at whom is the advice directed?

Reference

McLoughlin, Linda (2000) *The Language of Magazines*. London: Routledge.

⭐ Task C4.15: 'Sex difference' in spoken media discourse

➤ Over the course of a week, listen out for and note down references to and discussion of sex difference – linguistic and otherwise – in (a) spoken non-fictional media discourse (e.g. radio talk shows), and (b) media fiction (e.g. TV soaps, radio drama).

➤ How is this articulated?

➤ What sort of explanations are offered?

➤ Are any challenges raised?

Task C4.16: The variable status of gender and language study

Step 1
➤ Within your own academic institution, consider the status of any of the following? (Some of these will be more relevant to you than others.)

- gender and language as a topic within Women's Studies;
- gender and language as a topic within (Applied) Linguistics;
- gender and language as a topic within either mother-tongue or second-language teaching;
- feminist theory within gender and language study;
- a linguistic understanding of 'discourse analysis' in sociology.

Step 2
➤ Look at university or college departmental web sites and course handbooks.

Step 3
➤ If you can, interview academic staff who teach within the above areas (ideally, several short interviews with different staff).

Step 4
➤ Prepare a model or an electronic poster to represent your findings, and post it on your Gender and Language web site.

Task C4.17: Responses to the expression of gendered stereotypes

Step 1
➤ With others, enact a focus group, complete with facilitator. (To get you started, read Lia Litosseliti's [2003] *Using Focus Groups in Research.*) Your topic is 'Responses to the expression of gender-stereotypical views'. The facilitator starts the discussion and keeps it going with the following prompts:

- What do you do (if anything), when someone comes out with a stereotype about what women are like, and/or how this differs from what men are like?

- Do you think responses to this sort of situation might (or should) vary with the stereotype in question?
- Can you think of anything else that might make a difference to your response? (Prompts: the apparent degree of seriousness and sincerity with which the stereotype was expressed; the setting and the participants in that setting; your relationships with the participants.)

Step 2
➤ With reference to Unit B4.1, can you add to Deborah Cameron's list of possible responses to expressed stereotypes?

➤ Put together a chart which indicates possible and actual responses.

Step 3
➤ Post the chart on your Gender and Language web site.

Task C4.18: Visual models of gender

Step 1
➤ With others (if possible), brainstorm and produce one or more labelled visual representations of gender, taking into consideration possible relationships between masculinity and femininity. These representations can be two- or three-dimensional. Produce a computer graphic if possible.

Step 2
➤ Post the representations on your Gender and Language web site.

Task C4.19: Queer theory

Step 1
➤ Read three or more chapters from William Leap's book on gay men's language (1996) and the more recent edited collections on gay and lesbian language (Cameron and Kulick 2003, Livia and Hall 1997).

Step 2
➤ Make notes on how the field has changed between the publication of the last two books, and the Cameron and Kulick collection.

Step 3
➤ Read or reread what Cynthia Nelson (Unit B4.3) says about the role of language in queer theory.

Step 4

➤ How might a language teacher (or teacher of another subject) draw on queer theory in the classroom, in practice?

➤ Discuss some possibilities and problems here.

Task C4.20: Research projects for different understandings of gender

➤ Look at the bulleted list at the end of Unit A4.

➤ Taking all six possibilities for gender and language study, develop your own chart to show a possible research project with which each could be explored. Be as specific as you can in terms of the research questions you would ask and the data you would need for each.

Unit C5
Developing understandings of language: Language change

 Task C5.1: Gender, language and traditional dictionaries

Step 1
➤ Read some work on gender and 'standard' dictionaries: Hennessy 1994, Hoey 1996, Kaye 1989, Romaine 1999.

Step 2
➤ Choose a 'standard' dictionary for which you can find more than one edition.

➤ Trace the entries for several 'sexist' and 'non-sexist' linguistic items over time, i.e. in different editions. Words might include any of:

- Ms
- man
- chairman
- chairperson
- s/he
- girl
- themself
- gay
- partner

Step 3
➤ Choose one of these words and document its 'etymological history'. Refer if possible not only to different editions of the same dictionary, but to different (standard) dictionaries. Post this 'etymological history' on your Gender and Language web site.

 Task C5.2: Non-traditional dictionaries and wordbooks

Step 1
➤ Get hold of one of these 'non-traditional' dictionaries/wordbooks with a focus on gender and language: Daly 1987, Kramarae and Triechler 1997, Mills 1989.

Step 2
➤ Read the introduction to the book and then selected sections.

➤ Make notes on the following:

- ■ the purpose of the chosen book;
- ■ how the keywords/items have been selected;
- ■ how each entry is arranged.

Step 3
➤ In what ways would you update the book, i.e. for an edition published in the early twenty-first century?

➤ Consider both new keyword/items, as well as what is said about language use.

Step 4
➤ If you were publishing the *American Heritage School Dictionary* (see Unit B5.1) today, again with a brief to be non-sexist, but at the same to reflect actual usage, what guidelines would you give to your team of lexicographers?

➤ Produce a one-page document, with examples.

Step 5
➤ Write your own detailed dictionary entry for each of the following:

- ■ Ms
- ■ man
- ■ chairperson
- ■ s/he
- ■ girl

➤ If possible, compare these with others doing the same task.

Step 6
➤ Bring this work together in a report on 'Non-traditional dictionaries and wordbooks', using your own Step 5 entries as exemplification of what might be included in a more 'standard' dictionary.

➤ Post the results on your Gender and Language web site.

Task C5.3: Language, gender and science fiction

Step 1
➤ Consider why science fiction is a genre of interest to feminists, and why it might also be of interest to (some) linguists.

➤ If you are not a reader of science fiction, ask around to identify:

■ as many works of science fiction as you can which may be of particular
interest to feminists and/or scholars of gender and of women's studies;
■ other works of science fiction in which *language* is a focus of the work.

Step 2
➤ Read Suzette Haden Elgin's science-fiction work *Native Tongue* (1985),
published by The Women's Press (London).

➤ Write a short description of Láadan (the language spoken).

➤ In what ways does it 'represent' gender?

➤ Are there male and female third-person singular pronouns?

➤ Is there a word for 'human beings', and is this marked for gender?

➤ What lexical features might be of interest to feminist linguists?

➤ What is said about the language by the characters in the book? Does this shed
light on the language? Does this correspond to what might be said by linguists?

Step 3
➤ Look at some web sites on this author and this book, for example: <http://
www.sfwa.org/members/elgin/NativeTongue/Index.html>.

Step 4
➤ Investigate Esperanto, together with one other of the other 600 artificial
languages in existence.

➤ Ask and answer the first three questions you asked of Láadan (Step 2).

➤ Are there any other features of particular interest to gender and language
scholars in either of these two languages?

**Task C5.4: Gender change in dominant and non-dominant
languages**

Step 1
➤ Read *Women Changing Language*, by Anne Pauwels (1998), in its entirety.

Step 2
➤ Read two chapters from Hellinger and Bußmann (eds) *Gender Across Languages:
the linguistic representation of women and men* (2001–2). One chapter should

be on a language with which you are (relatively) familiar, one on a language with which you are not at all familiar.

➤ As follow-up, read Anne Pauwels' article on feminist language planning and titles for women (1996).

Step 3
➤ Develop a 'comparison chart' showing how gender varies across your two chosen languages, using as many different variables as are relevant. If either or both languages are undergoing change, indicate this on your chart.

Step 4
➤ If you are familiar with a language (or dialect) that is not included in the Hellinger and Bußmann collection, document your own knowledge.

➤ Indicate how gender 'works' in the language in question.

➤ Include also your personal experience of gender-related language change, if any, and of popular opinions and official practices here.

➤ Post your observations on your Gender and Language web site.

Step 5
➤ Choose a language that has not been explored in the Hellinger and Bußmann collections, with which you are not familiar, but of which you know speakers.

➤ Interview one or more speakers of that language to find out how gender 'works' in the language, and what, if anything, is happening in terms of language change.

Task C5.5: Teachers teaching language change

Step 1
➤ How *should* teachers of English as a foreign language (EFL) or English as a second language (ESL) deal with questions of language change in relation to gender?

➤ What are some different possibilities here?

➤ As preparation for this question, read and make notes on the following articles, identifying some different things that a teacher's decision might depend on: Cochran 1992, 1996, Florent et al. 1994, Pugsley 1991, 1992, Willeke and Sanders 1978.

Step 2
➤ Visit a library, language school or British Council office.

➤ Find out if and how questions of language change and gender are addressed in EFL or ESL textbooks and in teachers' guides to such textbooks. (Look at as many as you can.)

Step 3
➤ Recommendations of good practice are, of course, not the same as practice itself.

➤ Design a study to investigate how EFL and ESL teachers actually *do* deal with questions of gender and language *change* in class.

➤ Start by dealing with the question of how you would select a 'fruitful' lesson to observe.

➤ Continue by developing a set of interview questions for teachers.

Step 4
➤ Post your research plan on your Gender and Language web site.

➤ If you are interested in how language teachers deal with gender representation (as opposed to gendered language change) in textbooks, see also Unit B6.1, in which you can read an extract from Sunderland et al. (2002) 'From representation towards discursive practices'.

Task C5.6: Non-progressive uses of progressive language

Step 1
➤ Check the British National Corpus of written language for occurrences of 'non-sexist language' items such as 'chairperson' and 'she or he'.

Step 2
➤ Are these items being used in ways of which feminist language reformers would approve?

➤ Are there any instances of these uses being cited in order to be negatively evaluated, or ridiculed (or is ridicule implied)?

➤ What can we learn from such an exercise?

Task C5.7: The case of Japanese

Step 1
Much has been written about the 'sex-exclusive' nature of some aspects of Japanese – mainly phonology, morphology and syntax (for example, final particles such as *wa* and *ga*, and first and second pronominal forms), but also lexis. These patterns

tend to have the effect of making women's talk sound more formal and polite than that of men.

➤ Read at least two of the following references: Hasegawa 2005, Ide and McGloin 1991, Ide 1979, 1982, 1986, 1992, 2003, 1997, Okamoto and Shibamoto-Smith 2004, Sakata 1991, Shibamoto 1991, Tanaka 2004, Wetzel 1988.

Step 2
Importantly, the idea that this gender-differentiated language code is homogeneous across Japan, and unchanging, has been widely contested. There is evidence of women and girls using certain 'male' forms, in certain contexts.

➤ Read one or two of these articles and chapters: Akiba-Reynolds 1985, Matsumoto 2002, 2004, McMahill 2002, Okamoto 1995, Ozaki 1998.

Step 3
➤ Summarise what seems to be the state of affairs here, to date.

➤ What sort of debates are going on?

Task C5.8: Teaching and learning gendered Japanese

Step 1
➤ Find web sites which aim to teach the Japanese language, or aspects of it, to foreigners.

Step 2
➤ Given that, traditionally, women and men were and indeed often still are expected to speak Japanese in certain different ways, in what sense is this promoted *pedagogically* today? For example, is it 'required', 'recommended' or simply mentioned as a possibility? Is it critically addressed? What different reasons are given for such an expectation, and what consequences (if any) for transgression are indicated?

Step 3
➤ Interview a Japanese teacher about her or his own views and practices here, and about whether the Japanese language teaching profession shares any consensus about this.

➤ To what extent is there a debate in the profession?

Task C5.9: 'Post-feminism'

Step 1
➤ List some different possibilities for the meaning of 'post-feminism'. Start off by listing your own ideas, then ask around, and use the World Wide Web.

Step 2

➤ According to this list, what might be the role of language in post-feminism?

➤ Are any of your possibilities particularly helpful in terms of understanding current gender and language issues or particular texts?

References

Gamble, Sarah (ed.) (2000) *The Routledge Critical Dictionary of Feminism and Postfeminism.* New York: Routledge. (In particular, Mary Talbot's article on 'Feminism and language'.)

Mills, Sara (1998) 'Post-feminist text analysis', *Language and Literature* 7 (3): 235–53.

Step 3

➤ Create an annotated bibliography entitled 'Gender, language and post-feminism'.

➤ Post it on your Gender and Language web site.

 Task C5.10: Linguistic intervention

Step 1

➤ Make a list of different approaches to linguistic intervention in terms of the implementation of non-sexist language, i.e. what social and linguistic practices might help here?

Step 2

➤ Read Chapter 9 of *Gendered Discourses* (Sunderland 2004), which is entitled '"Damaging discourses" and intervention in discourse'. This, of course, refers to discourse(s) rather than individual linguistic items. Nevertheless, does it suggest ways in which you might amend your list?

 Task C5.11: Codes of practice

Step 1

In the 1970s and 1980s, numerous 'codes of practice' were drawn up that provided guidelines for various sorts of 'inclusive language' – to do with ethnicity, age and disability as well as gender.

➤ Read Florent et al. (1994), written for publishers of EFL textbooks (and discussed with them).

Step 2
➤ Track down more such codes of practice, for example those used by professional organisations, higher-education institutions or unions. (See also Unit A3 for extracts from the UK Society of Personnel Officers in Government Services (SOCPO) guidelines.) In particular, try and find any written in (and about) a language other than English.

Step 3
➤ Do you notice any changes in codes of practice over the 1970s, 1980s and 1990s?

➤ Can you find any current (twenty-first century) codes of practice that pertain specifically or *inter alia* to gender and language?

Task C5.12: Derogatory language

Step 1
➤ Investigate the derogatory use of 'slag', 'tart' and 'bitch' in modern English, as follows:

   ■ Ask native speakers of English of different ages about (a) their uses and understandings of these terms; (b) the practices of others; and (c) any changes they are aware of here.
   ■ Use corpora, especially of spoken English (e.g. British National Corpus).

Step 2
➤ Traditionally used of women, to what extent are these terms now used also of men, and, if they are used of men, what meanings do they carry?

➤ Are these terms as derogatory as when used of women?

➤ Are they as derogatory when used of women as they used to be?

Step 3
➤ Carry out a similar investigation for comparable terms for a language other than English, with which you are at least slightly familiar.

Step 4
➤ Document your findings from Steps 1–3 and post them on your Gender and Language web site.

Task C5.13: Men's use of non-sexist language

Step 1
Juliane Schwarz's study (Unit B5.3) focuses on women's conceptualisations of 'Ms'.

➤ Design a focus group study to investigate *men*'s conceptualisations of 'Ms'. The men should be of two different age groups but from similar backgrounds.

➤ Consider carefully:

- what you will tell the participants;
- whether they will do any 'warm-up' tasks (e.g. at the start of the discussion);
- facilitator's prompts;
- practical questions of time, place and payment;
- the audio-recording (do you need an assistant?).

Step 2
➤ Run the groups, audio-recording the discussions.

Step 3
➤ Transcribe the sessions (see Task C1.3).

Step 4
➤ Analyse the data by identifying the different conceptualisations.

➤ Try to explain your findings.

Step 5
➤ Post a report of your study on your Gender and Language web site.

References

Edley, Nigel (2001) 'Analysing masculinity: interpretive repertoires, ideological dilemmas and subject positions', in Wetherell, M. et al. *Discourse as Data: a guide for analysis*. London: Sage/Open University.
Litosseliti, Lia (2003) *Using Focus Groups in Research*. London: Continuum.
See also Silverman 2004.

 Task C5.14: Text rewriting

Step 1
➤ Re-write the following anthropological text *three times* using (1) gender-neutral pronouns; (2) the 'generic she'; (3) pluralisation.

The alchemist, like the smith, and like the potter before him, is a 'master of fire.' It is with fire that he controls the passage of matter from one state to another. The first potter who, with the aid of live embers, was successful in hardening those shapes which he had given to his clay, must have felt the intoxication of the demiurge: he had discovered a transmuting agent. That

274

which natural heat—from the sun or the bowels of the earth—took so long to ripen, was transformed by fire at a speed hitherto undreamed of. This demiurgic enthusiasm springs from that obscure presentiment that the great secret lay in discovering how to 'perform' faster than Nature, in other words (since it is always necessary to talk in terms of the spiritual experience of primitive man) how, without peril, to interfere in the processes of the cosmic forces. Fire turned out to be the means by which man could 'execute' faster, but it could also do something other than what already existed in Nature.

(Steven J. Pyne 1999, <http://www.findarticles.com/cf_dls/
m0GER/1999_Winter/58458625/p1/article.jhtml>)

Step 2
➤ Compare the four versions.

➤ What is the 'effect' of the these differently written texts?

Step 3
Either:

➤ Ask various people to read, compare and comment on the different versions. Do they agree on the 'effects' of each?

Or:

➤ Ask friends or fellow students to complete this exercise, and then compare your newly written versions.

Task C5.15: Creating a new pronoun

Step 1
➤ Read and make notes on the following, reminding yourself of why many users of the English language feel the need for a gender-neutral third-person singular pronoun: Baron 1981, Bodine 1975a, McKay 1980, Miller and Swift 1989.

Step 2
➤ Write a summary of what you have read.

Step 3
➤ If you were to devise such a pronoun in English, what might it be? Why?

➤ Produce a list of possibilities, together with the advantages and disadvantages of each.

Step 4
➤ Ask around for other possibilities and add these to your list. Limit the list to ten items maximum.

Step 5
➤ Ask people who did not contribute to Step 4 to rank the items in order of preference, and to give reasons for their choices. Record these systematically.

Step 6
➤ After doing this exercise, what do you think are the constraints on and opportunities for each pronoun?

➤ Post your conclusions on your Gender and Language web site.

Unit C6
Developing understandings
of language: Context

Task C6.1: Meanings of *context*

Step 1
➤ Read one or more of the following, on the notion of context: Bates 1976, Halliday and Hasan 1989, Lyons 1981.

Step 2
➤ Identify some definitions or explanations of 'context' in these or in other linguistics literature.

➤ In what ways are the definitions and explanations similar, and different?

➤ Are different aspects or dimensions of 'context' covered?

➤ Is gender referred to, either directly or indirectly?

Task C6.2: 'Talk around the text'

Step 1
➤ Read and make notes on the following two studies of 'talk around the text': Dombey 1992, Smith 1995.

Step 2
➤ What insights does each provide for our understanding of gender and language?

➤ Write a brief review of the two articles from the perspective of 'talk around the text' and post it on your Gender and Language web site.

Task C6.3: Communities of practice

Step 1
➤ Read Penny Eckert's paper 'The whole woman: sex and gender differences in variation' (1990).

➤ In what ways does Eckert's data anticipate and indeed provide empirical support for the community of practice (CofP) notion, which was to be developed for gender and language study shortly after?

Step 2
➤ Make a list of possible CofPs, using your own experience and the extract on CofPs in B6.2.

Step 3
➤ Add more examples of CofPs, as follows:

- those identified by Eckert and McConnell-Ginet (either 1992a or 1992b)
- examples from Lave and Wenger (1991)
- examples from the special CofP 1999 issue of *Language in Society*

Step 4
Lave and Wenger's (1991) pioneer work on CofPs was written primarily for education.

➤ Read it carefully.

➤ Is *language* seen as important?

➤ Is *gender* identified as something relevant to a CofP – or to which a CofP may be relevant? (These connections may be stated directly, or implied.)

Step 5
➤ Read Wenger's later (1998) piece, and ask the same questions.

Step 6
➤ Consider whether each CofP on your list (Steps 2 and 3) would be considered a CofP according to Lave and Wenger's (1991) list of characteristics.

Step 7
➤ What *linguistic* characteristics of a CofP might you add to Lave and Wenger's (1991) list?

Step 8
➤ Choose a fellow student, friend, relative, acquaintance or colleague whom you see as generally busy and sociable.

➤ Plan and develop a semi-structured interview to establish to which CofPs he or she belongs, using Lave and Wenger's (1991) list.

➤ Carry out and audio-record the interview.

➤ Use the recording to develop a diagram of this person's social networks, and decide whether or not s/he is a 'peripheral' or 'core' member of these.

References

Miles, M. and Huberman, M. (1994) *Qualitative Data Analysis: An Expanded Sourcebook.* London: Sage.

Silverman, David (ed.) (2004) *Qualitative Research: Theory, Method and Practice. London*: Sage.

See also Arksey and Knight 1999, Cohen et al. 2000, Ritchie and Spencer 1994, Strauss and Corbin 1990 and Strauss 1987.

Task C6.4: People on the margins of a CofP

Step 1
➤ Create a group of fellow students interested in the topics of context and CofPs.

➤ Appoint a group note-taker.

Step 2
➤ Discuss whether any of you has ever been a 'peripheral' or 'marginal' member of a CofP.

➤ If so, discuss whether you can relate to the idea of 'practice' not only as 'habitual social action' but also as 'rehearsal for later social action'?

➤ Was there something 'gendered' about this?

➤ Discuss why people on the 'margins' of a CofP are often at the 'centre of analysis'.

Step 3
➤ Develop a set of case studies of individual group members based on these discussions.

Step 4
➤ Write these up in the form of a report on 'People on the margins of a CofP'. Try to incorporate both a historical and a critical dimension.

Step 5
➤ Post the report on your Gender and Language web site.

Task C6.5: Relationships between large-scale surveys of linguistic behaviour and ethnographic studies

Step 1
In their 1992(a) paper (Unit B6.2), Eckert and McConnell-Ginet challenge an implication of Labov's that ethnographic studies should 'answer to' generalised correlations found in sociolinguistic surveys.

➤ Read Labov's (1990) paper on 'Sex and social class in linguistic change', in particular the section entitled 'Some methodological issues' (pp. 208–10).

➤ What do you see as Labov's position on ethnography in relation to 'controlled study of speech production'?

Step 2
Eckert and McConnell-Ginet go on to argue that 'ethnographic studies [of language and society] must answer to each other, and . . . survey and experimental studies in turn must answer to them' (1992a: 94).

➤ What do you think they mean by this?

➤ How might written ethnographies use and refer to survey and experimental sociolinguistic studies?

 Task C6.6: *Hlonipha*

Step 1
➤ Using print and electronic references, find out as much as you can about the practice and language of *hlonipha*.

Step 2
➤ Why is *hlonipha* of particular interest to sociolinguists and to gender and language scholars?

➤ Which words are characteristic of *hlonipha* use?

➤ In what ways, if any, may women benefit from this sociolinguistic practice?

➤ To what extent, and in what contexts, is this practice changing?

Step 3
➤ Create an annotated bibliography about *hlonipha*.

Step 4
➤ Read or reread Hanong Thetela's piece on *hlonipha* (Unit B6.3).

➤ Then, ask around to see if someone you know comes from an area in which *hlonipha* is spoken, or knows someone else who does, and would be willing to talk to you.

➤ Plan and carry out an interview, as follows:

■ Using your findings from Steps 1 and 2, prepare some interview questions, aimed at filling in some of the gaps in your understanding. (Remember that *hlonipha* practices are likely to vary across southern Africa.)
■ Arrange to audio-record the interview (this includes getting the permission of the interviewee to be recorded)
■ Ask in what ways he or she thinks that *hlonipha* is helpful or unhelpful for women.

Step 5
➤ Complete your account of *hlonipha*, so that it incorporates your interviewee's perspectives.

Step 6
➤ With your interviewee's permission, post the interview, your bibliography, and your account on your Gender and Language web site. Extracts from the interview should be used appropriately in your account to illustrate the points you make.

Task C6.7: 'Teacher talk around the text'

Step 1
➤ Read the study by Sunderland et al. (2002) from Unit B6.1 in full.

Step 2
➤ Replicate it, if possible as a small group. Each person should:

■ get access to a language classroom and the textbook used;
■ find out what units of the textbook will be taught, and when;
■ identify some possible 'gender critical points';
■ arrange to observe and audio-record the lesson;
■ during the lesson, pay particular attention to the 'gender critical point' (i.e. before and after as well as during); take fieldnotes here;
■ transcribe the part of the recording of the lesson that contains the 'gender critical point', plus enough of the talk before and after to provide relevant contextual background (see Task C1.3).

➤ Using the model on p. 154 as a starting point, identify how the 'gender critical point' in question was treated by the teacher.

Step 3
➤ Compare your findings.

Step 4
➤ As a group, consider whether the model on p. 154 needs modifying, i.e. did you find a form of textbook use (i.e. the use of a particular textbook text) which it does not acknowledge?

Step 5
➤ Write up your results and post them on your Gender and Language web site, including your revised version of the model.

 Task C6.8: Learner 'consumption' of texts

Step 1
➤ Consider how you would extend Task C6.7 to take account of how *learners* 'consume' a textbook text.

➤ Make notes of some initial ideas.

Step 2
➤ Plan the study in detail and write a 'Small Grant Research Proposal' for an imaginary research grant awarding body (e.g. 2000 US dollars maximum).

➤ Write your proposal using the following categories:

- Rationale for Study, i.e. why does it need to be done, why is it interesting and important, and who is it interesting to and important for?
- Research Questions, i.e. what exactly are you trying to find out?
- Data Required, i.e. the data needed to address the research questions, and why.
- Data Collection Methods, i.e. the way(s) you will collect the data, and prepare it for analysis.
- Analytical Framework, i.e. what you will do with the data in order to answer your research questions.
- Ethical Procedures, i.e. how you will protect, and even benefit, the classroom participants.
- Beneficiaries, i.e. who will gain from the research.
- Plans for Dissemination, i.e. where you will present it (e.g. Teachers' Association meeting, article in a newsletter or journal).
- Costs, e.g. for hardware, travel, expenses, transcription fees, 'thank you' gift to the educational institutions.

Step 3
➤ If possible, present your proposal to others in a mock competition for the research grant.

Unit C7
Developing understandings
of language: Discourse and discourses

Task C7.1: 'Celebrity fatherhood' media texts

Step 1
UK examples of 'celebrity fatherhood' are the recent birth of the babies of Gordon
Brown, Charles Kennedy and David Cameron (Gordon Brown of the Labour Party
is at the time of writing the UK Chancellor of the Exchequer, widely mooted to
be the next Prime Minister; Charles Kennedy was a recent leader of the Liberal
Democrats; David Cameron is the new, young leader of the Conservative Party). In
Germany, Gerhard Schroeder has adopted a little Russian girl. Readers in other
countries will be aware of other famous politicians who are also new fathers.

➤ Read the newspaper reports (or even editorials) that greeted the news of the
new fatherhood of a politician.

Step 2
➤ Identify some 'discourses of fatherhood' here?

➤ What might be some good names for these?

➤ To help you, reread Unit B7.1, and Sunderland (2002) 'Baby entertainer,
bumbling assistant and line manager: discourses of paternal identity in
parentcraft texts'.

Step 3
➤ Find other reports of the birth of a child to a famous father. Look in newspapers
or magazines (particularly celebrity magazines such as *Yes!* and *Hello*).

➤ Analyse the discourses of fatherhood and name them. Try to go beyond the
discourses identified in the above chapter and Unit B7.1, and indeed beyond
those you found in Step 2.

➤ To what extent do the discourses vary with the couple being reported on?

Task C7.2: 'Celebrity couples'

Step 1
➤ Put together a set of news reports or magazine articles about a 'celebrity couple', for example Michael Douglas and Catherine Zeta Jones or Anna Kournikova and Enrique Iglesias.

Step 2
➤ How are the couple constructed *as partners*?

➤ Identify linguistic traces of wider 'gender relations discourses' manifested in this set of texts. For example, can you see traces of what might be called a 'separate spheres' discourse, or perhaps an 'equal roles' discourse?

 Task C7.3: Foucault, feminism and discourses

Step 1
➤ Investigate Foucault's original conceptualisation of discourses, and, in particular, the role of language here.

Step 2
➤ Find out how feminist writers and/or writers on gender and language have both drawn on, and critiqued, the concept of discourse(s).

➤ To what extent is Foucault's work compatible with feminist linguistics?

References

Baxter, Judith (2003) *Positioning Gender in Discourse*. London: Palgrave Macmillan. (2): 300–16.
Foucault, Michel (1978) *The History of Sexuality: an introduction*. Harmondsworth: Penguin (also 1981, *The History of Sexuality: an introduction*, Vol. I. New York: Vintage/Random House).
Sunderland, Jane (2004) *Gendered Discourses*. London: Palgrave Macmillan. Chapters 1–2.
See also Coates 1997, Coupland and Williams 2002, Foucault 1984, 1989, Francis 1999, Hollway 1984, Hollway 1995, Rich 1980, Soper 1993, Wetherell et al. 1987.

 Task C7.4: Naming discourses

Step 1
➤ Familiarise yourself with some different ways discourses have been named. The references provided for Task C7.3 will help you here, but see especially Sunderland (2004) – Chapter 2 and the index. Make notes on these.

Step 2
➤ Using as many of these ways of discourse naming as you can, think of some other gendered discourses with which you are familiar, and name them in ways that make sense to you. Make a list.

Step 3
➤ For the next week, keep an eye open for linguistic 'traces' (Fairclough 1989, Talbot 1998) of these discourses in what you hear and read.

➤ Make a note of such 'traces' when you come across them.

Task C7.5: Feminist post-structuralist discourse analysis (FPDA)

Step 1
Judith Baxter carried out two case studies in which she put FPDA to the test: one of a classroom, and another of a management team.

➤ If you have not already done so, follow up these studies in *Positioning Gender in Discourse* (2003).

Step 2
➤ In what ways was FPDA used differently in the two studies?

➤ Do you feel that an FPDA approach was more successful in one of the contexts than the other?

Task C7.6: The development of FPDA

Step 1
➤ In 2002, Judith Baxter published two closely related articles: 'Competing discourses in the classroom: a post-structuralist discourse analysis of girls' and boys' speech in public contexts' (2002a) and 'A juggling act: a feminist post-structuralist analysis of girls' and boys' talk in the secondary classroom' (2002b). Read these carefully.

Step 2
➤ Although the article in *Gender and Education* (2002b) was published slightly earlier, it is in some ways a development of the *Discourse and Society* article (2002a). Taking the three works together (these two articles, and Baxter's (2003) book *Positioning Gender in Discourse*), do you notice any developments in Baxter's thinking here?

Task C7.7: The FPDA debate

Baxter's article in *Discourse and Society* (2002a) was responded to, in many ways very critically, by Candace West. In the same issue (13/6) it was also 'defended' by Baxter.

➤ Read West's (2002) critique and Baxter's response and then summarise the debate, highlighting

■ the important points of this debate;
■ the real differences of substance between Baxter and West;
■ any apparent cases of miscommunication.

 Task C7.8: Re-analysis of 'we're boys, miss!'

Scenario

Eleven- and twelve-year-old students in a German class are reading out dialogues they have been writing. They had been working in single sex pairs, by choice. The teacher was aware of the danger of talking to boys more than girls and was alternating between pairs of boys and pairs of girls:

T:	we're going to have two more boys I think . two more boys . what about Ray and Max
Ray/Max:	no
T:	no . why not
Lia/May:	we're boys
Kay/Bea:	we're boys
Kay:	we're boys miss
T:	all right we'll have two more girls and then we'll see if the boys have got any courage

[no-one laughed, the teacher let Kay have the next turn, and the lesson continued]

(Sunderland 1995, 1996)

Step 1
➤ Read ' "We're boys, miss!": finding gendered identities and looking for gendering of identities in the foreign language classroom' (Sunderland 1995).

Step 2
➤ Reanalyse the 'We're boys, miss!' stretch of data from an FPDA perspective.

➤ In particular, identify and name some different discourses by which the speakers seem to be positioned.

Task C7.9: 'Parenting' magazines

Step 1

➤ Make a list of the ways in which 'Parenting' magazines (e.g. those magazines on the care of babies and young children with titles such as *Parenting*, rather than *Mother and Baby*), might address fathers and mothers equally. The magazines could be written in any language.

Step 2

➤ Put together a collection of current commercial 'Parenting' magazines. Look at the following:

- visuals
- use of 'you'
- frequency and distribution of 'dad' and 'father'
- use of 'parent(s)' (Is 'parent(s)' what is meant?)
- the different 'voices' populating the various features.

Step 3

➤ In what way can these magazines be said to address fathers as well as mothers?

➤ In what way can they be said to be addressing mothers alone?

➤ Is the question of 'shared parenting' ever addressed, and, if so, how?

Step 4

➤ Compare your findings with those reported in Sunderland 2004 (Chapter 5) and Sunderland 2006.

Step 5

➤ Write up the study and post it on your Gender and Language web site, identifying similarities and differences between your findings and those of the above.

Task C7.10: Health texts

Step 1

➤ Collect some publicly available medical leaflets or brochures about one or more of the following:

- sex
- sex education
- contraception
- sexually transmitted diseases
- childbirth.

Step 2

➤ Identify as many gendered discourses as you can in these.

➤ Focusing on the text you consider the most 'discourse rich', would you say this leaflet/brochure is on the whole progressive or conservative in the way it represents (and linguistically constructs) gender relations?

 Task C7.11: The 'compulsory heterosexuality' discourse

Step 1

➤ Read 'Compulsory heterosexuality and lesbian existence' by Adrienne Rich (1980). Although she talked about 'compulsory' (i.e. highly normative) sexuality, Adrienne Rich did not use the phrase 'compulsory heterosexuality discourse'. However, this article is widely cited in the understanding that it in effect refers to such a discourse.

Step 2

➤ Collect textual evidence of the 'compulsory heterosexuality' discourse, i.e., linguistic 'traces' within particular texts, from as many different sources as you can. A good place to start would be the popular press. (An example: a letter to a newspaper arguing that women should not join the military since their presence is distracting to men.)

Key reference

Rich, Adrienne (1980) 'Compulsory heterosexuality and lesbian existence', *Signs* 5 (4): 631–60.

 Task C7.12: Subversive discourses in *Shrek*

Step 1

➤ Identify and name some gendered discourses evident in fairy tales (or at least in the Hollywood versions of these), linking these with the fairy tales in question.

➤ Produce a chart to show these, indicating recurrences of the same discourses.

Step 2

➤ Watch a video or DVD of the movie *Shrek* (and/or *Shrek 2*).

➤ Which of these 'traditional fairy tale' discourses are being actively subverted here, and how?

➤ Which are being recycled, and in what sense is this happening?

> If you are aware of other films which subvert fairytales in any way, carry out this talk with these other films too.

Step 3
> Download and read the Lancaster University Centre in Language for Social Life Working Paper 124 on this topic from <http://www.ling.lancs.ac.uk/groups/clsl/current.htm>.

Step 4
> Write a report on 'The recycling and subversion of gendered discourses in fairy tales', and post it on your Gender and Language web site.

References

Cosslett, Tess (1996) 'Fairytales: revising the tradition', in Tess Cosslett, Alison Easton and Penny Summerfield (eds) *Women, Power and Resistance*. Milton Keynes: Open University Press, pp. 81–90.
Zipes, Jack (1986) 'A second gaze at Little Red Riding Hood's trials and tribulations', in Jack Zipes (ed.) *Don't Bet on the Prince: contemporary fairy tales in North America and England*. London: Routledge & Kegan Paul, pp. 227–60.
See also Davies (1989a), Levorato (2003) and Sunderland (2004).

Task C7.13: Birth announcements

Step 1
> Collect as many birth announcement pages as you can, from different newspapers (local and national, tabloid and broadsheet, those whose aim is to entertain and those whose aim is to inform) and in different languages. With help, include some from outside the country in which you are living or studying.

Step 2
> Identify the different ways in which these announcements linguistically construct gender.

Step 3
> Write a brief report of this study, and post it on your Gender and Language web site.

Task C7.14: 'Wedding album' pages

Step 1
> Repeat Steps 1 and 2 of Task C7.13 using 'Wedding album' pages from different newspapers.

Step 2

➤ Compare the textual practices of different newspapers in this respect.

➤ Is it possible to identify 'conservative' and 'progressive' practices here?

➤ If so, in what sense?

Unit C8
Approaches to gender and language research

Task C8.1: 'Gender similarities' in corpus data

Step 1
➤ Rewrite the 'Gender variation' text (Text B8.1, pp. 180–3) in a way that emphasises 'gender similarities' rather than differences. You can add, delete and otherwise change words, sentences and paragraphs. (Leave the tables untouched, of course.)

Step 2
➤ If possible, compare your version with those of other students or colleagues.

Task C8.2: Using an existing corpus

Step 1
➤ Access a corpus of spoken English, for example:

- MICASE (Michigan Corpus of Academic Spoken English): <http://www.hti.umich.edu/m/micase>.
- British National Corpus: <http://www-dev.natcorp.ox.ac.uk>.
- Santa Barbara Corpus of Spoken American English: <http://www.ldc.upenn.edu/Projects/SBCSAE>.

Step 2
➤ Design and carry out a study to answer the following research questions (RQs):

- RQ1: What can we say about use of the word 'partner'?
- RQ2: Compare usages of the words 'girl' and 'boy' when the referents are in fact women and men.
- RQ3: Do women and men talk about (a) cars, (b) democracy, differently from each other?

Step 3
➤ Read the work of Janet Holmes and Robert Sigley (2002a, 2002b) and Michael Stubbs (1996) on gender and corpora.

Task C8.3: Developing your own small corpus

Step 1
➤ Compile your own simple small corpus of 'private talk' (around 15,000 words) as follows:

- Audio-record as many 'mealtime conversations' (between different groups of people) as you can.
- Ask friends to walk around with a Walkman for a day, and to record their conversations. (Make sure they carefully note down who they speak to, so that permission to use this data can be requested later.)
- Transcribe the talk. (You may be able to use speech recognition software such as ViaVoice to help you with this, see also Task C1.3.) Make sure you indicate the sex of the speakers.
- Put all your transcripts into one electronic file.

Step 2
➤ Ask the C8.2 research questions again, this time using your own small corpus as data. If this provides relevant data, but your findings do not reflect those in C8.2, why might this be?

Step 3
➤ Think of some new research questions you can now 'ask' your corpus, as regards word frequencies of interest to gender and language study.

➤ Answer these RQs.

Step 4
➤ Document your results and post them on your Gender and Language web site, together with a description of your development of this small corpus.

References

If you are interested in small corpora, the following may be of interest to you:

Cameron, Lynn and Deignan, Alice (2003) 'Combining large and small corpora to investigate tuning devices around metaphor in spoken discourse', *Metaphor and Symbol* 18 (3): 149–60.
Ghadessy, M., Henry, A. and Roseberry, R. (eds) (2001) *Small Corpus Studies and ELT: theory and practice*. Amsterdam: John Benjamins.

Task C8.4: Using corpora in conversation analysis

Step 1
➤ Complete Task C8.3.

Step 2
➤ Read or reread Units B8.2 and B8.3 on CA.

Step 3
➤ Starting with some obvious 'gender markers' like 'he', 'she', 'man', 'woman', 'lady', 'boy', 'girl', search your small corpus of talk for some possible 'participant orientations' to gender.

Step 4
➤ Based on this experience, consider and make notes on:

- the CA notion of 'orientation';
- the notion of 'orientation to gender';
- the special contribution of corpora as useful methodological tools for CA.

Task C8.5: Researcher/participant relationships and researcher commitment

Step 1
➤ Read the 'Introduction' to *Researching Language* (Cameron et al. 1992), which looks at the questions of research in terms of relationships with participants: research 'on' (ethics), research 'for' (advocacy) and research 'with' (empowerment).

Step 2
➤ Find examples of studies in the Gender and Language field (starting with those in this book) in which you can see evidence of one or more of these three approaches. Do not expect to find a study that is fully 'empowering'! You will find the various edited collections on gender and language listed on at the start of the Bibliography on p. 324.

Step 3
Feminist researchers clearly approach their work with a particular sense of 'commitment'. For some, this clashes with 'objectivity'. There is, of course, a debate as to whether 'objectivity' can ever be achieved, or even if it is desirable anyway.

➤ Read work on 'feminist research methods' and 'feminist epistemologies': for example, Hesse-Biber 1998, Nielson 1990, Reinharz with Davidmann 1992, Roberts 1981, Stacey 1988, Webb 1993.

Step 4
➤ Follow this up with readings around the topic of feminist approaches to gender and language study, for example Gill (1995).

Step 5
➤ Develop your own position on whether certain approaches are particularly appropriate for gender and language study and/or feminist research.

➤ Write a argument in favour of one particular approach. If you are working with other students, you should each try and argue in favour of different approaches.

Step 6
➤ Post your argument or set of arguments on your Gender and Language web site.

Task C8.6: Gender, conversation analysis and feminist research: the debate

Step 1
Elizabeth Stokoe and Janet Smithson, and Celia Kitzinger (Unit B8.2, B8.3), were contributing to a wider debate about CA and its value for feminist research.

Follow this debate through the various *Discourse and Society* issues, starting with the contribution by Emanuel Schegloff (1997).

Step 2
➤ Write the 'story' of how this debate developed, including how previous arguments were addressed and new ones advanced.

Step 3
➤ Document your own conclusion about the question.

➤ Post this, along with your 'story', on your Gender and Language web site.

Task C8.7: Identifying gender using conversation analysis

Step 1
➤ Collect some naturally occurring data by audio-recording an informal conversation of about 20 minutes.

Step 2
➤ Transcribe the tape (see Task C1.3).

Step 3

➤ Carefully reread the Unit B8 extracts by Stokoe and Smithson (B8.2), and Kitzinger (B8.3), as well as work on CA more widely (for example, Psathas 1995; see also references in Task C8.8).

Step 4

➤ Can you identify any points in your transcribed conversation in which speakers 'orient' to gender in some way.

➤ List these, and, for each, note down your 'warrant' for deciding that the speaker was, indeed, orienting to gender.

➤ Can you do this *without* researcher inference?

Task C8.8: Conversation analysis and transcription

You may have noted that conversation analysts use very detailed symbols or diacritics in their transcription systems. For example, from Charles Antaki's web-based tutorial on CA:

(.): Just noticeable pause

(.3), (2.6): Examples of timed pauses in seconds

↑word,↓word: Onset of noticeable pitch rise or fall (*can be difficult to use reliably*)

A: word |word

B: |word: Square brackets aligned across adjacent lines denote the start of overlapping talk. Some transcribers also use '|' brackets to show where the overlap stops.

.hh, hh: in-breath (note the preceding full stop) and out-breath respectively.

wo(h)rd: (h) is a try at showing that the word has 'laughter' bubbling within it.

wor-: A dash shows a sharp cut-off.

wo:rd: Colons show that the speaker has stretched the preceding sound.

(words): A guess at what might have been said if unclear.

(   ): Unclear talk. Some transcribers like to represent each syllable of unclear talk with a dash or an 'x'.

A: word=

B: =word: The equals sign shows that there is no discernible pause between two speakers' turns or, if put between two sounds within a single speaker's turn, shows that they run together.

word, WORD: Underlined sounds are louder, capitals louder still

°word°: material between 'degree signs' is quiet

>word word<

<word word>: Inwards arrows show faster speech, outward slower

→: Analyst's signal of a significant line

((*sobbing*)): Transcriber's attempt to represent something hard, or impossible, to write phonetically.

(<http://www-staff.lboro.ac.uk/~ssca1/intro1.htm>)

The person originally responsible for the development of these systems was Gail Jefferson.

Step 1
➤ Read one or more of the following articles below, looking carefully at the use of these various symbols and diacritics: Atkinson and Heritage 1984, Jefferson 2004, Ochs et al. 1996, Psathas 1995, Sacks et al. 1978 (a classic).

Step 2
➤ Apply the symbols shown above to a very small stretch of your own conversational data (e.g. 2 minutes). You will need to play and replay the tape.

➤ Does this more detailed transcription help at all in addressing the question of 'orientation to gender'?

Key reference

Jefferson, Gail (2004) 'Glossary of transcript symbols with an introduction', in G. H. Lerner (ed.) *Conversation Analysis: studies from the first generation.* Amsterdam: John Benjamins, pp. 13–31.

 Task C8.9: The politics of transcription

Step 1
➤ Collect a few minutes of conversational data. (If you have done Task C8.8, you can use the same data.)

Step 2
➤ With a friend or classmate, transcribe the conversation individually, without sharing your ideas. Do not use the symbols associated with CA (see above). Rather, keep the transcription simple – but do consider both pauses and overlaps.

➤ When you have finished, make a note of your key.

Step 3
➤ Compare your transcripts.

➤ What does each suggest about the conversation that the other does not?

Step 4
➤ Read and make notes on Mary Bucholtz's paper on 'The politics of transcription' (2000), and Eleanor Ochs' classic paper (1979) on 'Transcription as theory'.

Task C8.10: Gender and language study and critical discourse analysis

Step 1
➤ Critical discourse analysis (CDA) has, perhaps surprisingly, been less used for gender and language study than it might have been. Why might this be?

➤ Start by reading Michelle Lazar's introductory chapter to *Feminist Critical Discourse Analysis* (2005).

Step 2
➤ Identify examples of specific linkages between CDA and gender and language study by finding relevant articles/chapters which report how CDA has been explicitly drawn on.

➤ Begin by looking at the edited collections listed at the start of the Bibliography.

Step 3
➤ Create an annotated bibliography on 'CDA, Gender and Language' and post it on your Gender and Language web site.

References

Cameron, Deborah (1998b) 'Gender, language and discourse: A review essay', *Signs* 1: 945–73.
—— (1997b) 'Theoretical debates in feminist linguistics: questions of sex and gender', in R. Wodak (ed.) *Gender and Discourse*. London: Sage.
Lazar, Michelle (2005) *Feminist Critical Discourse Analysis*. London: Palgrave Macmillan.
Walsh, Clare (2001) *Gender and Discourse: language and power in politics, the church and organisations*. London: Longman.

Task C8.11: Gender and language study and discursive psychology

Discursive psychology is discussed in Unit A9, in relation to the epistemological site of 'Masculinity' exemplified in Unit B9. This task is included in Unit C8 since discursive psychology is, of course, an approach to gender and language study. Readers may however wish to read the relevant sections of Unit 9 before doing this task.

Step 1
Paul McIlvenny in *Talking Gender and Sexuality* (2002) observes that Discursive Psychology divides into two strands: the CA strand and the post-structuralist strand.

> Follow up and make notes on work done here, including by Potter and Edwards (the CA strand), and Edley and Wetherell (the post-structuralist strand).

References

(with useful brief annotations, taken from Edley 2001, see Unit B9)

Billig, M. (1996) *Arguing and Thinking: a rhetorical approach to social psychology*, 2nd edn. Cambridge: Cambridge University Press. (One of the truly foundational texts in the development of discursive psychology.)

Billig, M., Condor, S., Edwards, D., Gane, M., Middleton, D. and Radley, A. (1988) *Ideological Dilemmas: a social psychology of everyday thinking*. London: Sage. (For the original exposition of the concept of ideological dilemmas.)

Davies, B. and Harré, R. (1990) 'Positioning: the discursive production of selves', *Journal for the Theory of Social Behaviour*, 20: 43–65. (Reproduced in Wetherell et al. 2001: offers a more detailed discussion of the concept of subject positions.)

Edley, N. and Wetherell, M. (1997) 'Jockeying for position: the construction of masculine identities', *Discourse and Society*, 8: 203–17. (For an analysis of how social relations are conducted in and through the construction of masculine identities.)

Edwards, D., and Potter, J. (1992) *Discursive Psychology*. London: Sage.

Freeman, M. (1993) *Rewriting the Self: history, memory, narrative*. London: Routledge. (Offers a lucid account of how selves are both spoken and storied.)

Potter, J. and Wetherell, M. (1987) *Discourse and Social Psychology: beyond attitudes and behaviour*. London: Sage. (Another foundational text in the development of discursive psychology.)

Potter, J. (1996) Representing Reality: Discourse, Rhetoric and Social Construction. London: Sage.

Sampson, E. E. (1993) *Celebrating the Other: a dialogic account of human nature*. Hemel Hempstead: Harvester Wheatsheaf. (An accessible US-based account of the social or discursive production of selfhood.)

Wetherell, M. (1998) 'Positioning and interpretative repertoires: conversation analysis and post-structuralism in dialogue', *Discourse and Society*, 9: 387–412. (For a discussion of how critical discursive psychology differs from more conversation analytic forms of discourse analysis.)

Step 2
> Find out something about the status of Discursive Psychology for Psychology as a discipline, in one or more of the following ways:

■ Consult *recent* introductory and advanced books on Social Psychology.

■ If you have access to a Psychology department, consult their course handbooks for references to Discursive Psychology.

■ Arrange to interview a member of academic staff of a Psychology department.

Step 3
➤ Using comparable methods, find out something about the status of Discursive Psychology for Linguistics.

Step 4
➤ Write a short report on what Discursive Psychology has uniquely contributed to (a) Linguistics, in general, and (b) to gender and language study in particular.

➤ Post the report on your Gender and Language web site.

Unit C9
Data and data sites

Task C9.1: Epistemological sites

Step 1
➤ Read or reread Unit A9.

➤ Consider what *sort* of sites, in general terms, are interesting for gender and language study, and why.

➤ List some particular sites, with reasons why each is interesting.

Step 2
➤ Identify (a) the epistemological sites in question, and (b) the justifications for them, in the following studies: Coupland and Williams 2002, Speer 2002, Walsh 2001.

Step 3
➤ Identify a research project on language and gender with which you are or will be currently involved:

■ What is the epistemological site?
■ Why did you choose this site?
■ Is it a particularly fruitful site, in terms of gender and language study?

➤ Consider how best to justify your choice(s). If possible, explain them to colleagues or other students.

Task C9.2: Selecting a children's book for analysis

Step 1
➤ Read or reread the last section of Unit A9, on children's literature.

Step 2
➤ Think about each of the following possible principled ways of choosing which book(s) to analyse:

- books that have won particular awards;
- 'best-seller' children's books;
- reading schemes used widely by schools;
- books that have been published in different editions, and have changed accordingly over time;
- books/stories that appear in many different versions (fairy tales are the obvious case here);
- books that have been turned into films (to enable comparison);
- books that are 'parallels' in terms of content and gender representation (for example, the Harry Potter series by J. K. Rowling, and the Worst Witch series by Jill Murphy);
- books in which the characters include a girl-and-boy set of twins (for the purposes of comparison of representation);
- books with a clear female or male protagonist, including those about only boys (and men), or only girls (and women) (Is the gender representation as straightforward as it might appear?);
- animal stories in which the animals are given human-like characteristics.

➤ Identify the theoretical and methodological implications (and perhaps practical advantages and disadvantages) of each type of choice.

Step 3
➤ Follow up other work on gender and children's literature (bearing in mind that much of it does not have a linguistic focus).

➤ Identify the criteria for choice in this work.

References

(Can you find work on books written in other languages?)

Adler, Sue (1992) 'Aprons and attitudes: feminism and children's books', in H. Claire, J. Maybin and J. Swann (eds) *Equality Matters*. Clevedon: Multilingual Matters.

Berman, Ruth (1998) 'No Joe Marches', *Children's Literature in Education* 29 (4): 237–47.

Claire, H., Maybin, Janet and Swann, Joan (eds) (1993) *Equality Matters*. Clevedon: Multilingual Matters.

Cosslett, Tess (1996) 'Fairytales: revising the tradition', in Tess Cosslett, Alison Easton and Penny Summerfield (eds) *Women, Power and Resistance*. Milton Keynes: Open University Press, pp. 81–90.

Davies, Bronwyn (1989a) *Frogs and Snails and Feminist Tales*. Sydney: Allen & Unwin.

—— (1993) *Shards of Glass*. Sydney: Allen & Unwin.

Smith, Ruth (1995) 'Young children's interpretation of gender from visual text and narrative', *Linguistics and Education*, 7: 303–25.

Swann, Joan (1992) *Girls, Boys and Language*. Cambridge, Mass. and Oxford: Blackwell.

See also Chandler and Chappell 1993, Cherland 1994, Children's Rights Workshop 1976 , Dombey 1992, Freebody 1989, Hillman 1974, Kortenhaus and Demarest 1993, Moss 1989, Nilsen 1977, Petersen and Lach 1990, Stephens 1992, Stinton 1979, Stones 1983, Turner-Bowker 1996, Wharton 2005 and Zipes 1986.

 Task C9.3: The language classroom as a fruitful epistemological site

The article 'Girls being quiet: a problem for foreign language classrooms?' (Sunderland 1998) reports a study motivated by an interest in gendered classroom interaction in an under-explored site of study for gender and language: the foreign-language classroom. However the study is also motivated by the fact that in many contexts and levels (for example, GCSE examinations in British secondary schools, which students sit at around age sixteen), girls perform considerably better than boys in all subjects, and the difference is particularly marked in foreign languages. This does not however sit smoothly with the finding of many classroom studies that not only are girls in mixed-sex classrooms talked to less by the teacher than are boys, girls also talk less to the teacher than do boys (e.g. French and French 1984, Swann and Graddol 1988).

Sunderland's findings included that in this classroom (a German as a foreign language classroom in a British secondary school, in which the boys and girls were eleven and twelve), although the teacher did pay more attention to the boys as a whole, the girls on the whole talked to the teacher more than the boys did. This was not simply because of a few particularly articulate and assertive girls, but rather reflected the public classroom talk of around half the girls in the class.

The data for the study is qualitative (twelve lesson transcripts), the analysis for much of the study is quantitative. One unit of analysis was the 'student solicit', defined as 'an utterance which requires and often results in a verbal response (or which results in *or* requires a behavioural one) from the teacher very soon after the uttering of the solicit' (Sunderland 1998: 60).

Step 1
➤ Read the article to which the above notes refer.

➤ Focus on what the article says about the research questions, and the collection of the naturally occurring classroom data.

Step 2
➤ Read the article a second time, and make notes on the following:

■ access
■ ethics
■ the 'observer's paradox'

- data collection methods
- the role of the researcher
- relationships with research participants.

Step 3
➤ Think carefully about the main findings:

- The teacher directed more solicits to the 'average boy' and more 'solicit-words' to him (the latter statistically significantly so).
- The 'average girl' herself produced more solicits than the 'average boy', significantly more solicit-words, and more unsolicited solicits (this last again statistically significantly so).

➤ What factors might have brought about this (in some ways 'unbalanced') state of affairs?

➤ What would you need to know more about, in order to answer this question?

➤ How can we be sure that gender is what is relevant here? (See Swann 2002.)

➤ What might have been some other ways of analysing this data in relation to learner gender?

Step 5
➤ Summarise your work by writing a critical review of the article, and posting it on your Gender and Language web site.

Task C9.4: 'Telling cases' in the classroom

Eleven- and twelve-year-old students in a German class are reading out dialogues they have been writing. They had been working in single sex pairs, by choice. The teacher was aware of the danger of talking to boys more than girls and was alternating between pairs of boys and pairs of girls.

Step 1
➤ Look carefully at the data on teacher–student talk in relation to this in Unit C7.8.

Step 2
This episode can be analysed and interpreted in different ways.

➤ Consider:

- terms of abuse for girls/women;
- the concept of 'semantic derogation' (see Unit A2);

■ 'multiple positioning' by different 'gendered discourses' (see Unit A7) (you may already have done this as part of Unit C7.8).

Step 3

➤ Read the extract below which comes from an interview with two boys from the class about the event.

Int.:	if [Miss X] had said 'two girls' and if you wanted to have a go might you say 'we're girls'
Jim/Sam:	no [both laugh]
Int:	no [rising intonation]
Jim:	no way
Int.:	why why not
Jim:	I don't think boys like to (xxx) they're soft or stuff like that so they wouldn't say that they're girls but girls aren't really bothered about being shy and stuff so they just say 'we're boys'
Int.:	okay so you think if you said 'we're girls' it would look as if you were soft
Jim:	(xxx) stupid
Int.:	yeah why wouldn't you say it
Jim:	same reason as Jim everybody would think you were
Int.:	mm hm . do you think that's a funny thing the boys will say 'we're boys' but the boys wouldn't say 'we're girls'
Jim:	it's just something that the boys don't do girls will do anything to get a go at something but boys they have a limit what they can do and if they pass that limit they won't they won't they won't say anything they can't be bothered doing it
Int.:	so what would've happened if you'd said 'we're girls' or if some boys had said 'we're girls'
Sam:	the response would've been that everybody laughed their heads off
Int.:	everybody would've laughed their heads off so it wouldn't have worked right . when these girls said 'we're boys' nobody laughed
Sam:	it was sort of like normal
Int.:	yeah
Sam:	for a girl to shout out and stuff but like for a boy it's just not normal to say that you're a girl

The line numbers in the left margin are: 5 (Jim: no way), 10 (Int.: okay so...), 15 (Int.: mm hm...), 20 (won't say anything...), 25 (Int.: everybody would've...).

➤ By what limiting gendered discourses are boys and girls positioned, in this interview?

➤ Who do you think are the more limited?

➤ What does this sort of 'telling case' achieve that more 'representative' data cannot?

Reference

Mitchell, J. Clyde (1984) 'Typicality and the case study', in R. F. Ellen (ed.) *Ethnographic Research: a guide to general conduct.* London: Academic Press.

Task C9.5: Gender and workplace talk: Existing work

Step 1
➤ List possible workplaces which you think might constitute interesting epistemological sites for gender and language study, with reasons why they might be interesting. If you can, do this with other students as a group brainstorm.

Step 2
➤ Now compare this with workplaces actually studied. Start by checking the *Gender and Genre Bibliography* (2006) (<http://www.ling.lancs.ac.uk/groups/clsl/current.htm>). Then use a web search engine to find more.

➤ Which workplaces have been studied the most?

➤ Why?

➤ Do you think this is because of reasons of convenience or principled reasons of epistemology?

Step 3
➤ Read and make notes on the following articles on gender and workplace talk: Holmes 2000, 2003, Holmes and Stubbe 1998, 2003, McIlhenny 1995, Osterman 2003, Stubbe 2000, Tannen 1991.

Step 4
➤ Individually or, if you can, as a team, create an annotated bibliography on 'Gender and talk in the workplace'.

➤ Post this on your Gender and Language web site.

Task C9.6: Gender and workplace talk: Your study

Step 1
➤ Go into a workplace that is unconnected with education (e.g. a bank, a café).

Step 2
➤ Make fieldnotes on any 'gendered events' that appear to be going on.

Step 3

➤ Consider whether this workplace would make a good epistemological site for gender and language study, and why.

➤ What research questions might you ask of this site?

Step 4

➤ If possible, compare notes with fellow students who have been to different workplaces.

★ Task C9.7: Team research tasks

➤ Identify, plan and write a proposal for a study in the area of gender and language which could not be carried out by one individual researcher, but rather requires a team.

➤ Justify why a team of researchers is needed. (If you wish, refer back to the study by Sunderland et al. (2002), an extract from which appeared in Unit B6.1, which involved five researchers.)

➤ Your proposal should include:

- an explanation of why the topic is of interest;
- research questions;
- data required (nature and amount);
- data collection methods;
- ethical considerations;
- data analysis methods;
- beneficiaries of the research.

★ Task C9.8: Longitudinal studies

➤ Identify, plan and write a proposal for a research project in the area of gender and language which requires a longitudinal study to be done either (a) as a ten-week research programme (small-scale study); or (b) as a three-year research programme (large-scale study).

➤ Justify the need for an extended period of time.

➤ See Task C9.7 for what your proposal should include.

Two possibilities for longitudinal studies

➤ Change in individuals' uses of particular terms, such as Ms.

➤ Change in the gendered language use in a particular class of students.

Check the World Wide Web for reports of language-related longitudinal studies for more ideas.

Unit C10
Written texts

 Task C10.1: Science fiction

Step 1
➤ Makes notes on why science fiction novels and short stories might be considered an interesting genre in the study of gender and language.

➤ Consider these novels first as fiction and, second, as science fiction.

Step 2
➤ Choose a science fiction novel that is particularly interesting in terms of gender, for example one by Marge Piercy, or Ursula LeGuin. (If you are not sure which to pick, ask people you know who enjoy science fiction.) The novel can be written in any language.

➤ Read the novel.

➤ In what way does it expand our appreciation of the possibilities for gender?

 Task C10.2: Further work by Bronwyn Davies

Step 1
➤ Do a web search to find and read other work by Bronwyn Davies. This includes *Shards of Glass* (1993), the follow-up to *Frogs and Snails and Feminist Tales* (1989), as well as various pieces on post-structuralism in relation to gender and educational thought and practice.

Step 2
➤ Summarise Davies' contribution to the fields of gender and education, and gender and language.

➤ Post the summary on your Gender and Language web site.

Task C10.3: Fairy tales

Step 1

➤ Alessandra Levorato (2003) analysed a large number of versions of 'Red Riding Hood'. Choose another fairy tale and do the same.

➤ Focus on similarities and differences between the gendered representations of the female characters, drawing on some of the linguistic concepts used by Thornborrow (Unit B10.1).

➤ In particular, investigate one of more aspects of the way the characters talk, for example, in terms of:

- verbosity
- speech acts
- transitivity
- agency
- choice of lexis.

Step 2

➤ Visit some children's libraries and bookshops and see if you can find some of the feminist fairy tales mentioned in the bibliography of Bronwyn Davies' *Frogs and Snails and Feminist Tales* (1989).

➤ Then find some more recent children's books that might fall into the category of 'feminist fairy tales'. (Ask the librarians and booksellers about this – perhaps describe them as 'modern fairy tales.')

➤ Collect as many as you can.

Step 3

➤ Divide them into two groups, starting with Davies' own system in Chapter 3 of *Frogs and Snails.*

➤ Does this 'dichotomy' work, now?

➤ Does it need amending?

Step 4

➤ Post your list of feminist fairy tales, appropriately categorised, on your Gender and Language web site.

Task C10.4: Prize-winning children's books

Step 1
➤ Carry out an investigation into the different awards for children's books in the country in which you are studying.

➤ Assess to what extent, if at all, gender is considered here (explicitly or implicitly).

Step 2
➤ Choose one of the awards and have a look at one of the books that has received this over the past (say) ten years.

➤ Try to identify ways in which it is simultaneously progressive and traditional in its gender representation. (When doing this, remember that we cannot read a fictional text 'straight', and also that if something exists or happens, this cannot be straightforwardly read as the writer approving of that state of affairs.)

References

Stephens, John (1992) *Language and Ideology in Children's Fiction.* London: Longman.
Sunderland, Jane (2004) *Gendered Discourses.* London: Palgrave Macmillan, Chapter 7: 'Gendered discourses in children's literature'.

Step 3
John Burningham is twice a winner of the Kate Greenaway award (for 'distinguished illustration in a book for children'). His illustrations characteristically do not correspond to the texts they accompany.

➤ With a partner or small group, have a look at one or more of John Burningham's 'Shirley' books (e.g. *Come Away from the Water, Shirley, Time to Get Out of the Bath, Shirley*), published by HarperCollins.

➤ Is Burningham's illustrative technique in principle a useful strategy for progressive representations of female characters (in some sense), and perhaps for a subversive approach to gender?

➤ To what extent does Burningham in practice use the technique to progressive effect in these two (or other) books?

➤ If possible, compare your findings and conclusions with a partner or small group.

Task C10.5: *Barbie* comics

Step 1

➤ Buy a *Barbie* comic.

➤ Analyse one or more of the stories containing both male and female characters in the following way. In relation to gender, carry out:

- ■ a content analysis of the 'plots' of the stories;
- ■ a content analysis of the different characters' social practices and roles;
- ■ a linguistic analysis of verbosity;
- ■ an analysis of the different speech acts;
- ■ a 'case study' of the representation of Barbie herself, in terms of her social practices and language use.

➤ In the light of this, decide to what extent *Barbie* comic stories in general, and Barbie herself, offer positive role models for young girl readers.

Step 2

➤ Carry out a study of girl readers of *Barbie* comics, through a series of loosely structured interviews.

➤ Ask questions like:

- ■ Do you like the stories? Why? Why not?
- ■ Do you think Barbie does things that (older) girls actually do?
- ■ Would you like to be like Barbie? Why? Why not?

References

Caldas-Coulthard, Carmen and van Leeuwen, Theo (2002) 'Stunning, shimmering, iridescent: Toys as the representation of gendered social actors', in Lia Litosseliti and Jane Sunderland (eds) *Gender Identities and Discourse Analysis*. Amsterdam: John Benjamins.

Graue, M. E., and Walsh, D. J. (1998) *Studying Children in Context: theories, methods, and ethics*. Thousand Oaks, Calif.: Sage Publications.

Rogers, Mary (1999) *Barbie Culture*. London: Sage.

Scott, J. (2000) 'Children as respondents: the challenge for quantitative methods', in P. Christensen and A. James (eds) *Research with Children*. London and New York: Falmer Press, pp. 98–119.

Step 3

➤ Post the findings of the study on your Gender and Language web site.

Task C10.6: Girls' magazines

Step 1

➤ Find out what sort of girls' magazines are on the market.

➤ Look for magazines targeted at girls right up to their late teens.

➤ Purchase a set of girls' magazines for a given month (if weekly or twice-monthly, choose the first in the month). This is your (non-electronic) 'corpus'.

Step 2

➤ Identify magazine features that focus on language use (e.g. 'How to talk to your Mum').

  ■ Categorise these as far as possible.
  ■ Is there evidence of the promotion of particular uses of language?
  ■ Does this relate to popular stereotypes of the way women talk, or to claims made by writers such as Lakoff (1975), Coates (1996) or Tannen (1991)?

➤ Look for evidence of the discourse of 'consumer femininity' (see Talbot 1995, Andrews and Talbot 2000), and the discourse of 'mutual unintelligibility of the sexes' (Sunderland 2004).

➤ Categorise the speech acts in the fictional stories.

  ■ How often is each speech act used by the female and male characters?
  ■ What is the resultant 'gender profile' of speech act use?

Task C10.7: 'Talk around the text'

Step 1

➤ Read different stories to young children of the appropriate age.

➤ Experiment: vary the number and type of comments you make and questions you ask.

➤ What is the relationship between this and the contributions of the children being read to?

This is not a systematic study, rather, the idea is rather to get a feel for how 'talk around the text' by the 'reader aloud' can influence the talk (and possibly the ideas) of the child.

Step 2

➤ Choose any (age-appropriate) children's story, and read this same story to four children (perhaps all girls, or all boys).

➤ With two of the children, just read the story.

➤ With the other two: comment, ask questions, and perhaps express your own opinions and judgements. What you say here should where possible be relevant to gender in some way.

➤ After the readings, ask the children questions about the story. Again, some should pertain to gender issues.

➤ Assess to what extent your 'talk around the text' appears to have made a difference in the children's understandings.

Task C10.8: Foreign-language textbooks

Step 1

➤ Read some early articles critiquing gender representation in language textbooks, for example: Carroll and Kowitz 1994, Gupta and Lee 1990, Hellinger 1980, Porecca 1984, Poulou 1997, Pugsley 1992, Rees-Parnell 1976, Sunderland 1994, Talansky 1986, Willeke and Sanders 1978.

Step 2

➤ Read the pamphlet 'On Balance' (Florent et al. 1994). This was written to suggest to writers and publishers ways in which they could be more gender-inclusive and progressive in their English language textbooks.

Step 3

➤ Examine a selection of English as a foreign language (EFL) textbooks published since 2000 (new books, not reprints). Examine one unit from each book (e.g. the middle unit). To what extent do the 'On Balance' guidelines (or equivalent views and recommendations) appear to have been taken on board for each book?

Step 4

➤ Consider whether the guidelines themselves need amending, and make notes to this effect.

Step 5

➤ Write up this task and post it on your Gender and Language web site. You may like to structure it as follows:

   ▪ The Problem
   ▪ Early Investigations

■ Recommendations

■ The Situation in the Twenty-First Century.

Key reference

Florent, Jill et al. (1994) 'On balance: guidelines for the representation of women and men in English language teaching materials', in Jane Sunderland (ed.) *Exploring Gender: questions and implications for English language education.* Hemel Hempstead: Prentice Hall, pp. 112–20.

Task C10.9: Advertisements for products for women and men

Step 1
➤ Read or reread Unit B10.1.

Step 2
➤ Explore a current Filofax web site (e.g. <http://www.filofax.co.uk>).

➤ Can you find any evidence here of the construction of 'ideal reading positions' based on gender stereotypes?

Step 3
➤ Check magazine or newspaper advertisements for other products apparently designed for women and men alike.

➤ Can you identify 'ideal reading positions' for women and for men?

Step 4
➤ Find a magazine or newspaper advertisement for a particular product in which gender is an important feature, which you think can be read in more than one way.

➤ Interview ten people about their interpretation(s) of the advertisement, and document all these.

➤ Which interpretations can be seen as 'dominant' and which as 'alternative'?

Step 5
➤ Find a newspaper or magazine ad for a product aimed at men but featuring women (e.g. with a message that product X will make men more attractive to women).

➤ Redesign it using appropriate layout, fonts and, if you can, visuals. It should still be advertising the same sort of product, but should reverse the gender roles.

➤ Interview another ten people about their interpretations of your ad to find out if it 'works', and how. If possible, compare your findings with a partner or group.

Task C10.10: Personal ads

Step 1
➤ Read two articles on personal ads (for example, Hogben and Coupland 2000, Shalom 1997), or try the third (2006) edition of the *Gender and Genre Bibliography* (<http://www.ling.lancs.ac.uk/groups/clsl/current.htm>).

Step 2
➤ Find a set of personal ads (in any language) in one issue of a national newspaper.

➤ How are the ads categorised by the newspaper itself?

➤ Which category is the largest?

➤ What sort of characteristics are frequently 'Wanted'? How do these vary with the different categories?

➤ Look at a selection of ads – for example, every tenth one.

➤ Design a chart and show how and to what extent the different wanted characteristics vary with category.

Step 3
➤ Electronically scan the ads. These now constitute a small corpus.

➤ Using your findings from Step 2, devise a research question comparing a particular characteristic (e.g. 'GSOH', i.e. 'Good sense of humour').

Step 4
➤ Using the chart you designed in Step 2, analyse your corpus with this research question in mind.

➤ What can you now say about the textual construction of gender and sexual identity in relation to these ads?

Task C10.11: Texts on sex

Step 1
➤ Consider why texts broadly related to sex might constitute particularly useful sites for the study of gender and language, gender relations and the linguistic construction of gender.

➤ What sorts of 'texts on sex' might, in principle, be included here?

Step 2
➤ Create a bibliography of studies of gender and language that have used such texts, and post them on your Gender and Language web site.

⭐ Task C10.12: Magazine problem pages

Step 1
➤ Make copies of 'problem pages' from several different girls'/women's magazines.

Step 2
➤ Identify some different linguistic representations/constructions of women and/or girls in the language of these texts, in particular in the 'Answers'.

➤ Are these achieved in part through the use of certain stereotypical gendered presuppositions?

Step 3
➤ Ascertain whether there is much difference between the magazines here.

➤ Are there any surprises?

Step 4
➤ Write up your results as a report and post it on your Gender and Language web site.

⭐ Task C10.13: Travel brochures

Step 1
➤ Collect a set of travel brochures, for diverse audiences. You may need to ask the advice of travel agents here, or you may need to order particular brochures (use the World Wide Web, as well as newspapers and 'lifestyle' magazines).

Step 2
➤ Examining both texts and visuals, explore how women and men are constructed in these texts, in terms of both gender and sexuality.

➤ Think carefully about presupposition as well as questions of topic, interpellation (e.g. Mills 1992) and gaze.

➤ In particular, how is heterosexuality constructed?

➤ Can you find evidence of the 'compulsory heterosexuality' discourse (Rich 1980)? (See also Unit A7.)

Step 3
➤ If some of your brochures are aimed at young, single people, look carefully at whether and how the notion of 'safe sex' is addressed.

➤ Can this be said to contribute to the 'linguistic construction of gender'?

➤ Can you identify, and name, some discourses surrounding sex? (Again see Unit A7.)

Task C10.14: Jokes

CMC and e-mail lists have enabled sets of jokes to do the rounds of the globe, divorced from any author (which can also mean they can be altered, unnoticed). Many of these jokes are about gender and gender relations. This task asks you to explore different possible readings (including alternative and feminist ones) of jokes that may simultaneously be seen as anti-woman, sexist or downright misogynist.

Step 1
➤ Read Sara Mills' article (1992) on different readings of, and what we might call different 'reader self-positionings' in, the poem 'Valentine'.

Step 2
➤ Read the data: a set of jokes on the 'sex' of various objects.

Photocopier: Female, because once turned off, it takes a while to warm up. It's an effective reproductive device if the right buttons are pushed, but can wreak havoc, if the wrong buttons are pushed.

Sponges: Female, because they're soft and squeezable and retain water.

Web page: Female, because they're always getting hit on.

Hourglass (egg timer): Female, because over time, the weight shifts from top to bottom.

Remote control: Female . . . Ha! You thought it'd be male. But consider – it gives a man pleasure, he'd be lost without it, and while he doesn't always know the right buttons to push, he keeps trying!!

Step 3
➤ Did you find some of these offensive?

➤ Did you find some of these offensive and amusing at the same time?

➤ If Yes, did you experience this as rather a 'contradictory' experience?

➤ If Yes, how can we account for this?

Step 4
➤ If you did not answer 'Yes' to either of the first two questions in Step 3, consider the possibility that other readers may have found the jokes offensive and amusing, and may have experienced this as 'contradictory'.

➤ In either case, ask ten people to read and respond to the jokes, asking the four Step 3 questions.

➤ Audio-record or note down their responses.

Step 5
➤ Try to explain the various responses. Use the following notions and 'perspectives' (you may find one, or more than one, is particularly helpful):

- reader response;
- resistant reading/'reading against the grain';
- multiple and simultaneous positioning in/by different discourses;
- adopting different reading positions;
- transposition of the object of the joke (e.g. from, arguably, women, to men);
- 'double-voicing' (Bakhtin 1984).

Key references

Mills, Sara (1992) 'Knowing your place: Marxist feminist contextualised stylistics', in Michael Toolan (ed.) *Language, Text and Context: essays in stylistics.* London: Routledge, pp. 182–205.
Sunderland, Jane (2006) 'Contradictions in gendered discourses: feminist readings of sexist jokes?' *Lancaster University Centre for Language in Social Life Working Paper* 125 (<http://www.ling.lancs.ac.uk/groups/clsl/current.htm>)

 Task C10.15: Popular songs

Step 1
➤ Find a tape or CD which includes a popular song about women, men, or both. (This is not difficult!) Your chosen tape or CD should include the lyrics.

Step 2
➤ Play the song, noting how it appears to linguistically construct women, men and/or gender relations.

➤ Then read the lyrics, and refine your ideas. Consider humour and irony.

Step 3

➤ If you have chosen a song that constructs women in a traditional or stereotypical way, now choose another which you feel does not.

➤ Put it to the test.

Task C10.16: What is 'text'?

Extending the idea of 'text' to spoken as well as written language is now commonplace. However, we can ask whether 'text' can be extended still further. Theo van Leeuwen and Carmen Caldas-Coulthard (2002) address the possibility of 'toys as text', with particular reference to the stereotypically feminine range of Barbie dolls (see also Task C10.5). You might find it helpful to explore, and use, the notion of 'indexing' here (e.g. Ochs 1992, 1993).

Step 1

➤ Read van Leeuwen and Caldas-Coulthard's chapter 'Stunning, shimmering, iridescent: toys as the representation of gendered social actors' (2002).

Step 2
Either:

➤ Using a catalogue of children's toys, consider in what sense the visuals of the toys (ignore the written text) can be seen to 'construct gender'?

Or:

➤ Visit a toyshop and make notes on this question while you walk around.

Step 3

➤ Document your conclusions.

➤ Reread van Leeuwen and Caldas-Coulthard's chapter, and finish your piece of work with some observations on the question of the sense in which, or the extent to which, toys can be considered 'text'.

➤ If you are uncomfortable with this, you might prefer to address the question of the ways in which toys are *like* (written or spoken) text.

Step 4

➤ Post your conclusions and observations on your Gender and Language web site.

Further reading

UNIT A1 EARLY WORK ON GENDER AND LANGUAGE

Bodine, Anne (1975b) 'Sex differentiation in language', in B. Thorne and N. Henley (eds) *Language and Sex: difference and dominance*. Rowley, Mass.: Newbury House, pp. 130–51.

Cameron, Deborah (1992b) *Feminism and Linguistic Theory*, 2nd edn. London: Macmillan.

Coates, Jennifer (1993) *Women, Men and Language*, 2nd edn. Harlow: Longman.

Gal, Susan (1978) 'Peasant men can't get wives: language change and sex roles in a bilingual community', *Language in Society* 7: 1–17.

Greif, Esther Blank and Gleason, Jean Berko (1980) 'Hi, thanks, and goodbye: more routine information', *Language in Society* 9: 159–66.

Jespersen, Otto (1922) *Language: its nature, development and origin*. London: Allen & Unwin.

Kramarae, Cheris (1981) *Women and Men Speaking*. Rowley, Mass.: Newbury House.

Labov, William (1966) *The Social Stratification of English in New York City*. Washington, DC: Center for Applied Linguistics.

Trudgill, Peter (1972a) 'Sex, covert prestige and linguistic change in the urban British English of Norwich', *Language in Society* 1: 179–95.

UNIT A2 THE INFLUENCE OF FEMINISM AND FEMINIST LINGUISTICS (A)

Black, Maria and Coward, Ros (1981) 'Linguistic, social and sexual relations: a review of Dale Spender's *Man-Made Language*', *Screen Education* 39: 69–85.

Blaubergs, Maija (1980) 'An analysis of classic arguments against changing sexist language', *Women's Studies International Quarterly* 3: 135–47.

Cameron, Deborah (1995a) *Verbal Hygiene*. London: Routledge.

Fishman, Pamela (1978) 'What do couples talk about when they're alone?' in Douglas Butturff and Edmund L. Epstein (eds) *Women's Language and Style*. Akron, Ohio: L & S Books, pp. 11–22.

Miller, Casey and Kate Swift (1976) *Words and Women*. New York: Anchor Press.

Schultz, Muriel (1990) 'The semantic derogation of women', in Deborah Cameron (ed.) *The Feminist Critique of Language: a reader*, 1st edn. London: Routledge, pp. 134–47.

UNIT A3 THE INFLUENCE OF FEMINISM AND FEMINIST LINGUISTICS (B)

Coates, Jennifer (1996) *Women Talk.* Oxford: Blackwell.
—— (1989) 'Gossip revisited: an analysis of all-female discourse', in Jennifer Coates and Deborah Cameron (eds) *Women in their Speech Communities.* Harlow: Longman, pp. 94–122.
Holmes, Janet (1995) *Women, Men and Politeness.* London: Longman.
Tannen, Deborah (1991) *You Just Don't Understand! Women and men in conversation.* London: Virago.

UNIT A4 DEVELOPING UNDERSTANDINGS OF GENDER

Butler, Judith (1999) *Gender Trouble: feminism and the subversion of identity.* First published 1990. New York: Routledge.
Cameron, Deborah (1997b) 'Theoretical debates in feminist linguistics: questions of sex and gender', in Ruth Wodak (ed.) *Gender and Discourse.* London: Sage, pp. 21–36.
Jones, Alison (1993) 'Becoming a "girl": Post-structuralist suggestions for educational research', *Gender and Education* 5/2: 157–66.
Mathieu, Nicole-Claude (1996) 'Sexual, sexed and sex-class identities', in Diana Leonard and Lisa Adkins (eds) *Sex in Question: French materialist feminism*, first published in French, 1989. London: Taylor & Francis, pp. 42–71.
Weedon, Chris (1996) *Feminist Practice and Poststructuralist Theory*, first published 1987. Oxford: Blackwell.

UNIT A5 DEVELOPING UNDERSTANDINGS OF LANGUAGE: LANGUAGE CHANGE

Cameron, Deborah (2003) 'Gender and language ideologies', in Janet Holmes and Miriam Meyerhoff (eds) *Handbook of Gender and Language Research.* Oxford: Blackwell, pp. 447–67.
Cooper, Robert (1984) 'The avoidance of androcentric generics', *International Journal of Social Language* 50: 5–20.
Eckert, Penelope and McConnell-Ginet, Sally (1999) 'New generalisations and explanations in language and gender research', *Language in Society* 28: 185–201.
Labov, William (1990) 'The intersection of sex and social class in the course of linguistic change', *Language Variation and Change* 2 (2): 205–51.
Pauwels, Anne (1998) *Women Changing Language.* London: Longman.
Sunderland, Jane (1994) 'Pedagogical and other filters: the representation of non-sexist language change in British pedagogical grammars', in J. Sunderland (ed.) *Exploring Gender: questions and implications for English language education.* Hemel Hempstead: Prentice Hall.

UNIT A6 DEVELOPING UNDERSTANDINGS OF LANGUAGE: CONTEXT

Hymes, Dell (1972) 'Models of the interaction of language and social life', in John Gumperz and Dell Hymes (eds) *Directions in Sociolinguistics: the ethnography of communication*. New York: Holt, Rinehart & Winston.

Lave, Jean and Wenger, Etienne (1991) *Situated Learning: legitimate peripheral participation*. Cambridge: Cambridge University Press.

Maybin, Janet (1996) 'Everyday talk', in Janet Maybin and Neil Mercer (eds) *Using English: from conversation to canon*. London: Routledge, pp. 5–41.

O'Barr, William and Atkins, Bowman (1980) 'Women's language or powerless language?' in Sally McConnell-Ginet, Ruth Borker and Nelly Furman (eds) *Women and Language in Literature and Society*. New York: Praeger, pp. 93–110.

Talbot, Mary (1992) 'I wish you'd stop interrupting me!: interruptions and asymmetries in speaker rights in equal encounters', *Journal of Pragmatics* 16: 451–66.

West, Candace (1984b) 'When the doctor is a "lady": power, status and gender in physician-patient dialogues', *Symbolic Interaction* 7: 85–105.

UNIT A7 DEVELOPING UNDERSTANDINGS OF LANGUAGE: DISCOURSE AND DISCOURSES

Chouliaraki, Lilie and Fairclough, Norman (1999) *Discourse in Late Modernity: rethinking critical discourse analysis*. Edinburgh: Edinburgh University Press.

Fairclough, Norman (2003) *Analysing Discourse: textual analysis for social research*. London: Routledge.

Foucault, Michel (1990) *The History of Sexuality*, Vol. I. New York: Random House.

Mills, Sara (1997) *Discourse*. London: Routledge.

Rich, Adrienne (1980) 'Compulsory heterosexuality and lesbian existence', *Signs* 5 (4): 631–60.

Talbot, Mary (1998) *Language and Gender*. London: Polity.

Walsh, Clare (2001) *Gender and Discourse: language and power in politics, the church and organisations*. London: Longman.

Wetherell, Margaret, Stiven, Hilda and Potter, Jonathan (1987) 'Unequal egalitarianism: a preliminary study of discourses concerning gender and employment opportunities', *British Journal of Social Psychology* 26: 59–71.

Wilkinson, Sue and Kitzinger, Celia (eds) (1995) *Feminism and Discourse: psychological perspectives*. London: Sage.

Wodak, Ruth (ed.) (1997) *Gender and Discourse*. London: Sage.

UNIT A8 APPROACHES TO GENDER AND LANGUAGE RESEARCH

Cameron, Deborah, Frazer, Elizabeth, Harvey, Penelope, Rampton, Ben and Richardson, Kay (1992) *Researching Language: issues of power and method*. London: Routledge.

Cameron, Deborah (1998b) 'Gender, language and discourse: a review essay', *Signs* 23(4): 945–73.

Gill, Ros (1995) 'Relativism, reflexivity and politics: interrogating discourse analysis from a feminist perspective', in Sue Wilkinson and Celia Kitzinger (eds) *Feminism and Discourse: psychological perspectives*. London: Sage, pp. 165–186.

Holmes, Janet and Sigley, Robert (2002) 'Looking at girls in corpora of English', *Journal of English Linguistics* 30: 138–57.

Lazar, Michelle (2005) *Feminist Critical Discourse Analysis: gender, power and ideology in discourse*. London: Palgrave Macmillan.

Schegloff, Emanuel (1997) 'Whose text? Whose context?' *Discourse and Society* 8 (2): 165–87.

Stubbs, Michael (2001) 'Texts, corpora, and problems of interpretation: a response to Widdowson', *Applied Linguistics* 22 (2): 149–72.

Wetherell, Margaret (1998) 'Positioning and interpretative repertoires: conversation analysis and post-structuralism in dialogue', *Discourse and Society* 9 (3): 387–412.

UNIT A9 DATA AND DATA SITES

Mason, Jennifer (2002) *Qualitative Researching* (2nd edn). London: Sage.

McIlhenny, Bonnie (1995) 'Challenging hegemonic masculinities: female and male police officers handling domestic violence', in K. Hall and M. Bucholtz (eds) *Gender Articulated: language and the socially constructed self*. London: Routledge, pp. 217–43.

Pavlenko, Aneta and Piller, Ingrid (2001) 'Introduction' , in Aneta Pavlenko, Adrian Blackledge, Ingrid Piller and Marya Teutsch-Dwyer (eds) *Multilingualism, Second Language Learning and Gender*. Berlin: Mouton de Gruyter, pp. 1–52.

Speer, Susan (2002) 'Sexist talk: gender categories, participants' orientations and irony', *Journal of Sociolinguistics* 6 (3): 347–77.

Taylor, Stephanie (2001) 'Locating and conducting discourse analytic research', in Margaret Wetherell, Stephanie Taylor and Simon Yates (eds) *Discourse as Data: a guide for analysis*. London: Sage (in association with The Open University), pp. 5–48.

Weatherall, Anne (2002) *Gender, Language and Discourse*. New York: Routledge.

UNIT A10 WRITTEN TEXTS

Baker, Paul (2001) 'Moral panic and alternative identity construction in Usenet', *Journal of Computer Mediated Communication* 17: 1 (e-journal).

Cosslett, Tess (1996) 'Fairytales: revising the tradition', in Tess Cosslett, Alison Easton and Penny Summerfield (eds) *Women, Power and Resistance*. Open University Press, pp. 81–90.

Herring, Susan (1996) 'Two variants of an electronic message schema', in Susan C. Herring (ed.) *Computer-Mediated Communication: linguistic, social, and cross-cultural perspectives*. Amsterdam: John Benjamins, pp. 81–108.

Jones, Martha, Kitetu, Catherine and Sunderland, Jane (1997) 'Discourse roles, gender and language textbook dialogues: who learns what from John and Sally?' *Gender and Education* 9 (4): 469–90.

Stephens, John (1992) *Language and Ideology in Children's Fiction*. London Longman.

Sunderland, Jane (2004) *Gendered Discourses*. London: Palgrave Macmillan.

Bibliography

EDITED COLLECTIONS

Bergvall, Victoria, Bing, Janet and Freed, Alice (eds) (1996) *Rethinking Language and Gender Research*. London: Longman.

Bucholtz, Mary, Liang, A. C. and Sutton, Laurel (eds) (1999) *Reinventing Identities – the gendered self in discourse*. Oxford: Oxford University Press.

Cameron, Deborah (ed.) (1998a, 2nd edition) *The Feminist Critique of Language*. London: Routledge.

Coates, Jennifer (ed.) (1998) *Language and Gender: a reader*. Oxford: Blackwell.

Coates, Jennifer and Cameron, Deborah (eds) (1988) *Women in their Speech Communities*. London: Longman.

Hall, Kira and Bucholz, Mary (eds) (1995) *Gender Articulated: language and the socially constructed self*. New York: Routledge.

Harvey, Keith and Shalom, Celia (eds) (1997) *Language and Desire: encoding sex, romance and intimacy*. London: Routledge.

Holmes, Janet and Meyerhoff, Miriam (eds) (2003) *Handbook of Language and Gender*. Oxford: Blackwell.

Johnson, Sally and Meinhof, Ulrike Hanna (eds) (1997) *Language and Masculinity*. Oxford: Blackwell.

Kotthoff, Helga and Wodak, Ruth (eds) (1997) *Communicating Gender in Context*. Amsterdam: John Benjamins.

Kramarae, Cheris (ed.) (1981) *Women and Men Speaking*. Rowley, Mass: Newbury House Publishers, Inc.

Lazar, Michelle (ed.) (2005) *Feminist Critical Discourse Analysis: Studies in Gender, Power and Ideology*. London: Palgrave Macmillan.

Leap, William L. (ed.) (1995) *Beyond the Lavender Lexicon: Authenticity, Imagination and Appropriation in Lesbian and Gay Languages*. New York: Gordon & Breech Press.

Litosseliti, Lia and Sunderland, Jane (eds) (2002) *Gender Identity and Discourse Analysis*. Amsterdam: John Benjamins.

Livia, Anna and Hall, Kira (eds) (1997) *Queerly Phrased: Language, Gender and Sexuality*. Oxford: Oxford University Press.

McConnell-Ginet, Sally, Borker, Ruth and Furman, Nelly (eds) (1980) *Women and Language in Literature and Society*. New York: Praeger.

Mills, Sara (ed.) (1994) *Gendering the Reader*. Hemel Hempstead: Harvester Wheatsheaf.

Mills, Sara (ed.) (1995b) *Language and Gender: interdisciplinary perspectives*. London: Longman.

Penfield, Joyce (ed.) (1987) *Women and Language in Transition*. Albany: SUNY Press.

Philips, Susan U., Steele, Susan and Tanz, Christine (eds) (1987) *Language, Gender, and Sex in Comparative Perspective*. New York: Cambridge University Press.

Sunderland, Jane (ed.) (1994a) *Exploring Gender: questions and implications for English language education*. Hemel Hempstead: Prentice Hall.

Tannen, Deborah (ed.) (1993) *Gender and Conversational Interaction*. New York: Oxford University Press.

Thorne, Barrie and Henley, Nancy (eds) (1975) *Language and Sex: difference and dominance*. Rowley, Mass.: Newbury House.

Thorne, Barrie, Kramarae, Cheris and Henley, Nancy (eds) (1983) *Language, Gender and Society*. Rowley. Mass.: Newbury House.

Thorne, Barrie and Henley, Nancy (eds) (1975) *Language and Sex: difference and dominance*. Rowley, Mass.: Newbury House.

Todd, Alexandra Dundas, and Sue Fisher (eds) (1988) *Gender and Discourse: The Power of Talk*. Norwood, NJ: Ablex.

Vetterling-Braggin, Mary (ed.) (1981) *Sexist Language*. Totowa, NJ: Littlefield, Adams.

Wilkinson, Sue and Kitzinger, Celia (eds) (1995) *Feminism and Discourse: psychological perspectives*. London: Sage.

Wodak, Ruth (ed.) (1997) *Gender and Discourse*. London: Sage.

GENERAL SOURCES

Abdul Rahim, Fauziah (1997) 'Gender – if "it's part of the climate", what do language teachers do?: looking at teachers' treatment of gender in teaching materials'. MA dissertation, Lancaster University.

Abraham, John (1989) 'Teacher ideology and sex roles in curriculum texts', *British Journal of Sociology of Education* 10 (1): 33–51.

Abrahams, Roger D. (1975) 'Negotiating respect: patterns of presentation among black women', in C. R. Farrar (ed.) *Women and Folklore*. Austin, Tex.: University of Texas Press.

—— (1976) *Talking Black*. Rowley, Mass.: Newbury House.

Adler, Sue (1992) 'Aprons and attitudes: feminism and children's books', in H. Claire, J. Maybin and J. Swann (eds) *Equality Matters*. Clevedon: Multilingual Matters.

Ainsworth-Vaughn, Nancy (1992) 'Topic transitions in physician-patient interviews: power, gender, and discourse change', *Language in Society* 21: 409–26.

Akiba-Reynolds, Katsue (1985) 'Female speakers of Japanese in transition', *Proceedings of the First Berkeley Women and Language Conference*, Berkeley, Calif.: Berkeley Women and Language Group, pp. 183–96.

Alberts, J. K. (1992) 'Teasing and sexual harassment: double-bind communication in the workplace', in Linda A. M. Perry, Lynn H. Turner and Helen M. Sterk (eds), *Constructing and Reconstructing Gender: the links among communication, language, and gender*. Albany: SUNY Press, pp. 185–97.

Alderson, Charles (1997) 'Models of language: whose? what for? what use?' in A. Ryan and A. Wray (eds) *Evolving Models of Language*. British Studies in Applied Linguistics 12. Clevedon: BAAL/Multilingual Matters, pp. 1–22.

Allwright, Dick (1988) *Observation in the Language Classroom*. London: Longman.

Allwright, Dick and Bailey, Kathleen (1991) *Focus on the Language Classroom*. Cambridge: Cambridge University Press.

Althusser, Louis (1971) *Lenin and Philosophy and Other Essays*, London: New Left Books.

Anderson, Judy (1996) 'Not for the faint of heart: contemplations on Usenet', in Lynn Cherny and Elizabeth Reba Weise (eds) *Wired Women: gender and new realities in cyberspace*, Seattle, Wash.: Seal Press, pp. 126–38.

Andrews, Margaret and Talbot, Mary (eds) (2000) *All the World and Her Husband: women in twentieth-century consumer culture.* London: Cassell.

Antaki, Charles (1995) 'Conversation analysis and social psychology', *British Psychological Society Social Psychology Section Newsletter* (winter): 21–34.

Antaki, Charles and Widdicombe, Sue (eds) (1998) *Identities in Talk.* London: Sage.

Aries, Elizabeth (1976) 'Interaction patterns and themes of male, female, and mixed groups', *Small Group Behaviour* 7: 7–18.

Arksey, Hilary and Knight, Peter (1999) *Interviewing for Social Scientists.* London: Sage.

Arminem, I. (2000) 'On the context sensitivity of institutional interaction', *Discourse and Society* 11: 435–58.

Atkinson, John Maxwell (1984) *Our Master's Voices: the language and body language of politics.* London: Methuen.

Atkinson, John Maxwell and Heritage, John (eds) (1984) *Structures of Social Action: studies in conversation analysis.* Cambridge: Cambridge University Press.

Austin, John (1962) *How To Do Things with Words.* London: Oxford University Press.

Baker, Paul (2001) 'Moral panic and alternative identity construction in Usenet', *Journal of Computer Mediated Communication* 17: 1 (e-journal).

—— (2002) *Polari: the lost language of gay men.* London: Routledge.

Bakhtin, Mikhail (1981) *The Dialogic Imagination: four essays.* Austin, Tex.: University of Texas.

—— (1984) *Problems of Dostoevsky's Poetics* (ed. and trans. Caryl Emerson). Minneapolis, Minn.: University of Minnesota Press.

Baron, Dennis E. (1981) 'The epicene pronoun: the word that failed', *American Speech* 56: 83–97.

Barrett, Rusty (1999) 'Indexing polyphonous identity in the speech of African American drag queens', in Mary Bucholtz, A. C. Liang and Laurel Sutton (eds) *Reinventing Identities: the gendered self in discourse.* New York: Oxford University Press, pp. 313–31.

Barthes, Roland (1973) *Mythologies.* London, Paladin.

—— (1977) *Image-Music-Text.* New York: Hill & Wang.

—— (1982) 'Inaugural lecture, Collège de France', in Susan Sontag (ed.) *A Barthes Reader.* London, Jonathan Cape.

Barton, Ellen (2002) 'Inductive discourse analysis: discovering rich features', in Ellen Barton and Gail Stygall (eds) *Discourse Studies in Composition.* Creskill, NJ: Hampton Press, pp. 19–42.

Bate, Barbara (1978) 'Non-sexist language use in transition', *Journal of Communication* 28: 139–49.

Bates, Elizabeth (1976) *Language and Context.* New York: Academic Press.

Baumann, Richard (1972) 'Belsnickling in a Nova Scotia island community', *Western Folklore* 31 (4): 229–43.

Baxter, Judith (2002a) 'Competing discourses in the classroom: a post-structuralist discourse analysis of girls' and boys' speech in public contexts', *Discourse and Society* 13 (6): 827–42. (Also 'Is PDA really an alternative? A reply to Candace West', pp. 843–52.

—— (2002b) 'A juggling act: a feminist post-structuralist analysis of girls' and boys' talk in the secondary classroom', *Gender and Education* 14 (1): 5–19.

—— (2003) *Positioning Gender in Discourse: a feminist methodology.* London: Palgrave Macmillan.

—— (ed.) (2006) *Speaking Out: the female voice in public contexts.* London: Palgrave Macmillan.

Beach, Wayne (2000) 'Inviting collaborations in stories about a woman', *Language in Society* 29: 379–407.

Beattie, Geoffrey (1981) 'Interruption in conversational interaction, and its relation to the sex and status of the interactants', *Linguistics* 19: 15–35.

Bell, Jan and Gower, Roger (1992) *Upper Intermediate Matters.* Harlow: Longman.

Bem, Sandra and Bem, Daryl (1973) 'Does sex-biased job advertising "aid and abet" sex discrimination?' *Journal of Applied Social Psychology* 3: 6–18.

Benwell, Bethan (2002) 'Is there anything "new" about these lads? The textual and visual construction of masculinity in men's magazines', in Lia Litosseliti, and Jane Sunderland (eds) *Gender Identity and Discourse Analysis.* Amsterdam: John Benjamins, pp. 149–74.

—— (ed.) (2003) *Masculinity and the Men's Lifestyle Magazine.* Oxford: Blackwell.

—— (2004) 'Ironic discourse: evasive masculinity in men's lifestyle magazines', *Men and Masculinities* 7 (1): 3–21.

Berger, Maurice, Wallis, Brian and Watson, Simon (eds) (1995) *Constructing Masculinity.* London: Routledge.

Berger, Peter and Kellner, Hansfried (1970) 'Marriage and the construction of reality', in Hans Peter Dreitzel (ed.) *Recent Sociology 2.* London: Macmillan, pp. 50–72.

Berger, Peter and Luckmann, Thomas (1967) *The Social Construction of Reality.* New York: Anchor Books.

Bergvall, Victoria (1999) 'Towards a comprehensive theory of language and gender', *Language in Society* 28: 273–93.

—— (2000) 'The continuum of gender construction in on-line discourse', paper presented at the First International Gender and Language Association (IGALA) Conference, Stanford University.

Bergvall, Victoria and Bing, Alice (1996) 'The question of questions: beyond binary thinking', in Victoria Bergvall, Janet Bing and Alice Freed (eds) *Rethinking Language and Gender Research.* London: Longman.

Bergvall, Victoria and Remlinger, Kathryn (1996) 'Reproduction, resistance and gender in educational discourse: the role of Critical Discourse Analysis', *Discourse and Society* 7 (4): 453–79.

Berman, Ruth (1998) 'No Joe Marches', *Children's Literature in Education* 29 (4): 237–47.

Billig, Michael (1991) *Ideology and Opinions: studies in rhetorical psychology.* London: Sage.

—— (1996) *Arguing and Thinking: a rhetorical approach to social psychology*, 2nd edn. Cambridge: Cambridge University Press.

—— (1999) 'Whose terms? Whose ordinariness? Rhetoric and ideology in conversation analysis', *Discourse and Society* 10: 543–58.

Billig, Michael, Condor, Susan, Edwards, Derek, Gane, Mike, Middleton, David and Radley, Andrew (1988) *Ideological Dilemmas: a social psychology of everyday thinking.* London, Sage.

Black, Maria and Coward, Ros (1981) 'Linguistic, social and sexual relations: a review of Dale Spender's *Man-Made Language*', *Screen Education* 39: 69–85.

Blaubergs, Maija (1978) 'Changing the sexist language: the theory behind the practice', *Psychology of Women Quarterly* 2/3: 244–61.

—— (1980) 'An analysis of classic arguments against changing sexist language', *Women's Studies International Quarterly* 3: 135–47.

Bodine, Anne (1975a) 'Androcentrism in prescriptive grammar', *Language in Society* 4: 129–46.

—— (1975b) 'Sex differentiation in language', in B. Thorne and N. Henley (eds) *Language and Sex: difference and dominance.* Rowley, Mass.: Newbury House, pp. 130–51.

Bohan, Janis S. (1993) 'Regarding gender: essentialism, constructionism and feminist psychology', *Psychology of Women Quarterly* 17: 5–21.

Boissevain, Jeremy (1974) *Friends of Friends: networks, manipulators and coalitions*. Oxford: Blackwell.

Bonkowski, Frank (1995) *Teacher Use and Interpretation of Textbook Materials in the Secondary ESL Classroom in Quebec*. PhD thesis, Lancaster University.

Bourdieu, Pierre (1977) *Outline of a Theory of Practice*. Cambridge: Cambridge University Press.

Brail, Stephanie (1996) 'The price of admission: harassment and free speech in the Wild, Wild West', in Lynn Cherny and Elizabeth Reba Weise (eds) *Wired Women: gender and new realities in cyberspace*. Seattle, Wash.: Seal Press, pp. 141–57.

Brannen, Julia (1992) 'Combining qualitative and quantitative approaches: an overview', in J. Brannen (ed.) *Mixing Methods: qualitative and quantitative research*. Aldershot: Avebury, pp. 3–37.

Britzman, Deborah (1995) 'Is there a queer pedagogy? Or, stop reading straight', *Educational Theory* 45 (2): 151–65.

Brooks-Gunn, Jeanne and Matthews, Wendy S. (1979) *He and She: how children develop their sex-role identity*. Englewood Cliffs, NJ: Prentice-Hall.

Brown, Penelope and Levinson, Stephen C. (1987) *Politeness: some universals in language usage*. Cambridge: Cambridge University Press.

Bruckman, Amy S. (1993) 'Gender swapping on the Internet', paper presented at the Internet Society, San Francisco, August. Available via FTP from the author at: <http://www.cc.gatech.edu/fac/Amy.Bruckman/papers/#INET>.

Bryman, Alan and Burgess, Robert (eds) *Analysing Qualitative Data*. London: Routledge, pp. 173–94.

Bucholtz, Mary (1998) 'Geek the girl: language, femininity, and female nerds', in Natasha Warner et al. (eds) *Gender and Belief Systems: proceedings of the Fourth Berkeley Women and Language Conference*. Berkeley, Calif.: Berkeley Women and Language Group, pp. 119–31.

—— (1999a) 'Why be normal?: language and identity practices in a community of nerd girls', *Language in Society* 28 (2): 203–23.

—— (1999b) 'Bad examples: transgression and progress in language and gender studies', in Mary Bucholtz, A. C. Liang and Laurel Sutton (eds) *Reinventing Identities: the gendered self in discourse*. New York: Oxford University Press, pp. 3–24.

—— (1999c) 'Purchasing power: the gender and class imaginary on the shopping channel', in M. Bucholtz, A. C. Liang and L. A. Sutton (eds) *Reinventing Identities: the gendered self in discourse*. New York: Oxford University Press, pp. 348–68.

—— (2000) 'The politics of transcription', *Journal of Pragmatics* 32: 1439–65.

—— (2002) 'Geek feminism', in *Gendered Practices in Language: proceedings of the First IGALA Conference*. Stanford, Calif.: CSLI Publications, pp. 277–307.

Burbules, Nicholas C. (1997) 'A grammar of difference: some ways of rethinking difference and diversity as educational topics', *Australian Educational Researcher* 24 (1): 97–116.

Burnard, Lou (compiler) (1995) *The Users Reference Guide for the British National Corpus*. Oxford: Oxford University Computing Services.

Butler, Judith (1991) 'Imitation and gender insubordination', in Diana Fuss (ed.) *Inside/Out: lesbian theories, gay theories*. London: Routledge, pp. 13–31.

—— (1990) 'Performative acts and gender constitution: an essay in phenomenology and feminist theory', in Sue-Ellen Case (ed.) *Performing Feminism: feminist critical theory and theatre*. Baltimore, Md.: Johns Hopkins University Press, pp. 270–82.

—— (1999) *Gender Trouble: feminism and the subversion of identity*. First published 1990. New York: Routledge.

—— (2004a) *Precarious Life: the power of mourning and violence*. London: Verso.

—— (2004b) *Undoing Gender*. London: Routledge.

Buttny, Richard (1993) *Social Accountability in Communication*. London: Sage.

Cain, Roy (1996) 'Heterosexism and self-disclosure in the social work classroom', *Journal of Social Work Education* 32: 65–76.

Caldas-Coulthard, Carmen (1995) 'Man in the news: the misrepresentation of women speaking in news as narrative discourse', in Sara Mills (ed.) *Language and Gender: interdisciplinary perspectives*. London: Longman, pp. 226–39.

—— (1996) '"Women who pay for sex. And enjoy it": transgression versus morality in women's magazines', in Carmen Rosa Caldas-Coulthard and Malcolm Coulthard (eds) *Texts and Practices: readings in critical discourse analysis*. London: Routledge, pp. 250–70.

Cameron, Deborah (1992a) 'Review: Deborah Tannen: You Just Don't Understand! Women and Men in Conversation', *Feminism and Psychology* 2 (3): 465–89.

—— (1992b) *Feminism and Linguistic Theory*, 2nd edn. London: Macmillan.

—— (1994) 'Problems of sexist and non-sexist language', in Jane Sunderland (ed.) *Exploring Gender: questions for English language education*. London: Prentice-Hall, pp. 26–33.

—— (1995a) *Verbal Hygiene*. London: Routledge.

—— (1995b) 'Rethinking language and gender studies: some issues for the 1990s', in Sara Mills (ed.) *Language and Gender: interdisciplinary perspectives*. Harlow: Longman, pp. 31–44.

—— (1996) 'The language-gender interface: challenging co-optation', in Victoria Bergvall, J. M. Bing and Alice Freed (eds) *Rethinking Language and Gender Research*. London: Longman, pp. 31–53.

—— (1997a) 'Performing gender identity: young men's talk and the construction of heterosexual masculinity', in Sally Johnson and Ulrike Hanna Meinhof (eds) *Language and Masculinity*. Oxford: Blackwell, pp. 47–64.

—— (1997b) 'Theoretical debates in feminist linguistics: questions of sex and gender', in Ruth Wodak (ed.) *Gender and Discourse*. London: Sage, pp. 21–36.

—— (1998b) 'Gender, language and discourse: a review essay', *Signs* 23(4): 945–73.

—— (2000) *Good to Talk? Living and working in a communication culture*. London: Sage.

—— (2001) *Working with Spoken Discourse*. London: Sage.

—— (2003) 'Gender and language ideologies', in Janet Holmes and Miriam Meyerhoff (eds) *Handbook of Gender and Language Research*. Oxford: Blackwell, pp. 447–67.

—— (2006) 'Language, sexism and advertising standards' in D. Cameron (ed.) *On Language and Sexual Politics*. New York: Routledge.

Cameron, Deborah and Kulick, Don (2003) *Language and Sexuality*. Cambridge: Cambridge University Press.

Cameron, Deborah, Frazer, Elizabeth, Harvey, Penelope, Rampton, Ben and Richardson, Kay (1992) *Researching Language: issues of power and method*. London: Routledge.

Cameron, Deborah, McAlinden, Fiona and O'Leary, Kathy (1989) 'Lakoff in context: the social and linguistic functions of tag questions', in Jennifer Coates and Deborah Cameron (eds) *Women in their Speech Communities*. Harlow: Longman, pp. 74–93.

Cammack, J. Camille and Kalmback Phillips, Donna (2002) 'Discourses and subjectivities of the gendered teacher', *Gender and Education* 14 (2): 123–33.

Camp, L. Jean (1996) 'We are geeks, and we are not guys: the systers mailing list', in Lynn Cherny and Elizabeth Reba Weise (eds) *Wired Women: gender and new realities in cyberspace*. Seattle, Wash.: Seal Press, pp. 114–25.

Carroll, David and Kowitz, Joanne (1994) 'Using concordancing techniques to study gender stereotyping in ELT textbooks', in Jane Sunderland (ed.) (1994) *Exploring Gender: questions and implications for English language education.* Hemel Hempstead: Prentice Hall.

Chalmers, Alan F. (1978) *What Is This Thing Called Science? An assessment of the nature and status of science and its methods.* Milton Keynes: Open University Press.

Chandler, A. and Chappell, D. (1993) Review of Reynold, Kimberly (1990) *Girls Only: gender and popular children's fiction in Britain 1880–1910*, *Signs* 18 (3): 674–8.

Channell, Joanna (1994) *Vague Language.* Oxford: Oxford University Press.

Cherland, Meredith R. (1994) *Private Practices: girls reading fiction and constructing identity.* London: Taylor & Francis.

Cherny, Lynn and Weise, Elizabeth Reba (eds) (1996) *Wired Women: gender and new realities in cyberspace*, Seattle, Wash.: Seal Press.

Cheshire, Jenny (1982) *Variation in an English Dialect: a sociolinguistic study* (Cambridge Studies in Linguistics no. 37). Cambridge: Cambridge University Press.

Children's Rights Workshop (1976) *Sexism in Children's Books: facts, figures and guidelines.* London: Writers and Readers Publishing Co-operative.

Chiles, Tina (2003) 'Titles and surnames in the linguistic construction of women's identity', *New Zealand Studies of Applied Linguistics* 9 (1).

Chodorow, Nancy (1978) *The Reproduction of Mothering: psychoanalysis and the sociology of gender.* Berkeley, Calif.: University of California Press.

Chouliaraki, Lilie (1994) 'The case of *Task Way English*: alternative gender constructions in EFL textbooks. Interview with Bessie Dendrinos', in Jane Sunderland (ed), *Exploring Gender: questions and implications for English language education.* Hemel Hempstead: Prentice Hall, pp. 121–33.

Chouliaraki, Lilie and Fairclough, Norman (1999) *Discourse in Late Modernity: rethinking critical discourse analysis.* Edinburgh: Edinburgh University Press.

Cicourel, Aaron (1992) 'The interpenetration of communicative contexts: examples from medical encounters', in Alessandro Duranti and Charles Goodwin (eds) *Rethinking Context: language as an interactive phenomenon.* Cambridge: Cambridge University Press, pp. 293–310.

Cincotta, Madeleine (1978) 'Textbooks and their influence on sex-role formation', *Babel: The Journal of the Australian Federation of MLTS Association* 14 (3): 24–9.

Claire, Hilary, Maybin, Janet and Swann, Joan (eds) (1993) *Equality Matters.* Clevedon: Multilingual Matters.

Clatterbaugh, Kenneth (1990) *Contemporary Perspectives on Masculinity.* Boulder, Col.: Westview Press.

Coates, Jennifer (1989) 'Gossip revisited: an analysis of all-female discourse', in Jennifer Coates and Deborah Cameron (eds) *Women in their Speech Communities.* Harlow: Longman, pp. 94–122.

—— (1993) *Women, Men and Language*, 2nd edn. Harlow: Longman.

—— (1996) *Women Talk.* Oxford: Blackwell.

—— (1997) 'Competing discourses of femininity', in Helga Kotthof and Ruth Wodak (eds) *Communicating Gender in Context.* Amsterdam: John Benjamins, pp. 285–314.

—— (1999) 'Changing femininities: the talk of teenage girls', in Mary Bucholtz, A. C. Liang and Laurel Sutton (eds) *Reinventing Identities: the gendered self in discourse.* Oxford: Oxford University Press, pp. 123–44.

—— (2003) *Men Talk.* Oxford: Blackwell.

Cochran, Effie (1992) 'Towards degendered English in the ESL classroom', *Working Papers on Language, Gender and Sexism* 2 (2): 27–35.

—— (1996) 'Gender and the ESL classroom', *TESOL Quarterly* 30 (1): 159–62.

Cohen, Louis, Manion, Lawrence and Morrison, Keith (2000) *Research Methods in Education*. London: Routledge.

Cohen, David (1990) *Being a Man*. London: Routledge.

Conefrey, Theresa (1997) 'Gender, culture and authority in a university life sciences laboratory', *Discourse and Society* 8 (3): 313–40.

Connell, Robert W. (1995) *Masculinities*. Cambridge: Polity.

Connor-Linton, Jeff (1999) 'Competing communicative styles and crosstalk: a multifeature analysis', *Language in Society* 28 (1): 25–56.

Conrick, Maeve (1999) *Womanspeak*. Dublin: Marino Books.

Cooper, Robert (1984) 'The avoidance of androcentric generics', *International Journal of Social Language* 50: 5–20.

Corbett, Greville (2004) *Gender*. First published 1991. Cambridge: Cambridge University Press.

Cornwall, Andrea and Lindisfarne, Nancy (eds) (1994) *Dislocating Masculinity: comparative ethnographies*. London: Routledge.

Cosslett, Tess (1996) 'Fairytales: revising the tradition', in Tess Cosslett, Alison Easton and Penny Summerfield (eds) *Women, Power and Resistance*. Milton Keynes: Open University Press, pp. 81–90.

Coupland, Justine and Williams, Angie (2002) 'Conflicting discourses, shifting ideologies: pharmaceutical, "alternative" and feminist emancipatory texts on the menopause', *Discourse and Society* 13 (4): 419–45.

Crawford, Mary (1995) *Talking Difference: on gender and language*. London: Sage.

Crowdy, Steve (1993) 'Spoken corpus design and transcription', *Literary and Linguistic Computing* 8 (4): 259–65.

—— (1995) 'The BNC Spoken Corpus', in Geoff Leech, Greg Myers and Jenny Thomas (eds) *Spoken English on Computer: transcription, mark-up and application*. London: Longman, pp. 224–34.

Crowther, Barbara and Leith, Dick (1995) 'Feminism, language and the rhetoric of television wildlife programmes', in Sara Mills (ed.) *Language and Gender: interdisciplinary perspectives*. London: Longman, pp. 207–25.

Cushing, Pamela J. (1996) 'Gendered conversational rituals on the Internet: an effective voice is based on more than simply what one is saying', *Anthropologica* 38 (1): 47–80.

Dalley, Gillian (1996) *Ideologies of Caring*. Basingstoke: Macmillan.

Daly, Mary (1987) *Webster's First New Intergalactic Wickedary*. Boston, Mass.: Beacon Press.

Davies, Bronwyn (1988) 'Romantic love and women's sexuality', unpublished paper.

—— (1989a) *Frogs and Snails and Feminist Tales: pre-school children and gender*. Sydney: Allen & Unwin (2nd edition 2003).

—— (1989b) 'Education for sexism: a theoretical analysis of the sex/gender bias in education', *Educational Philosophy and Theory* 21 (1): 1–19.

—— (1993) *Shards of Glass*. Sydney: Allen & Unwin.

—— (1997) 'The subject of post-structuralism: a reply to Alison Jones', *Gender and Education* 9 (1): 271–83.

Davies, Bronwyn and Harré, Rom (1990) 'Positioning: the discursive production of selves', *Journal for the Theory of Social Behaviour*, 20: 43–65.

Davis, Kathy (1988) 'Paternalism under the microscope', in A. Dundas Todd and S. Fisher (eds) *Gender and Discourse: the power of talk*. Norwood, NJ: Ablex, pp. 19–54.

de Beauvoir, Simone (1949) *The Second Sex*. Harmondsworth: Penguin.

De Francisco, Victoria (1991) 'The sounds of silence: how men silence women in marital relations', *Discourse and Society* 2 (4): 413–23.

DeLosh, Shelley (1993) 'Etiquette books as vehicles for gender stereotypes', available online at <http://courses.lib.odu.edu/engl/jbing/delosh.html>.

Dee, Catherine (1999) *The Girls' Book of Wisdom: empowering, inspirational quotes from over 400 fabulous females.* New York: Megan Tingley.

Dendrinos, Bessie (1988) *Task Way English.* Athens: N.C. Grivas Publications.

—— (1992) *The EFL Textbook and Ideology.* Athens: N. C. Grivas Publications.

Dennis, N., Henriques, F.M. and Slaughter, C. (1957) *Coal is our Life.* London: Eyre & Spottiswode.

Dibbell, Julian (1998) *My Tiny Life: crime and passion in a virtual world.* New York: Henry Holt.

Dombey, Henrietta (1992) 'Lessons learnt at bedtime', in K. Kimberly, M. Meek and J. Miller (eds) *New Readings: contributions to an understanding of literacy.* London: A & C Black, pp. 29–36.

Doyle, Margaret (1994) *The A-Z of Non-Sexist Language.* London: Women's Press.

Drew, Paul and Heritage, John (eds.) *Talk at Work: interaction in institutional settings.* Cambridge: Cambridge University Press.

Dubois, Betty Lou and Crouch, Isobel (1975) 'The question of tag questions in women's speech: they don't really use more of them, do they?' *Language in Society* 4: 289–94.

—— (eds) (1976) *The Sociology of the Languages of American Women.* San Antonio, Tex.: Trinity University.

Dunant, Sara (ed.) (1994) *The War of the Words: the political correctness debate.* London: Virago Press.

Eagleton, Terry (1991) *Ideology: an introduction.* London, Verso.

Eble, Connie (1975) 'Girl Talk: a Bicentennial Perspective.' *Views on Language.* Murfressboro, Tenn.: Intrauniversity Publishing, pp. 77–86.

—— (1976) 'Etiquette books as linguistic authority', in Peter Reich (ed.) *LACUS Forum II.* Columbia, SC: Hornbeam Press.

—— (1996) *Slang and Sociability: in-group language among college students.* Chapel Hill, NC: University of North Carolina Press.

Eckert, Penelope (1990) 'The whole woman: sex and gender differences in variation', *Language Variation and Change* 1: 245–67.

—— (2000) *Linguistic Variation as Social Practice.* Oxford: Blackwell.

Eckert, Penelope and McConnell-Ginet, Sally (1992a) 'Communities of practice: where language, gender, and power all live', in Kira Hall et al. (eds) *Locating Power: proceedings of the Second Berkeley Women and Language Conference.* Berkeley, Calif.: Women and Language Group, pp. 89–99.

—— (1992b) 'Think practically and look locally: language and gender as community-based practice', *Annual Review of Anthropology* 21: 461–90.

—— (1995) 'Constructing meaning, constructing selves: snapshots of language, gender and class from Belten High', in Kira Hall and Mary Bucholtz (eds) *Gender Articulated.* London: Routledge, pp. 469–507.

—— (1998) 'Communities of practice: where language, gender and power all live', in J. Coates (ed.) *Language and Gender: a reader.* Oxford: Blackwell.

—— (1999) 'New generalisations and explanations in language and gender research', *Language in Society* 28: 185–201.

—— (2003) *Language and Gender.* Cambridge: Cambridge University Press.

Edelsky, Carole (1977) 'Acquisition of an aspect of communicative competence: learning what it means to talk like a lady', in Susan Ervin-Tripp and Claudia Mitchell-Kernan (eds) *Child Discourse.* New York: Academic Press.

Edgar, Timothy (1994) 'Self-disclosure strategies of the stigmatized: strategies and outcomes for the revelation of sexual orientation', in R. J. Ringer (ed.) *Queer Words, Queer Images: communication and the construction of homosexuality*. New York: New York University Press, pp. 221–37.

Edge, Julian and Richards, Keith (1998) 'May I see your warrant, please? Justifying claims in qualitative research', *Applied Linguistics* 19 (3): 334–56.

Edley, Nigel (1993) 'Prince Charles – our flexible friend: accounting for variations in constructions of identity', *Text* 13: 397–422.

—— (2001) 'Analysing masculinity: interpretative repertoires, ideological dilemmas and subject positions', in Margaret Wetherell, Stephanie Taylor and Simon Yates (eds) *Discourse as Data*. London: Sage/Open University Press, pp. 189–228.

Edley, Nigel and Wetherell, Margaret (1995) *Men in Perspective: practice, power and identity*, Hemel Hempstead: Prentice Hall/Harvester Wheatsheaf.

—— (1996) 'Masculinity, power and identity', in Mairtin Mac An Ghaill (ed.) *Understanding Masculinities: social relations and cultural arenas*. Milton Keynes: Open University Press.

—— (1997) 'Jockeying for position: the construction of masculine identities', *Discourse and Society* 8: 203–17.

—— (1999) 'Imagined futures: young men's talk about fatherhood and domestic life', *British Journal of Social Psychology* 38: 181–94.

—— (2001) 'Jekyll and Hyde: men's constructions of feminism and feminists', *Feminism and Psychology* 11 (4): 439–57.

Edwards, Derek (1997) *Discourse and Cognition*. London: Sage.

—— (1998) 'The relevant thing about her: social identity categories in use', in Charles Antaki and Sue Widdicombe (eds) *Identities in Talk*. London: Sage, pp. 15–33.

Edwards, Derek and Potter, Jonathan (1992) *Discursive Psychology*. London: Sage.

Eggins, Suzanne and Iedema, Rick (1997) 'Difference without diversity: semantic orientation and ideology in competing women's magazines', in R. Wodak (ed.) *Gender and Discourse*. London: Sage.

Ehrlich, Eugene H. (1996) *The International Thesaurus of Quotations: revised edition*. London: Collins.

Ehrlich, Susan (2001) *Representing Rape: language and sexual consent*. London: Routledge.

Ehrlich, Susan and King, Ruth (1992) 'Gender-based language reform and the social construction of meaning', *Discourse and Society* 3 (2): 151–66.

Eichler, Margrit (1991) *Non-Sexist Research Methods: a practical guide*. New York: Allen & Unwin.

Ekstrand, Lars (1980) 'Sex differences in second language learning? Empirical studies and a discussion of related findings', *International Review of Applied Psychology* 29: 205–59.

Elliott, Anthony (1996) *Subject to Ourselves*. Oxford: Polity Press.

Fairclough, Norman (1989) *Language and Power*. London: Longman.

—— (1992a) *Discourse and Social Change*. Cambridge: Polity Press.

—— (ed.) (1992b) *Critical Discourse Analysis*. London: Longman.

—— (1995) *Critical Discourse Analysis*. London: Longman.

—— (2000) *New Labour, New Language?* London: Routledge.

—— (2001) 'The discourse of New Labour: critical discourse analysis', in Margaret Wetherell, Stephanie Taylor and Simon Yates (eds) *Discourse as Data: a guide for analysis*. London: Sage and Open University Press, pp. 229–66.

—— (2003) *Analysing Discourse: textual analysis for social research*. London: Routledge.

Faris, James C. (1966) 'The dynamics of verbal exchange: a Newfoundland example', *Anthropologica* (Ottawa) 8 (2): 235–48.

Farrar, C. R. (ed.) *Women and Folklore*. Austin, Tex.: University of Texas Press.

Fausto-Sterling, Anne (1998) 'The five sexes: why male and female are not enough', in Dina L. Anselmi and Anne L. Law (eds) *Questions of Gender: perspectives and paradoxes.* London: McGraw-Hill, pp. 29–34.

Finlayson, Rosalie (1995) 'Women's language of respect: *isihlonipho sabafazi*', in R. Mesthrie (ed.) *Language and Social History: studies in South African Sociolinguistics.* Cape Town: David Philip, pp. 141–53.

Fishman, Pamela (1978) 'What do couples talk about when they're alone?' in Douglas Butturff and Edmund L. Epstein (eds) *Women's Language and Style.* Akron, Ohio: L & S Books, pp. 11–22.

—— (1980) 'Conversational insecurity', in Howard Giles, Peter Robinson and Philip M. Smith (eds) *Language: social psychological perspectives.* New York: Pergamon Press, pp. 127–32.

—— (1983) 'Interaction: the work women do', in Barrie Thorne et al. (eds) *Language, Gender and Society.* Rowley, Mass.: Newbury House, pp. 89–101. First published 1978 in *Social Problems* 25: 397–406.

Florent, Jill et al. (1994) 'On balance: guidelines for the representation of women and men in English language teaching materials', in Jane Sunderland (ed.) *Exploring Gender: questions and implications for English language education.* Hemel Hempstead: Prentice Hall, pp. 112–20.

Foucault, Michel (1972) *The Archaeology of Knowledge.* London: Tavistock.

—— (1977) *Discipline and Punish.* London: Penguin.

—— (1978) *The History of Sexuality: an introduction.* Harmondsworth: Penguin.

—— (1980) *Power/Knowledge: selected interviews and other writings, 1972–1977.* Trans. by C. Gordon, L. Marshall, J. Mepham, and K. Soper. New York: Pantheon.

—— (1981) 'The order of discourse', in R. Young (ed.) *Untying the Text: a post-structuralist reader.* London: Routledge & Kegan Paul.

—— (1984) 'What is enlightenment?' in P. Rabinov (ed.) *The Foucault Reader.* London: Penguin.

—— (1989) *Foucault Live (Interviews, 1966–84).* New York: Semiotext(e).

—— (1990) *The History of Sexuality*, Vol. I. New York: Random House.

Fowler, Roger, Hodge, Robert, Kress, Gunther and Trew, Tony (1979) *Language and Control.* London: Routledge & Kegan Paul.

Fox-Keller, Evelyn (1985) *Reflections on Gender and Science.* New Haven, Conn.: Yale University Press.

Francis, Becky (1999) 'An investigation of the discourses children draw on [in] their constructions of gender', *Journal of Applied Social Psychology* 29 (2): 300–16.

—— (2000) 'The gendered subject: students' subject preferences and discussion of gender and subject ability', *Oxford Review of Education* 26 (1): 35–48.

Franke, R. and Leary, M. R. (1991) 'Disclosure of sexual orientation by lesbians and gay men', *Journal of Social and Clinical Psychology* 10: 262–9.

Franklin, Clyde W. (1984) *The Changing Definition of Masculinity.* New York: Plenum.

Freebody, Peter (1989) *Children's First Schoolbooks.* Oxford: Blackwell.

Freebody, Peter and Baker, Carolyn (1987) 'The construction and operation of gender in children's first school books', in Anne Pauwels (ed.) *Women, Language and Society in Australia and New Zealand.* Sydney: Australian Professional Publications.

Freeman, Donald (ed.) (1981) *Essays in Modern Stylistics.* London: Methuen.

Freeman, Mark (1993) *Rewriting the Self: history, memory, narrative.* London: Routledge.

French, Jane and French, Peter (1984) 'Gender imbalances in the primary classroom: an interactional account'. *Educational Research* 26 (2): 127–36.

Freudenstein, Reinhold (1978) *The Role of Women in Foreign Language Textbooks: a collection of essays*. Collection d'Etudes Linguistiques 24. Ghent: Fédération Internationale des Professeurs de Languages Vivantes.

Frith, Hannah (1998) 'Constructing the "Other" through talk', *Feminism & Psychology* 8 (4): 530–6.

Furger, Roberta (1998) *Does Jane Compute? Preserving our daughters' place in the cyber revolution*. New York: Time Warner.

Fuss, Diana (1991) 'Inside/Out', in Diana Fuss (ed.) *Inside/Out: lesbian theories, gay theories*. New York: Routledge, pp. 1–10.

Gaff, Robin (1982) 'Sex-stereotyping in modern language teaching – an aspect of the hidden curriculum', *British Journal of Language Teaching* 20 (3): 71–8.

Gagné, Patrica, Tewksbury, Richard and McGaughey, Deanna (1997) 'Coming out and crossing over: identity formation and proclamation in a transgender community', *Gender & Society* 11 (4): 478–508.

Gal, Susan (1978) 'Peasant men can't get wives: language change and sex roles in a bilingual community', *Language in Society* 7: 1–17.

Gamble, Sarah (ed.) (2000) *The Routledge Critical Dictionary of Feminism and Postfeminism*. New York: Routledge.

Garcia, Angela (1998) 'The relevance of interactional and institutional contexts for the study of gender differences: a demonstrative case study', *Symbolic Interaction* 21 (1): 35–58.

Gardner, Carol Brooks (1980) 'Passing by: street remarks, address rights, and the urban female', *Sociological Inquiry* 50 (3–4): 328–56.

Garfinkel, Harold (1967) *Studies in Ethnomethodology*. Englewood Cliffs, NJ: Prentice-Hall.

Gatens, Moira (1990), in A. Jaggar and I. M. Young (eds) *A Companion to Feminist Philosophy*. Oxford: Basil Blackwell.

Gaudio, Rudolph (1997) 'Not talking straight in Hausa', in Anna Livia and Kira Hall (eds) *Queerly Phrased: language, gender and sexuality*. New York: Oxford University Press, pp. 416–29.

Geertz, Clifford (1973) *The Interpretation of Cultures*. New York: Basic Books.

—— (1993) *Local Knowledge: further essays in interpretive anthropology*. London: Fontana.

Gilbert, Nigel and Mulkay, Michael (1984) *Opening Pandora's Box: a sociological analysis of scientists' discourse*. Cambridge: Cambridge University Press.

Gilbert, Sandra and Gubar, Susan (1979) *The Madwoman in the Attic: the woman writer and the nineteenth century literary imagination*. New Haven, Conn.: Yale University Press.

Giles, Howard and Coupland, Nikolas (1991) *Language: contexts and consequences*. Milton Keynes: Open University Press.

Giles, Howard, Coupland, Justine and Coupland, Nikolas (eds) (1992) *Contexts of Accommodation: developments in applied sociolinguistics*. Cambridge: Cambridge University Press.

Gill, Ros (1995) 'Relativism, reflexivity and politics: interrogating discourse analysis from a feminist perspective', in Sue Wilkinson and Celia Kitzinger (eds) *Feminism and Discourse: psychological perspectives*. London: Sage, pp. 165–86.

Gleason, Jean Berko (1973) 'Code switching in children's language', in T. E. Moore (ed.) *Cognitive Development and the Acquisition of Language*. New York: Academic Press, pp. 159–67.

Gleason, Jean Berko and Ratner, Nan Bernstein (1998) (eds) *Psycholinguistics*. Austin, Tex.: Harcourt Brace.

Gleason, Jean Berko and Greif, Esther Blank (1983) 'Men's speech to young children', in Barrie Thorne, Cheris Kramarae and Nancy Henley (eds) *Langage, Gender and Society*. Rowley, Mass.: Newbury House, pp. 140–50.

Goddard, Angela and Patterson, Lyndsey Mean (2000) *Language and Gender*. London: Routledge.

Goodwin, Marjorie Harness (1980) 'Directive-response speech sequences in girls' and boys' task activities', in Sally McConnell-Ginet, Ruth Borker and Nelly Furman (eds) *Women and Language in Literature and Society*. New York: Praeger, pp. 157–73.

—— (1990) *He-Said-She-Said: talk as social organization among black children*. Bloomington, Ind.: Indiana University Press.

Graddol, David, Cheshire, Jenny and Swann, Joan (1995) *Describing Language*, 2nd edn. Milton Keynes: Open University Press.

Gramsci, Antonio (1971) *Selections from Prison Notebooks*. London: Lawrence & Wishart.

Greater Manchester Police (2001a) 'Mind our language', no longer available but see <http://www.gmp.police.uk>.

—— (2001b) 'Reporting a hate crime', see <http://www.gmp.police.uk/mainsite/pages/reporthatecrime.htm>.

Greater Manchester Police Appropriate Language Working Group (2000) 'The power of language: a practical guide to the use of language', no longer available but see <http://www.gmp.police.uk>.

Greer, Germaine (1972) *The Female Eunuch*. London: Paladin.

Greif, Esther Blank and Gleason, Jean Berko (1980) 'Hi, thanks, and goodbye: more routine information', *Language in Society* 9: 159–66.

Gumperz, John (1977) 'Sociocultural knowledge in conversational inference', in M. Saville-Troike (ed.) *Linguistics and Anthropology* (Georgetown Round Table on Languages and Linguistics, 1977). Washington, DC: Georgetown University Press.

—— (1978a) 'The conversational analysis of interethnic communication', in E. L. Ross (ed.), *Interethnic Communication*, Proceedings of the Southern Anthropological Society. Athens, Ga.: University of Georgia Press.

—— (1978b) 'Dialect and conversational inference in urban communication', *Language in Society* 7 (3): 393–409.

—— (1979) 'The sociolinguistic basis of speech act theory', in J. Boyd and S. Ferrara (eds) *Speech Act Ten Years After*. Milan: Versus.

—— (1982a) (ed.) *Language and Social Identity*. Cambridge: Cambridge University Press.

—— (1982b) *Discourse Strategies*. Cambridge: Cambridge University Press.

Gumperz, John and Cook-Gumperz, Jenny (1982) 'Introduction: language and the communication of social identity', in J. J. Gumperz (ed.) *Language and Social Identity*. Cambridge: Cambridge University Press, pp. 1–21.

Gumperz, John and Tannen, Deborah (1979) 'Individual and social differences in language use', in W. Wang and C. Fillmore (eds) *Individual Differences in Language Ability and Language Behaviour*. New York: Academic Press.

Gumperz, John, Agrawal, Arun and Aulakh, G. (1977) 'Prosody, paralinguistics and contextualisation in Indian English', Language Behaviour Research Laboratory, typescript. Berkeley, Calif.: University of California.

Gupta, Anthea and Lee, Ameline Lee Su (1990) 'Gender representation in English language textbooks used in the Singapore primary classroom: an interactional account', *Language and Education* 4 (1): 29–50.

Haas, Adelaide (1979) 'The acquisition of genderlect', in J. Orasnu, M. Slater and L. Adler (eds) *Language, Sex and Gender: does la différence make a difference?*, *Annals of the New York Academy of Sciences* 327: 101–13.

Haas, Mary (1944) 'Men's and women's speech in Koasati', *Language* 20: 142–9.

Hall, Kira (1996) 'Cyberfeminism', in Susan C. Herring (ed.) *Computer-Mediated*

Communication: linguistic, social, and cross-cultural perspectives. Amsterdam: John Benjamins, pp. 147–70.

—— (2003) 'Exceptional speakers: contested and problematized gender identities', in Miriam Meyerhoff and Janet Holmes (eds) *Handbook of Language and Gender.* Oxford: Basil Blackwell, pp. 352–80.

Hall, Kira and O'Donovan, Veronika (1996) 'Shifting gender positions among Hindi-speaking hijras', in Victoria Bergvall, Janet Bing and Alice Freed (eds) *Rethinking Language and Gender Research: theory and practice.* London: Longman, pp. 228–66.

Hall, Stuart (1988) 'Minimal selves', in ICA documents 6, *Identity: the real me.* London: Institute of the Contemporary Arts.

Halliday, Michael (1981) 'Linguistic function and literary style: an inquiry into the language of William Golding's *The Inheritors*', in Donald C. Freeman (ed.) *Essays in Modern Stylistics.* London: Methuen, pp. 325–60.

—— (1985) *Introduction to Functional Grammar.* London: Edward Arnold.

Halliday, Michael and Hasan, Ruqaiya (1989) *Language, Context and Text: aspects of language in a social-semiotic perspective.* Oxford: Oxford University Press.

—— (1976) *Cohesion in English*, London: Longman.

Hammersley, Martin (1990) 'What's wrong with ethnography? The myth of theoretical description', *Sociology* 24 (4): 579–615.

Hannerz, Ulf (1969) *Soulside.* New York: Columbia University Press.

Hanong Thetela, Puleng (2002) 'Sex discourses and gender construction in Southern Sotho: a case study of police interviews of rape/sexual assault victims', *Southern African Linguistics and Applied Language Studies* 20: 177–89.

Haraway, Donna (1991) *Simians, Cyborgs, and Women: the reinvention of nature.* New York: Routledge.

Harding, Susan (1975) 'Women and words in a Spanish village', in R. Reiter (ed.) *Towards an Anthropology of Women.* New York: Monthly Review Press.

Hare-Mustin, Rachel T. and Maracek, Jeane (eds) (1994) *Making a Difference: psychology and the construction of gender.* New Haven, Conn.: Yale University Press.

Harris, Sandra (1984) 'Questions as a mode of control in magistrates' courts', *International Journal of the Sociology of Language* 49: 5–27.

Harrison, Linda (1975) 'Cro-magnon woman – in eclipse', *Science Teacher* (April): 8–11.

Hartman, Pat and Judd, Elliot (1978) 'Sexism and TESOL materials', *TESOL Quarterly* 12 (4): 383–92.

Hasegawa, Yoko (2005) 'Japanese as a gendered language', available online at <http://ist-socrates.berkeley.edu/~hasegawa/Papers/GenderedLanguage.pdf>.

Hellinger, Marlis (1980) 'For men must work and women must weep: sexism in English language textbooks used in German schools', *Women's Studies International Quarterly* 3: 267–75.

Hellinger, Marlis and Bußmann, Hadumod (eds) (2001–2) *Gender across Languages: the linguistic representation of women and men*, Vols I–III. Amsterdam: John Benjamins.

Henley, Nancy (1986) *Body Politics: power, sex and nonverbal communication*, New York, Simon & Schuster.

—— (1987) 'This new species that seeks a new language: on sexism in language and language change', in Joyce Penfield (ed.) *Women and Language in Transition.* Albany, NY: SUNY Press, pp. 3–27.

Hennessy, Margaret (1994) 'Propagating half a species: gender in learners' dictionaries', in Jane Sunderland (ed.) *Exploring Gender: questions and implications for English language education.* Hemel Hempstead: Prentice Hall, pp. 104–11.

Heritage, John (1984) *Garfinkel and Ethnomethodology.* Cambridge: Polity.

Herring, Susan C. (1994) 'Politeness in computer culture: why women thank and men flame', in Mary Bucholtz et al. (eds) *Cultural Performances: proceedings of the Third Berkeley Women and Language Conference.* Berkeley, Calif.: Berkeley Women and Language Group, pp. 278–94.

—— (1996) 'Two variants of an electronic message schema', in Susan C. Herring (ed.) *Computer-Mediated Communication: linguistic, social, and cross-cultural perspectives.* Amsterdam: John Benjamins, pp. 81–108.

—— (1999) 'The rhetorical dynamics of gender harassment on-line'. *Information Society* 15 (3): 151–67.

Herring, Susan C., Johnson, Deborah A. and DeBenedetto, Tamra (1995) ' "This discussion is going too far!": male resistance to female participation on the Internet', in Kira Hall and Mary Bucholtz (eds) *Gender Articulated: language and the socially constructed self,* New York: Routledge, pp. 67–96.

Hesse-Biber, Sharlene, Gilmartin, Christina and Lydenberg, Robin (1998) *Feminist Approaches to Theory and Methodology.* Oxford: Oxford University Press.

Hester, Stephen and Eglin, Peter (eds) (1997) *Studies in Culture in Action: membership categorisation analysis.* Boston, Mass.: International Institute for Ethnomethodology and University Press of America.

Hillman, Judith S. (1974) 'An analysis of male and female roles in two periods of children's literature', *Journal of Education Research* 68: 84–8.

Hirschman, Lynette (1973) 'Female-male differences in conversational interaction'. Paper presented at Linguistics Society of America, San Diego.

—— (1994) 'Female-male differences in conversational interaction', *Language in Society* 23: 427–42.

Hoch, Paul (1979) *White Hero, Black Beast: racism, sexism and the mask of masculinity.* London: Pluto Press.

Hoey, Michael (1996) 'A clause-relational analysis of selected dictionary entries: contrast and compatibility in the definitions of 'man' and 'woman', in Carmen Caldas-Coulthard and Malcolm Coulthard (eds) *Texts and Practices: readings in critical discourse analysis.* London: Routledge.

Hogben, Susan and Coupland, Justine (2000) 'Egg seeks sperm. End of story?: articulating gay parenting in small ads for reproductive partners', *Discourse and Society* 11 (4): 459–86.

Hollway, Wendy (1984) 'Gender difference and the production of subjectivity', in J. Henriques, W. Holloway, C. Unwin, C. Venn and V. Walkerdine (eds) *Changing the Subject: psychology, social regulation and subjectivity.* London, Methuen, pp. 227–63.

—— (1989) *Subjectivity and Method in Psychology.* London: Sage.

—— (1994) 'Beyond sex differences: a project for feminist psychology', *Feminism and Psychology* 4 (4): 538–46.

—— (1995) 'Feminist discourses and women's heterosexual desire', in Sue Wilkinson and Celia Kitzinger (eds) *Feminism and Discourse: psychological perspectives.* London: Sage, pp. 86–105.

Holmes, Janet (1984) 'Hedging your bets and sitting on the fence: some evidence for hedges as support structures', *Te Reo* 27: 47–62.

—— (1992a) 'Language and gender: a state-of-the-art survey article', *Language Teaching,* 24 (4): 207–20.

—— (1992b) *An Introduction to Sociolinguistics.* London: Longman.

—— (1995) *Women, Men and Politeness.* London: Longman.

—— (2000) 'Doing collegiality and keeping control at work: small talk in government departments', in Justine Coupland (ed.) *Small Talk.* London: Longman, pp. 32–61.

—— (2003) *Power and Politeness in the Workplace.* London: Longman.

Holmes, Janet and Sigley, Robert (2002a) 'What's a word like *girl* doing in a place like this? Occupational labels, sexist usages and corpus research', in Pam Peters, Peter Collins, Adam Smith (eds) *New Frontiers of Corpus Linguistics: papers from the 21st International Conference on English Language Research on Computerized Corpora. Sydney 2000.* Amsterdam: Rodopi, pp. 247–63.

—— (2002b) '*Girl*-watching in corpora of English', *Journal of English Linguistics* 30 (2): 138–57.

—— (2002c) 'Looking at girls in corpora of English', *Journal of English Linguistics* 30: 138–57.

Holmes, Janet and Meyerhoff, Miriam (1999) 'The community of practice: theories and methodologies in language and gender research', *Language in Society* 28: 173–83.

Holmes, Janet and Stubbe, Maria (1998) 'Small talk, business talk: oiling the wheels of business', *People and Performance* (June): 28–31.

—— (2003) ' "Feminine" workplaces: stereotype and reality', in Janet Holmes and Miriam Meyerhoff (eds) *The Handbook of Language and Gender.* Oxford: Blackwell, pp. 573–99.

Hopper, Robert and LeBaron, Curtis (1998) 'How gender creeps into talk', *Research on Language and Social Interaction* 31 (3): 59–74.

Huckin, Thomas (1997) 'Critical discourse analysis', in T. Miller (ed.) *Functional Approaches to Written Text: classroom applications.* Washington DC: United States Information Agency.

Hudson, Richard A. (1994) 'About 37% of word-tokens are nouns', *Language* 70: 331–39.

Hurford, James and Heasley, Brendan (1983) *Semantics: a coursebook.* Cambridge: Cambridge University Press.

Hutchby, Ian (1996) 'Power in discourse: the case of arguments on talk radio', *Discourse and Society* 7 (4): 481–97.

Hutchby, Ian and Wooffitt, Robin (1998) *Conversation Analysis.* Cambridge: Polity.

Hutchinson, Eunice (1996) What do teachers and learners actually do with textbooks? Teacher and learner use of a fisheries-based ELT textbook in the Philippines', PhD thesis, Lancaster University.

Hymes, Dell (1972) 'Models of the interaction of language and social life', in John Gumperz and Dell Hymes (eds) *Directions in Sociolinguistics: the ethnography of communication.* New York: Holt, Rinehart & Winston.

Ide, Sachiko (1979) *Onna no kotoba. Otoko no kotoba* (*Women's language. Men's language*). Tokyo: Nihon Keizai Tsushinsha.

—— (1982) 'Japanese sociolinguistics: politeness and women's language', *Lingua* 57 (2/4): 357–85.

—— (1986) 'Sex difference and politeness in Japanese', *International Journal of the Sociology of Language* 58: 25–36.

—— (1992) 'Gender and function of language use: quantitative and qualitative evidence from Japanese', *Pragmatics and Language Learning* 3: 117–29.

—— (2003) 'Women's language as a group identity marker in Japanese', in M. Hellinger and H. Bußmann (eds) *Gender Across Languages: the linguistic representation of women and men.* Amsterdam: John Benjamins, pp. 227–38.

—— (ed.) (1997) *Joseigo no sekai* (*The World of Women's Language*). Tokyo: Meiji Shoin.

Ide, Sachiko and McGloin, Naomi H. (1991) 'Aspects of Japanese women's language', *Journal of Pragmatics* 16: 596–99.

Jackson, David (1990) *Unmasking Masculinity: a critical autobiography*, London, Unwin Hyman.

Jaffe, Alexandra (2003) 'Talk around text: literacy practices, cultural identity and authority in a Corsican bilingual classroom', *International Journal of Bilingual Education and Bilingualism* 6 (3): 202–20.

Jagose, Annemarie (1996) *Queer Theory: an introduction*. New York: New York University Press.

Jaworski, Adam and Coupland, Nick (1999) *The Discourse Reader*. London, Routledge.

Jayyusi, Lena (1984) *Categories and the Moral Order*. London: Routledge.

Jefferson, Gail (1984) 'Transcript notation', in John Atkinson and John Heritage (eds) *Structures of Social Action: studies in conversation analysis*. Cambridge: Cambridge University Press, pp. ix–xvi. Also in Adam Jaworski and Nikolas Coupland (eds) (1999) *The Discourse Reader*. London: Routledge, pp. 158–66.

—— (2004) 'Glossary of transcript symbols with an introduction', in G. H. Lerner (ed.) *Conversation Analysis: studies from the first generation*. Amsterdam: John Benjamins, pp. 13–31.

Jespersen, Otto (1922) *Language: its nature, development and origin*. London: Allen & Unwin.

Johnson, Sally (1997) 'Theorising language and masculinity: a feminist perspective', in Sally Johnson and Ulrike Hanna Meinhof (eds) *Language and Masculinity*. Oxford: Blackwell, pp. 8–26.

Johnson, Sally and Finlay, Frank (1997) 'Do men gossip? An analysis of football talk on television', in Sally Johnson and Ulrike Hanna Meinhof (eds) *Language and Masculinity*. Oxford: Blackwell, pp. 130–343.

Jones, Alison (1993) 'Becoming a "girl": post-structuralist suggestions for educational research', *Gender and Education* 5 (2): 157–66.

Jones, Deborah (1990) 'Gossip: notes on women's oral culture', in Deborah Cameron (ed.) *The Feminist Critique of Language*, 1st edn. London: Routledge, pp. 242–50.

Jones, Martha, Kitetu, Catherine and Sunderland, Jane (1997) 'Discourse roles, gender and language textbook dialogues: who learns what from John and Sally?' *Gender and Education* 9 (4): 469–90.

Jordan, K. M. and Deluty, R. H. (1998) 'Coming out for lesbian women: its relation to anxiety, positive affectivity, self-esteem, and social support', *Journal of Homosexuality* 35: 41–63.

Kalçik, Susan (1975) ' "... Like Anne's gynecologist or the time I was almost raped": personal narratives in women's rap groups', *Journal of American Folklore* 88 (347): 3–11.

Kapferer, Bruce (1969) 'Norms and the manipulation of relationships in a work contexts', in J. Clyde Mitchell (ed.) (1969) *Social Networks in Urban Situations*. Manchester: Manchester University Press, pp. 181–244.

Katz, Jack (1997) 'Ethnography's warrants', *Sociological Methods and Research* 25 (4, May), 391–423.

Kaye, Patricia (1989) ' "Women are alcoholics and drug addicts", says dictionary', *ELT Journal* 43 (3): 192–5.

Kendall, Lori (1998) ' "Are you male or female?" Gender performances on MUDs', in Jody O'Brien and Judith A. Howard (eds) *Everyday Inequalities: critical inquiries*. Malden, Mass.: Basil Blackwell, pp. 131–53.

Kessler, Suzanne and McKenna, Wendy (1978) *Gender: an ethnomethodological approach*. Chicago, Ill.: University of Chicago Press.

Kirkby, John (1746) *A New English Grammar*. London. Reprinted by R. C. Alston 1974.

Kissling, Elizabeth Arveda (1991) 'Street harassment: the language of sexual terrorism', *Discourse and Society* 2 (4): 451–60.

Kissling, Elizabeth A. and Kramarae, Cheris (1991) 'Stranger compliments: the interpretation of street remarks', *Women's Studies in Communication* 14 (1): 75–93.

Kitetu, Catherine and Sunderland, Jane (2000) 'Gendered discourses in the classroom: the importance of cultural diversity', *Temple University of Japan Working Papers* 17. Tokyo: Temple University, pp. 26–40. Also as *Centre for Research in Language Education (CRILE) Working Paper* 43, Department of Linguistics and Modern English Language, Lancaster University.

Kitzinger, Celia (2000) 'Doing feminist conversation analysis', *Feminism and Psychology* 10 (2): 163–93.

Kitzinger, Celia and Frith, Hannah (1999) 'Just say no? The use of conversation analysis in developing a feminist perspective on sexual refusal', *Discourse and Society* 10 (3): 293–316.

Kortenhaus, Carole and Demarest, Jack (1993) 'Gender role stereotyping in children's literature: an update', *Sex Roles* 29 (3/4): 219–32.

Kramarae, Cheris (1986) 'Speech crimes which the law cannot reach; or, compliments and other insulting behavior', in Sue Bremner, Noelle Caskey and Birch Moonwomon (eds) *Proceedings of the First Berkeley Women and Language Conference 1985*. Berkeley, Calif.: Berkeley Women and Language Group, pp. 84–95.

—— (1995) 'A backstage critique of virtual reality', in Steven G. Jones (ed.) *Cybersociety: computer-mediated communication and community*. Thousand Oaks, Calif.: Sage, pp. 36–56.

Kramarae, Cheris and Treichler, Paula (1985, 1997) *A Feminist Dictionary*. London: Pandora.

Kristeva, Julia (1986) *The Kristeva Reader*, ed. by Toril Moi. Oxford: Blackwell.

Krol⊘kke, Charlotte and S⊘rensen, Anne Scott (2006) *Gender Communication Theories and Analyses*. London: Sage.

Kulick, Don (1996) 'Gender in the speech of Brazilian transvestite prostitutes'. Paper presented at the annual meeting of the American Association of Applied Linguistics (AAAL), Chicago.

Kumaravadivelu, B. (1999) 'Critical classroom discourse analysis', *TESOL Quarterly* 33 (3): 453–84.

Labov, William (1962) 'The social history of a sound change on the island of Martha's Vineyard, Massachusetts', Master's essay, Columbia University.

—— (1966) *The Social Stratification of English in New York City*. Washington, DC: Center for Applied Linguistics.

—— (1972a) *Language in the Inner City*. Philadelphia, Pa.: University of Pennsylvania Press.

—— (1972b) 'The social motivation of a sound change', in *Sociolinguistic Patterns*. Philadelphia, Pa.: University of Pennsylvania Press, Chapter 1.

—— (1972c) *Sociolinguistic Patterns*. Philadelphia, Pa.: University of Pennsylvania Press.

—— (1990) 'The intersection of sex and social class in the course of linguistic change', *Language Variation and Change* 2 (2): 205–51.

Lakoff, Robin (1975) *Language and Woman's Place*. New York: Harper & Row. Reprinted 2004, ed. by Mary Bucholtz.

—— (2004) *Language and Woman's Place: text and commentaries*. ed. Mary Bucholtz. Oxford: Oxford University Press.

Lather, Patti (1991) *Getting Smart: feminist research and pedagogy with/in the postmodern*. London: Routledge.

Lave, Jean and Wenger, Etienne (1991) *Situated Learning: legitimate peripheral participation*. Cambridge: Cambridge University Press.

Lazar, Michelle (1993) 'Equalising gender relations: a case of double talk', *Discourse and Society* 4 (4): 443–65.

—— (2005) 'Politicising gender in discourse: feminist critical discourse analysis as political perspective and praxis', in M. Lazar (ed.) *Feminist Critical Discourse Analysis*. London: Palgrave, pp. 1–29.

Leap, William (1996) *Word's Out: gay men's english*. Minneapolis, Minn.: University of Minnesota Press.

Lees, Sue (1997) *Ruling Passions: sexual violence, reputation and the law*. Milton Keynes: Open University Press.

LeMasters, E. E. (1975) *Blue Collar Aristocrats: life-styles at a working class tavern*. Madison, Wisc.: University of Wisconsin Press.

Leontzakou, Cristina (1997) 'How teachers deal with gendered EFL textbook material', MA dissertation, Lancaster University.

Le Page, Robert and Tabouret-Keller, Andrée (1985) *Acts of Identity*. Cambridge: Cambridge University Press.

Lepper, Georgia (2000) *Categories in Text and Talk*. London: Sage.

Lever, Janet (1976) 'Sex differences in the complexity of children's play and games', *American Sociological Review* 43: 471–83.

Levorato, Alessandra (2003) *Language and Gender in the Fairy Tale Tradition*. Basingstoke: Palgrave Macmillan.

Liang, A. C. (1997) 'The creation of coherence in coming-out stories', in Anna Livia and Kira Hall (eds) *Queerly Phrased: language, gender and sexuality*. Oxford: Oxford University Press, pp. 287–309.

Litosseliti, Lia (2002) ' "Head-to-head": gendered repertoires in newspaper articles', in Lia Litosseliti and Jane Sunderland (eds) *Gender Identity and Discourse Analysis*. Amsterdam: John Benjamins, pp. 129–48.

—— (2003) *Using Focus Groups in Research*. London: Continuum.

Lofland, John and Lyn Lofland (1995) *Analyzing Social Settings: a guide to qualitative observation and analysis*, 3rd edn, Belmont, Calif.: Wadsworth Publishing Company.

Lyons, John (1981) *Language, Meaning and Context*. London: Fontana.

Lyotard, Jean-Francois (1984) *The Postmodern Condition*. Manchester: Manchester University Press.

Mac An Ghaill, Mairtin (1994) '(In)visibility: sexuality, race and masculinity in the school context', in Debbie Epstein (ed.) *Challenging Lesbian and Gay Inequalities in Education*. Buckingham: Open University Press, pp. 152–76.

McConnell-Ginet, Sally (1978) 'Address forms in sexual politics', in Douglass Butturff and Edmund L. Epstein (eds) *Women's Language and Style*. Akron, Ohio: L & S Books, pp. 23–35.

—— (1988) 'Language and gender', in Frederick Newmeyer (ed.) *Linguistics: the Cambridge Survey*, Vol. IV: *The Sociocultural Context*. Cambridge: Cambridge University Press.

Macdonell, Diane (1987) *Theories of Discourse: an introduction*. Oxford: Blackwell.

McEnery, Anthony and Xiao, Richard Z. (2004) 'Swearing in modern British English: the case of *fuck* in the BNC', *Language and Literature* 13 (3): 235–68.

McIlhenny, Bonnie (1995) 'Challenging hegemonic masculinities: female and male police officers handling domestic violence', in Kira Hall and Mary Bucholtz (eds) *Gender Articulated: language and the socially constructed self*. New York: Routledge.

McIlvenny, Paul (ed.) (2002) *Talking Gender and Sexuality*. Amsterdam: John Benjamins.

McKay, Donald G. (1980) 'Psychology, prescriptive grammar and the pronoun problem', *American Psychologist* 35: 444–9.

MacKinnon, Richard (1997) 'Virtual rape', *Journal of Computer-Mediated Communication* 2 (4), <http://www.ascusc.org/jcmc/vol2/issue4/mackinnon.html>.

McLellan, David (1986) *Ideology*. Buckingham: Open University Press.

McLoughlin, Linda (2000) *The Language of Magazines*. London: Routledge.

McMahill, Cheiron (2002) 'Dry winds and bossy women: acquiring a second language and social identity in Gunma, Japan', *The Language Teacher* 26 (6): 27–31.

McMillan, Julie A., Clifton, A. K., McGrath, Diane and Gale, Wanda S. (1977) 'Women's language: uncertainty of interpersonal sensitivity and emotionality?' *Sex Roles* 3: 545–59.

McWilliam, Erica (1997) 'Performing between the posts: authority, posture and contemporary feminist scholarship', in W. G. Tierney and Y. Lincoln (eds) *Representation and the Text: reframing the narrative voice*. Albany, NY: SUNY Press, pp. 219–32.

Maccoby, Eleanor and Jacklin, Carol (1974) *The Psychology of Sex Differences*. Stanford, Calif.: Stanford University Press.

Malinowski, Bronislaw (1923) 'The problem of meaning in primitive languages', Appendix to C. K. Ogden and I. A. Richards *The Meaning of Meaning: a study of the influence of language upon thought and of the science of symbolism*, 8th edn, p. 307.

Maltz, Daniel and Borker, Ruth (1982) 'A cultural approach to male-female miscommunication', in John Gumperz (ed.) *Language and Social Identity*. Cambridge: Cambridge University Press, pp. 196–216.

Martyna, Wendy (1978) 'What does "he" mean?' *Journal of Communication* 28: 131–8.

—— (1980) 'The psychology of the generic masculine', in Sally McConnell-Ginet, Ruth Borker and Nelly Furman (eds) *Women and Language in Literature and Society*. New York: Praeger, pp. 69–78.

Mashberg, Tom (2000) 'Bad hair, pocket protector – and proud!' *Boston Herald*, 2 April, available at <http://www.bostonherald.com/news/local_regional/geek04022000.htm>.

Mason, Jennifer (2002) *Qualitative Researching*, 2nd edn. London: Sage.

Mathieu, Nicole-Claude (1989) 'Identité sexuelle/sexuée/de sexe? Trois modes de conceptualisation du rapport entre sexe et genre', in A.-M. Daune-Richard, M.-C. Hurtig and M.F. Pichevin (eds) *Catégorisation de sexe et constructions scientifiques*. Aix-en-Provence: Université de Provence, pp. 109–47.

—— (1996) 'Sexual, sexed and sex-class identities', in Diana Leonard and Lisa Adkins (eds) *Sex in Question: French materialist feminism*. London: Taylor & Francis, pp. 42–71. First published 1989 in French.

Matoesian, Gregory (1993) *Reproducing Rape: domination through talk in the courtroom*. Cambridge: Polity Press.

Matsumoto, Yoshiko (2002) 'Gender identity and the presentation of self in Japanese', in Sarah Benor, Mary Rose, Devyani Sharma and Julie Sweetland (eds) *Gendered Practices in Language* Stanford, Calif.: CSLI Publications, pp. 339–54.

—— (2004) 'Alternative femininity and the presentation of self in Japanese', in Janet (Shibamoto) Smith and Shigeko Okamoto (eds) *Japanese Language, Gender, and Ideology* (Studies in Language and Gender Series). Oxford: Oxford University Press.

Maybin, Janet (1996) 'Everyday talk', in Janet Maybin and Neil Mercer (eds) *Using English: from conversation to canon*. London: Routledge, pp. 5–41.

—— (2001) 'The Bakhtin/Volosinov writings on heteroglossia, dialogism and reported speech', in Margaret Wetherell, Stephanie Taylor and Simon Yates (eds) *Discourse Theory and Practice: a reader*. London: Sage (in association with The Open University), pp. 64–71.

Maynard, Douglas W. (1992) 'On clinicians co-implicating recipients' perspectives in the delivery of diagnostic news', in P. Drew and J. Heritage (eds) *Talk at Work: interaction in institutional settings*. Cambridge: Cambridge University Press, pp. 331–58.

Maynard, Mary and Purvis, June (eds) (1994) *Researching Women's Lives from a Feminist Perspective*. London: Taylor & Francis.

Meditch, Andrea (1975) 'The development of sex-specific speech patterns in young children', *Anthropological Linguistics* 17 (1): 19–24.

Millar, Melanie Stewart (1998) *Cracking the Gender Code: who rules the wired world?* Toronto: Second Story Press.

Miller, Casey and Swift, Kate (1976) *Words and Women*. New York: Anchor Press

—— (1989) *The Handbook of Non-Sexist Writing*. First published 1982. London: The Women's Press.

Mills, Jane (1989) *Womanwords: a vocabulary of culture and patriarchal society*. Harlow: Longman.

Mills, Sara (1992) 'Knowing your place: Marxist feminist contextualised stylistics', in Michael Toolan (ed.) *Language, Text and Context: essays in stylistics*. London: Routledge, pp. 182–205.

—— (1995a) *Feminist Stylistics*. London: Routledge.

—— (1997) *Discourse*. London: Routledge.

—— (1998) 'Post-feminist text analysis', *Language and Literature* 7 (3): 235–53.

—— (2002a) 'Third wave feminist linguistics and the analysis of sexism and naming practices', Plenary Lecture, IGALA2, University of Lancaster, UK.

—— (2002b) 'Rethinking politeness, impoliteness and gender identity', in Lia Litosseliti and Jane Sunderland (eds), *Gender Identity and Discourse Analysis*, Amsterdam: John Benjamins, pp. 69–89.

—— (2003a) 'Caught between sexism, anti-sexism and "political correctness": feminist women's negotiations with naming practices', *Discourse and Society* 14 (1): 87–110.

—— (2003b) 'Third wave feminist linguistics and the analysis of sexism', *Discourse Analysis Online* 2, 1.

—— (2003c) *Gender and Politeness*. Cambridge: Cambridge University Press.

—— (forthcoming) *Third Wave Feminist Linguistics and the Analysis of Sexism*. Cambridge: Cambridge University Press.

Milroy, Lesley (1980) *Language and Social Networks*. Oxford: Basil Blackwell.

Mitchell, J. Clyde (ed.) (1969) *Social Networks in Urban Situations*. Manchester: Manchester University Press.

—— (1984) 'Typicality and the case study', in Ellen, R. F. (ed.) *Ethnographic Research: a guide to general conduct*. London: Academic Press, pp. 238–41.

Moeketsi, Rosemary (1999) *Discourse in a Multilingual and Multicultural Courtroom: a court interpreter's guide*. Pretoria: J. L. van Schaik.

Moerman, Michael (1988) *Talking Culture: ethnography and conversation analysis*. Philadelphia, Pa.: University of Pennsylvania Press.

Montgomery, Martin (1986) *An Introduction to Language and Society*. London: Methuen.

Morgan, John (1999) *Debrett's New Guide to Etiquette and Modern Manners*. London: Headline Book Publishing Ltd.

Morgan, Robin (1977) *Going Too Far*. New York: Random House.

Morse, Margaret (1997) 'Virtually female: body and code', in Jennifer Terry and Melodie Calvert (eds) *Processed Lives: gender and technology in everyday life*. London: Routledge, pp. 23–36.

Moss, Gemma (1989) *Unpopular Fictions*. London: Virago.

Mouffe, Chantal (1992) 'Feminism, citizenship and radical democratic politics', in J. Butler and J. W. Scott (eds) *Feminists Theorize the Political*. New York: Routledge, pp. 369–84.

Nelson, Cynthia (2002) 'Why Queer theory is useful in teaching: a perspective from English as a Second Language teaching', in K. Robinson, J. Irwin and T. Ferfolja (eds) *From Here to Diversity: the social impact of lesbian and gay issues in education in Australia and New Zealand*. Binghampton, NY: Haworth Press, pp. 43–53.

Newton, Sarah E. (1994) *Learning to Behave: a guide to American conduct books before 1900*. Westport, Conn.: Greenwood Press.

Nielson, Joyce M. (1990) *Feminist Research Methods: exemplary readings in the social sciences*. Boulder, Col.: Westview Press.

Nilan, Pam (1995) 'Membership categorization devices under construction: social identity boundary maintenance in everyday discourse', *Australian Review of Applied Linguistics* 18: 69–94.

Nilsen, Alleen Pace (1973) 'Grammatical gender and its relationship to the equal treatment of males and females in children's books', unpublished PhD thesis, University of Iowa.

—— (1977) 'Sexism in children's books and elementary classroom materials', in Nilsen, Alleen Pace et al. (eds) *Sexism and Language*. Urbana, Ill.: National Council for Teachers of English. [pages?]

O'Barr, William and Atkins, Bowman (1980) 'Women's language or powerless language?', in Sally McConnell-Ginet, Ruth Borker and Nelly Furman (eds) *Women and Language in Literature and Society*. New York: Praeger, pp. 93–110.

Ochs, Eleanor (1979) 'Transcription as theory', in Eleanor Ochs and Bambi Schieffelin (eds) *Developmental Pragmatics*. New York: Academic Press, pp. 43–72.

—— (1992) 'Indexing gender', in Alessandro Duranti and Charles Goodwin (eds) *Rethinking Context*. Cambridge: Cambridge University Press, pp. 335–58.

Ochs, Eleanor (1993) 'Constructing social identity: a language socialisation perspective', *Research on Language and Social Interaction* 26 (3): 287–306.

Ochs, Eleanor, Schegloff, Emanuel A. and Thompson, S. A. (eds) (1996) *Interaction and Grammar*. Cambridge: Cambridge University Press.

Ogbay, Sarah (1999) 'Gendered perceptions, silences and resistance in two Eritrean secondary schools: reasons for girls' lower performance than boys', PhD thesis, Lancaster University.

Okamoto, Shigeko (1995) ' "Tasteless Japanese": less "feminine" speech among young Japanese women', in Kira Hall and Mary Bucholtz (eds) *Gender Articulated: language and the socially constructed self*. London: Routledge.

Okamoto, Shigeko and Shibamoto-Smith, Janet S. (eds) (2004) *Japanese Language, Gender, and Ideology: cultural models and real people*. Oxford: Oxford University Press.

Olins, R. and Rafferty, F. F. (1990) 'No to the sexy sell', *Sunday Times*, 11 February, 5.

Ostermann, Ana Cristina (2003) 'Communities of practice at work: gender, facework and the power of habitus at an all-female police station and a feminist crisis intervention center in Brazil', *Discourse and Society* 14 (4): 473–505.

O'Sullivan, T., Hartley, J., Saunders, D. and Fiske, J. (1978) *Key Concepts in Communication*. London: Routledge.

Ozaki, Wakako (1998) ' "Gender-appropriate" language in transition: a study of sentence-final particles in Japanese', in Suzanne Wertheim, Ashlee C. Bailey and Monica Corston-Oliver (eds) *Engendering Communication: proceedings of the Fifth Berkeley Women and Language Conference*. Berkeley, Calif. : Berkeley Women and Language Group, University of California, pp. 427–38.

Pallotta-Chiarolli, M. (1996) ' "A rainbow in my heart": interweaving ethnicity and sexuality studies', in L. Laskey and C. Beavis (eds) *Schooling and Sexualities: teaching for a positive sexuality*. Geelong, Victoria: Deakin Centre for Education and Change, pp. 53–67.

Parker, Ian (1992) *Discourse Dynamics: critical analysis for social and individual psychology*. London: Routledge.

—— (1998) *Social Constructionism, Discourse and Realism*. London: Sage.

Pauwels, Anne (1987) 'Language in transition: a study of the title *Ms* in contemporary Australian society', in Anne Pauwels (ed.) *Women and Language in Australian and New Zealand Society*. Sydney: Australian Professional Publications, pp. 129–54.

—— (1996) 'Feminist language planning and titles for women: some crosslinguistic perspectives', in Ulrich Ammon and Marlis Hellinger (eds) *Contrastive Sociolinguistics*. Berlin: Mouton De Gruyter, pp. 251–69.

—— (1998) *Women Changing Language*. London: Longman.

—— (2001) 'Spreading the feminist word: the case of the new courtesy title *Ms* in Australian English,' in Marlis Hellinger and Hadumod Bußmann (eds) *Gender Across Languages: the linguistic representation of women and men*. Amsterdam: Benjamins, pp. 115–36.

—— (2003) 'Linguistic sexism and feminist linguistic activism', in Janet Holmes and Miriam Meyerhoff (eds) *The Handbook of Language and Gender*. Oxford: Blackwell, pp. 550–70.

Pavlenko, Aneta and Piller, Ingrid (2001) 'Introduction', in Aneta Pavlenko, Adrian Blackledge, Ingrid Piller and Marya Teutsch-Dwyer (eds) *Multilingualism, Second Language Learning and Gender*. Berlin: Mouton de Gruyter, pp. 1–52.

Pavlenko, Aneta, Blackledge, Adrian, Piller, Ingrid and Teutsch-Dwyer, Marya (eds) (2001) *Multilingualism, Second Language Learning and Gender*. Berlin: Mouton de Gruyter, pp. 1–52.

Pecheux, Michel (1982) *Language, Semantics and Ideology*. Basingstoke: Macmillan.

Petersen, Sharyl and Lach, Mary Alyce (1990) 'Gender stereotypes in children's books: their prevalence and influence on cognitive and affective development', *Gender and Education* 2 (2): 185–97.

Peterson, Shelley (2002) 'Gender meanings in grade eight students' talk about classroom writing', *Gender and Education* 14 (4): 351–66.

Phelan, Shane (1994) *Getting Specific: postmodern lesbian politics*. Minneapolis, Minn.: University of Minnesota Press.

Philips, Susan U. (1998). *Ideology in the Language of Judges*. New York: Oxford University Press.

Philipsen, Gerry (1975) 'Speaking "like a man" in Teamsterville: cultural patterns of role enactment in an urban neighborhood', *Quarterly Journal of Speech* 61: 13–22.

—— (1990/1) 'Situated meaning, ethnography and conversation analysis', *Research on Language and Social Interaction* 24: 225–38.

Plant, Sadie (1996) 'On the matrix: cyberfeminist simulations', in Rob Shields (ed.) *Cultures of Internet: virtual spaces, real histories, living bodies*. London: Sage, pp. 170–83.

Platt, Suzy (1989) *Respectfully Quoted*. Washington, DC: Library of Congress. Also available online at <http://www.bartleby.com/73>.

Plummer, Ken (1995) *Telling Sexual Stories: power, change and social worlds*. London: Routledge.

Pomerantz, Anita (1989) 'Epilogue', *Western Journal of Speech Communication* 53: 242–6.

Poole, Joshua (1646) *The English Accidence*. Scholar Press Facsimile, 1967.

Pop, Sever (1950) *La Dialectologie: aperçu historique et méthodes d'enquêtes linguistiques*. Louvain: Chez L'Auteur.

Porecca, Karen (1984) 'Sexism in current ESL textbooks', *TESOL Quarterly* 18 (4): 705–24.

Potter, Jonathan (1996) *Representing Reality: discourse, rhetoric and social construction*. London: Sage.

Potter, Jonathan and Wetherell, Margaret (1987) *Discourse and Social Psychology: beyond attitudes and behaviour*. London: Sage.

—— (1995) 'Discourse analysis', in J. Smith, R. Harre and L. van Langenhove (eds) *Rethinking Methods in Psychology*. London: Sage, pp. 80–92.

Potter, Jonathan, Wetherell, Margaret, Gill, Ros and Edwards, Derek (1990) 'Discourse: noun, verb or social practice?' *Philosophical Psychology* 3: 205–17.

Poulou, Sofia (1997) 'Sexism in the discourse roles of textbook dialogues', *Language Learning Journal* 15: 68–73.

Poynton, Cate (1997) 'Language, difference and identity: three perspectives', *Literacy and Numeracy Studies* 7 (1): 7–24.

Psathas, George (1995) *Conversation Analysis: the study of talk-in-interaction.* London and Thousand Oaks, Calif.: Sage.

Pugsley, Jenny (1991) 'Language and gender in the EFL classroom', *The Teacher Trainer* 5 (1): 27–9.

—— (1992) 'Sexist language and stereotyping in ELT materials', *Working Papers on Language, Gender and Sexism* 2 (2): 5–13.

Rayson, Paul, Leech, Geoff, and Hodges, Mary (1997) 'Social differentiation in the use of English vocabulary: some analyses of the conversational component of the British National Corpus', *International Journal of Corpus Linguistics* 2 (1): 133–52.

Rees-Parnell, Hilary (1976) 'Women in the world of *Kernel Lessons Intermediate*', *ARELS Journal* 2 (2): 29–31.

Register, Cheri (1975) 'American feminist literary criticism: a bibliographical introduction', in Josephine Donovan (ed.) *Feminist Literary Criticism*, Lexington, Ky.: University Press of Kentucky, pp. 1–28.

Reinharz, Shulamit (with Davidmann, Lynn) (1992) *Feminist Methods in Social Research.* New York: Oxford University Press.

Rich, Adrienne (1980) 'Compulsory heterosexuality and lesbian existence', *Signs* 5 (4): 631–60.

Ritchie, Jane and Spencer, Liz (1994) 'Qualitative data analysis for applied policy research', in A. Bryman and R. Burgess (eds) *Analysing Qualitative Data.* London: Routledge, pp. 173–94.

Robert, Kirrily 'Skud' (1998) 'Female geeks: do they exist?' *Slashdot*, 24 November, <http://slashdot.org/features/98/11/24/0941201.shtml>. Also available at <http://infotrope.net/writing/>.

—— (2000) 'Geek chicks: second thoughts', *Freshmeat*, 5 February, <http://freshmeat.net/articles/view/145/>. Also available at http://infotrope.net/writing>.

Roberts, Helen (ed.) (1981) *Doing Feminist Research.* London: Routledge & Kegan Paul.

Robertson, Kirsten and Murachver, Tamar (2003) 'Children's speech accommodation to gendered language styles', *Journal of Language and Social Psychology* 22 (3): 321–33. Abstract available online at <http://jls.sagepub.com/cgi/content/refs/22/3/321>.

Rogers, Mary (1999) *Barbie Culture.* London: Sage.

Romaine, Suzanne (1999) 'From dictionaries to dick-tionaries: *Websters* old and new', *Communicating Gender*, London and Mahwah, NJ: L.Erlbaum, pp. 293–7.

Rowe, Clarissa (2000) ' "True Gay – hegemonic homosexuality?" Representations of gayness in conversations between gay men', MA dissertation, Lancaster University.

Rumney, Philip (1999) 'When rape isn't rape: Court of Appeal sentencing practice in cases of marital and relationship rape', *Oxford Journal of Legal Studies* 19 (2): 243–70.

Sacks, Harvey (1972) 'On the analyzability of stories by children', in John Gumperz and Dell Hymes (eds) *Directions in Sociolinguistics: the ethnography of communication.* New York: Holt, Rinehart & Winston, pp. 325–45. Also in R. Turner (ed.) *Ethnomethodology: selected readings.* Harmondsworth: Penguin Books, pp. 216–32.

—— (1984) 'Notes on methodology', in John Atkinson and John Heritage (eds) *Structures of Social Action: studies in conversation analysis.* Cambridge: Cambridge University Press, pp. 21–7.

—— (1992, 1995) *Lectures on Conversation*, ed. Gail Jefferson. Oxford: Blackwell.

Sacks, Harvey, Schegloff, Emanuel and Jefferson, Gail (1974) 'A simplest systematics for the organization of turn-taking for conversation', *Language* 50: 696–735. Also 1978 in J. N. Schenkein (ed.) *Studies in the Organization of Conversational Interaction.* New York: Academic Press, pp. 7–55.

Sakata, Minako (1991) 'The acquisition of Japanese "gender" particles', *Language and Communication* 11 (3): 117–25.

Sampson, Edward E. (1993) *Celebrating the Other: a dialogic account of human nature.* Hemel Hempstead: Harvester Wheatsheaf.

Sanders, Robert (1999) 'The impossibility of a culturally contexted conversation analysis: on simultaneous, distinct types of pragmatic meaning', *Research on Language and Social Interaction* 32 (1–2): 129–40.

Savicki, Victor, Lingenfelter, Dawn and Kelley, Merle (1996) 'Gender, language, style and group composition in internet discussion groups', *Journal of Computer Mediated Communication* 2/3, <http://www.ascusc.org/jcmc/vol2/issue3/savicki.html>.

Schachar, S. A. and Gilbert, L. A. (1983) 'Working lesbians: role conflicts and coping strategies', *Psychology of Women Quarterly* 7: 244–56.

Schegloff, Emanuel (1972) 'Sequencing in conversational openings', in John Gumperz and Dell Hymes (eds) *Directions in Sociolinguistics: the ethnography of communication.* New York: Holt, Rinehart & Winston, pp. 346–80.

—— (1982) 'Discourse as an interactional achievement: some uses of "uh huh" and other things that come between sentences', in Deborah Tannen (ed.) *Georgetown University Roundtable on Languages and Linguistics (1981) Analyzing Discourse: text and talk.* Washington, DC: Georgetown University Press.

—— (1988) 'On an actual virtual servo-mechanism for guessing bad news: a single case conjecture', *Social Problems* 35 (4): 442–57.

—— (1992) 'In another context', in Alessandro Duranti and Charles Goodwin (eds) *Rethinking Context: language as an interactive phenomenon.* Cambridge: Cambridge University Press, pp. 193–227.

—— (1997) 'Whose text? Whose context?' *Discourse and Society* 8 (2): 165–87.

—— (1998) 'Reply to Wetherell', *Discourse and Society* 9 (3): 413–16.

—— (1999a) ' "Schegloff's Texts" as "Billig's Data": a critical reply', *Discourse and Society* 10 (4): 558–72.

—— (1999b) 'Naivety vs. sophistication or discipline vs. self-indulgence: a rejoinder to Billig', *Discourse and Society* 10 (4): 577–82.

Schegloff, Emanuel and Sacks, Harvey (1974) 'Opening up closings', in Roy Turner (ed.), *Ethnomethodology.* Harmondsworth: Penguin Education, pp. 197–215.

Scher, Murray, Stevens, Mark, Good, Glenn and Eichenfield, Gregg A. (eds) (1993) *Handbook of Counselling and Psychotherapy with Men.* London, Sage.

Schipper, Mineke (1991) *Source of All Evil: African proverbs and sayings on women.* Chicago, Ill. and London: Ivan Dee.

—— (2003) *Never Marry a Woman with Big Feet: women in proverbs from around the world.* New Haven, Conn.: Yale University Press.

Schneider, Joseph and Hacker, Sally (1973) 'Sex role imagery and use of the generic "man" in introductory texts', *American Sociologist* 8: 12–18.

Schultz, Muriel (1975) 'The semantic derogation of women'. In Barrie Thorne and Nancy Henley (eds) *Language and Sex: difference and dominance.* Rowley, Mass.: Newbury House. pp. 64–73.

—— (1990) 'The semantic derogation of women', in Deborah Cameron (ed.) *The Feminist Critique of Language: a reader,* 1st edn. London: Routledge, pp. 134–47.

Schwarz, Juliane (2003) 'Quantifying non-sexist language: the case of Ms', in Srikant Sarangi and Theo van Leeuwen (eds) *Applied Linguistics and Communities of Practice.* London: BAAL/Continuum, pp. 169–83.

—— (2006) 'Non-sexist language beyond second-wave feminism: interpretative repertoires in the metalinguistic accounts of female undergraduate students of different disciplines and different generations', PhD thesis, Lancaster University.

Scott, David and Usher, Robin (eds) (1996) *Understanding Educational Research*. London: Routledge.

Sedgwick, Eve K. (1990) *Epistemology of the Closet*. London: Penguin.

Seidler, Victor J. (1989) *Rediscovering Masculinity: reason, language and sexuality*. New York: Routledge.

—— (1994) *Unreasonable Men: masculinity and social theory*. New York: Routledge.

Seidman, Steven (1993) 'Identity and politics in a "postmodern" gay culture: some historical and conceptual notes', in M. Warner (ed.), *Fear of a Queer Planet: queer politics and social theory*. Minneapolis, Minn.: University of Minnesota Press, pp. 105–42.

—— (1995) 'Deconstructing queer theory or the under-theorization of the social and the ethical', in Linda Nicholson and Steven Seidman (eds) *Social Postmodernism: beyond identity politics*. Cambridge: Cambridge University Press, pp. 116–41.

Seseke, A. (1999) *Mekhoa le Maele a Basotho*. Maseru: Morija Sesuto Book Depot.

Shakespeare, T. (1999) 'Coming out and coming home', *Journal of Gay, Lesbian and Bisexual Identity* 4 (1): 39–51.

Shalom, Celia (1997) 'That great supermarket of desire: attributes of the desired other in personal advertisements', in Keith Harvey and Celia Shalom (eds) *Language and Desire: encoding sex, romance and intimacy*. New York: Routledge, pp. 186–203.

Shattuck, Julie (1996) 'The interplay between EFL textbooks, teacher behaviour and gender', MA dissertation, Lancaster University.

Shapiro, Michael (1992) *Reading the Postmodern Policy*. Minneapolis, Minn.: University of Minnesota Press.

Shibamoto, Janet (1991) 'Sex-related variation in the ellipsis of *wa* and *ga* in Japanese', in Sachiko Ide and Naomi McGloin (eds) *Aspects of Japanese Women's Language*. Tokyo: Kurosio.

Shotter, John and Gergen, Kenneth (eds) (1989) *Texts of Identity*. London: Sage.

Sigley, Robert and Holmes, Janet (2002) 'Looking at *girls* in corpora of English', *Journal of English Linguistics* 30: 138–57.

Silverman, David (1993) 'The machinery of interaction: remaking social science', *Sociological Review* 41 (4): 731–51.

—— (2000) *Doing Qualitative Research: a practical handbook*. London: Sage.

—— (ed.) (2004) *Qualitative Research: theory, method and practice*. London: Sage.

Smith, Patricia (ed.) (1993) *Feminist Jurisprudence*. New York: Oxford University Press.

Smith, Ruth (1995) 'Young children's interpretation of gender from visual text and narrative', *Linguistics and Education* 7: 303–25.

Smithson, Janet (1999) 'Equal choices, different futures: young adults talk about work and family expectations', *Psychology of Women Section Review* 1 (2): 43–57.

Soper, Kate (1993) 'Productive contradictions', in C. Ramazanoglu (ed.) *Up Against Foucault: some tensions between Foucault and feminism*. London: Routledge.

Speer, Susan (1999) 'Feminism and conversation analysis: an oxymoron?' *Feminism and Psychology* 9 (4): 471–8.

—— (2002) 'Sexist talk: gender categories, participants' orientations and irony', *Journal of Sociolinguistics* 6 (3): 347–77.

Speer, Susan and Potter, Jonathan (2000) 'The management of heterosexist talk: conversational resources and prejudiced claims', *Discourse and Society* 11 (4): 543–72.

Spender, Dale (1980) *Man Made Language*. London: Routledge.

—— (1995) *Nattering on the Net*. North Melbourne, Victoria: Spinifex Press.

Stacey, Judith (1988) 'Can there be a feminist ethnography?' *Women's Studies International Forum* 11 (1): 21–7.

Stanley, Julia (1977) 'Gender-marking in American English: usage and reference', in Alleen

Pace Nilsen, Haig Bosmajian, H. Lee Gershuny and Julia Stanley (eds) *Sexism and Language*. Urbana, Ill.: National Council of Teachers of English, pp. 43–74.

—— (1978) 'Sexist grammar', *College English* 39 (7): 800–11.

Stanley, Liz and Wise, Sue (1983) *Breaking Out: feminist consciousness and feminist research*. London: Routledge.

Stephens, John (1992) *Language and Ideology in Children's Fiction*. London: Longman.

Stephens, Kate (1990) 'The world of John and Mary Smith: a study of Quirk and Greenbaum's *University Grammar of English*', *CLE Working Papers* 1: 91–107.

Stewart, Concetta M., Shields, Stella F., Monolescu, Dominique and Taylor, John Charles (1999) 'Gender and participation in synchronous CMC: an IRC case study', *Interpersonal Computing and Technology* 7 (1–2), <http://www.emoderators.com/ipct-j/1999/n1–2/stewart.html>.

Stinton, J. (1979) *Racism and Sexism in Children's Books*. London: Writers & Readers Publishing Cooperative.

Stodolsky, Susan (1989) 'Is teaching really by the book?', in P. Jackson and S. Haroutian-Gordon (eds) *From Socrates to Software: the teacher as text and the text as teacher*. Chicago, Ill.: National Society for the Study of Education, pp. 159–84.

Stokoe, Elizabeth (1997) 'An evaluation of two studies of gender and language in educational contexts: some problems in analysis', *Gender and Education* 9 (2): 233–44.

—— (1998) 'Talking about gender: the conversational construction of gender categories in academic discourse', *Discourse and Society* 9 (2): 217–40.

—— (2000) 'Towards a conversation analytic approach to gender and discourse', *Feminism and Psychology* 10: 590–601.

Stokoe, Elizabeth and Smithson, Janet (2001) 'Making gender relevant: conversation analysis and gender categories in interaction', *Discourse and Society* 12 (2): 217–44.

Stones, Rosemary (1983) *'Pour out the Cocoa, Janet': sexism in children's books*. York: Longman Resources Unit (Schools Council Programme, 3: Developing the Curriculum for a Changing World).

Strauss, Anselm (1987) *Qualitative Analysis for Social Scientists*. Cambridge: Cambridge University Press.

Strauss, Anselm and Corbin, Juliet (1990) *Basics in Qualitative Research*. London: Sage.

Stringer, Jeffrey and Hopper, Robert (1998) 'Generic *he* in conversation?' *Quarterly Journal of Speech* 84: 209–21.

Stubbe, Maria (2000) 'Talk that works: evaluating communication in a factory production team', *New Zealand English Journal* 14: 55–65.

Stubbs, Michael (1996) *Text and Corpus Analysis: computer-assisted studies of language and culture*. Oxford: Blackwell.

—— (2001) 'Texts, corpora, and problems of interpretation: a response to Widdowson', *Applied Linguistics* 22 (2): 149–72.

Suhr, Stephanie and Johnson, Sally (2003) 'Re-visiting "PC": introduction to special issue on "political correctness"', *Discourse and Society* 14 (1): 5–16.

Sunderland, Jane (1991) 'The decline of "man"', *Journal of Pragmatics* 16: 505–22.

—— (1994b) 'Pedagogical and other filters: the representation of non-sexist language change in British pedagogical grammars', in Jane Sunderland (ed.) *Exploring Gender: questions and implications for English language education*. Hemel Hempstead: Prentice Hall.

—— (1994c) 'Differential teacher treatment-by-gender in the EFL classroom: using ex-participants' perspectives', in Jane Sunderland (ed.) *Exploring Gender: questions and implications for English language education*. Hemel Hempstead: Prentice Hall, pp. 148–54.

—— (1995) ' "We're boys, miss!": finding gendered identities and looking for gendering of identities in the foreign language classroom', in Sara Mills (ed.) *Language and Gender: interdisciplinary perspectives.* Harlow: Longman, pp. 160–78.

—— (1996) 'Gendered discourse in the foreign language classroom: teacher-student and student-teacher talk, and the social construction of children's femininities and masculinities'. PhD thesis, Lancaster University.

—— (1998) 'Girls being quiet: a problem for foreign language classrooms?' *Language Teaching Research* 2 (1): 48–82.

—— (2002) 'Baby entertainer, bumbling assistant and line manager: discourses of paternal identity in parentcraft texts', in Jane Sunderland and Lia Litosseliti (eds) *Gender Identity and Discourse Analysis.* Amsterdam: John Benjamins, pp. 293–324.

—— (2004) *Gendered Discourses.* London: Palgrave Macmillan.

—— (2006) '"Parenting" or "mothering"?: the case of modern childcare magazines', *Discourse and Society* 17 (4): 503–27.

Sunderland, Jane and Litosseliti, Lia (2002) 'Gender identity and discourse analysis: theoretical and empirical considerations', in Lia Litosseliti and Jane Sunderland (eds) *Gender Identity and Discourse Analysis.* Amsterdam: John Benjamins, pp. 1–39.

Sunderland, Jane, Cowley, Maire, Rahim, Fauziah Abdul, Leontzakou, Christina and Shattuck, Julie (2000) 'From bias "in the text" to "teacher talk around the text": an exploration of teacher discourse and gendered foreign language textbook texts'. *Linguistics and Education* 11 (3): 251–86.

—— (2002) 'From representation towards discursive practices: gender in the foreign language classroom revisited', in Lia Litosseliti and Jane Sunderland (eds) *Gender Identity and Discourse Analysis.* Amsterdam: John Benjamins, pp. 223–55.

Sutton, Laurel A. (1994) 'Using Usenet: gender, power, and silence in electronic discourse', *Berkeley Linguistics Society* 20: 506–20.

Swann, Joan (1992) *Girls, Boys and Language.* Cambridge, Mass. and Oxford: Blackwell.

—— (2000) 'Gender and language use', in Rajend Mesthrie, Joan Swann, Andrea Deumert and William L. Leap (eds) *Introducing Sociolinguistics.* Edinburgh: Edinburgh University Press, pp. 216–47.

—— (2002) 'Yes, but is it gender?', in Lia Litosseliti and Jane Sunderland (eds) *Gender Identity and Discourse Analysis.* Amsterdam: John Benjamins, pp. 43–67.

Swann, Joan and Graddol, David (1988) 'Gender inequalities in classroom talk'. *English in Education* 22 (1): 48–65.

Talansky, Sandra (1986) 'Sex role stereotyping in TEFL teaching materials', *Perspectives* 11 (3): 32–41.

Talbot, Mary (1992) 'I wish you'd stop interrupting me! Interruptions and asymmetries in speaker rights in equal encounters', *Journal of Pragmatics* 16: 451–66.

—— (1995a) *Fictions at Work: language and social practice in fiction.* London: Longman.

—— (1995b) 'A synthetic sisterhood: false friends in a teenage magazine', in Kira Hall and Mary Bucholtz (eds) *Gender Articulated.* London: Routledge, pp. 143–65.

—— (1998) *Language and Gender.* London: Polity.

Tanaka, Lidia (2004) 'Gender, language and culture: a study of Japanese television interview discourse'. *Studies in Language Companion Series* 69. La Trobe University.

Tannen, Deborah (1991) *You Just Don't Understand! Women and men in conversation.* London: Virago.

—— (1992) 'Response to Senta Troemel-Ploetz's "Selling the apolitical"', *Discourse and Society* 3 (2): 249–54.

—— (1999) 'The display of (gendered) identities in talk at work', in M. Bucholtz et al. (eds) *Reinventing Identities: the gendered self in discourse.* New York: Oxford University Press, pp. 221–40.

Taylor, Stephanie (2001) 'Locating and conducting discourse analytic research', in Margaret Wetherell, Stephanie Taylor and Simon Yates (eds) *Discourse as Data: a guide for analysis.* London: Sage (in association with Open University Press), pp. 5–48.

Taylor, Yolande and Sunderland, Jane (2003) ' "I've always loved women": representation of the male sex worker in *FHM*', in Bethan Benwell (ed.) *Men's Lifestyle Magazines.* Edinburgh: Edinburgh University Press, pp. 69–187.

ten Have, Paul (1999) *Doing Conversation Analysis: a practical guide.* London: Sage.

Terry, Jennifer and Calvert, Melodie (1997) 'Introduction: machine/lives', in Jennifer Terry and Melodie Calvert (eds) *Processed Lives: gender and technology in everyday life.* London: Routledge, pp. 1–19.

Thomas, Beth (1988) 'Differences of sex and sects: linguistic variation and social networks in a Welsh mining village', in Jennifer Coates and Deborah Cameron (eds) *Women in their Speech Communities.* London: Longman, pp. 51–60.

Thomas, Jenny (1995) *Meaning in Interaction: an introduction to pragmatics.* London: Longman.

Thornborrow, Joanna (1991) 'Orderly discourse and background knowledge', *Text* 11 (4): 581–606.

—— (1994) 'The woman, the man and the Filofax: gender positions in advertising', in Sara Mills (ed.) *Gendering the Reader.* London: Harvester Wheatsheaf, pp. 128–51.

Thorne, Barrie, Kramarae, Cheris and Henley, Nancy (eds) (1983) *Language, Gender and Society.* Rowley, Mass.: Newbury House.

Todd, Alexandra and Fisher, Sue (1988) 'Theories of gender, theories of discourse', in Alexandra Todd and Sue Fisher (eds) *Gender and Discourse.* Norwood: Ablex Publishing Corporation, pp. 1–16.

Tong, Rosemarie (1992) *Feminist Thought: a comprehensive introduction.* First published 1989. Boulder, Col.: Westview Press.

Toth, Emily (1970) 'How can a woman "man" the barricades?' *Women: a journal of liberation* 2 (1): 57.

Toulmin, S. (1969) *The Uses of Argument,* 2nd edn. Cambridge: Cambridge University Press.

Tracy, Karen (1998) 'Analysing context: framing the discussion', *Research in Language and Social Interaction* 31 (1): 1–28.

Trade Union Congress (1998) *Words Can Never Hurt Me: a TUC briefing on avoiding language which may be offensive to disabled people.* London: TUC.

Troemel-Ploetz, Senta (1991) 'Review essay: selling the apolitical', *Discourse and Society* 2 (4): 489–502. [On Deborah Tannen's *You Just Don't Understand!* (1991)]

Trouwborst, A. (1973) 'Two types of partial network in Burundi', in J. Boissevain and J. C. Mitchell (eds) *Network Analysis: studies in human interaction.* The Hague: Mouton.

Trudgill, Peter (1972a) 'Sex, covert prestige and linguistic change in the urban British English of Norwich', *Language in Society* 1: 179–95.

—— (1972b, 1974) *The Social Differentiation of English in Norwich.* Cambridge: Cambridge University Press.

—— (1974, 1983, 1995) *Sociolinguistics.* London: Penguin.

Turkle, Sherry (1995) *Life on the Screen: identity in the age of the Internet.* New York: Simon & Schuster.

—— (1988) 'Computational reticence: why women fear the intimate machine', in Cheris Kramarae (ed.) *Technology and Women's Voices: keeping in touch.* New York: Routledge & Kegan Paul, pp. 41–61.

Turner-Bowker, Diane M. (1996) 'Gender stereotyped descriptions in children's future books: does "Curious Jane" exist in the literature?' *Sex Roles,* 35 (7–8): 461–88.

Uchida, Aki (1992) 'When "difference" is "dominance": a critique of the "anti-power-based" cultural approach to sex differences', *Language in Society* 21: 547–68.

Usher, Pat (1996) 'Feminist approaches to research', in D. Scott and R. Usher (eds) *Understanding Educational Research*. London: Routledge, pp. 120–42.

Van Dijk, Teun (1997) 'Discourse and interaction in society', in Teun Van Dijk (ed.) *Discourse Studies: a multidisciplinary introduction*, Vol. II. London: Sage, pp. 1–34.

—— (1998) *Ideology: a multidisciplinary approach*. London: Sage.

—— (1999) 'Critical discourse analysis and conversation analysis', *Discourse and Society* 10 (4): 459–60.

Van Dijk, Teun, Ting-Toomey, Stella, Smitherman, Geneva and Troutman, Denise (1997) 'Discourse, ethnicity, culture and racism', in Teun Van Dijk (ed.) *Discourse as Social Interaction*. London: Sage, pp. 144–80.

van Leeuwen, Theo (1995) 'Representing social action'. *Discourse and Society* 6 (1): 81–106.

—— (1996) 'The representation of social actors', in Carmen Caldas-Coulthard and Malcolm Coulthard (eds) *Texts and Practices: readings in critical discourse analysis*. London: Routledge, pp. 32–70.

van Leeuwen, Theo and Caldas-Coulthard, Carmen (2002) 'Stunning, shimmering, iridescent: toys as the representation of gendered social actors', in Lia Litosseliti and Jane Sunderland (eds) (2002) *Gender Identity and Discourse Analysis*. Amsterdam: John Benjamins.

Van Lier, Leo (1988) *The Classroom and the Language Learner: ethnography and second-language classroom research*. London: Longman.

Wakeford, Nina (1997) 'Networking women and grrrls with information/communication technology: surfing tales of the World Wide Web', in Jennifer Terry and Melodie Calvert (eds) *Processed Lives: gender and technology in everyday life*. London: Routledge, pp. 51–66.

Walby, Sylvia (1990) *Theorising Patriarchy*. Oxford: Blackwell.

Walkerdine, Valerie (1984) 'Some day my prince will come', in Angela McRobbie and M. Nava (eds) *Gender and Generation*. London: Macmillan, pp. 162–84.

—— (1990) *Schoolgirl Fictions*. London: Verso.

Wallace, Michele (1979) *Black Macho and the Myth of the Superwoman*. New York: Dial Press.

Walsh, Clare (2001) *Gender and Discourse: language and power in politics, the church and organisations*. London: Longman.

Wareing, Sian (1990) 'Women in fiction: stylistic modes of reclamation', *Parlance* 2 (2): 72–85.

Warner, Michael (1993) 'Introduction', in Michael Warner (ed.) *Fear of a Queer Planet: queer politics and social theory*. Minneapolis, Minn.: University of Minnesota Press, pp. vii-xxxi.

Warnick, Barbara (1999) 'Masculinizing the feminine: inviting women on line ca 1997', *Critical Studies in Mass Communication* 16: 1–19.

Watson, Graham and Seiler, Robert M. (eds) (1992) *Text in Context: contributions to ethnomethodology*. London: Sage.

Weatherall, Anne (2000) 'Gender relevance in talk-in-interaction and discourse', *Discourse and Society* 11 (2): 286–8.

—— (2002) *Gender, Language and Discourse*. New York: Routledge.

Webb, Christine (1993) 'Feminist research: definitions, methodology, methods and evaluation', *Journal of Advanced Nursing* 18 (3): 416–23.

Weber, Max (1969) *The Theory of Social and Economic Organization*. New York: The Free Press.

Weedon, Chris (1987) *Feminist Practice and Poststructuralist Theory*. Oxford: Basil Blackwell. 2nd edn. 1996.

Wenger, Etienne (1990) *Toward a Theory of Cultural Transparency*. Palo Alto, Calif.: Institute for Research on Learning.

—— (1998) *Communities of Practice: learning, meaning and identity*. Cambridge: Cambridge University Press.

Wertsch, James W. (1990) *Voices of the Mind: a sociocultural approach to mediated action*. London: Harvester Wheatsheaf.

West, Candace (1979) 'Against our will: male interruptions of females in cross-sex conversation', in Judith Orsanu, Mariam K. Slater and Leonore Loeb Adler (eds) *Language, Sex and Gender*, Annals of the New York Academy of Sciences, Vol. 327. New York: New York Academy of Sciences, pp. 81–97.

—— (1984a) *Routine Complications: trouble with talk between doctors and patients*. Bloomington, Ind.: Indiana University Press.

—— (1984b) 'When the doctor is a "lady": power, status and gender in physician–patient dialogues', *Symbolic Interactionism* 7: 85–105.

—— (1995) 'Women's competence in conversation', *Discourse and Society* 6 (1): 107–31.

—— (2002) 'Peeling an onion: a critical comment on "competing discourses"'. *Discourse and Society* 13 (6): 843–51.

West, Candace and Zimmerman, Don (1977) 'Women's place in everyday talk: reflections on parent-child interaction', *Social Problems* 24, 521–9.

—— (1983) 'Small insults: a study of interruptions in cross-sex conversations between unacquainted persons', in Barrie Thorne et al. (eds) *Language, Gender and Society*. Rowley, Mass.: Newbury House, pp. 103–17.

—— (1987) 'Doing gender', *Gender and Society* 1: 125–51. Also (1991) in J. Lorber and S. A. Farrell (eds) *The Social Construction of Gender*. London: Sage, pp. 13–37.

West, Candace and Fenstermaker, Sarah (1993) 'Power, inequality, and the accomplishment of gender: an ethnomethodological view', in P. England (ed.) *Theory on Gender/Feminism on Theory*. New York: Aldine de Gruyter, pp. 151–74.

—— (1995) 'Doing difference', *Gender and Society* 9 (1): 8–37.

—— (2002) 'Accountability in action: the accomplishment of gender, race and class in a meeting of the University of California Board of Regents'. *Discourse and Society* 13 (4): 537–63.

West, Candace and Garcia, Angela (1988) 'Conversational shift work: a study of topical transitions between women and men', *Social Problems* 35: 551–75.

Wetherell, Margaret (1994) 'Men and masculinity: a socio-psychological analysis of discourse and gender identity', ESRC grant No. R000233129.

—— (1998) 'Positioning and interpretative repertoires: conversation analysis and post-structuralism in dialogue', *Discourse and Society* 9 (3): 387–412.

Wetherell, Margaret, Stiven, Hilda and Potter, Jonathan (1987) 'Unequal egalitarianism: a preliminary study of discourses concerning gender and employment opportunities', *British Journal of Social Psychology* 26: 59–71.

Wetherell, Margaret and Edley, Nigel (1998) 'Gender practices: steps in the analysis of men and masculinities', in K. Henwood, C. Griffin and A. Phoenix (eds) *Standpoints and Differences: essays in the practice of feminist psychology*. London: Sage, pp. 157–73.

—— (1999) 'Negotiating hegemonic masculinity: imaginary positions and psycho-discursive practices', *Feminism and Psychology* 9: 335–56.

Wetherell, Margaret and Potter, Jonathan (1988) 'Discourse analysis and the identification of interpretative repertoires', in Charles Antaki (ed.) *Analysing Everyday Explanation: a casebook of methods*. London: Sage, pp. 154–88.

Wetherell, Margaret, Taylor, Stephanie and Yates, Simon (eds) (2001) *Discourse Theory and Practice: a reader.* London: Sage (in association with Open University Press).

Wetzel, Patricia J. (1988) 'Are "powerless" communication strategies the Japanese norm?' *Language in Society* 17 (4): 555–64.

Wex, Marianne (1979) *Let's Take Back Our Space.* Hamburg and Longmead: Element Books.

Wharton, Sue (2005) 'Invisible females, incapable males: gender construction in a children's reading scheme', *Language and Education* 3: 238–51.

Widdicombe, Sue and Wooffitt, R. (1995) *The Language of Youth Sub-Cultures: social identity in action.* Hemel Hempstead: Harvester Wheatsheaf.

Widdicombe, Sue (1998) ' "But you don't class yourself": the interactional management of category membership and non-membership', in Charles Antaki and Sue Widdicombe (eds) *Identities in Talk.* London: Sage, pp. 52–70.

Widdowson, Henry (1995) 'Discourse analysis: a critical view', *Language and Literature* 4 (3): 157–72.

Wilkinson, Sue (1997) 'Feminist psychology', in Dennis Fox and Isaac Prilleltensky (eds) *Critical Psychology.* London: Sage, pp. 247–65.

Willeke, Audrone and Sanders, Ruth (1978) '*Walter ist intelligent und Brigitte ist blond*: dealing with sex bias in language texts', *Unterrichtspraxis* 11: 60–5.

Williams, Raymond (1965) *The Long Revolution.* Harmondsworth: Pelican Books.

Williamson, Judith (1978) *Decoding Advertisements: ideology and meaning in advertising.* London: Marion Boyars.

Wilson, Thomas (1553) [1962] *Arte of Rhetorique.* Scholar's Facsimiles and Reprints. New York: Delmar.

Winter, Debra, and Huff, Chuck (1996) 'Adapting the Internet: comments from a women-only electronic forum', *American Sociologist* 27 (1): 30–54

Wise, Sue and Stanley, Liz (1987) *Georgie Porgie: sexual harassment in everyday life.* London: Pandora Press.

Wood, Kathleen M. (1997) 'Narrative iconicity in electronic-mail lesbian coming out stories', in Anna Livia and Kira Hall (eds) *Queerly Phrased: language, gender and sexuality.* Oxford: Oxford University Press, pp. 257–73.

Woolf, Virginia (1974) [1929] *A Room of One's Own.* London: Penguin.

Woolgar, Steve (ed.) (1988) *Knowledge and Reflexivity: new frontiers in the sociology of science.* London: Sage.

Yerian, Keli (2001) 'Strategic constructivism: the discursive body as a site for identity display in women's self-defense courses', in Sarah Benor, Mary Rose, Devyani Sharma, Julie Sweetland and Qing Zhang (eds) *Gendered Practices in Language.* Stanford, Calif.: CSLI Publications, pp. 389–405.

Zdenek, Sean (2002) 'Scripting Sylvie: language, gender, and humanness in public discourse about software agents', in Sarah Benor, Mary Rose, Devyani Sharma, Julie Sweetland and Qing Zhang (eds) *Gendered Practices in Language.* Stanford, Calif.: CSLI Publications, pp. 255–73.

Zimmerman, Don and Candace West (1975) 'Sex roles, interruptions and silences in conversation', in Barrie Thorne and Nancy Henley (eds), *Language and Sex: difference and dominance.* Rowley, Mass.: Newbury House, pp. 105–29.

Zimmerman, Don and Pollner, Melvin (1971) 'The everyday world as a phenomenon', in Jack Douglas (ed.) *Understanding Everyday Life: toward the reconstruction of sociological knowledge.* London: Routledge & Kegan Paul, pp. 83–103.

Zipes, Jack (1986) 'A second gaze at little Red Riding Hood's trials and tribulations', in Jack Zipes (ed.) *Don't Bet on the Prince: contemporary fairy tales in North America and England.* Aldershot: Gower, pp. 227–60.

Index